Becoming and Unbecoming White

Critical Studies in Education and Culture Series

Becoming and Unbecoming White

Owning and Disowning a Racial Identity

EDITED BY

Christine Clark and James O'Donnell

Critical Studies in Education and Culture Series
Edited by Henry A. Giroux

BERGIN & GARVEY
Westport, Connecticut • London

Library of Congress Cataloging-in-Publication Data

Becoming and unbecoming white : owning and disowning a racial identity
/ edited by Christine Clark, James O'Donnell.
    p.   cm.—(Critical studies in education and culture series,
ISSN 1064–8615)
    Includes bibliographical references and index.
    ISBN 0–89789–620–3 (alk. paper).—ISBN 0–89789–621–1 (pbk. :
alk. paper)
    1. Whites—United States—Race identity.   2. Racism—United
States.   3. United States—Race relations.   I. Clark, Christine,
1962–   . II. O'Donnell, James, 1951–   . III. Series.
E184.A1B29   1999
305.8′00973—dc21   98–34240

British Library Cataloguing in Publication Data is available.

Library of Congress Catalog Card Number: 98–34240
ISBN: 0–89789–620–3
      0–89789–621–1 (pbk.)
ISSN: 1064–8615

First published in 1999

Bergin & Garvey, 88 Post Road West, Westport, CT 06881
An imprint of Greenwood Publishing Group, Inc.

Printed in the United States of America

The paper used in this book complies with the
Permanent Paper Standard issued by the National
Information Standards Organization (Z39.48–1984).

10 9 8 7 6 5 4 3 2

Copyright Acknowledgments

For my mother, Jerine, and my sister, Carolyn,
who, in all of their contradictions,
exemplify life-long commitment to the antiracist racist struggle;
toward becoming more fully human.
—C. Clark

For my son, Zak,
and his generation for a rainbow tomorrow.
—J. O'Donnell

Contents

Series Foreword

Educational reform has fallen upon hard times. The traditional assumption that schooling is fundamentally tied to the imperatives of citizenship designed to educate students to exercise civic leadership and public service has been eroded. The schools are now the key institution for producing professional, technically trained, credentialized workers for whom the demands of citizenship are subordinated to the vicissitudes of the marketplace and the commercial public sphere. Given the current corporate and right wing assault on public and higher education, coupled with the emergence of a moral and political climate that has shifted to a new Social Darwinism, the issues which framed the democratic meaning, purpose, and use to which education might aspire have been displaced by more vocational and narrowly ideological considerations.

The war waged against the possibilities of an education wedded to the precepts of a real democracy is not merely ideological. Against the backdrop of reduced funding for public schooling, the call for privatization, vouchers, cultural uniformity, and choice, there are the often ignored larger social realities of material power and oppression. On the national level, there has been a vast resurgence of racism. This is evident in the passing of anti-immigration laws such as Proposition 187 in California, the dismantling of the welfare state, the demonization of Black youth that is taking place in popular media, and the remarkable attention provided by the media to forms of race talk that argue for the intellectual inferiority of Blacks or dismiss calls for racial justice as simply a holdover from the "morally bankrupt" legacy of the 1960s.

Poverty is on the rise among children in the United States, with 20 percent of all children under the age of eighteen living below the poverty line. Unemployment is growing at an alarming rate for poor youth of color, especially in the urban centers. While Black youth are policed and disciplined in and out of the nation's schools, conservative and liberal educators define education through the ethically limp discourses of privatization, national standards, and global competitiveness.

Many writers in the critical education tradition have attempted to challenge the right wing fundamentalism behind educational and social reform in both the United States and abroad while simultaneously providing ethical signposts for public discourse about education and democracy that is both prophetic and transformative. Eschewing traditional categories, a diverse number of critical theorists and educators have successfully exposed the political and ethical implications of the cynicism and despair that has become endemic to the discourse of schooling and civic life. In its place, such educators strive to provide a language of hope that inextricably links the struggle over schooling to understanding and transforming our present social and cultural dangers.

At the risk of overgeneralizing, both cultural studies theorists and critical educators have emphasized the importance of understanding theory as the grounded basis for "intervening into contexts and power . . . in order to enable people to act more strategically in ways that may change their context for the better."[1] Moreover, theorists in both fields have argued for the primacy of the political by calling for and struggling to produce critical public spaces, regardless of how fleeting they may be, in which "popular cultural resistance is explored as a form of political resistance."[2] Such writers have analyzed the challenges that teachers will have to face in redefining a new mission for education, one that is linked to honoring the experiences, concerns, and diverse histories and languages that give expression to the multiple narratives that engage and challenge the legacy of democracy.

Equally significant is the insight of recent critical educational work that connects the politics of difference with concrete strategies for addressing the crucial relationships between schooling and the economy, and citizenship and the politics of meaning in communities of multicultural, multiracial, and multilingual schools.

Critical Studies in Education and Culture attempts to address and demonstrate how scholars working in the fields of cultural studies and the critical pedagogy might join together in a radical project and practice informed by theoretically rigorous discourses that affirm the critical but refuse the cynical, and establish hope as central to a critical pedagogical and political practice but eschew a romantic utopianism. Central to such a project is the issue of how pedagogy might provide cultural studies theorists and educators with an opportunity to engage pedagogical practices that are not only transdisciplinary, transgressive, and oppositional, but also connected to a wider project designed to further racial, economic, and political democracy.[3] By taking seriously the relations between culture and power, we further the possibilities of resistance, struggle, and change.

Critical Studies in Education and Culture is committed to publishing work that opens a narrative space that affirms the contextual and the specific while simultaneously recognizing the ways in which related debates on pedagogy are understood and addressed within the larger context of social responsibility, civic courage, and the reconstruction of democratic public life. We must keep in mind Raymond Williams's insight that the "deepest impulse (informing cultural politics) is the desire to make learning part of the process of social change itself."[4] Education as a cultural pedagogical practice takes place across multiple sites, which include not only schools and universities but also the mass media,

popular culture, and other public spheres, and signals how within diverse
contexts, education makes us both subjects of and subject to relations of power.

This series challenges the current return to the primacy of market values and
simultaneous retreat from politics so evident in the recent work of educational
theorists, legislators, and policy analysts. Professional relegitimation in a
troubled time seems to be the order of the day as an increasing number of
academics both refuse to recognize public and higher education as critical public
spheres and offer little or no resistance to the ongoing vocationalization of
schooling, the continuing evisceration of the intellectual labor force, and the
current assaults on the working poor, the elderly, and women and children.[5]

Emphasizing the centrality of politics, culture, and power, *Critical Studies in
Education and Culture* will deal with pedagogical issues that contribute in
imaginative and transformative ways to our understanding of how critical
knowledge, democratic values, and social practices can provide a basis for
teachers, students, and other cultural workers to redefine their role as engaged and
public intellectuals. Each volume will attempt to rethink the relationship
between language and experience, pedagogy and human agency, and ethics and
social responsibility as part of a larger project for engaging and deepening the
prospects of democratic schooling in a multiracial and multicultural society.
Critical Studies in Education and Culture takes on the responsibility of
witnessing to and addressing the most pressing problems of public schooling and
civic life and engages culture as a crucial site and strategic force for productive
social change.

Henry A. Giroux

NOTES

1. Lawrence Grossberg, "Toward a Genealogy of the State of Cultural Studies," in
Cary Nelson and Dilip Parameshwar Gaonkar, eds. *Disciplinarity and Dissent in
Cultural Studies* (New York: Routledge, 1996), 143.
2. David Bailey and Stuart Hall, "The Vertigo of Displacement," Ten 8 2:3 (1992),
19.
3. My notion of transdisciplinary comes from Mas'ud Zavarzadeh and Donald
Morton, "Theory, Pedagogy, Politics: The Crisis of the 'Subject' in the Humanities,"
in *Theory Pedagogy Politics: Texts for Change*, Mas'ud Zavarzadeh and Donald
Morton, eds. (Urbana: University of Illinois Press, 1992), 10. At issue here is neither
ignoring the boundaries of discipline-based knowledge nor simply fusing different
disciplines, but creating theoretical paradigms, questions, and knowledge that cannot
be taken up within the political boundaries of the existing disciplines.
4. Raymond Williams, "Adult Education and Social Change," in *What I Came to
Say* (London: Hutchinson-Radus, 1989), 158.
5. The term "professional legitimation" comes from a personal correspondence
with Professor Jeff Williams of East Carolina University.

Acknowledgments

We would like to thank each of the contributors for sharing their stories and analyses, thereby enhancing the quality of the project this book represents. Further, we would like to extend additional thanks to Peter McLaren, Beverly Daniel Tatum, and Henry A. Giroux for providing in their chapters contexts for furthering our understanding of the cultural, social, economic, political, ideological, and psychological circumstances and impacts of racism. Further still, we would like to give a special thanks to Peter McLaren for his support and guidance throughout our work on this project. To the outside reviewers, thank you for your keen, thoughtful insights and comments. Finally, too numerous to mention, are past and present colleagues who, as teachers, mentors, and friends, have assisted us in deepening our understanding of racial oppression and strengthening our commitment to eradicating it.

   Many thanks.

Christine Clark
James O'Donnell

Rearticulating a Racial Identity: Creating Oppositional Spaces to Fight for Equality and Social Justice

Christine Clark and James O'Donnell

INTRODUCTION

We are two White multicultural educators who, like many other White and of color multicultural educators, have worked with students who are not receptive to the ideas embedded in multicultural education. In particular, the idea that no one social issue (e.g., racism) or social group membership (e.g., Native American, Black, Latina/o, Asian, or White) is more important than another (e.g., sexual orientation or gay men and lesbians, respectively) is generally difficult for all students to embrace who tend to feel the issue or group membership they prioritize should be the one everyone does (Nieto, 1998). Student opposition to and nonengagement with multicultural issues is a common topic of discussion among multicultural educators (hooks, 1993; McCarthy & Crichlow, 1993; Chávez Chávez & O'Donnell, 1998).

If we narrow the discussion of the ideas embedded in multicultural education to issues of race, specifically antiracism, we find that the composition of students who are not receptive also narrows, converging around almost exclusively all White students. Coincidentally, we know that 80% of all in-service teachers in the United States are White (Chávez Chávez, 1995). Although we work at a "minority-majority" university (an Hispanic[1] [sic] serving institution), the enrollment in our pre-service teacher education program reflects these in-service demographics. If the majority of those teaching (as well as those currently pursuing teacher licensure) are White, paying close attention to the impact of whiteness on all students' achievement (or rather the lack thereof) makes sense.

Perhaps out of our own necessity to move the conversation regarding our confrontations with student resistance into a discourse of positiveness, of hope, we began to ask ourselves this question: What about White students that *don't* resist multicultural education? Wouldn't it be interesting to develop a project around interviews with White students who embrace rather than resist multicultural education in which they spoke about the experiences that caused and/or influenced this disposition to develop in them? As we discussed this idea, we realized that we were describing ourselves in the past tense. We were previously two White students who had championed multicultural education even when White classmates desecrated it. How did we move from a racist to an antiracist consciousness? What experiences facilitated this movement, this transformation? Might these experiences be instructive and informative to others?

From this conversation, the idea for this book emerged. In addition to telling our own stories of transformation, we decided to invite other White multicultural educators to detail their experiences and the processes of transformation in their racial identity as White Americans from a racist to an antiracist consciousness (Wellman, 1977; Katz, 1978; Hardiman, 1979; Young, 1979; Kovel, 1984; McIntosh, 1989; Helms, 1990a; Terkel, 1992; Frankenberg, 1993). Further, the stories in this book explore the implications of racist to antiracist transformation for our work as multicultural educators (Tatum, 1994).

We use the phrase "White Americans" to describe, collectively, U. S. citizens of European ancestry who are generally considered, anthropologically speaking, to be predominantly Caucasian or White (Bowser & Hunt, 1981). Because the concept of race is sociopolitically constructed (Webster, 1992), to reference it perpetuates its reification, to refrain from referencing it obscures the persistent, pervasive, and seemingly permanent reality of racism (Bell, 1992; Nieto, 1996). To become White, to own a racial identity as White people, we must come to (1) see racism, (2) admit that it exists, (3) acknowledge that we benefit from it whether or not we want to and even in spite of other oppressions we may experience (e.g., as working class, women, ethnic minorities, religious minorities, gay, lesbian, physically disabled, and so forth), and (4) learn to define it as separate and distinct from simply the racial prejudice that people from all racial groups have toward one another because *our* racial prejudice is reinforced at the institutional and cultural levels of society (Terry, 1981).

Additionally, antiracist White consciousness must be characterized by a willingness to interrupt, actively resist, at the level of thought and practice, enjoyment of White race privilege (Jackson, 1976a; Hardiman, 1979). Thus, the process of transformation in our racial identity development as White Americans ultimately forces us to embrace ourselves as both racist and antiracist.

It is ironic that Whites in active and passive acceptance of racism (Jackson, 1976a; Hardiman, 1979), feign color-blindness, conceptualize racism as an individual rather than cultural and institutional pathology, and deny the existence of racism and their associated race privilege. Many Whites also find the discussion of antiracist consciousness to be somehow strange, perhaps dangerous and at odds with self-interest. Nonengagement in the process of becoming White leaves Whites attempting to define racism as a nonentity while simultaneously subversively holding onto the trappings they earn from its continuation. In cutting through the pathology here, the prevailing unanswered question in the literature remains: *What is required for Whites to come to the realization that the benefits of being antiracist far outweigh the benefits of being racist?*

The literature on antiracist White consciousness and/or the role of Whites as allies (Tatum, 1994) in the struggles of people of color, including that engaged in to engender the acceptance of comprehensive, critically conscious multicultural education, while growing is still sparse. A handful of scholars assert that this sparseness is part and parcel of the problem given the enormity of racism and its manifestations (Welsing, 1970; Dennis, 1981). In one early relevant study, *Beyond Racism* (Young, 1969), a plea is articulated: "Perhaps sociologists will oblige us by dropping their preoccupation with the alleged pathologies of Black America and study the very real, corroding sickness of White America" (p. 87). This plea, for the most part, remains unheeded.

CRITICAL WHITE STUDIES

In the last five years, the field of "critical White studies" has emerged within academia. The literature in the field is oriented to challenging White privilege toward the realization of the eradication of racism of White Americans. Most texts in this area examine how the concept of whiteness is constructed to ensure social, political, and economic benefits for Whites (Roediger, 1991; Haney López, 1996). Some texts, however, argue that the social and political arrangements may only benefit middle and upper class Whites and hence call for the abolition of Whiteness altogether (Roediger, 1994; Ignatiev & Garvey, 1996). That is, the attention focused on race and the problem of whiteness diminishes the attention necessary for forging interracial allegiances, especially across the working class.

Because race has been socially constructed as a social and political category, it will most likely continue to function as such for some time to come despite efforts to deconstruct this. Racism cannot simply be removed from the cultural, social, and political arenas by calling for its abolition or by appealing to calls for justice. Because of the entrenched nature of the ideology of whiteness, race remains an active part of the cultural, social, and political configuration of group relationships that characterize life in the United States (Omi & Winant, 1994). While dismantling racial constructs remains a distant goal, facilitating critical dialogue about these constructs may prove more valuable to realizing this goal than we have previously believed, that is, talk may not be so cheap after all. As Giroux (1997) delineates:

Analyzing Whiteness opens a theoretical space for teachers and students to articulate how their own racial identities have been shaped within a broader racist culture and what responsibilities they might assume for living in a present in which Whites are accorded privileges and opportunities (though in complex and different ways) largely at the expense of other racial groups. (p. 314, emphasis added)

Clearly, Giroux is calling for a rearticulation, not an abolition, of whiteness through critical multicultural pedagogy. Whiteness, like other forms of positionality (maleness, heterosexuality, ableness, and so forth) is not to be essentialized but rather to be understood as a social, political, and ideological construction that can be redefined to realize a democratic space for equality and social justice.

We two educators are products of whiteness and its forms of racism. But, we are also Whites who have been transformed by our experiences such that we are able to see the efficacy of border crossing as conceived by Rosaldo (1993) and Giroux (1992; 1993) and exemplified by David Wellman in chapter 5 in this volume. In coming to understand what led us from our previous world views and consciousnesses to our present ones, we have realized that what is White is not in fact what is "right" and essentialized truth, but rather a culturally, socially, and politically constructed perspective. That is, we have come to the realization that the images of life depicted on television, in the media, in our school textbooks, and so forth, are not images defined by and/or for everyone. Our informal and formal learning experiences enable us to dislodge the psychic dissonance that Whites often deal with in coming to deconstruct the so-called ideals of liberty and justice for all of the United States (Dennis, 1981; Tatum, 1992). Further, we know and acknowledge the individual, cultural, and institutional manifestations of racism and the corresponding opportunity structures that support the ideology of whitenes as discussed by Peter McLaren in chapter 2.

No one incident or event or revealed contradiction caused us to shed our blinders to the realities of racism and White privilege. Rather, it was a series of events, informal (inadvertently experienced) and formal (sought out), that enabled us to "see" these things. Further, it was the series of conversations with actual people or the books they wrote that enabled us to realize the contradictions in our lives and in our society vis-à-vis the social construction of race and, especially, whiteness.

Given that the curriculum in most of our nation's schools continues to be Eurocentric, male-oriented, and middle class; given our schools' penchant for a stratified classification system based on pseudo-scientific IQism and EQism, sad and consistent examples of institutional racism, as well as sexism and classism; given most schools continue to mark the "Other" as different and that different in this context means deficit; and given our own struggle to understand racism, we realize that though White students will be resentful, angry, and defensive when confronted with critical antiracism dialogue, we believe that this is a necessary and important step in the transformative process from being racist to becoming antiracist (Oakes, 1985; Gay, 1985, 1990; hooks, 1995; Pinar et. al., 1995; Slattery, 1995; Gould, 1996; Nieto, 1996). We believe this volume will facilitate other multicultural educators in engaging students, especially White students, in the process of identifying how whiteness is constructed and how racism is manifested particularly at institutional levels in our society. In so doing, we believe that all students may be facilitated in learning to join together in taking collective action to dismantle this system of differential privilege and punishment.

WHITE FETISHISM

Because the field of critical White studies is growing so rapidly, critics have begun to talk about the phenomenon of "White fetishism." Simply put, critics wonder if the surge of interest in even *critical* White studies by leftists genuinely committed to antiracist struggle is but another way dialogue becomes centered and/or recentered around whiteness. Even dialogue that seriously problematizes whiteness and its social construction taken to an extreme, dominating the discourse at multicultural education conferences, in multicultural education textbooks, and in the multicultural education classroom, puts Whites at the center again and again, perhaps not as the good guys, as with the White right's centering and recentering of Whiteness, but as the bad guys, which may be how the White left manifests its racist pathology to be at the center.

In thinking about this book as a resource for multicultural education classes, we come face-to-face with this dilemma posed by the White fetishism critics of critical White studies. A powerful rationale for focusing the learning of all students in multiculturally oriented teacher education programs on issues of White identity development exists and, as mentioned previously, has to do with the reality that 80% of all students in teacher education programs, as well as of in-service teachers, in the United States are White (Chávez Chávez, 1995).

In some interesting research done by Chávez Chávez (1995), the potential for horribly negative educational outcomes resulting from teacher racism (and other discriminatory attitudes) is made stark. Chávez Chávez postulates that out of a class of twenty-five pre-service teacher education students, if only two (most likely both White) remain completely resistant to multicultural education ideals, unengaged in the importance of commitment to the practice of multicultural education in the classroom, one would think that is not so bad. After all, twenty-three will go into teaching committed to it. But, he goes on to calculate that out of approximately 250 teacher education programs in the country, with, on average, twenty faculty members, each who teach, on average, six courses a year with, conservatively, twenty-five students per class, two persistently multiculturally hostile students becomes 60,000 who graduate each year and become in-service teachers with the power to greatly impact students of their own. If each of these graduates has, again conservatively, twenty-five students of their own each year and teaches for an average of twenty-five years, these 60,000 will touch the lives of over 37,500,000 young hearts and minds in their career. Those two resistant pre-service teacher education students that did not initially seem all that important suddenly become revealed as a reactionary army who touch, in devastatingly negative ways, the lives of millions of school age children and adolescents in school today.

Clearly, the argument for focusing on eroding White student resistance by prioritizing White identity issues in the multicultural education classroom is compelling. But, as compelling as this argument is, it is also problematic. It simply exacerbates White supremacy by putting Whites and whiteness at the center again; yet another expression of White fetishism. It makes concepts related to whiteness the standard for learning even in the multicultural education classroom where, at least theoretically, the argument has been that surely and at least in this kind of classroom, students of color will finally find their issues and identities centered. This is not said, however, to support a view of multicultural education as compartmentalized ethnic studies, "feel good" curriculum for only students of color (Nieto, 1996) rather, it is said to encourage the ongoing political interrogation of whiteness in the multicultural education classroom as suggested by Giroux (1997b; Chapter 15 in this volume) and McLaren (Chapter 2).

So then, how do we recommend this text be used? We believe that all of the contradictions just discussed should be part and parcel of the classroom dialogue of this text. We believe, too, that this text should be used in conjunction with other texts that radically decenter Whites and whiteness; for example, bell hooks's *Teaching to Transgress: Education as the Practice of Freedom* (1993), which centers Blacks and blackness as well as women and feminism, working-class status and struggle, and, to a lesser extent, lesbian sexual orientation.

NARRATIVE RESEARCH

In the process of telling the stories of our experiences with racism, we became aware of the cognitive and affective signifiers and markers of racism. The telling of our stories occurred not only as individual acts of self-reflection or in informal conversations with friends, but also in more formal discussions with other White students and students of color in the multicultural education classroom. It was through the use of story-telling as pedagogy (Fay, 1977; hooks, 1993; Nieto, 1996) that we began to build a "collective text" (Bigelow, 1990). In this text, the idiosyncratic nature of our experiences became less and instead revealed the systemic construct of racism.

Autobiographical research, or research based on the narrative and critical analysis of the experiences of the researcher, has come into its own in the past decade in the social sciences (Mitchell, 1981; Polkinghorne, 1988; Bruner, 1990) and in education as well (Connelly & Clandnin, 1990). Narrative research is highly congruent with the philosophy of multicultural education, which argues that for any learning to be meaningful, to engage the learner, all learning must be relevant to students' life experiences to their autobiographies (Nieto, 1996). It must also encourage the development of each and every student voice, their narrative (Walsh, 1991). Given this, it made sense to develop this multicultural education resource in an autobiographical fashion.

To focus learning *only* on the autobiography, however, would be a mistake (Giroux, 1993; hooks, 1993; Macedo, 1994). Each and every autobiography has to be contested with critical and reflective analysis in order for the learner to realize that their point of entry into the debate is not the only one, that the way they view and perceive the world is not the only way. The dialectic juxtaposition of autobiography and critical consciousness is the key (hooks, 1993). Heeding this critique, the narratives presented herein are problematized with dialogic inquiry.

In exploring the totality of these experiences as both negative (racist) and positive (antiracist), informal (inadvertent) and formal (sought out) (Clark, 1993), each author identifies, via convergence among the positive, formal ones, factors that encouraged antiracist White consciousness to come about. These factors are then explored to inform multicultural education theory and practice toward the confrontation and erosion of racism in even more deliberate and effective fashion (Nieto, 1996).

The authors of the narrative chapters (chapters 4 through 14) represented in this volume have several things in common. They are all White and dedicated to the realization of a critical, multicultural democratic society. They are female and male from diverse ethnicities, socioeconomic class backgrounds, first language groups, religious and spiritual affiliations, and sexual orientations. They are professors of education, psychology, and sociology as well as community activists. The stories that they share reveal the history of racism in this country over a fifty-year period beginning in the late 1930s and continuing into the early 1980s. The stories are most diverse in this respect, sharing what it was like growing up White during and after Jim Crow segregation, the civil rights movement, and busing and "integration." Thus, there is a history here of our country's racism yesterday and today. Inviting students to experience this history may encourage them to further explore its ongoing manifestations.

It is important to recognize that the vast majority of these authors' narratives detail their antiracist conscientization vis-à-vis their experience with Blacks as opposed to Native Americans, and especially Latinas/os and Asians. Only one author, Carolyn O'Grady, made a concerted effort to recount her experiences with members of each of color group. While the rest of the authors, ourselves included, certainly have had experiences with members of of color groups other than Blacks, the experiences we chose to focus on were those having to do with Blacks. For most of us, this was a function of geography; we grew up in locales where the only or the vast majority of people of color were Black. When we solicited chapters for this volume, we did so from people nationwide. Oddly, while both of us, as well as many of those who responded to our solicitation live in communities today in which the vast majority of people of color are Native American, Latina/o, and/or Asian, none of us grew up in these communities. In thinking about the most poignant experiences impacting our antiracist development, while we had many such experiences with Native Americans, Latinas/os, and Asians later in life, we tended to focus on those from our early childhood and/or adolescence with Blacks.

Consequently, a clear weakness of this volume is that the stories in it do not focus adequately on the emergence of White antiracism with more specific respect to members of of color groups other than Blacks and especially Latinas/os and Asians. We believe that such stories might be very different from the ones related herein and in so being would add greater depth to this work. At the same time, we also believe that the social construction of racial conflict and race-related dialogue in the United States that encourages the dichotomizing of racial identity into only and either White or Black, ignoring the experiences of other people of color altogether, is magnified in this volume as it stands. Either one identifies and attempts to assimilate with those in power, "acts" White, or one challenges power relations, "acts" Black (Ogbu, 1986; Haney López, 1996).

Eurocentric schooling teaches us that the history of this continent began when the Europeans arrived, the indigenous Native American peoples already living here for as long as 500 years apparently had no history (Delgado, 1995; Delgado & Stefancic, 1997). Eurocentric schooling also teaches us that U.S. history emanates from East to West, as opposed to from South to North as is the case for Chicanas/os (most of who were crossed by the border as opposed to having crossed the border), Puertoriqueñas/os, as well as Central and South Americans and Caribbean Islanders (Takaki, 1993). Furthermore, U.S. immigration laws dating from 1863 (the year of the Emancipation Proclamation) to 1952 forced people trying to enter the country, particularly Asians, to argue that they were either of African ancestry or "White" (Haney López, 1996). Given the at least second-class status of those already here identified as of African ancestry, every would-be immigrant argued that they were "White." Those with other than

European ancestry, again, particularly Asians, were routinely denied entry even when they were able to produce "expert" anthropologists to argue their cases from the Western scientific perspective (Haney López, 1996). The "rule of common knowledge" which argued that even if a scientific argument could be made for a person's "whiteness," common knowledge about what a "White" person "looks like" that contradicts the so-called science was routinely and successfully invoked to challenge these experts and deny immigration to plaintiffs (Haney López, 1996).

Given all of this, it should not surprise us that we think in terms of White and Black instead of in terms of shades of Brown. At the same time, bringing this dynamic of racism to our conscious attention begs us to engage in the erosion of such linear and modernistically, either/or, constructed thinking (Giroux, 1993). As a result, an important piece of the classroom discussion of this text might include having White students who have had experiences with the lesser represented of color groups share their experiences with the class, comparing and contrasting their narratives with ours. Especially Students of Color, but generally every student, should also be strongly encouraged to contest all of these narratives, ours and those shared by White classmates, for the continued racist bias they are able to discern in them.

Following this introductory chapter, chapter 2, by Peter McLaren, locates the construct of "whiteness" within the sociopolitical realm. The third chapter, by Beverly Daniel Tatum, sets forth a theoretical construct of White racial identity development which focuses on the psychosocial dynamics of racism. The subsequent narrative chapters by both of us as well as Becky Thompson, David Wellman, Arnold Cooper, Carolyn O'Grady, Mary Gannon, Pritchy Smith, Patti DeRosa, Elizabeth Aaronsohn, and Gary Howard detail our individual struggles as "White" people to become committed antiracist, multicultural educators. The final chapter, by Henry Giroux, looks further at the pedagogical issues raised in the narrative chapters by calling for a radical rearticulation of whiteness, especially as it impacts the multicultural education terrain.

Though each of our stories is idiosyncratic given our own diverse backgrounds, several thematic strands emerge in all of our stories that illuminate how racism functions systematically, at institutional levels in our society. To persist in being racist we had to believe the following:

1. Racism is a pathology of the individual racist only, not a function of a racist culture and political structure.
2. Whiteness is "normal" and "American."
3. People of color are "Other" and as such are "abnormal" and "deficit."
4. Eurocentric schooling taught the absolute "truth."

To become antiracist we had to do the following:

1. Be exposed to educational experiences (books, newspapers, films, speakers, and so forth) outside the Eurocentric norm.
2. Engage with people of color in books, in newspapers, in films, and in person by chance in public spaces, in alternative classrooms, and so forth.

3. Engage with antiracist Whites in books, in newspapers, in films, and in person by chance in public spaces, in alternative classrooms, and so forth.

Though these seven strands are woven throughout the stories presented, no two stories are alike. Each story is different in its telling of the who, what, when, where, why, and how of the author's transformation from racist to antiracist. In addition, each of us as multicultural educators employ various curricular structures and pedagogical strategies to engage our students in the task of "creating an oppositional space to fight for equality and social justice" (Giroux, 1997, p. 296).

In wanting this work to be one that holds a promise for of color and White solidarity, we struggled with how to more comprehensively include the voices of people of color in it, given its topic. Toward that end, we involved people of color in the entirety of the review, critique, and editing process of this work.

CONCLUSION

This book contributes to the previous paucity of research in the area of critical White studies vis-à-vis White fetishism and of color solidarity (Dennis, 1981). The blame-the-victim master narrative, which dictates that the collective White unconscious remain just that, unconscious, is a fierce giant to attempt to topple. Yet, we believe that to infuse a refocusing of the discussion of racism onto its perpetrators is the first big step in the slaying of this giant. It is toward the realization of this refocusing and the positive impact that such will necessarily have on our continued efforts as multicultural educators that this book is directed.

NOTES

The phrase, "creating oppositional spaces to fight for equality and social justice," in this chapter's title comes from Giroux (1997, p. 296). See, Giroux, chapter 15, in this volume.

1. The word "hispanic" is a U. S. government census term that was institutionalized by the Nixon administration. The term is considered problematic (1) because it was chosen as a name for a group by nonmembers instead of by group members, and (2) because it identifies a people of multicultural heritage (Indigenous American, African, and European) by referencing only their European heritage, creating the perception that this is the only desirable heritage with which to identify.

Unthinking Whiteness, Rethinking Democracy: Critical Citizenship in Gringolandia

Peter McLaren

To the memory of Emiliano Zapata, el lider campesino necho mártir en 1917
and El Ejército Zapatista de Liberacíon Nacional.
Also dedicated to the environmental activist and revolutionary, Judi Bari.

A given society is racist or it is not.
—Franz Fanon, *Black Skin, White Masks*

All forms of exploitation resemble one another. They all seek the source of their
necessity in some edict of a Biblical nature. All forms of exploitation are identical
because all of them are applied against the same "object": man. When one tries to
examine the structure of this or that form of exploitation from an abstract point of view,
one simply turns one's back on the major, basic problem, which is that of restoring man
to his proper place.
—Franz Fanon, *Black Skin White Masks*

Don't mourn. Organize!
—Joe Hill, 1915

CAPITALISM'S INCOMPATIBILITY WITH DEMOCRACY

This chapter is an attempt to link—albeit provisionally and quite
modestly—what is occurring in our cities and inside our schools to structures of
imperialism and advanced capitalism that appear to be intractably globalized. It
is simultaneously an effort to put forward a series of pronouncements and
questions. In Paulo Freire's terms, it is an exercise in problem-posing rather than
answer-giving.

I shall discuss critical pedagogy in three basic contexts: that of the
internationalization of capital and labor markets, postmodern cultures and
critical multiculturalism and the abolition of whiteness, and the development of

the "ethical self" and critical citizen. In my view, these three contexts mutually inform one another in important ways. I argue that we cannot sufficiently understand our purpose and role as ethical agents and cultural workers without first examining critically how both we and our students are shaped and informed by current characteristics of late capitalism, how late capitalism shapes and is shaped by global cultures (including cultures within the United States), and how capital and culture are connected to the formal and informal practices of citizenship. My commentary unhesitatingly assumes the position that critical citizenship must be directed toward the creation of self-consciously ethical subjects of history and should be redistributive of society's material wealth and resources.

The specific struggle that I wish to address is that of choosing against whiteness. Yet is it possible for us to choose against whiteness given that, historically, the practice of whiteness has brought about such a devastating denial, disassembly, and destruction of other races? One would think that such a choice against whiteness would be morally self-evident. However, precisely because whiteness is so pervasive, it remains difficult to identify, to challenge, and to separate from our daily lives. My message is that we must create a new public sphere where the practice of whiteness is not only identified and analyzed but also contested and destroyed. For choosing against whiteness is the hope and promise of the future.

Most school systems now live in pathetic prostration to the capitalist marketplace and in the thrall of the new technocapitalist social order. We are everywhere witnessing the progressive enlargement of the capitalist economic domain. Everything has been turned into a commodity, including curricula, courses, instructional materials, lifestyles, and belief systems. The economy is impinging on people's lives today more than at any other time in history, largely as a result of economic transactions occurring through mass communications. In fact, television has colonized even our most private thoughts, suturing them to the cultural logic of the marketplace. Bureaucracy has increased and has become more interventionary and has created conditions for transnational corporations to thrive. Market democracy has spawned market justice for the rich. Moneyed interests prevail over the construction of identity.

Capitalism is traversed by the irrational and exists at the level of insanity, and this state of dementia is infecting the globe. I want to be clear about this. Capitalism nourishes political forms of repression in the way it organizes power through rituals in schools, in the workplace, in churches. It unites private desire and fantasy with economic infrastructure. Postmodern culture provides another, smoother way of facilitating the marriage of time and money. The church was able to invent the idea of international power in the Middle Ages; capitalism has emerged as the magnificent new religious order with more converts than the church. Its cultlike "get rich" hysteria is of the same order of fanaticism as that of Heaven's Gate or Order of the Solar Temple. Old forms of capitalist production, as well as former relations of production, are disappearing, including the class system of classical capitalism. We have now entered the world of commodity forms that function as purchasing power through instantaneous telematic transactions. We live in a digital economy of information and data and superprofits.

Technocapitalism operates through financial transactions undertaken through cyberspace technologies. These technologies efface the contradictions of labor and power; they create a reaction formation against materiality, a kind of packaged sublimity and secular morphology in which the world is reduced to one's subjective constellation of ideas. Here, the realities of pain and suffering no longer exist. Capital subordinates and coordinates all forms of subjectivities within late capitalist culture, creating forms of citizenship supinely weak yet falsely presumed to possess growing autonomy and democratic self-determination. Capitalism has become the most powerful arbiter of our new technodemocracy. It is intimately tied to the resurgent racism we are presently witnessing throughout the country. It is a racism made respectable through its legitimization by politicians who, after the collapse of the Cold War, are turning the immigrant into the new hated "Other."

Consider the comments made by Boston University president John Silber during his campaign for governor of Massachusetts in 1990: "Why has Massachusetts suddenly become so popular for people who are accustomed to living in a tropical climate? Amazing. There has got to be a welfare magnet going on here, and right now I am making a study to find out what that magnet is . . . . Why should Lowell be the Cambodian capital of America?" (Boston Globe, 1990, cited in Macedo and Bartholome, forthcoming).

Donaldo Macedo and Lilia Bartholome (forthcoming) point out that if Silber had conducted such a study he would have soon learned that the majority of Lowell's welfare recipients are White Americans. He would also have discovered that the Asian community is a powerful economic force greatly needed after the flight of jobs and capital out of Lowell.

Current species of consumer capitalism are all about low growth, low wages, and high profits. We live at a juncture of "fast capitalism;" deindustrialization; mass migrations; union-bashing, economic dislocation; the progressive deregulation of national economies; widescale unemployment resulting in part from a declining importance of the national economy as an unitary, cohesive category; and a transition to a post-Fordist phase of capitalism. It is an era consisting of large-scale diasporic migrations of oppressed peoples, the racialization of spatial reconfigurations resulting from global flows of populations, and incoherences in public narratives of nationalism. Wealth is being transferred from the poor to the rich while the state protects its social and economic practices. There has been a powerful decline in real wages for the vast majority of the working population with high levels of un- and underemployment in many of the so-called industrial economies. The contemporary two-parent family with two children has added numerous hours of work per week outside the home. Blue collar workers will be nearly obsolete in several decades, and 90% of job loss is occurring as part of technological replacement; white-collar service-sector jobs are also on the decline. Business after-tax profit rates continue to grow not as a result of profitability or investment but as a result of declining wages. The rich see their tax bills fall and CEOs now earn 170 times more than the average worker. The agonies and sufferings of the oppressed, whose memories and voices we have buried in the sealed vaults of this country's structural unconscious, continue to haunt us.

What's worse, we can see within the context of globalization that some areas of the world are depressingly becoming holograms of the United States.

Jeff Sachs of Harvard University, noted economist and principle architect of the economic transition for the former communist region of Eastern Europe and the USSR, labeled the "shock therapy model," has been assisting the United States in reorganizing the political balance of power across the entire continent. Sachs is masterminding the transformation of the old Soviet command economy. Leading the charge for globalized capitalism, Sachs is helping the United States accomplish such a daunting challenge through the exclusion of Russia from a reorganized Europe and through working for the absorption of East-Central Europe into the Western sphere, creating a European community institutional order along the lines of a U.S.-crafted neoliberal zone. Years ago, such global behavior had a name—imperialism. Today it is known under the rubric of global democratization.

The fall of communism in the former Soviet Union is still being celebrated in the United States by self-righteous bourgeois columnists in newspapers such as the *Los Angeles Times*. We read that in order to get work, young Russian women who want to be secretaries, accountants, and would-be managers are having to describe their physical attributes in job-wanted advertisements, to include their breast and hip measurements on their job applications, and to squeeze into tight miniskirts and high heels and prance around hotel ballrooms at Western-style job fairs. This is what the *Times* calls the "wild side" of the job hunt in Russia, making unemployment seem almost thrilling and definitely sexy. While mildly lamenting the sexism and unemployment situation, columnist Stephanie Simon calls the former Soviet system that made unemployment a crime and résumés unnecessary, a "cushy system" (1996, p. 1). The current unemployment problem is reduced to the failure of Russians in writing effective résumés, developing job-interview skills, and creating enough placement services. The answer to the unemployment problem offered by the *Times* is that the unemployed need to "network to the hilt." Capitalism itself is never criticized. What is blamed for Russian economic malaise is the stubborn and woeful inability of Russians to adjust to that necessary and inevitable transition toward a capitalist system. Of course, the failure of new levels of economic growth, productivity, job creation, and living standards to materialize cannot seriously be linked to the lousy résumés of unemployed Russians but rather to the guiding ideology of the World Bank and International Monetary Fund, which want as little government intervention and as few social programs as possible during the present period of economic shock therapy. Very few newspaper articles link the 42% rise in the 1992 Russian murder rate (and the additional 27% in 1993) (Boggs, 1995) along with rising drug and alcohol addiction, mental illness, and suicide to shock therapy capitalism. Carl Boggs, columnist for an alternative Los Angeles newspaper, describes the situation in Russia thus:

Under the rubric of "democracy," the real actors in this process were to be the mechanisms of global capitalism—not the Russian (or Polish or Hungarian) people. Not only was shock therapy too abrupt and too authoritarian, it was much too capitalist. The established planning and welfare structures were largely junked, plunging the country into chaos and stripping it of its ability to carry out any developmental policies. Thus the new order, such as it was, lacked any semblance of coherence and legitimacy. The transition from state to private enterprise had no social basis: the only people with large amounts of capital were either foreign investors looking to make a quick fortune or homegrown mafiosi and black marketers, none of whom had much interest in long-term social goals. The old Communist guarantees (inadequate and bureaucratic as they were)—of work, decent public services, and orderly social life—simply vanished. The economy was ransacked. The significant gains in political and cultural freedom presided over first by Gorbachev and then by Yeltsin were essentially ransomed at the altar of shock therapy. (1995, p. 8)

Of course, the model democracy, that of the United States, is not without its serious challenges in Americanizing the globe. In a recent cover story in the *Los Angeles Times*, Nora Zamichow describes the role of the U.S. military in Bosnia by quoting Captain Bob Rector of the U.S. Army's civil affairs division, who notes that, for the young officers, "it's like a cavalry mission from the 1800s and they're taming the Wild Wild West" (1996, p. 1). There was no recognition by Captain Rector that the taming of the Wild Wild West historically included the extermination of hundreds of thousands of native peoples and the enslavement and exploitation of others. Captain James "J. J." Love, touring Bosnian trenches, declares: "I swear to God, it's like touring a civil war battlefield" (Zamichow, 1996, p. 10). Apparently the U.S. military can't escape the powerful and popular U.S. mythology surrounding their own history, a mythology that supports the conviction that Americans are a singular species of humanity attempting to mediate between more primitive parties.

Consider some remarks made closer to home—on Capitol Hill, to be exact—by Riordan Roett, an authority on Mexico who serves as a consultant for the Chase Bank. Roett's advice to the Institutional Revolutionary Party—Mexico's ruling party—to facilitate the NAFTA agreement and stimulate its economy was reported in *Time* magazine: "The Mexican government, still reeling from the peso crisis, must 'eliminate' the opposition in the rebellious southern state of Chiapas . . . and should 'consider carefully whether or not to allow opposition victories [even] if fairly won at the ballot box.' And indeed, President Ernesto Zedillo's soldiers rolled into Chiapas last Thursday to crack down on the rebels and arrest their leaders as criminals" (*Time*, 1995, p. 9). Roett's remarks echo the official U.S. ideological disposition toward Mexico and other Third World countries, where not only bankers but also the Central Intelligence Agency have played central roles in attempting to destabilize regimes considered inhospitable to U.S. economic interests.

Noam Chomsky (1996) argues that capitalism requires privatizing profit but socializing cost and risk. In the U.S., many politicians want money to be controlled by the states, not the federal government. But lack of federal regulations only helps the private sector use the money for its own interests, and the average citizen is even further exploited.

All too often, schools are serving the interests of the capitalist social order, which is designed to serve the rich (Darder, 1992). It has been a standard insight of critical educators for decades that schools reproduce class interests (although not without resistance). They do this, for instance, by producing particular ideologies such as individualism and consumerism; by promoting certain character structures that respond to personal responsibility rather than collective responsibility; and by producing producing creative thinkers and using such creativity more often that not in the service of the entrepreneurial spirit rather than in the service of equality and social justice. I want to argue that capitalist relations, while powerful, are not over determining in the last instance such that individuals and groups are reduced to the simple reflexes of moneyed interests. Critical class consciousness is possible and necessary, and critical pedagogy is one means to facilitate it.

If corporate ownership is more globally situated and consolidated, and the means of exploitation more sophisticated, is there any hope for the development of a critical class consciousness in sites such as public schools? For years, I have been arguing that we need to rethink class struggle in cultural terms as well as economic terms. But I have never suggested that we forget the production system, the social division of labor, or the social relations of production or consumption. Rather, I have suggested that we expand our understanding of class in ways that broaden the concept of class as only material production.

Stanley Aronowitz and William DiFazio (1994) have developed the idea of class in ways that are worth repeating. They note, for instance, that class identities are contextually specific and multidimensional, especially in this era of globalization in which ownership is highly centralized in a tightly organized transnational corporate system but where production has been radically deterritorialized. Class, therefore, "is operative in the multiple relations of economic, political, and cultural power that together constitute the ruling systems of production and *reproduction* of goods, services, and knowledge" (p. 231).

What we need to grasp here is the idea that individuals and groups are differentially located within overlapping power systems, and it is in the context of such differential locations that we need to understand and problematize class struggle. In other words, the cultural and social aspects of class need to be understood. We still need to consider individuals to be living, breathing, subjects of history who posses some relative autonomy rather than dismissing them as simply the inventions of discourse or the offspring of discursive formations. Social classes are more than individual actors, they are formations that struggle for and over power; they are historical struggles for specific forms of life (Aronowitz and DiFazio, 1994). Class has not so much to do with individual assets or lack of them. As Aronowitz and DiFazio point out, it is not a question of using distribution-centered class analysis against production-centered analyses. Or positing the capitalist market as the independent variable and cultural and collective relations as dependent variables determined in the last instance by the marketplace. Doing so misses my point about agency. Class structure influences but does not irrevocably determine class consciousness. Knowledge and culture possess a relative autonomy through which critical agency can be produced. Class must be seen as a conscious struggle for specific forms of community. As Aronowitz and DiFazio note, "Class relations are social relations. But social relations are not governed by systematic economic relations. They are overdetermined, but not by economics. Class relations are not limited only to the social relations of the labor process; they continue outside the labor process as well. They occur in all aspects of everyday life . . . the question is, how do social actions produce class culture, which is necessary and indispensable if class struggle is going to occur?" (1994, pp. 292–293)

Class, race, gender, and sexual orientation are mutually determining sets of social relations and practices, and not all of these sets of social relations are subordinate to moneyed capital. Aronowitz and DiFazio maintain that class is "a social movement" that is engaged in a "struggle to transform its own cultural representation and formulate a new cultural representation of class, work, and power" (1994, p. 297). This is not, of course, to deny the growing proletarianization of workers as well as members of the "new class" of intellectual and cultural workers. Neither is it to deny that class struggle is important and imperative within a revolutionary multicultural project. In fact, as I have argued throughout this book, the struggle for a revolutionary socialism is the preeminent struggle of our time. While not all social relations are subordinate to capital or overdetermined by economic relations, most social relations constitutive of racialized and gendered identities are considerably shaped by the social division of labor and the social relations of production. Capitalism is an overarching totality that is dropping out of sight in many analyses undertaken by poststructuralists and postmoderninsts. This can only have dire consequences for a rejuvenated leftist struggle. I agree with Ellen Meiksins Wood that "at the very heart of the new pluralism is a failure to confront (and often an explicit denial of) the overarching totality of capitalism as a social system, which is constituted by class exploitation but which shapes all 'identities' and social relations" (1995, p. 260).

I maintain that we need to move beyond formal equity by way of legal principles and political procedures (as in the case of new pluralism) by struggle to transform global capitalist society. This challenge would seem ludicrous to the new pluralists who view capitalism as having identities and social relations that are irrevocably fragmented and pulverized into an endless plurality of competing interests and heterogeneous lifestyles. Such a view ignores the ways in which commodities create a powerful global homogeneity, and it disables our capacity to both recognize and resist the unifying cohesiveness of capitalist relations and overarching structures of coercion that inscribe identities within the abstract and exploitative requirements of the market.

What does ethics have to do with global capitalism and the concept of class as collective agency and struggle? In order to answer this question, I will turn to the work of sociologist Zygmunt Bauman (1992) with specific reference to his reflections on postmodernity. I want to connect Bauman's commentary about mortality and immortality to the theme of the construction of identity within current circuits and flows of transnational capitalism.

Bauman's central premise is that modernity was preoccupied with the deconstruction of mortality, whereas postmodernity is preoccupied with the deconstruction of immortality. The age of modernity constructed the present as having no value outside of reason and, furthermore, constructed it within the framework of a project whose value, legitimacy, and authenticity resided in judgment drawn from the future. The modernist present, in other words, delayed its own fulfillment, projecting it instead teleologically into the "not-yet." The age of modernity or Enlightenment (which some would argue has not been abandoned) deconstructed or unsettled the idea of mortality, or death, by transforming death into a series of temporary afflictions that can be overcome (through modern medicine, technology, progress, and so forth). In current postmodern times, however, we no longer live within the telic, linear project of creating a better future because the future is accepted as having already arrived and therefore is as fully erasable as the present or the past.

According to Bauman, each moment in postmodernity flows into the next, and the orphans of modernity (I think of the young people in the movies *Kids* and *Welcome to the Dollhouse*) presently occupy the existential condition of nomadic, transient, or evanescent immortality. Whereas the inhabitants of modernity lived within the project such that the present was meaningless unless it was lived in deference to and in the service of the future, postmodernity creates identities that are motivated by roles rather than by future-oriented goals. Modern pilgrims who possessed *connexity* in relation to the time and space of everyday have given way to postmodern nomads who betray a *disconnexity* of the time/space canvas upon which modern pilgrims plotted their life plans. The postmodern nomad lives moment to moment in an ex post facto sense, that is, lives always already in retrospect or in relation to the "now."

Postmodern nomads live their lives in the contingency of a present in which the future self-destructs into an infinite repetition of the same. The only variable that matters is intensity. The past and future have, in this sense, no claim on the present as simultaneity has replaced history. Life becomes a series of "self-canceling determinations" (Bauman, 1992, p. 169). Postmodern culture decomposes eternity and transforms history into "the right to be recorded" on videotape, film, radio, or in newspaper or magazine articles. Access to historicity is accorded the utmost importance. We disturbingly witness "prime-time" serial killers, wife-beaters, butchers of human flesh, and torturers who eat their victims and keep body parts as fetish objects; these actors enjoy as much currency in our collective historical narrative as do poets, scholars, or saints (I am thinking of themes of the movies *Natural Born Killers* and *Pulp Fiction*, and women and men who fall in love with assassins and murderers). Major law breakers can become millionaires by selling their stories to television or the film industry. The notorious atrocities of Republika Srpska's, its war crimes and practices of ethnic cleansing, were tolerated in the West because they were directed against Muslims. But the same cultural logic can be seen here in the United States in the practices of class warfare and institutional racism that prohibit access to equality and social justice for people of color—an access that should be the birthright of all U.S. citizens.

Bauman reports that the most postmodern of games is "the great twentieth century institution of the quiz," in which the past is instantly recoverable and in a state of "perpetual resurrection" (1992, p. 171). Mahatma Ghandi or Dr. Martin Luther King, Jr. carry no more prestige value by postmodern standards than Jeffrey Dahmer or Ted Bundy. Andy Warhol was already grasping this phenomena when he noted that everyone will one day become a celebrity for fifteen minutes. In the era of postmodernity, nothing disappears through death; death is always overcome and is replaced by the fractal moment of dispersion. Even in the worst case scenarios, death can always be put on temporary hold. According to Bauman, "In the world in which *disappearing* has replaced the dying, immortality dissolves in the melancholy of presence, in the monotony of endless *repetition*" (p. 175). Repetition has replaced representation because now everything is mass-produced, and it is impossible to discern what is original. Singularity has dissolved into reassemblances. Nothing, therefore, is real. In theoretical terms, the signifier has no real referent and can be found referring to another signifier ad infinitum. In the postmodern world of unlimited semiosis, all signs are autocopulating, they create no meaning outside of their own self-evidence. They stand for nothing but themselves. In Bauman's terms, "There is no division among things that mean and things that are meant" (p. 183). Everything is fiction, and life is as good as the media wants it to be. Welcome, brother and sister educators, to what I call "predatory culture" (McLaren, 1995).

Whereas the modern world was ruled by the law, postmodernity is guided by the rule. Laws suggest right and wrong, good and evil, oppressors and oppressed. Rules simply describe how the game is played, and one need not worry about the rules when there are infinite number of games to play. There is nothing outside of the game. While you might choose to exit a game you are always constructed by another game. If you are troubled by the thought of hungry and homeless people or reports of torture, imperialist invasions, or oppressive politics or laws, just quickly leave that game and play another. It's that simple. Or is it? Postmodernism does emphasize communities but, as Bauman notes, "The *sociality* of the postmodern community does not require sociability" (1992, p. 198).

Built into the structure of everyday postmodern life is a deferral of death; objects do not die but are merely discarded and then replaced by newer, more trend-setting, sophisticated, and expensive commodities. Familiar, trustworthy objects are undermined by the creation of infinitely new possibilities for prestige capacity and status distinction. We are being programmed by image managers and marketing firms for desirable citizenship conduct (which is the same as consumer conduct), and it doesn't take much: just enough time to detract us from our present thoughts long enough to process a commercial message. Even after a single moment of attention to a commercial message, the ground is prepared and the semiotic manure spread for a reforging of the same message, for endless repetition. This is the postmodernist sublime. Are we having fun yet? Postmodernism has surrendered the self-reflexive subject.

It is in the conceit of postmodern dream-makers that they can turn the world into a factory for immortality through endless television reruns. We can witness people being blown up by bombs and rockets, rebels being killed by government forces in Chiapas, and resign ourselves in inertia. It's all a fiction anyway. And then we, as academics, can invest our time in debating about whether or not to write the obituary of philosophy. After all, in a world without history or future, who needs philosophy? The postmodern moment is autocopulatory; it has already reproduced itself forever. It cannibalizes itself as soon as it is born so it can recreate the same moment again, over and over.

Let me try to expand upon what I have just said, this time in the context of talking about democracy and citizenship. We live at a time of what James Holston and Arjun Appadurai (1996) call liberal procedural justice or the liberal compact. Yet within postmodern conditions, where the disparity among the rich and poor has grown so frighteningly and dangerously wide, oppressed peoples and even the middle class no longer believe in the democratic vision of shared goals. Everybody sees through the hoax. People are just out to get as much as they can get, to acquire as much purchasing power as possible. We can refer to this as the devaluation of citizenship membership in the nation-state or the death of the American dream. In cities known for their urban sprawl, such as Los Angeles, people are barricading themselves in fortress communities where numerous urban incorporations have been able to operate with the sanction of local governments and implant zoning regulations to keep "outsiders" away from their communities. Witness the increasing emphasis on the growth of private security forces and, for that matter, the privatization of everything still considered public.

As I pointed out earlier, the transnationalization and globalization of capital has created a new dynamics of inequality and a new criminalization of poor and marginalized communities. There exists a new asymmetry within relations of power and privilege. The liberal compact of shared values and active citizenship participation toward a common good is in crisis due to this "unprecedented growth of economic and social inequalities during the last few decades" (Holston and Appadurai, 1996, p. 192).

Let me now rehearse the argument made by Appadurai and Holston (1996). The current postmodern social imaginary operates as a priority of right over good. This is a process of liberal democracy based not on constitutive or substantive ends but on procedural justice. Procedural justice permits the same principles of justice to regulate each and every individual the same way. No specific content—or no particular interests—are subscribed by the res publica. Individual ends can point to almost any interest whatsoever as long as it is officially within the law. In this sense, the liberal compact of shared commitment gives a lie to the concept of community upon which it depends because, as Holston and Appadurai (1996) point out, its lack of moral vision—its content-free aspect—precludes the sense of "prior affiliation" and "shared allegiance" that the liberal compact requires. They write: "Procedural liberalism leaves citizens more entangled in obligations they do not choose and less attached to common identifications that would render these obligations not just bearable but even virtuous" (p. 193). In advanced capitalist contexts, procedural liberalism produces not active, self-reflexive citizens but passive subjects of history. Procedural liberal democracy is to some extent a prophylaxis to liberation.

Procedural liberalism is officially proclaimed to be difference-neutral and universal but is predicated upon group membership in which the White, heterosexual Anglo male of property is the prime signifier. As Bauman (1992) has written:

The West-European-born modern civilization had won the right to narrate the history of the world; the right which until quite recently it enjoyed and practiced unchallenged. (It is today challenged all over the place—by the once "weaker" sex, by ethnic groups denied their language and by aborigines denied their land—but this challenge can easily be taken in its stride by a society not any more excessively worried with immortality.) The right to tell history was gained by force, but the superior killing potential of guns was interpreted as the superiority of Western reason and form of life, so that its practical impact could be in good conscience taken for the clinching argument, if one was needed, on behalf of the peak historical position on which the gun-carriers were perched. (p. 120)

Noam Chomsky (1996) has put forward convincing arguments claiming that what government officials within a procedural democracy fear the most—from conservatives to liberals—is "the crisis of democracy." This "crisis" refers to popular democracy by the people. Government officials fear democracy as a problem that must be eliminated because they believe that the ignorant masses will make decisions that will force the government to be more responsible to the people and less responsive to moneyed interests. The answer to this crisis, as Chomsky persuasively suggests, is "the manufacture of consent"—that is, reducing the masses to obedient, passive subjects and keeping power in the hands of an elite class that is able to manage the people through sophisticated forms of public relations. Chomsky proclaims that in this context government officials provide the people with the means of ratifying decisions that other people have already made, they eliminate the means whereby people can educate themselves and organize themselves, and they find ways to engineer the decision making while giving the public the appearance that it is in control. That's not too difficult when those who have the freedom to persuade or convince others of their opinion are the moneyed interests who own and run the public relations industry. Democracy—procedural democracy—is the power to manufacture agreement in a way that enables moneyed interests to further maximize their advantage at the expense of most of the population, who, as I have noted, are growing poorer.

Displaced in the practice of procedural liberalism is a politics of difference, that is, difference-specific democracy. In fact, difference-neutral or procedural democracy actually amounts to little more than an ideology and practice of discrimination. Just as those who espouse a difference-neutral democracy often decry affirmative action on the basis of promoting a "color-blind" society, we can see the destruction of affirmative action (from the difference-specific perspective) as largely the practice of affirmative action on behalf of White, Anglo, heterosexual males of privilege.

Why do we, as educators, wittingly and unwittingly advance our views about what it means to be an American on the graveyards of other peoples' cultures, values, and social practices? Marginalized minority groups, the economically disenfranchised, and those under assault from the English Only movement's policies of linguistic apartheid, the colonialist *pronunciamientos* in Propositions 187 and 209, and generous offerings of Latina/ophobia and an extralegalization of justice will often argue for a difference-specific form of citizenship that recognizes their inalienable right to retain, honor, and nurture their unique, specific identities. From their perspective, they have only *formal* rights, not substantive rights. Consequently, they argue for equal opportunity on the basis of a politics of difference. And while there can be problems with difference-specific claims for citizenship (e.g., defining identities in a narrow, militantly particularistic, or essentialist way), critical educators need to constantly struggle around the issue of naming and defining democracy in ways that unsettle and destabilize Eurocentric and White supremacist forms of procedural, difference-neutral citizenship based on the liberal compact as the telic point of history and civilization.

Critical educators must first recognize that democracy exists in a state of paradox, that it has no universal vision of the common good; democracy does, however, enable particular struggles to determine how it should be defined. The nature of such struggles is what critical pedagogy should be all about. A difference-specific democracy is always relational and never pure; it is always temporary, historically conditional, and contradictorily mediated according to the shifting standpoints of its citizens and their changing circumstances. Here we can follow Ernesto Laclau (1992) in understanding the foundation of democracy to be its own constitutive lack, its own impossibility. Proponents of difference-specific democracy are correct in arguing for the detranscendentalizing of universality and the decentering of Eurocentrism and in so doing differentiating between universal Western selves and the particular lived experiences of concrete social actors, such as the experiences of our Chicana/o sisters and brothers here in the Southwest. Critical educators need to ask: How do democratic institutions such as schools *restrict* the universalism of our shared political ideals by legitimizing only or mainly White Anglo perspectives? How are students turned into identities without properties, without contents, stripped and denuded of their ethnic and cultural particularities in order to become raised to the abstract level of the universal American citizen? What are the rights, for instance, of the undocumented worker? Have they been reduced simply to their market worth? In this case, what does entitlement mean?

Racism and the exploitation of peoples considered to be ontologically inferior to European Americans have always been historical allies to the White supremacist, capitalist, and patriarchal hegemony that characterizes the United States. Procedural, difference-neutral democracy does little to challenge the taken-for-granted White privilege that undergirds it. The non-European American world produced by discourses or "regimes of truth" (that include multiform texts, linguistic practices, and representations) is an ethnocentric projection and the result of assigning to the Other values married to the narcissism and arrogance of the colonial mind. It has been engendered by a militantly systematized hierarchization of values and social, cultural, and economic practices of inferiorization, exclusion, peripheralization, and discrimination that have found a safe, institutional home in our schools. Here, whiteness (*gabachismo*) remain the uncontested, implacable marker against which the non-Anglo-American is judged, often leading to a process of *engabachamiento,* in which marginalized groups are forced to act white in order to succeed. (Of course, *engabachamiento* is a discursive relay of sorts—"White but not quite": Latina/os are never really accepted as White because paranoid fantasies about the Latin Other on the part of Whites keep Latina/os peripheralized and on the cultural and economic sidelines.)

Hypocritical Whites, often singing the praises of *mestizaje* consciousness, refuse to create the conditions whereby the *mestizo* can be politically empowered. The structural ambivalence of the term "mestizo" erroneously implies that border-crossing (the creation of *mestizaje* consciousness through the crossing of cultural, social, and political borders) poses the same challenges for

Whites as it does for people of color. Yet as some Chicana/o groups in California have expressed: "We didn't cross the border; the border crossed us."

What kind of optics of representation frames the Chicana/o student while at the same time denying permission to contribute a verse to the ongoing play of life, a play whose topology regrettably celebrates the civilizational narratives of empire, late-capitalist cultural formations, and the tropes of the Western unconscious?

I am currently a citizen of a country who supplies the United States with a substantial number of undocumented workers—Canada. But you don't see the U. S. government militarizing its northern border. I don't have to be too concerned about harassment from *la migra* if California's Propositions 187 or 209 someday take effect. Consider the vehemently racist comments directed against Mexican and other immigrants of color by Patrick Buchanan, a recent Republican candidate for the U.S. presidency: "If British subjects, fleeing a depression, were pouring into this country through Canada, there would be few alarms. The central objection to the present flood of illegals is they are not English-speaking White people from Western Europe; they are Spanish-speaking Brown and Black people from Mexico, Latin America and the Caribbean" (Bradlee, Jr., 1996, pp. 1 and 12).

I would ask you to consider Buchanan's remarks along with John Silber's earlier comments in light of U. S. history. I offer some comments made by Abraham Lincoln during a speech made in southern Illinois in 1858:

"I am not," he told his audience, "nor ever have been, in favor of bringing about in any way the social or political equality of the white and black races . . . . I will say in addition that there is a physical difference between the white and black races which, I suppose, will forever forbid the two races living together upon terms of social and political equality; and in as much as they cannot so live, that while they do remain together there must be a position of the superiours and the inferiors; and that I, as much as any other man, am in favor of the superior being assigned to the white man." (cited in Zinn, 1970, p. 148)

Another U.S. hero, Benjamin Franklin, wrote: "Why increase the Sons of *Africa*, by planting them in *America*, where we have so fair an Opportunity, by excluding all Blacks and Tawneys, of increasing the lovely White and Red?" (cited in Perea, 1995, p. 973).

Or consider the views of Thomas Jefferson, who was concerned about the presence of Africans in America, and referred to them as an impure "blot" on the purity of the land. "It is impossible not to look forward to distant times, when our rapid multiplication will expand itself . . . & cover the whole northern, if not the southern continent, with a people speaking the same language, governed in similar forms by similar laws; *nor can we contemplate with satisfaction either blot or mixture on that surface*" (cited in Perea, 1995, p. 974). Armed with a Protestant Hebralism, an Augustinian conviction, a Spartan virtue of service to the public sphere, an antinomian iconoclasm, a classical republicanist image of liberty and civic virtue, and models of character development founded on Lycurgus, Cato the Elder, and Calvin, Jefferson hid his racism under the higher calling of establishing God's New Jerusalem on the golden soil of America (Murphy, 1996).

Not only was Thomas Jefferson a mean-spirited racist and slave owner, he also can be arguably considered the central ideological founder of American apartheid. He advocated an approach to democracy, inspired by a mystical reading of the French Revolution, that justified mass slaughter in the name of liberty and justice for Whites only. It is perhaps no coincidence that when Timothy McVeigh was arrested driving away from Oklahoma City on the day the Federal Building was bombed, he was wearing a T-shirt that bore the celebrated words of Jefferson: "The tree of liberty must be refreshed from time to time by the blood of patriots and tyrants." Although Jefferson eventually favored the abolition of slavery, he unhesitatingly called for the banishment of free Blacks from the United States, since he believed that "nature, habit, opinion has drawn indelible lines of distinction" between White people and Black people such that they "cannot live in the same government" (O'Brien, 1996, p. 57).

Although Jefferson preached against slavery, he had one of his many slaves, James Hubbard, severely flogged for escaping. In addition, he proposed an amendment to the Virginia legal code that would ban free Blacks from coming to Virginia of their own accord or taking up residence for more than a year. His amendment was rejected by his contemporaries as being too severe. Jefferson had even proposed that White women who had children by Black fathers were to be ordered out of Virginia within a year of the child's birth. Failure to leave the state would place these women "out of the protection of the law," which meant, of course, that they could be lynched. Jefferson also suggested that the government purchase newborn slaves from their owners and pay for their maintenance until the children were old enough to find jobs. They would work up to their date of deportation to Santo Domingo (O'Brien, 1996). Fortunately, these other suggestions were also rejected by his contemporaries.

Not to be outdone in the racist department, we have Senator John Calhoun, speaking on the Senate floor in 1848, where he opposed annexation by the United States of land belonging to Mexico on the grounds of preserving a homogeneous White nation: "I know further, sir, that we have never dreamt of incorporating into our Union any but the Caucasian race—the free white race. To incorporate Mexico, would be the very first instance of the kind of incorporating an Indian race; . . . I protest against such a union as that! *Ours, sir, is the Government of a white race"* (cited in Perea, 1995, p. 976).

Compare the ideological logic behind California's Proposition 187 with the statements provided by Calhoun, Jefferson, Franklin, Buchanan, and Silber. Compare, toc, Proposition 187's logic to its precursor—California's 1855 "Greaser Act." The Greaser Act was an antiloitering law that applied to "all persons who are commonly known as 'Greasers,' or the issue of Spanish and Indian blood . . . and who go armed and are not peaceable and quiet persons" (cited in López, p. 145).

This is the same racist logic that fueled David Duke's 1992 comments: "Immigrants 'mongrelize' our culture and dilute our values" (cited in López, p. 143). More recent comments made by Duke, in California in 1996, were in support of Proposition 209, an anti-affirmative-action effort to create a "color-blind" society. The proposition was orchestrated by Ward Connerly, an African

American who is a University of California regent and chairman of the Proposition 209 initiative. In addition to accusing minority men of raping White women "by the thousands" and claiming that Black New Orleans police officers rape and kill local citizens, Duke remarked: "I don't want California to look like Mexico . . . . I don't want to have their pollution. I don't want the corruption. I don't want their disease. I don't want their superstition. I don't want us to look like that country. If we continue this alien invasion, we will be like Mexico" (Bernstein, 1996, A14).

Duke reflects a perspective that hasn't changed since the days of the Zoot Suit massacre and Operation Wetback or those days when public Los Angeles swimming pools were frequently drained by Whites after they were used by Mexican Americans. It is a perspective also shared by the British extreme right, which sexualizes racism in order to "generate fear among women and masculine protectiveness among men" in relation to the presence of Black men in British inner cities (Rattansi, 1994, p. 63). Such perspectives connote earlier ideas of the Empire as a dangerous place where White women need protection (Rattansi, p. 63). One example is a story that appeared in the National Front youth newspaper, *Bulldog*. The story was titled "Black Pimps Force White Girls into Prostitution" and exhorted "White Man! You Have a Duty to Protect Your Race, Homeland and Family" (p. 63). Of course, this fear of the rape of the White woman is not projected solely onto the African American male. Underwriting Duke's comments on Mexico, for instance, was the image of the Mexican as rapist and beast. In his discussion of the relationship between San Diegans and Tijanenses, Ramón Gutiérrez describes how Tijuana—"as a place of unruly and transgressive bodies" (1996, p. 256)—has become fixed in the American psyche. He reports that "Tijuana first developed as an escape valve for the sexually repressed and regulated American Protestant social body of San Diego" (p. 255). He writes that "the international boundary between Mexico and the United States has long been imagined as a border that separates a pure from an impure body, a virtuous body from a sinful one, a monogamous conjugal body regulated by the law of marriage from a criminal body given to fornication, adultery, prostitution, bestiality and sodomy" (pp. 255–256).

The United States is constructed as a country governed by nature and the law; such codes of civility that regulate kinship and the body are thought not to exist in Mexico, where only unregulated desire and criminality exist to menace all who come into contact with Mexicans. The image of the undocumented worker as an illegal alien, as a "migrant" living in squalor, spreading disease, raping White women, extorting lunch money from White school children, creating squatter communities, hanging out in shopping centers, and forcing Anglo schools to adopt bilingual education programs to accommodate the offspring of criminals and to appease the foreigner living on U.S. soil has served to identify Mexicans with dirt, filth, and unnatural acts while symbolically constructing European Americans citizens as pure, law-abiding, and living in harmony with God's natural law (Gutiérrez, 1996).

One of the nation's relatively unblemished heroes of history is Woodrow Wilson. Many U.S. citizens have little, if any, knowledge about Wilson's Palmer raids against left-wing unions, his segregation of the federal government, and his military interventions in Mexico (eleven times beginning in 1914) and in Haiti in 1915, the Dominican Republic in 1916, Cuba in 1917, and Panama in 1918. Wilson also maintained forces in Nicaragua (Loewen, 1995, p. 23). Wilson was an unrepentant White supremacist who believed that Black people were inferior to White people. In fact, Wilson ordered that Black and White workers in federal government jobs be segregated. Wilson vetoed a clause on racial equality in the Covenant of the League of Nations. Wilson's wife told "darky" stories in cabinet meetings, and Wilson's administration drafted a legislative program designed to curtail the civil rights of African Americans. Congress refused to pass it. However, Wilson did manage to appoint Southern Whites to offices traditionally given to Blacks (Loewen, 1995).

President Warren G. Harding was inducted into the Ku Klux Klan in a ceremony at the White House (Loewen, 1995). How many students can boast knowledge of this event? How can U.S. history books cover up these events, and hundreds of others, including the 1921 race riot in Tulsa, Oklahoma, in which Whites dropped dynamite from an airplane onto a Black community, destroying 1,000 homes and killing 75 people (Loewen, 1995, 165)?

How can we forget the evils of slavery, including the 10,000 Native Americans shipped from Charleston, South Carolina, to the West Indies (in one year) in exchange for Black slaves? Must we forget that the United States is a country conceived in slavery and baptized in racism?

The Protocols of the Learned Elders of Zion was an influential book for another American hero, Henry Ford. His newspaper ran a series of anti-Semitic articles in the 1920s that were made available to the public in book form under the title *The International Jew*. In this particular sense, the U.S. is not "post-Fordist" at all. Within many right-wing Christian movements, many fervently believe that White people are the true Israelites, that Blacks are subhuman, and that Jews are the issue of Satan. The organization known as Christian Identity is linked to British Israelism, which began as a White supremacist Protestant organization in Victorian England. White Europeans were believed to be the twelve lost tribes of Israel. Like many post-millennial religions, Christian Identity proclaims that God gave the Constitution of the United States to the White Christian Founding Fathers and only White Christian men can be true sovereign citizens of the Republic. Identity followers are set to destroy the "Beast"—the government of the United States—in order to hasten forth Armageddon (Southern Poverty Law Center, 1996). Members of Pat Robertson's Christian Coalition are aligned with the Patriot movement. This movement wants to establish God's law on earth, which in the view of some of the members of the movement, calls for the execution of homosexuals, adulterers, juvenile delinquents, and blasphemers (Southern Poverty Law Center, 1996).

During the Persian Gulf War, over 7,000 White U.S. soldiers were sent letters from neo-Nazi skinheads, urging them not to fight for Israel. Some of these letters were signed by a "racially pure white woman" and called on White GIs to return home and father White children in order to ensure the survival of the White race (Novik, 1995). Buchanan, Duke, Silber, Pete Wilson, and countless other conservative politicians currently enjoying the considerable popularity among growing sectors of the U.S. population owe a great deal to the racist perspectives that they inherited from historical figures such as Jefferson,

Franklin, and Lincoln, figures who have been sanctified and hagiographied in the larger political culture. It appears that it is as patriotic now for White people to proclaim racist sentiments as it was 150 years ago. Today, however, one has to camouflage one's racism in deceptive and sophisticated ways by hiding it in a call for family values, a common culture of decency, and a "color-blind" society, but the racist formations underwriting such a call are clearly in evidence to the discerning cultural critic.

Of course, the populist and nativist sentiments expressed by Buchanan (and reflected in the resurgence of racist groups such as The Order, Posse Comitatus, the Ku Klux Klan, White Aryan Resistance, Aryan Nations, Christian Identity, Gun Owners of America, and various militia movements) are on the rise in the United States. What he and others like him appear to be saying is that undocumented British subjects (whose countrymen invaded the North American continent and stole it from the native inhabitants) would represent a less serious immigrant problem than those groups (such as Mexicans) who had their land stolen from them by the U.S. military (whom some Mexicans still consider an "occupying force"). The real "illegal" in this case is Patrick Buchanan himself, whose repugnant White supremacist and neo-liberal ideology prohibits him from critically examining the economic and sociocultural forces surrounding recent diasporic movements affecting the United States. He remorselessly retires the identities of people of color before they have the opportunity to become established. The Latina/ophobic perspective of Buchanan and other White supremacists symbolically decapitates the immigrant and ultimately works to decenter and demonize the efforts of immigrants to maintain their dignity through identitarian forms of thinking and belonging. Shohat and Stam (1994) remark that "multicultural bellies, full of tacos, falafel, and chow mein, are sometimes accompanied by monocultural minds" (p. 21). It is the monolithic, monocultural perspective of the White Anglo majority population that is responsible, in large part, for the current state of Latina/ophobia and the demonization of people of color in general.

Recent scapegoating has been unparalleled in its acrimony and scope of blame. It can be seen in the example of southeastern Klan groups trying to create all-White trade unions or in the operation of rogue border patrols designed to catch (and sometimes torture and kill) undocumented Mexican workers or in the efforts of Bruder Schweigen, American Spring, SPIKE, Stop Immigration Now, Americans for Border Control, White Aryan Resistance, the Stompers, the Populist Party, the Liberty Lobby, the English Only movement, American Immigrant Reform, English First, Students for America, U.S. English, and Federation for American Immigration Reform. Or it can be witnessed in the "stealth candidate" tactics of Pat Robertson's Christian Coalition. The World Wide Web site of the Carolinian Lords of the Caucuses features and image of a burning cross. Broad strata of the population are being mobilized by these groups, which continue their war against leftist organizations of all stripes, such as the United Farm Workers Union, eco-feminist groups, gay and lesbian groups, Chicana/o activists, African American resistance groups, Asian activists, Native American groups, and radical educational organizations. Here in California the police and La Migra are feared nearly as much as these vigilante groups for reasons that, in recent years, have gained national exposure.

I suspect that many educators remain unaware of the fact that U.S. English is linked to the Federation for American Immigration Reform (FAIR) and has bankrolled Americans for Border Control. FAIR is financially supported by the Pioneer Fund, dedicated to eugenics and White racial superiority. Pioneer was created in the 1930s to support Hitler's theories of "Aryan superiority" and the Nazi program of forced sterilization of undesirables. In the 1970s, Pioneer funded the genetic research of William Schockley and Arthur Jensen and supported their claims that Blacks have hereditarily lower IQ scores than Whites (Novik, 1995). Jensen served on the advisory board of *Neue Anthropologie*, a German neo-Nazi publication, and his work paved the way for studies like the recent *The Bell Curve*. U.S. English is also supported by Cordelia Scaife May, an heiress to the Mellon family fortune who also sponsored, through her Laurel Foundation, the futuristic fantasy *The Camp of Saints*, a book that depicts Third World immigrants invading Europe and destroying its foundations of civilization. This book was required reading among staffers at U.S. English (Novik, 1995).

English First is an organization underwritten by an equally insidious White supremacy. It's founder, Larry Pratt, is a former Virginia legislator and officer of the Council on Inter-American Security (CIS). The CIS authored much of Ronald Reagan's and George Bush's Latin American policy. Pratt also heads Gun Owners of America and has steered the CIS toward a position that equates bilingual education and services with terrorism. The CIS describes the Indian ancestors of Latina/os as "uncivilized barbaric squatters" with "a penchant for grotesque human sacrifices, cannibalism, and kidnapping women" (Novik, 1995, p. 189). Not surprisingly, the CIS has major ties to the Reverend Sun Myung Moon's Unification Church and boasts Pat Buchanan as a member.

U.S. English and English First have jointly funded LEAD (Learning English Advocates Drive), a parent group that opposes bilingual education and has tried to conscript the support of the United Teachers of Los Angeles to oppose bilingual education.

UNTHINKING WHITENESS, REARTICULATING DIASPORIC PRAXIS

Now, this is the road that White Men tread
When they go to clean a land—Iron underfood and the vine overhead
And the deep on either hand.
We have trod that road—and a wet and windy road—
Our chosen star for guide.
Oh, well for the world when the White Men tread
Their highway side by side!
—Rudyard Kipling (cited in Said, 1985, p. 226)

Who can deny that the use of gunpowder against pagans is the burning of incense to our Lord.
—Oviedo, a governor of the settlement at Hispaniola (cited in Todorov, 1984, p. 151)

In 1996, the following article appeared in *Crosscurrents*:
It was not until March 2, 1996, that the mystery surrounding Ly's murder ended. That day, police arrested Gunner Lindberg, age twenty-one, and Dominic Christopher, age seventeen, after discovering a letter that Lindberg had written to a former prison inmate in New Mexico. The letter contained graphic details about the murder, as well as the writer's apparent insolence about the whole incident. Sandwiched between birthday plans, news about a friend's baby, and talk about the need for a new tattoo was this boastful account of what happened the night of January 29:

"*Oh, I killed a jap a while ago. I stabbed him to death at Tustin High School. I walked up to him; Dominic was with me and I seen this guy rollerblading and I had a knife. We walked in the tennis court where he was; I walked up to him. Dominic was right there; I walked right up to him and he was scared; I looked at him and said, 'Oh, I thought I knew you,' and he got happy that he wasn't gonna get jumped. Then I hit him . . . .*

"*I pulled the knife out, a butcher knife, and he said 'no' then I put the knife to his throat and asked him, 'Do you have a car?' And he grabbed my hand that I had the knife in and looked at me, trying to get a description of me, so I stomped on his head 3 times and each time said, 'Stop looking at me,' then he was kinda knocked out, dazed, then I stabbed him in the side about 7 or 8 times; he rolled over a little, so I stabbed his back out 18 or 19 times, then he lay flat and I slit one side of his throat on his jugular vein. Oh, the sounds the guy was making were like, 'Uhhh.' Then Dominic said, 'do it again,' and I said, 'I already did, Dude. Ya, do it again,' so I cut his other jugular vein and Dominic said, 'Kill him, do it again' and I said 'he's already dead.' Dominic said, 'Stab him in the heart.' So I stabbed him about 20 or 21 times in the heart . . . .*

"*Then I wanted to go back and look, so we did and he was dying just then, taking in some bloody gasps of air so I nudged his face with my shoe a few times, then I told Dominic to kick him, so he kicked the f___ out of his face and he still has blood on his shoes all over . . . here's the clippings from the newspaper . . . we were on all the channels*" ("Grisly Account of Ly Killing Believed Penned by Suspect," *Los Angeles Times* Orange County Edition, March 7, 1996).

Was there racial motivation behind the crime? White supremacist paraphernalia were found at Linberg's and Christopher's home (Mai Pham, "Former UCLA Student Leader Murdered in Hate Crime," *Crosscurrents* [Fall/Winter 1996], p 11).

The concept of whiteness became lodged in the discursive crucible of colonial identity by the early 1860s. Whiteness at that time had become a marker for measuring inferior and superior races. Interestingly, Genghis Khan, Attila the Hun, and Confucius were at this time considered "White." Blackness was evaluated positively in European iconography from the twelfth to the fifteenth centuries, but after the seventeenth century and the rise of European colonialism, blackness became conveniently linked to inferiority (Cashmore, 1996). For instance, during the sixteenth and seventeenth centuries, blood purity (*limpieza de sangre*) became raised to a metaphysical—perhaps even sacerdotal—status, as it became a principle used to peripheralize Indians, Moors, and Jews.

Blackness was not immediately associated with slavery. In the United States, the humanistic image of Africans created by the abolitionist movement was soon countered by new types of racial signification in which White skin was identified with racial superiority. Poor Europeans were sometimes indentured and were in some sense *de facto* slaves. They occupied the same economic categories as African slaves and were held in equal contempt by the lords of the plantation and legislatures (Cashmore, 1996). So poor Europeans were invited to align themselves with the plantocracy as "White" in order to avoid the most severe forms of bondage. This strategy helped plantation owners form a stronger social control apparatus; hegemony was achieved by offering "race privileges" to poor Whites as acknowledgment of their loyalty to the colonial land (Cashmore, 1996).

By the early twentieth century, European maritime empires controlled over half the land (72 million square kilometers) and a third of the world's population (560 million people). Seventy-five million Africans died during the centuries-long transatlantic slave trade (West, 1993). The logics of empire are still with us, bound to the fabric of our daily being-in-the-world, woven into our posture toward others, connected to the muscles of our eyes, dipped in the chemical relations that excite and calm us, structured into the language of our perceptions. We cannot will our racist logics away. We need to work hard to eradicate them. We need to struggle with a formidable resolve in order to overcome what we are afraid to confirm exists, let alone to confront it, in the battleground of our souls.

Cornel West has identified three White supremacist logics: the Judeo-Christian racist logic, the scientific racist logic, and the psychosexual story of Ham, son of Noah, who in failing to cover Noah's nakedness, had his progeny blackened by God. In this logic, unruly behavior and Catholic rebellion are linked to racist practices. The "scientific" racist logic is identified with the evaluation of physical bodies in light of Greco-Roman standards. Within this logic racist practices are identified with physical ugliness, cultural deficiency, and intellectual inferiority. The psychosexual racist logic identifies Black people with Western sexual discourses associated with sexual prowess, lust, dirt, and subordination. A serious question is raised by West's typology in relation to the construction of whiteness: What are the historically concrete and sociologically specific ways that White supremacist discourses are guided by Western philosophies of identity and universality and capitalist relations of production and consumption? West has located racist practices in the commentaries by the church fathers on the Song of Solomon and the Ywain narratives in medieval Brittany, to name just a few historical sources. West has also observed that human bodies were classified according to skin color as early as 1684 (before the rise of modern capitalism) by French physician François Bernier. The famous eighteenth-century naturalist Carolus Linnaeus produced the first major written account of racial division in *Natural System* (1735). White supremacy is linked to the way culture is problematized and defined. As we have seen, theories of culture are themselves by-products of and symptoms of theorists' relation to an ongoing global struggle over issues of social class.

George Lipsitz (1995) argues that understanding the destructive quality of White identity requires what Walter Benjamin termed "presence of mind" or "an abstract of the future, and precise awareness of the present moment more decisive than foreknowledge of the most distant events" (1995, p. 370). Noting that "race" is not merely a "cultural construct" but a construct that has "sinister structural causes and consequences," Lipsitz argues that from colonial times to the present there has existed systematic efforts "to create a possessive investment in whiteness for European Americans" (p. 371). Identifying what he calls a new form of racism embedded in "the putatively race-neutral liberal social democratic reforms of the past five decades" (p. 371), Lipsitz asserts that the possessive investment in whiteness can be seen in legacies of socialization bequeathed to U.S. citizens by federal, state, and local policies toward African Americans, Native Americans, Mexican Americans, Asian Americans "and other groups designated by whites as 'racially other.'"

Lipsitz impressively covers a great deal of historical ground in his discussion of White privilege—from colonial legal systems and racialized chattel slavery to contemporary efforts at urban renewal and highway construction that victimized mainly minority neighborhoods. For instance, Lipsitz tells us that while Blacks in Houston, Texas, make up a little more than one-quarter of the local population, more than 75% of municipal garbage incinerators and 100% of city-owned garbage dumps are located in Black neighborhoods. Lipsitz reports that in response to 1,177 toxic waste cases, the Environmental Protection Agency exacted penalties on polluters near the greatest White population that were 500% higher than penalties imposed on polluters in minority areas (income did not account for these differences). Not only were penalties for violating all federal environmental laws about air, water and waste pollution in minority communities found to be 46% lower than in White communities, minority communities had to wait longer for cleanups, sometimes 42% longer than at White sites, and endure a 7% greater likelihood of "containment" (walling off a hazardous site) than clean-up. White sites enjoyed treatment and clean-ups 22% more often than containment.

Urban renewal also favored the rich by constructing luxury housing units and cultural centers, rather than affordable housing for the poor, in order to help cities compete for corporate investment. After providing a long litany of policies and practices infused with institutionalized forms of racism that have persisted over decades—forms that included government subsidies to private sectors, tax breaks for the wealthy, tax increment redevelopment programs, industrial development bonds, tax reforms, and federal house loan policies—Lipsitz goes on to argue that Americans produce largely cultural explanations for structural social problems. They do so, Lipsitz maintains, because they are "largely ignorant of even the recent history of the possessive investment in whiteness" (1995, p. 379). For instance, Whites are often unaware that nationwide financial institutions receive more money in deposits from Black neighborhoods than they invest in them in the form of home mortgage loans. Home lending has thus become a vehicle for the transfer of capital away from Black savers and toward White investors. Disturbingly, some polls have revealed that Whites believe that Blacks have the same opportunity to acquire a middle-class life as Whites. While at the same time, Whites persist in viewing negatively Blacks abilities, work habits, and character.

Charles Gallagher (1994) has worked as a professor with working-class and middle-class White students at an urban U.S. university. He makes the important point that the efforts of the media and racial politics in general has made whiteness more distinct as a racial category and has prompted Whites to see themselves other than "colorless or racially transparent" (p. 166). Unlike other critics who maintain that whiteness is largely invisible to Whites themselves, Gallagher maintains that the political and cultural mobilization of racially defined minorities has positioned Whites to think about themselves in relation to other racial groups and that the decline of ethnicity among late-generation Whites has created an "identity vacuum" that has been, in part, replaced by radicalized identity. In this milieu, right-wing factions are currently attempting to reconstruct being "White" as a nonracist cultural identity informed by decent citizens trying to preserve their White heritage and by White students trying to create an identity in ways "that do not demonize white as a racial category" (p. 167).

Gallagher argues that "white reconstruction" is occurring "among a sizable part of the white population, particularly among young people" (1994, p. 168). White males especially feel under assault by non-Whites "even though the 47 percent of white males in the labor force account for almost 92 percent of corporate officers and 88 percent of corporate directors" (p. 169). According to Gallagher, many White students view themselves as being victimized by Black racists and used as targets because they are White. They feel further under attack by "university-sanctioned race-based curricula" and "social clubs" such as the NAACP and La Raza. But Gallagher believes that this is a construction of White students' "own racist projections about what blacks think about whites" (p. 171). Feeling that their status is under siege, Whites are now constructing their identities in reaction to what they feel to be the "politically correct" challenge to White privilege. Many Whites, Gallagher notes, feel that being a minority is actually an asset and advantage in the job market and, furthermore, believe that "what is 'great' for minorities must be a handicap to whites" (p. 176).

Many White students reportedly still "believe the United States is an egalitarian, colorblind society" and thus refuse to define themselves as oppressors or recipients of White privileges. Gallagher found that among college students a legitimate, positive narrative of one's own whiteness was often created by constructing an identity that negated White-oppressor accusations and framed whiteness as a liability. Not only do White students deny U.S. racial history but they believe that their skin color provides them with no benefits. Embracing a color-blind society permits White people to construct ideologies to avoid the issue of racial inequality while simultaneously benefiting from it. The creation or invention of whiteness described by Gallagher suggests that the ways in which the White population "get raced" points to a process that needs to be better understood. White identity needs to be understood as "a reaction to the entrance of historically marginalized racial and ethnic groups into the political arena and the ensuing struggle over social resources" (1994, p. 183). It appears as if whiteness is beginning to be formed within the context of its own racial logics and essences. Gallagher explains:

The explicit reinsertion of whiteness into politics is possible only by creating the illusion that being white is no different than belonging to any other racial group in the United States. If that illusion can be maintained a white identity and white culture modeled on a

Disney America theme park, with its purified historic revisionism, will allow whites to reinvent a cultural history that does not evoke such matters as the Ku Klux Klan or Japanese internment during World War II but instead is synonymous with egalitarianism, rugged individualism, and democracy. (p. 184)

In her article "Whiteness as Property" (1993), Cheryl I. Harris makes the compelling case that within the legal system and within popular reasoning, there exists an assumption that whiteness is a property interest entitled to legal protection. Whiteness as property is essentially the reification in law of expectations of White privilege. Not only has this assumption been supported by systematic White supremacy through the law of slavery and "Jim Crow" laws but also by recent decisions and rationales of the Supreme Court concerning affirmative action. Harris is correct in arguing that White racial identity provides the basis for allocating societal benefits in both public and private spheres. Whiteness as a property of status continues to assist in the reproduction of the existing system of racial classification and stratification that protects the socially entrenched White power elite. According to Harris, rejecting race-conscious remedial measures as unconstitutional under the equal-protection clause of the Fourteenth Amendment "is based on the Court's chronic refusal to dismantle the institutional protection of benefits for whites that have been based on white supremacy and maintained at the expense of Blacks" (1993, p. 1767).

Current legal definitions of race embrace the norm of color blindness and thus disconnect race from social identity and race consciousness. Within the discourse of color blindness, blackness and whiteness are seen as neutral and apolitical descriptions reflecting skin color and as unrelated to social conditions of domination and subordination and to social attributes such as class, culture, language, and education. In other words, color blindness is a concept that symmetrizes relations of power and privilege and flattens them out so that they appear symmetrical or equivalent. But blackness and whiteness exist symmetrically only as idealized oppositions; in the real world they exist as a dependent hierarchy, with whiteness constraining the social power of blackness by colonizing the definition of what is normal, by institutionalizing a greater allocation of resources for White constituencies, and by maintaining laws that favor Whites. According to Harris,

To define race reductively as simply color, and therefore meaningless is as subordinating as defining race to be scientifically determinative of inherent deficiency. The old definition creates a false linkage between race and inferiority; the new definition denies the real linkage between race and oppression under systemic white supremacy. Distorting and denying reality, both definitions support race subordination. As Neil Gotanda has argued, colorblindness is a form of race subordination in that it denies the historical context of white domination and Black subordination. (1993, p 1768)

Affirmative action needs to be understood not through privatizing social inequality through claims of bipolar corrective justice between Black and White competitors but rather as an issue of distributive social justice and rights that focus not on guilt or innocence but on entitlement and fairness.

According to Alex Callinicos (1993), racial differences are invented. Racism occurs when the characteristics that justify discrimination are held to be inherent in the oppressed group. This form of oppression is peculiar to capitalist societies; it arises in the circumstances surrounding industrial capitalism and the attempt to acquire a large labor force. Callinicos points out three main conditions for the existence of racism as outlined by Marx: economic competition among workers; the appeal of the racist ideology to White workers; and efforts of the capitalist class to establish and maintain racial divisions among workers. Capital's constantly changing demands for different kinds of labor can be met only through immigration. Callinicos remarks that "racism offers for workers of the oppressing 'race' the imaginary compensation for the exploitation they suffer of belonging to the '*ruling* nation'" (1993, 39).

Callinicos notes how Marx grasped the fact that racial divisions between "native" and immigrant workers could weaken the working class. U.S. politicians take advantage of this division, which the capitalist class understands and manipulates only too well. George Bush, Jesse Helms, Pat Buchanan, Phil Gramm, David Duke, and Pete Wilson have effectively used racism to divide the working class.

At this point you might be asking yourselves: Doesn't racism predate capitalism? Here I agree with Callinicos that the heterophobia associated with precapitalist societies was not the same as modern racism. Precapitalist slave and feudal societies Greece and Rome did not rely on racism to justify the use of slaves. The Greeks and Romans had no theories of White superiority. If they did, they must have been unsettling news to Septimus Severus, Roman emperor from C.E. 193 to 211, who was, many historians claim, a Black man. Racism developed at a key turning point in capitalism during the seventeenth and eighteenth centuries of colonial plantations in the New World, where slave labor stolen from Africa was used to produce tobacco, sugar, and cotton for the global consumer market (Callinicos, 1993). Callinicos cites Eric Williams, who remarks: "Slavery was not born of racism; rather, racism was the consequence of slavery" (cited in Callinicos, 1993, p. 24). Racism has emerged as the ideology of the plantocracy. It began with the class of sugar planters and slave merchants that dominated England's Caribbean colonies. Racism developed out of the "systemic slavery" of the New World. The "natural inferiority" of Africans was used by Whites to justify enslaving them. According to Callinicos,

Racism offers white workers the comfort of believing themselves part of the dominant group; it also provides, in times of crisis, a ready made scapegoat, in the shape of the oppressed group. Racism thus gives white workers a particular identity, and one moreover which unites them with white capitalists. We have here, then, a case of the kind of "imagined community" discussed by Benedict Anderson in his influential analysis of nationalism. (1993, p. 38)

To abolish racism, we need to abolish global capitalism. Callinicos is very clear on this point.

The educational left has largely failed to address the issue of whiteness and the insecurities that young Whites harbor regarding their future during times of diminishing economic expectations. With their "racially coded and divisive rhetoric," neoconservatives may be able to enjoy tremendous success in helping insecure young White populations develop White identity along racist lines. Consider the comments by David Stowe:

The only people nowadays who profess any kind of loyalty to whiteness *qua* whiteness (as opposed to whiteness as an incidental feature of some more specific identity) are Christian Identity types and Ayran Nation diehards. Anecdotal surveys reveal that few white Americans mention whiteness as a quality that they think much about or particularly value. In their day-to-day cultural preferences—food, music, clothing, sports, hairstyles—the great majority of American whites display no particular attachment to white things. There does seem to be a kind of emptiness at the core of whiteness. (1996, p. 74)

People don't discriminate against groups because they are different but rather the act of discrimination constructs categories of difference that hierarchically locate people as "superior" or "inferior" and then universalize and naturalize such differences. When I refer to whiteness or to the cultural logics of whiteness, I need to qualify what I mean. Here I adopt Ruth Frankenberg's injunction that cultural practices considered to be White need to be seen as contingent, historically produced, and transformable. White culture is not monolithic, and its borders must be understood as malleable and porous. It is the historically specific confluence of economic, geopolitical, and ethnocultural processes. According to Alastair Bonnett (1996), whiteness is neither a discrete entity nor a fixed, asocial category. Rather, it is an "immutable social construction" (p. 98). White identity is an ensemble of discourses, contrapuntal and contradictory. Whiteness—and the meanings attributed to it—are always in a state of flux and fibrillation. Bonnett notes that "even if one ignores the transgressive youth or ethnic borderlands of Western identities, and focuses on the 'center' or 'heartlands' of 'whiteness,' one will discover racialised subjectivities, that, far from being settled and confidant, exhibit a constantly reformulated panic over the meaning of 'whiteness' and the defining presence of 'non-whiteness' within it" (p. 106). According to Frankenberg, White culture is a material and discursive space that: "is inflected by nationhood, such that whiteness and Americanness, though by no means coterminous, are profoundly shaped by one another . . . Similarly, whiteness, masculinity, and femininity are coproducers of one another, in ways that are, in their turn, crosscut by class and by the histories of racism and colonialism" (1993, p. 233).

Whiteness needs to be seen as *cultural*, as *processual*, and not ontologically different from processes that are non-White. It works, as Frankenberg notes, as "an unmarked marker of others' differentness—whiteness not so much void or formlessness as norm" (1993, p. 198). Whiteness functions through social practices of assimilation and cultural homogenization; whiteness is linked to the expansion of capitalism in the sense that "whiteness signifies the production and consumption of commodities under capitalism" (p. 203). Yet capitalism in the United States needs to be understood as contingently White, since White people participate in maintaining the hegemony of institutions and practices of racial dominance in different ways and to greater or lesser degrees. Frankenberg identifies the key discursive repertoires of whiteness as follows:

[First,] modes of naming culture and difference associated with west European colonial expansion; second, elements of "essentialist" racism . . . linked to European colonialism but also critical as rationale for Anglo settler colonialism and segregationism in what is now the USA; third, "assimilationist" or later "color- and power-evasive strategies for thinking through race first articulated in the early decades of this century; and, fourth, . . . "race-cognizant" repertoires that emerged in the latter half of the twentieth century and were linked both to U.S. liberation movements and to broader global struggles for decolonization. (p. 239)

    While the entire range of discursive repertoires may come into play, jostling against, superceding, and working in conjunction with each other, White identity is constructed in relation to an individual's personal history, geopolitical situatedness, contextually specific practices, and location in the materiality of the racialized social order. In other words, many factors determine which discursive configurations are at work and the operational modalities present.
    Whiteness has no formal content. It works rhetorically by articulating itself out of the semiotic detritus of myths of European superiority. These are myths that are ontologically empty, epistemologically misleading, and morally pernicious in the way that they privilege descendants of Europeans as the truly civilized in contrast to the quaint, exotic, or barbaric character of non-European cultures. Whiteness is a sociohistorical form of consciousness, given birth at the nexus of capitalism, colonial rule, and the emergent relationships among dominant and subordinate groups. Whiteness operates by means of its constitution as a universalizing authority by which the hegemonic White bourgeois subject appropriates the right to speak on behalf of everyone who is non-White while denying voice and agency to these Others in the name of civilized humankind. Whiteness constitutes and demarcates ideas, feelings, knowledge, social practices, cultural formations, and systems of intelligibility that are identified with or attributed to White people and that are invested in by White people as "White." Whiteness is also a refusal to acknowledge how White people are implicated in certain social relations of privilege and relations of domination and subordination. Whiteness, then, can be considered as a form of social amnesia associated with modes of subjectivity within particular social sites considered to be normative. As a lived domain of meaning, whiteness represents particular social and historical formations that are reproduced through specific discursive and material processes and circuits of desire and power. Whiteness reflects a conflictual sociocultural, sociopolitical, and geopolitical process that animates commonsensical practical action in relationship to dominant social practices and normative ideological productions. Whiteness constitutes the selective tradition of dominant discourses about race, class, gender, and sexuality hegemonically reproduced. Whiteness has become the substance and limit of our common sense articulated as cultural consensus. As an ideological formation transformed into a principle of life, into an ensemble of social relations and practices, whiteness needs to be understood as conjunctural, as a composite social hieroglyph that shifts in denotative and connotative emphasis depending on how its elements are combined and on the contexts in which it operates (Haymes, 1995).
    Whiteness is not a pregiven, unified ideological formation but is a multifaceted collective phenomenon resulting from the relationship between the self and the

ideological discourses, which are constructed out of the surrounding local and global cultural terrain. Whiteness is fundamentally Euro- or Western-centric in its episteme, as it is articulated in complicity with the pervasively imperializing logic of empire. Whiteness in the United States can be understood largely through the social consequences it provides for those who are considered to be non-White. Such consequences can be seen in the criminal justice system, in prisons, in schools, and in the board rooms of corporations such as Texaco. It can be defined in relation to immigration practices and social policies and practices of sexism, racism, and nationalism. It can be seen historically in widespread acts of imperialism and genocide and can be linked to an erotic economy of "excess." Eric Lott writes:

In rationalized Western societies, becoming "white" and male seems to depend upon the remanding of enjoyment, the body, and aptitude for pleasure. It is the other who is always putatively "excessive" in this respect, whether through exotic food, strange and noisy music, outlandish bodily exhibitions, or unremitting sexual appetite. Whites in fact organize their own enjoyment through the other, Slavoj Zizek has written, and access pleasure precisely by fantasizing about the other's "special" pleasure. hatred of the other arises from the necessary hatred of one's own excess; ascribing this excess to the "degraded" other and indulging it—by imaging, incorporating, or impersonating the other—one conveniently and surreptitiously takes and disavows pleasure at one and the same time. This is the mixed erotic economy, what Homi Bhabha terms the "ambivalence," of American whiteness. (1993, p. 482)

Whiteness is a type of articulatory practice that can be located in the convergence of colonialism, capitalism, and subject formation. It both fixes and sustains discursive regimes that represent self and "Other"; that is, whiteness represents a regime of differences that produces and racializes an abject Other. In other words, whiteness is a discursive regime that enables real effects to take place. Whiteness displaces blackness and brownness—specific forms of nonwhiteness—into signifiers of deviance and criminality within social, cultural, cognitive, and political contexts. White subjects discursively construct identity through producing, naming, "bounding," and marginalizing a range of others (Frankenberg, 1993, p. 193).

Whiteness constitutes unmarked (European American male) practices that have negative effects on and consequences for those who do not participate in them. Inflected by nationhood, whiteness can be considered an ensemble of discursive practices constantly in the process of being constructed, negotiated, and changed. Yet it functions to instantiate a structured exclusion of certain groups from social arenas of normativity. Coco Fusco remarks: "To raise the specter of racism in the here and now, to suggest that despite their political beliefs and sexual preferences, white people operate within, and benefit from, white supremacist social structures is still tantamount to a declaration of war" (1995, p. 76).

Whiteness is not only mythopoetical in the sense that it constructs a totality of illusions formed around the ontological superiority of the European American subject, it is also metastructural in that it connects whiteness across specific differences; it solders fugitive, break-away discourses and rehegemonizes them.

Consumer utopias and global capital flows rearticulate whiteness by means of relational differences (Kinchloe and Steinberg, in press).

Whiteness is dialectically reinitiated across epistemological fissures, contradictions, and oppositions through new regimes of desire that connects the consumption of goods to the everyday logic of Western democracy. The cultural encoding of the typography of whiteness is achieved by remapping Western European identity onto economic transactions, by recementing desire to capitalist flows, by concretizing personal history into collective memory linked to place, to a myth of origin. Whiteness offers a safe "home" for those imperiled by the flux of change.

Whiteness can be considered as a conscription of the process of positive self-identification into the service of domination through inscribing identity into an ontoepistemological framework of "us" against "them." For those who are non-White, the seduction of whiteness can produce a self-definition that disconnects the subject from her or his history of oppression and struggle, exiling identity into the unmoored, chaotic realm of abject otherness (while tacitly accepting the positioned superiority of the Western subject). Whiteness provides the European American subject with a known boundary that places nothing "off limits" yet which provides a fantasy of belongingness. It's not that whiteness signifies preferentially one pole of the White-non-White binarism. Rather, whiteness seduces the subject to accept the idea of polarity as the limit-text of identity, as the constitutive foundation of subjectivity.

In his important volume, *Psychoanalytic-Marxism*, Eugene Victor Wolfenstein describes the whiteness of domination as the "one fixed point" of America's many facisms. He argues that whiteness is a social designation and a "history disguised as biology" (1993, p. 331). Whiteness is also an attribute of language. Wolfenstein claims that "languages have skin colors. There are white nouns and verbs, white grammar and white syntax. In the absence of challenges to linguistic hegemony, indeed, language is white. If you don't speak white you will not be heard, just as when you don't look white you will not be seen" (p. 331).

Describing White racists as "virtuosos of denigration," Wolfenstein maintains that the language of White racism illustrates "a state of war" (1993, p. 333). Yet the battles are fought through lies and deceit. One such lie is the idea of "colorblindness."

Wolfstein notes that colorblindness constitutes more than a matter of conscious deceit:

White racism is rather a mental disorder, an ocular disease, an opacity of the soul that is articulated with unintended irony in the idea of "color blindness." To be color blind is the highest form of racial false consciousness, a denial of both difference and domi-nation. But one doesn't have to be color blind to be blinded by white racism . . . . Black people see themselves in white mirrors, white people see black people as their own photographic negatives. (1993, p. 334)

Wolfenstein suggests that two epistemological tasks be undertaken. Black people need to look away from the White mirror; White people need to attempt to see Black people as they see themselves and to see themselves as they are seen by other Black people. Wolfenstein links White racism to what he terms "epidermal fetishism." Epidermal fetishism reduces people to their skin color and renders them invisible. It is a type of social character that is formed within a process of exchange and circulation. As such, whiteness represents the superego (the standard of social value, self-worth, and mortality). Since the ego is affirmatively reflected in the superego, it must be White What is therefore repressed is blackness, which "becomes identified with the unwanted or bad parts of the self" (1993, p. 336).

At the level of social character, white racism is self-limiting for white people, self-destructive for black people. White people alienate their sensuous potentialities from themselves. They are devitalized and sterilized. Blackness, officially devalued, comes to embody their estranged life and desire. They are able, however, to see themselves reflected in the mirrors of selfhood. But is black people have their selfhood structured by the whitened-out from of social character, they become fundamentally self-negating. Their blackness, hated and despised, must be hidden away. Hair straighteners and skin lighteners testify to the desire to go further and eradicate blackness altogether. (1993, pp. 336–337)

The incorporeal luminescence of whiteness is achieved, according to Wolfenstein, by the subsumption of blackness within whiteness. What cannot be subsumed and digested is excreted. White people both despise and lust after blackness. Wolfenstein describes some forms of interracial romantic heterosexual relationships as epidermally mediated erotic domination, as an epidermalized sexual rebellion against a repressive social morality, and as an epidermally mediated double violation of the oedipal incest taboo. In order to resist epidermal fetishism, oppressed people need a language and a politics of their own.

It is important to recognize that White racism is neither purely systemic nor purely individual. rather, it is a complex interplay of collective interests and desires. White racism in this instance "becomes a rational means to collective ends" (Wolfenstein, 1993, p. 341) when viewed from the standpoint of ruling-class interests. yet for the White working class it is irrational and a form of false consciousness. White racism also circumscribes rational action for Black people in that they are encouraged to act in terms of their racial rather than class interests.

Whiteness offers coherency and stability in a world in which capital produces regimes of desire linked to commodity utopias where fantasies of omnipotence must find a stable home. Of course, the "them" is always located within the "us." The marginalized are always foundational to the stability of the central actors. The excluded in this case establish the condition of existence of the included. So we find that it is impossible to separate the identities of both oppressor and oppressed. They depend upon each other. To resist whiteness means developing a politics of difference. Since we lack the full semantic availability to understand whiteness and to resist it, we need to rethink difference and identity outside of sets of binary oppositions. We need to view identity as coalitional, as collective, as processual, as grounded in the struggle for social justice.

Alistair Bonnett notes that reified notions of whiteness "enables 'white' people to occupy a privileged location in antiracist debate; they are allowed the luxury of being passive observers, of being altruistically motivated, of knowing that their 'racial' identity might be reviled and lambasted but never actually made slippery, torn open, or, indeed, abolished" (1996, p. 98). Bonnett further notes: "To dismantle 'blackness' but leave the force it was founded to oppose unchallenged is to display both a political and theoretical naïveté. To subvert 'blackness' without subverting 'whiteness' reproduces and reinforces the 'racial' myths, and the 'racial' dominance, associated with the latter" (1996, p. 99).

Ian Haney López's book, *White by Law* (1996), offers a view of White transparency and invisibility that is at odds with Gallagher's thesis that Whites are growing more conscious of their whiteness. López cites an incident at a legal feminist conference in which participants were asked to pick two or three words to describe themselves. All of the women of color selected at least one racial term, but not one White woman selected a term referring to her race. This prompted Angela Harris to remark that only White people in this society have the luxury of having no color. An informal study conducted at Harvard Law School underscores Harris's remark. A student interviewer asked ten African Americans and ten White Americans how they identified themselves. Unlike the African Americans, most of the White Americans did not consciously factor in their "whiteness" as a crucial or even tangential part of their identity.

López argues that one is not born White but becomes White "by virtue of the social context in which one finds oneself, to be sure, but also by virtue of the choices one makes" (1996, p. 190). But how can one born into the culture of whiteness, who is defined as White, undo that whiteness? López addresses this question in his formulation of whiteness. He locates whiteness in the overlapping of *chance* (e.g., features and ancestry that we have no control over, morphology); *context* (context-specific meanings that are attached to race, the social setting in which races are recognized, constructed, and contested); and *choice* (conscious choices with regard to the morphology and ancestries of social actors in order to "alter the readability of their identity" (p. 191).

In other words, López maintains that chance and context are not racially determinative. He notes that: "Racial choices must always be made from within specific contexts, where the context materially and ideologically circumscribes the range of available choices and also delimits the significance of the act. Nevertheless, these are racial choices, if sometimes only in their overtone or subtext, because they resonate in the complex of meanings associated with race. Given the thorough suffusion of race throughout society, in the daily dance of life we constantly make racially meaningful decisions" (p. 193).

López's perspective offers potential, it would seem, for abolishing racism, since it refuses to locate whiteness only as antiracism's "Other." I agree with Bonnett when he remarks that "to continue to cast 'whites' as anti-racism's 'other,' as the eternally guilty and/or altruistic observers of 'race' equality work, is to maintain 'white' privilege and undermine the movement's intellectual and practical reach and utility" (1996, p. 107). In other words, Whites need to ask themselves to what extent their identity is a function of their whiteness in the process of their ongoing daily lives and what choices they might make to escape whiteness. López outlines—productively in my view—three steps in dismantling whiteness. They are worth quoting in full: "First, Whites must overcome the omnipresent effects of transparency and of the naturalization of race in order to recognize the many racial aspects of their identity, paying particular attention to the daily acts that draw upon and in turn confirm their whiteness. Second, they must recognize and accept the personal and social consequences of breaking out of a White identity. Third, they must embark on a daily process of choosing against Whiteness" (p. 193).

Of course, the difficulty of taking such steps is partly due to the fact that, as López notes, the unconscious acceptance of a racialized identity is predicated upon a circular definition of the self. It's hard to step outside of whiteness if you are White because of all the social, cultural and economic privilege that accompany whiteness. Yet, whiteness must be dismantled if the United States is to overcome racism. Lipsitz remarks: "Those of us who are 'white' can only become part of the solution if we recognize the degree to which we are already part of the problem—not because of our race, but because of our possessive investment in it" (1995, p. 384).

The editorial in the book *Race Traitor* puts it thus: "The key to solving the social problems of our age is to abolish the white race. Until that task is accomplished, even partial reform will prove elusive, because white influence permeates every issue in U.S. society, whether domestic or foreign . . . . Race itself is a product of social discrimination; so long as the white race exists, all movements against racism are doomed to fail" (Ignatiev and Garvey, 1996, p. 10).

While we lack the semantic availability to fully capture the meaning and function of whiteness, we can at least describe it as a discursive strategy, articulation, or modality; or we can refer to it perhaps as a form of discursive brokerage, a pattern of negotiation that takes place in conditions generated by specific discursive formations and social relations. Historically, whiteness can be seen as a tattered and bruised progeny of Western colonialism and imperialism.

Whiteness is crisscrossed by numerous social dynamics. It is produced through capitalist social relations or modes of domination. The marker "whiteness" serves as a discursive indicator or social hieroglyph (Cruz, 1996)—an "effect" of systematic social relations of which those who are marked as "White" have little conscious understanding. Whiteness, therefore, is socially and historically embedded; it's a form of racialization of identity formation that carries with it a history of social, cultural, and economic relations. Whiteness is unfinalizable, but compared to other ethnic formations, its space for maneuvering in the racialized and genderized permutations of U.S. citizenship is infinitely more vast. The task here for critical educators is to denaturalize whiteness by breaking its codes and the social relations and privileging hierarchies that give such codes normative power. The codification of whiteness as a social hieroglyph associated with civility, rationality, and political advancement is part of inherited social and cultural formations, formations that were given birth after the early capitalist marriage of industrialism and militarism. Whiteness is linked in a fundamental—if not dramatic—way to the racialization of aggression. Inherited categories and classifications that made whiteness the privileged signifier over blackness is a theme I have addressed in, "White Terror" (McLaren, 1995), and I will not rehearse that argument here.

I think that the relation between whiteness and privilege can be better understood by locating whiteness in the context of what Howard Winant calls "racial formation" (1994) and what David Theo Goldberg (1993b) calls "racial modality." A racial modality refers to "a fragile structure of racist exclusions at a space-time conjuncture" that is sustained by the power of socioeconomic interests and the intersection of discursive fields and strategies of representation (Goldberg, 1993b, p. 210). Winant defines race as "*a concept that signifies and symbolizes sociopolitical conflicts and interests to different types of human bodies*" (1994, p. 115). This signals an understanding of race as an everyday phenomenon, one that is historically and socially constructed and is implicated in social structures, identities, and signification systems. The concept of racial formation also addresses the "*expansion and intensification of racial phenomena*" on a global basis (p. 116). Further, it suggests "*a new conception of racial history and racial time*" (p. 116). Concerning the latter, then, whiteness can be seen as implicated in the progressive expansion of capitalism throughout the world and the genealogical racial time of European conquest, what Winant calls an "archetypal *longue durée*: a slow agony of inscription upon the human body, a murder mystery, if you will, but on a genocidal scale. The phenotypical signification of the world's body took place in and through conquest and enslavement, to be sure, but also as an enormous act of expression, of narration" (p. 117).

Whiteness, of course, is also a product of historical time in terms of what Winant calls "contingency," or the contextual specificity of its hegemonic articulations. Whiteness is implicated on a global basis in the internationalization of capital, which is being accompanied by the internationalization of race. We are witnessing growing diasporic movements as former colonial subjects immigrate to the Western metropoles, challenging the majoritarian status of European groups. Winant remarks that we are also witnessing "the rise of 'diasporic' models of blackness, the creation of 'panethnic' communities of Latinos and Asians (in such countries as the United Kingdom and the United States), and the breakdown of borders in both Europe and North America all [which] seem to be hybridizing and racializing previously national policies, cultures and identities" (p. 118). I would follow Winant in maintaining that the focus of our struggle at this present juncture should be on the racial dimensions of capitalism and the mobilization of White racial antagonisms. Prior to World War II in the United States there existed a well-developed racial ideology, "a caste-based social structure developed to guarantee white workers their racial identity as a signifier of their 'freedom'" (p. 125). White people represented the "*Herenvolk*"—a democracy of White males. Winant observes that the *Herenvolk's* supremacy was seriously eroded during the civil rights era. Of course, the post-civil rights era is another matter situation altogether. As racial domination gave way to racial hegemony, the task was no longer to subdue the masses of disenfranchised minorities but to accommodate them. The caste-based logic of race was discarded by White folks in favor of an egalitarian politics underwritten by a culture of poverty thesis: People of color should pull themselves up out of the "underclass" through their own initiatives.

Consider the recent case in point of the University of California's (UC) dismantling of affirmative action, championed by Ward Connerly, a conservative African American UC regent. When reports commissioned by the UC provost projected that the numbers of White and Asian UC undergraduates would markedly grow and numbers of underrepresented minority students would diminish, Connerly responded: "This is the most tacit admission of the extent that we are using race for underrepresented students that one could ever find" (cited in Wallace, 1996, pp. 1, 18). Connerly's comment is underwritten by a belief that African American and Latina/o students, for instance, are being given an unfair advantage by affirmative action programs. This presumes that the playing field is now equal and that we have arrived at a point in our society where meritocracy actually exists. It ignores issues of culture, economics, and ideology and how these factors and others work in relation to public institutions and the (re)production of structural racism. Consequently, Connerly is unable to fathom how his position on affirmative action acts in the service of White privilege.

I don't believe in reverse racism since I don't believe White people have transcended race; nor do I believe that Latina/os or African Americans have acquired a systematic power to dominate Whites. Yet along with the editors of *Race Traitor*, I believe in reversing racism by systematically dismantling whiteness. Even so, I am acutely aware that people of color might find troubling the idea that Whites populations can simply reinvent themselves by making the simple choice of not being White. Of course, this is not what López and others appear to be saying. The choices one makes and the reinvention one aspires to as a race traitor are not "simple;" nor are they easy choices for groups of Whites to make. Yet from the perspective of some people of color, offering the choice to White people of opting out of their whiteness could seem to set up an easy path for those who don't want to assume responsibility for their privilege as White people. Indeed, there is certainly cause for concern. David Roediger captures some of this when he remarks: "Whites cannot fully renounce whiteness even if they want to" (1994, p. 16). Whites are, after all, still accorded the privileges of being White even as they ideologically renounce their whiteness, often with the best of intentions. Yet the potential for nonwhiteness and anti-White struggle is too important to ignore or dismiss as wishful thinking or associate with a fashionable form of code-switching. Choosing not to be White is not an easy option for White people, not as simple as deciding to make a change in one's wardrobe. To understand the processes involved in the racialization of identity and to consistently choose nonwhiteness is a difficult act of apostasy, for it implies a heightened sense of social criticism and an unwavering commitment to social justice (Roediger, 1994). Of course, the question needs to be asked: If we can choose to be non-White, then can we choose to be Black or Brown? Insofar as blackness is a social construction (often "parasitic" on whiteness), I would answer yes.

Theologian James H. Cone, author of *A Black Theology of Liberation*, urges White folks to free themselves from the shackles of their whiteness: "If whites expect to be able to say anything relevant to the self-determination of the black community, it will be necessary for them to destroy their whiteness by becoming members of an oppressed community. Whites will be free only when they become new persons—when their white being has passed away and they are created anew in black being. When this happens, they are no longer white but free" (1986, p. 97).

I want to be clear that I am not arguing for constructing a positive White identity where whiteness is define with the best intentions as part of an antiracist and antiimperialist ideology. I argue for a self-consciousness about one's whiteness in terms of recognizing the danger of its transparency but do not advocate celebrating whiteness in any form. Rather, I argue for the disassembly and destruction of whiteness and advocate its rearticulation as a form of critical agency dedicated to struggles in the interests of the oppressed. López notes that "because races are constructed diacritically, celebrating Whiteness arguably requires the denigration of Blackness. Celebrating Whiteness, even with the best of antiracist intentions, seems likely only to entrench the status quo of racial beliefs" (1996, p. 172). Since White identity is the antonym to the identity of non-Whites, as López maintains, it is a sobering acknowledgment to make that the only positive identification one can offer with respect to whiteness is to call for the disassembly of whiteness and for its eventual destruction. López remarks, that "whiteness can only retain its positive meanings through the denial at every turn of social injustices associated with the rise and persistence of this racial category" (p. 185). The celebration of whiteness in any form is inseverably linked to the peripheralization and demonization of non-Whites. White identity serves implicitly as the positive mirror image to the explicit negative identities imposed on non-Whites (López, 1996). Even in the case of White U.S. citizens who claim European American identity as a way of avoiding the White versus non-White opposition, such a move is actually based on the double negative of not being non-White (López, 1996).

But again I would stress that becoming non-White is not a "mere" choice but a self-consciously political choice, a spiritual choice, and a critical choice. To choose blackness or brownness merely as a way to escape the stigma of whiteness and to avoid responsibility for owning whiteness is still very much an act of whiteness. To choose blackness or brownness as a way of politically disidentifying with White privilege and instead identifying and participating in the struggles of non-White peoples is an act of transgression, a traitorous act that reveals a fidelity to the struggle for justice. Lipsitz sums up the problems and the promise of the abolition of whiteness as follows:

Neither conservative "free market" policies nor liberal social democratic reforms can solve the "white problem" in America because both of them reinforce the possessive investment in whiteness. But an explicitly antiracist pan-ethnic movement that acknowledges the existence and power of whiteness might make some important changes. Pan-ethnic, antiracist coalitions have a long history in the United States—in the political activism of John Brown, Sojourner Truth, and the Magon brothers, among others—but we also have a rich cultural tradition of pan-ethnic antiracism connected to civil rights activism . . . . Efforts by whites to fight racism, not out of sympathy for someone else but out of a sense of self-respect and simple justice, have never completely disappeared; they remain available as models for the present. (1995, p. 384)

George Yúdice gives additional substance to Lipsitz's concerns related to coalition-building when he points out some of the limitations of current identity politics: "The very difficulty in imagining a new social order that speaks convincingly to over 70 percent of the population requires critics to go beyond pointing out the injustices and abuses and move on to an agenda that will be more effective in transforming structures. What good is it to fight against white supremacy unless whites themselves join the struggle?" (1995, p. 268). Stowe echoes a similar sentiment when he writes: "Race treason has its limits as a workable strategy. Consider the economistic language in which it is described. Whites are exhorted to renounce the wages of whiteness, to divest from their possessive investment in whiteness, to sabotage the exchange value of racial privilege . . . . How many social movements have gotten ahead through the renunciation of privilege, though?" (1996, p. 77).

Yúdice makes a lucid point when he criticizes the journal *Race Traitor* for lacking a notion of political articulation. I agree with him that it is not enough to simply have faith in Whites of goodwill to disidentify with their whiteness. He argues that change will not come suddenly as Whites rise up against their whiteness. This position ignores that: "(1) we are living in a time of diminishing expectations and (2) what binds together a society is an overdetermined configuration or constellation of ideologemes: democracy, individuality, free enterprise, work ethic, upward mobility, and national security are articulated in complex ways that do not simply split apart when anyone of them is challenged. Social formations tend to undergo processes of rearticulation, according to Ernesto Laclau, rather than the kind of upheaval that *Race Traitor* seeks" (Yúdice, 1995, pp. 271–272).

What is needed, argues Yúdice, is a multicultural politics that is capable of projecting "a new democratic vision that makes sense to the white middle and working classes" (1995, p. 273). Whites must be interpolated in rearticulating the whiteness of the dominant class. Whites need to "feel solidarity with those who have suffered deprivation as members of subordinated groups" (p. 276). They must be offered more than a rationalized rights discourse. They need to struggle over the interpretation of needs through the proliferation of public spheres in which the struggle for democracy can take place. The key, Yúdice maintains, is to center the struggle for social justice around resource distribution rather than identity: "Shifting the focus of struggle from identity to resource distribution will also make it possible to engage such seemingly nonracial issues as the environment, the military, the military-industrial complex, foreign aid, and free-trade agreements as matters impacting local identities and thus requiring a global politics that works outside of the national frame" (p. 280).

That whiteness was reproduced in the petri dish of European colonialism cannot be disputed, but it is wrong to think of whiteness as an incurable disease. Multiculturalists whose identities depend on whiteness being the static Other to antiracist efforts will perhaps resist the abolition of whiteness even though its destruction is their stated aim. We need to transgress the external determinations of White identity, which has brought about the unique conjuncture I have labeled the social hieroglyphics of whiteness, an ensemble of discourses informed, in part, by a perceived lack of ethnicity and also by issues of race, sexual identification, religion, and nation. Since the meanings that suture whiteness to special options denied to other groups within the United States are socially and historically constituted through circuits of investment and exchange, such meanings are mutable and can be transformed, but certainly not by self-willed efforts at refashioning whiteness into a new liturgy of self-critique accompanied by a new White cultural etiquette. Not until the social relations of (re)production and consumption are recognized as class relations linked to whiteness and thus challenged and transformed can new ethnicities emerge capable of eliminating White privilege.

European Americans still constitute the gatekeepers of the White racial order known as the United States. Its *Herrenvolk* democracy of White supremacy remains largely camouflaged under the logic of egalitarianism and meritocracy and the denial of the significance of race expressed by calls to abolish the "color line" through anti-affirmative action measures. This "color line" is no longer bipolar—Black versus White—but rather multipolar; Asians and Latina/os increase their pressure on White majoritarian constituencies in the larger struggle for racial democracy. Winant argues for the elimination of racial discrimination and inequality but emphasizes as well the liberation of racial identity itself. I agree with Winant that this will involve "a reenvisioning of racial politics and a transformation of racial difference" (1994, p. 169). This means making racial identity a matter of choice rather than an ascription of meaning to phenotype and skin color. Today the racist state still polices the "color line" as it did in the past, but this time by arguing that it is actually created by affirmative action. Important questions that still need to be raised involve the refiguring of whiteness in the context of globalization, diasporic identities, and the increasing dissolution of the nation-state. How might the construction of postnational identities cause us to rethink whiteness?

THE STRUGGLE FOR DEMOCRACY

In this final section will try to raise some of the concerns touched upon by Yúdice in the call for a radical vision of democratic practice. It is a vision that in my view is compatible with the struggle for a socialist democratic imaginary. Universal and particular rights will always be struggled over; they will never be fully compatible. For the critics of the universal, there are no universal rights provided by the nation-state, only further exclusion and demonization as the "enemies of America." Paradoxically, if the universal and the particular ever achieve compatibility, democracy will have disappeared and fascism taken its place. And while the practice of justice will always contain contradictions and ambiguities, critical educators still need to ask the tough question: How, for instance, do schools and other institutions restrict the universalisms of our shared political ideals mainly to privileged, White Anglo groups? But in asking the tough questions, critical educators should not subsume the universal quest for liberty and equality into the particular. Rather, the spheres of the universal should be considerably widened, and as this widening occurs, the contents of this universality should be reformulated to include the voices of those already marginalized and excluded (Laclau, 1992).

Etienne Balibar reflects a similar idea when he stresses the importance of understanding the social as well as the ideological conditions of democracy:

If democracy as a system of living traditions finds its expression in both the representation of the governed and the control of those who govern—by a sufficient appropriateness of the representation of the population's interests and ideas and by a sufficient degree of popular control over the controllers themselves—it is never more than a fragile equilibrium between the functions of consensus and the functions of conflict. Ultimately, democracy lies on the inverse excesses of these functions. In this way, democracy depends at least as much upon *fortuna* as upon *virtú*, as much upon favorable circumstances as upon the initiative of the ruling class, the parties, and the citizens. It is essential, if we want to understand history, that we not exaggerate the importance of consensus to the detriment of conflict. (1996, p. 370)

I want to argue that critical educators need to embrace what Nancy Fraser (1993) calls a "democratic socialist-feminist political imaginary." This imaginary entails, among other things, the following: expanding the vision of a fully social wage; defending the importance of public goods against commodities; challenging the technocratic discourses of the state that reduce citizens to clients and consumers; advocating for the importance of unwaged domestic work and the child-raising labor of women; enlarging the view of entitlement; criticizing "the hyperbolic masculinist-capitalist view that individual 'independence' is normal and desirable while 'dependence' is avoidable and deviant" (p. 21); insisting on a view of public provision as a system of social rights; rejecting the idea of "personal responsibility" and "mutual responsibility" in favor of "social responsibility;" and promoting social solidarity through confronting racism, sexism, homophobia, and class exploitation. We need a sense of shared responsibility without necessarily having to depend upon a shared identity (Darder, 1992).

Broadly speaking, Bauman sees communitarian democracy as community without freedom and liberal democracy as freedom without community. Bauman argues that the liberal concept of difference is "external" to the individual and stands for "the profusion of choices between the ways of being human and living one's life" (1996, p. 81). For communitarians, however, difference is "internalized" and represents "the refusal, or inability to consider other forms of life as options" (p. 81). Liberal difference has to do with affirming individual freedom; the difference spoken about by communitarians often has to do with the necessity of imposing limits on human freedom. In this latter view, freedom should be exercised in order to choose unfreedom. For communitarians, outcomes of choices need to be understood before the actual choice is made. On the other hand, Bauman notes that liberal freedom of choice "has become a major stratifying variable in our multi-dimensionally stratified society" (p. 88). In postmodern/consumer society, we are all fated to choose, but there exists a range of realistic choices because resources are needed to make those choices. While individual responsibility for choice is equally distributed, equality disappears, maintains Bauman, when we are considering the means to act on that responsibility: "What the liberal vision of the universal and equally awarded right to choose failed to take account of, is that 'adding freedom of action to the fundamental inequality of social condition will result in inequality yet deeper than before.' What liberal society offers with one hand, it tends to take back with the other; the duty of freedom without the resources that would permit a truly free choice is, for many affected a recipe for life without dignity, filled instead with humiliation and self deprecation" (p. 88).

Scott Lash (1996) argues against some of Bauman's criticisms of communication ethics, noting favorably that communitarian ethics has provided a "groundedness" necessary to promote an ethics linked to political collectivity and action. Lash offers some criticisms of the work of Emmanual Lévinas and his ethical imperative of unconditional responsibility for the Other. According to Lévinas, totality must be deconstructed and infinitely embraced. Totality—referring to tradition and contractual individualism and institutions such as law, politics, and history—permits the judgment of the individual as a universal "I." Whatever is left once ontological justification is removed constitutes the ethical moment for Lévinas. The ethical relation is therefore based on an originary, transcendental intersubjectivity prior to language. However, Lash presciently observes that upon closer examination of Lévinas's work, the concrete, particular "I" in its radical singularity and the "Other" appear to be both excluded in such an act of judgment. Lash criticizes Lévinas for offering a choice only between a politics of institutions (totality) and a politics of radical difference (infinity) and consequently rejecting a "subinstitutional politics of practice." (Lash, 1996, p. 94).

Lash maintains that in order for social transformation to take place, the singular "I" must be grounded in a set of political practices. According to Lash, Lévinas might respond that such practices are necessarily "egotistical." Lash maintains that this is not necessarily the case, and on this point I agree with him. It is not mandatory that ethics be world-denying and focus solely on the "event" of the moral relationship between subjectivity and the Other (Lash, 1996, p. 94). Lévinas's "event" takes place at every instant of revelation that consciousness encounters its own singularity. Lash reports that the construction of meaning, or the "pretemporal event," of revelation in which consciousness relates to the very act of saying is highly problematic in Lévinas's conceptualization. For instance, the subject in this case is reduced to the signifier, that brings about being in the event horizon of the word. Whereas a communitarian ethics would inhere in the world of social life and formations as regulative practices, for Lévinas the ethical relation is constitutive, not regulative, and occurs only when subjectivity turns away from the messiness of social life and toward infinity and the voice of the Other (the excluded, the oppressed, the strangers among us) is recognized.

Lash does concede that a communitarian ethics cannot sufficiently address the singularity of the Other. Yet still Lash argues that a community-oriented ethics of practice is necessary and can be carefully fashioned so that a space is left open "for the inscrutability of the other's singularity" (1996, p. 98). Rather than conceiving of the stranger as the featureless Other (as in Lévinas's work), Lash argues for an understanding of aspects of the horizon of the Other through dialogue. This dialogue would be grounded in diasporic understanding, that is, in communities of practice and the rhythms of shared languages and practices.

In Lash's view, a politics of difference should recognize the singularity of the Other through a dialogical praxis, through the overlapping of horizons, and through an ethics of sociality. Lévinas's space of infinity (where subjectivity confronts the face of the Other in an economy of being) must be made to extend beyond moral relationships in order to include dimensions of social relationships that exist exterior to totality and that embrace violence and death. Lash correctly points out that the ethical agent lives an infinite temporality that is not an empty eternity but rather one that is peopled and meaningful. He further observes—correctly in my view—that the concepts of patience and suffering in the work of Lévinas do not open up to the world of flesh and body. In Lévinas's ethical universe, pain takes place exterior to forms of social life. I should note, in passing, that Lash's position in reminiscent of my concept of *enfleshment*, in which subjectivity is formed in the temporal archives of the flesh and the historical moments of lived experience (see McLaren, 1995).

According to Lash, Lévinas gives us the polar opposite of the Third Reich's politics of spectacle, of the ethicization of aesthetics. We are offered an *éthique/esthétique*, which begins with a subjectivity facing toward infinity. Yet, paradoxically, this Lévinsian sublime does not mirror the Kantian sublime and the terror of aesthetic space but rather the ethical space of Kant's *Second Critique*, the realms of pure practical reason of *The Critique of Pure Reason*. Here, Lévinas's figures of singular subjectivity encounter the face of the Other in the sphere of reason where ethics becomes the primordial ground of knowledge and of truth. In this view we become our most moral selves when we are the furthest away from the constraints of time and space. I am arguing for a detranscendalized ethics of location grounded in one's situatedness in the messy web of social relations, and the worldiness of space and locality.

In arguing for an ethics grounded in the concrete practice and situatedness of dialogical relations, we need to turn to the writings of Mikhail Bahktin. Bahktin's perspectives can also help to forge an ethics that can take us past some of the limit conditions of Lévinas's position and in doing so bring us closer to a position compatible with that of the concept of "praxis" found in the work of the early Marx (Gardiner, 1996, p. 138; see also the important book on Volosinov and bilingual education by Marcia Morales, [1996]).

The materiality of ethics that is being discussed here, including Bahktin's notion of multivocality and dialogue, undergirds a concept of revolutionary multiculturalism that I consider to be fundamental to a pedagogy of liberation. The perspective on multiculturalism that I am advancing here I have referred to elsewhere as "critical multiculturalism" (see McLaren, 1995), and it bears a strong affinity to what Shohat and Stam (1994) refer to as "polycentric multiculturalism." Polycentric multiculturalism disidentifies with liberal pluralist multiculturalism premised on ethical universals; it is not simply about describing cultural history but about analyzing social power and transforming discourses, institutions, and social practices of privilege. It does not order cultures hierarchically against the invisible norm of whiteness in a liberal swirl of diversity but rejects the idea of a pre-existing center. That is, polycentric multiculturalism is articulated "from the margins" and views minoritarian communities "as active, generative participants at the very core of a shared, conflictual history" (Shohat and Stam, 1994, p. 48). It does not view identities as stable or fixed or essentialized but rather as unstable and historically situated. It is reciprocal and dialogical and rejects narrow definitions of identity politics as simply the work of discrete, bounded communities. Accompanied by a strategy of political articulation, critical multiculturalism can be a crucial practice in cutting racism at the joints and working toward a vision of cultural democracy premised on social and economic justice.

Dear brothers and sisters in struggle, I have been slowly leading up to a conclusion. Let me summarize some of the more prescriptive points which follow from my previous discussions. It seems clear to me that we must steadfastly refuse to cut our ties to the lifeworld of our students and the communities in which they live. We must work collectively to try to help our students better understand both what is occurring at the global level of capitalist flows and transactions and how consumer culture within late capitalism is producing marketplace justice for the privileged and poverty for the rest. This means inviting our students to challenge the cultural logics of late capitalism and how such logics and relations are not only turning individual subjects into servants of transnational regulatory banking institutions and corporations but are also coordinating identities and subjectivities into a cybercitizenship. This cybercitizenship promotes character structures that respond to personal responsibility and the entrepreneurial spirit rather than to collective responsibility and equality and social justice. In other words, we need to provide for our students the conditions for critical consciousness and struggle not only for economic justice (although this is crucial) but also for justice in the political arenas of race, gender, and sexuality.

What can we say about critical pedagogy in light of the contexts I have discussed? Broadly speaking, critical pedagogy is about struggling at the level of the social relations of production for economic justice for all working people. It is also about recreating culture and agency through the practice of criticism and a criticism of practice. I have tried to rescue in this chapter some undisputably Marxist foundations for critical pedagogy. Of course, much more work needs to be done in the area of pedagogy and class struggle, as unfashionable as this may seem in our current era of "post-Marxism."

"Is critical pedagogy about creating cultural heroes?" a student revolutionary once asked me following a lecture in Jalapa City, Mexico, a few years ago. Let me answer that question as a way of concluding my discussion. In my view, critical pedagogy is not mainly about struggling for cultural values (although values are certainly—fundamentally—important); it is, however, most emphatically about struggling with and for the oppressed. Critical citizenry is not about becoming a cultural hero by serving as a watchdog for family or civic values. Cultural heroes espouse certain values and may even die to defend them. They might even implore others to do the same (Bauman, 1992). While cultural heroes fight for cultural values, critical citizens, in contrast, sacrifice themselves for disenfranchised Others, and not necessarily for unpopular ideals. Life lived in service to others—rather than in service to abstract values—is one of the few measures that can give life within postmodern Gringolandia revolutionary meaning. Willingness to sacrifice ourselves for others is, as Lévinas, Bakhtin, and Bauman argue, the only revolutionary way to live amid the debris of existential uncertainty and alienation.

THE STRUGGLE FOR THE ETHICAL SELF

I am advocating here for the development of the ethical self as a way of living within and challenging the historical present of postmodern culture and transnational capitalism. Of the ethical self, Bauman writes:

Only in the shape of the ethical self is humanity complete. Only in that shape does it attain the subtle blend and sought-for reconciliation of uniqueness and togetherness. Only when raised to the level of the ethical self, individuality does not mean loneliness, and togetherness does not mean oppression. "Concern for the other, up to the sacrifice, up to the possibility of dying for him; responsibility for the other"—this is, as Lévinas insists, the "otherwise than being," the only exit from what otherwise would be self-enclosed, selfish, lonely, voiced (and ultimately meaningless) existence. (1992, p. 201)

I agree with Bauman when he explains that heroes traffic in ideas and die for them whether these happen to be ideas about freedom, justice, race, class, or God. Ethical selves, unlike heroes, die for the dignity of other human beings and for their well-being and in doing so they cannot justify any death or sacrifice *but their own*. Heroes often exhort others to die in the name of a cause (Bauman, 1992), whereas ethical selves cannot live at the expense of their responsibility to others.

As Bauman points out, "Death itself becomes a cause for the hero of a cause" (p. 201) whereas for the ethical self, life becomes the cause for those who are willing to die for the dignity and liberation of the Other. As critical citizens, we need to act as if the elimination of the needless suffering of all Others depended upon the day-to-day choices that we make. We must refuse to allow postmodern culture to domesticate the people, to render them useless, and we must struggle to deny contemporary democracy the license to proclaim the people unworthy servants of the common good. That is what is meant by acting critically, and that is the power, promise, and sacrifice of critical pedagogy.

Acting critically also means acting with aesthetic sensibility, since in some fundamental ways, aesthetic culture inevitably shapes political culture. Wolfgang Welsch (1996) suggests that relations of plurality, specificity, and partiality—as these operate within the realm of aesthetics—are structurally similar to the way in which they operate in everyday conditions of social life. Consequently, what is needed in contemporary formulations of critical pedagogy is an aesthetically reflexive awareness of difference in which social subjects are sensitized "for basic differences and for the peculiarity and irreducibility of different ways of life" (p. 19). Welsch notes that aesthetically reflective awareness "perceives deviant principles, sees through imperialisms, is allergic to injustice and encourages one to intervene for the rights of the oppressed" (p. 19). For example, Welsch claims that tolerance for difference without aesthetic sensibility is insufficient. He writes:

The example of tolerance serves to make clear just how dependent political culture is on aesthetic culture. Tolerance without sensibility would be just a bare principle. One imagines a person who has made all of the maxims of tolerance their own, but who in day-to-day life lacks the sensitivity to even notice that the perceptions of others are different in principle and not just subject to some arbitrary lapse, that is, that it's a case not of a deficit as such, but of a cultural difference. A person of this sort would never be embarrassed by so much as having to make use of his tolerance, but rather would incessantly practice imperialisms and oppression with the clearest of consciences and in the securest of beliefs that he's a tolerant person. Sensitivity for differences is then a real condition for tolerance. Perhaps we live in a society which talks too much of tolerance but has too little command of sensitivity. (1996, p. 19)

In fact, I would extend Welsch's example of tolerance by arguing that critical muliculturalism move beyond tolerance in order to embrace a politics of respect and affirmation. One way of extending Welsch's insights on aesthetic reflection—a project that I do not have time to develop here—would be to follow Paul Trembath (1996) in utilizing Gilles Deleuze's work on "affective capacities" in conjunction with a revised Marxian theory of sensuous activity in ways that are compatable with poststructuralist theories of difference and cultural materialism's opposition to the idealization of sense. In other words, we need a new language and politics of the body (McLaren, 1995).

The charge that I have leveled at U.S. democracy throughout this chapter is more than an arraignment of American civic-mindedness or national character but speaks to deep-seated structural arrangements prohibitive of equality and social justice. I am drawing attention to the ominous historical moment of citizen abdication of democracy to the powers of capital and to the false prophets of the antigovernment Patriot movement. It is a time of capitulation of government to corporations and of the fundamental incompatibility of unbridled capitalism and democracy. In this historical moment, we witness the marriage of dominant cultural life to *engabachamiento*.

I make this charge because the cause of liberation through schooling and other public spheres is too important to be left to narrow-minded educational researchers and pundits. The liberation of our schools is too vital a project to abandon to those who would domesticate critical pedagogy—such as some micro-ethnographers who either neutralize the social relations of production and consumption by ignoring the larger context of capitalism or pretend that it doesn't exist—or to right-wing journalists, conservative talk-show hosts, or conservative or liberal think tanks that seek democracy in our schools in only the most narrow functionalist or procedural sense. There are many arenas of struggle occupied by various groups offering strategies of hope: the EZLN (Ejército Zapatista se Liberación Nacional) in Chiapas; the EPR (Ejército Popular Revolutionario) and PROCUP-PDLP (Partido Revolutionario Obrero Clandestino Unión de Pueblo–Partido de los Pobres) in Oaxaca, Guerrero, and Hidalgo; ecofeminists struggling in southeastern Mexico; educational activists trained at the Centro de Estudios sobre la Universidad UNAM (Universidad Nacional Autonoma de Mexico) in Mexico City; African American urban activists in Detroit; student activists struggling to keep affirmative action in California; Puerto Rican students in Chicago politicizing their community; Nuyoricans struggling for justice in El Barrio; Chicana/o activists in Los Angeles fighting for *la raza*. Which arenas we are called to occupy will depend a great deal on the extent to which we can force democracy to provide for the basic needs of the people. Up to this point, the situation is unequivocal: We have failed democracy, and it has failed us.

Whites need to do more than remember the history of colonialism as it affected the oppressed; the need to critically re-member such history. As Homi Bhabha (1986, xxiii) reminds us, "Remembering is never a quiet act of introspection or retrospection. It is a painful re-membering, a putting together of the dismembered past to make sense of the trauma of the present." This means piercing the vapors of mystification surrounding the objectification of human relations within bourgeois consciousness in order to construct new forms of subjectivity and agency that operate within a socialist political imaginary.

What I am advocating, dear sisters and brothers in struggle, is a postcolonial multiculturalism that moves beyond the ludic, metrocentric focus on identities as hybrid and hyphenated assemblages that exist alongside or outside of the larger social totality. Postcolonial multiculturalism, as I am articulating the term, takes as its condition of possibility the capitalist world system; it moves beyond a monoculturalist multiculturalism that fails to address identity formation in a global context and focuses instead on the idea that identities are shifting, changing, overlapping, and historically diverse (Shohat, 1995). Multiculturalism is a politics of difference that is globally interdependent and raises questions about intercommunal alliances and coalitions. According to Ella Shohat, intercommunal coalitions are based on historically shaped affinities, and the multicultural theory that underwrites such a coalitionary politics needs "to avoid either falling into essentialist traps or being politically paralyzed by deconstructionist formulations" (1995, p. 177). Shohat articulates the challenge as follows:

Rather than ask who can speak, then, we should ask how we can speak together, and more important, how we can move the dialogue forward. How can diverse communities speak in concert? How might we interweave our voices, whether in chorus, in antiphony, in call and response, or in polyphony? What are the modes of collective speech? In this sense, it might be worthwhile to focus less on identity as something one "has," than on identification as something one "does." (p. 177)

Revolutionary multiculturalism recognizes that the objective structure in which we live, the material relations tied to production in which we are situated, and the determinate conditions that produce us are all reflected in our everyday lived experiences. In other words, lived experiences constitute more than subjective values, beliefs, and understandings; they are always mediated through ideological configurations of discourse, political economies of power and privilege, and the social division of labor. revolutionary multiculturalism is a socialist-feminist multiculturalism that challenges those historically sedimented processes through which race, class, and gender identities are produced within capitalist society. Therefore, revolutionary multiculturalism is not limited to transforming attitudinal discrimination but is dedicated to reconstituting the deep structures of political economy, culture, and power in contemporary social arrangements. It is not about reforming capitalist democracy but rather transforming it by cutting at its joints and then rebuilding the social order from the vantage point of the oppressed.

Revolutionary multiculturalsim must not only accommodate the idea of capitalism; it must also advocate a critique of capitalism and a struggle against it. The struggle for liberation on the basis of race and gender must not remain detached from anticapitalist struggle. Often the call for diversity and pluralism by the apostles of postmodernism is a surrender to the ideological mystifications of capitalism. The fashionable apostasy of preaching difference from the citadels of postmodernist thought has dissolved resistance into the totalizing power of capitalist exploitation. In this regard, Ellen Meiksins Wood rightly warns: "We should not confuse respect for the plurality of human experience and social struggles with a complete dissolution of historical causality, where there is nothing but diversity, difference and contingency, no unifying structures, no logic of process, no capitalism and therefore no negation of it, no universal project of human emancipation" (1995, p. 263).

The challenge is to create at the level of everyday life a commitment to solidarity with the oppressed and an identification with past and present struggles against imperialism, against racism, against sexism, against homophobia, against all those practices of unfreedom associated with living in a White supremacist capitalist society. As participants in such a challenge we become agents of history by living the moral commitment to freedom and justice, by maintaining a loyalty to the revolutionary domain of possibility, by speaking truth to power, and by creating a collective voice out of the farthest reaching "we"—one that unites all those who suffer under capitalism, patriarchy, racism, and colonialism throughout the globe.

Through critical pedagogy we can begin to ask questions about how we can live modernity's quest for emancipation within postmodern cultural climates without at the same time being deformed by its sufferings and practices of destruction. We can struggle to fathom how the goals of liberation can be won without dragooning less privileged groups into the service of our unacknowledged capitalist will to power. We need to do more than simply invert relations of power because then the oppressed, newly freed from their bondage, would inevitably recuperate the logic of the oppressor so long as the same system of power informs their identities as emancipated agents. Consequently, we must define liberation from whiteness outside of the particular goals of such a struggle. We must invariably ask: From whiteness to *where*? Addressing such a question will play a crucial role in the struggle for social justice, in the decades ahead. And this will be no small task in a world in which the theoretical pirouettes of the postmodern left have replaced a Marxian emphasis on concrete struggle and community activism; where a playful decentering of the signifier has replaced the struggle against oppression; and where the notion of oppression itself has been psychologized to mean anything that happens to be bothering you at the time, like the weeds in your front lawn. In this instance, resistance is co-opted and reduced to a variation of the monolithic theme of procedural democracy.

A revolutionary multiculturalism must begin with an immanent rather than a transcendent critique, revolutionary praxis rather than melioristic reforms. It must engage what Enrique Dussel (1993) calls "the Reason of the Other." The debates over modernity and postmodernity have a different set of valences for *los olvidados* in Latina/oamerica, for the peripheralized, for the marginalized, for the wretched of the earth. Dussell writes about this distinction from his Latin American context: "Unlike the postmodernists, we do not propose a critique of reason as such; but we do accept their critique of a violent, coercive, genocidal reason. We do not deny the rational kernel of the universalist rationalism of the Enlightenment, only its irrational moment as sacrificial myth. We do not negate reason, in other words, but the irrationality of the violence generated by the myth of modernity. Against postmodernist irrationalism, we affirm the 'Reason of Other'" (p. 75).

I wish to present critical pedagogy not as a set of classroom teaching practices but rather position it within a larger political problematic; here critical pedagogy is located as a politically informed disposition and commitment to marginalized Others in the service of justice and freedom. Justice is conceptualized in this context from within the spirit of a transformative diasporic consciousness and encompasses issues of class, race, gender, and sexual orientation because all of these ongoing relations inform each other. A critical pedagogy grounded in a rearticulation of whiteness must seek to create a larger context in which it shares values with other struggles. We need, in other words, to fight for each other's differences and not just our own. This stipulates that we must identify a common ground of struggle in which a universality of rights and the common good pass into particular social struggles and then is reinitiated dialectically at a higher level of universality, and so on, without final closure. I am pointing to a nonabsolutist form of cultural politics, one that is never quite free from historically given languages, cultural codes, positionings of time and space, and forms of memory and narration that make political articulation and expression possible in the first place (Rattansi, 1994, p. 76). The new political subject that will emerge will be constituted by deessentializing forms of agency and syncretic forms of political consciousness. An example of such syncretic tactics in the realm of music can be seen in the work of Britain's Apache Indian (Stephen Kuper), a Hindu Punjabi who was raised in a multiethnic area of working-class Birmingham. Apache has been voted best newcomer at the British Reggae Industry Awards and is popular among African Caribbean and South Asian disaporic communities, and his work topped the reggae and bhangra charts in 1991 (Bhachu, 1996). Similarly, the group PBN—Punjabi by Nature—is a Toronto-based group of Canadian-born South Asians whose music has been influenced by four continents, resulting in what Parminder Bhachu calls a "quadruple diasporic consciousness" (1996, p. 286). George Lipsitz tells the story of an African man who grew up believing that Pete Seeger was Black, because he knew Seeger was a civil rights activist, sang freedom songs, and included Paul Robeson among his personal friends. After coming to the United States, the man got into an argument over Seeger's ethnicity and was shown a picture of Seeger that showed him to be White. Yet still the man replied: "I know that Pete Seeger is Black . . . why should I change my mind just because I see his face" (1996, p. 409).

Only through a multidimensional approach to agency and a transformation of the human condition created by capitalism can we begin the task of transforming the overwhelming power of transnational capital and truly live as liberated subjects of history.

—————————— 3 ——————————

Lighting Candles in the Dark: One Black Woman's Response to White Antiracist Narratives

Beverly Daniel Tatum

Several months ago, I had a conversation with a White woman actively engaged in antiracist education. As we talked about our mutual interest in this work, our conversation became more personal, and we shared stories of our growing-up experiences. I, an African American woman raised in New England, was fascinated to learn that my colleague had grown up in the South in an affluent family that made its money "in cotton," she said. That fact was a source of embarrassment to her, it seemed, because wealthy people who owned cotton had also owned slaves. At least that was true for her family. That ancestral past had taken the form of Black household servants in her family's present. With her childhood deeply steeped in concrete reminders of an ideology of White supremacy, I was extremely curious to know what her path had been to her present life as a woman deeply committed to antiracist education. As she shared her story of turning points and the ongoing struggle to move beyond her early socialization, I asked if she had ever written about it.

Though she had often thought about it, she said, she never had, perhaps for fear of feeling too exposed or even self-indulgent, afraid of being yet another White person who was shining the spotlight on herself in what might be seen as a self-congratulatory way. I sympathized with her hesitation but urged her to push past these fears and write it down anyway. My White students need to read these stories, I said. And they do.

As a Black woman who has been teaching about racism for almost twenty years, I have learned how desperate White students are for positive images of whiteness. In the process of learning about racism, White students are forced to confront their whiteness in ways that most have not done before,—to recognize their racial privilege and the assumption of White superiority that has been so interwoven in most of their educational experiences. The feelings of sadness and guilt, shame and anger, even betrayal, are quite intense for many, overwhelming for some. Many move in a matter of a few class sessions from having taken their whiteness so much for granted that it was barely acknowledged to a painful state of embarrassment about it, an unfolding process of racial identity development familiar to many of the authors represented in this collection.

UNDERSTANDING WHITE RACIAL IDENTITY DEVELOPMENT

As a psychologist who has used the lens of White racial identity theory[1] to understand the responses of White students in my classes for many years, I cannot help but use that same lens in my reading of these essays in this book. For those readers whose introduction to the model has been limited to the occasional references made to it in the previous chapters, it may be useful to briefly describe Helms's model here. In general, racial identity development theory refers to the belief systems that evolve in response to the racial group categorizations given meaning by the larger society. In societies like the United States, where racial-group membership is an important determinant of social status, it is assumed that the development of a racial identity will occur to some degree in everyone. For Whites, the process involves becoming aware of one's "whiteness," accepting this aspect of one's identity as socially meaningful and personally salient, and ultimately internalizing a realistically positive view of whiteness that is not based on assumed superiority. Though without necessarily using the language of Helms's model, each author in this collection has recounted his or her own experience of this process.

Janet Helms (1995) identified six identity statuses (formerly called stages) that characterize a White individual's pattern of responding to racial situations in his or her environment. Though a person may use more than one strategy or pattern of responding to racial situations, one pattern often predominates.

The first status, Contact, is best described as obliviousness. Being White is viewed as a "normal" state of being that is rarely reflected upon, and the privileges associated with being White are simply taken for granted. Particularly for those Whites who have lived, worked or gone to school in predominantly White settings, contact with people of color has usually been quite limited, and therefore "knowledge" of communities of color is limited to media stereotypes, sometimes further distorted by the prejudiced comments of family and friends. The initial "contact" perspective is well illustrated in several of the narratives included here (see chapters 7, 9, and 12). The authors of these chapters give vivid descriptions of the way this perspective dominated their early experiences of race.

A shift from this pattern to the second status, Disintegration, is often precipitated by increased interactions with people of color and/or exposure to new information about the reality of racism, heightening awareness of White racial privilege and the systematic disadvantages experienced by people of color. A powerful example of the impact of a personal relationship is provided by G. Pritchy Smith in chapter 11. Yet other authors illustrate the power of formal learning opportunities in college classrooms to raise consciousness (see chapters 6, 8, and 13), a pattern I have seen repeatedly with my own students (Tatum, 1992, 1994, 1997).

This greater awareness is often accompanied by feelings of guilt, anger, and sadness. These emotions can lead to denial and resistance to this new learning, but they can also be a catalyst for action. People operating from this standpoint often try to "convert" others to their new way of thinking. Such actions are not always wellreceived, and individuals may feel considerable social pressure to "not notice" racism and to maintain the *status quo*.

The discomfort of the learning process and fear of social isolation can result in a psychological shift to the Reintegration status. Feelings of guilt and denial may be transformed into fear and anger toward people of color. Resentful "blaming of the victim" may be used as a strategy to avoid dealing with the uncomfortable issue of racism, as well as avoiding the struggle to abandon racist assumptions and define a new, antiracist identity.

The fourth status, Pseudoindependence, is marked by an intellectual understanding of the unfairness of racism as a system of advantage and a recognition of the need to assume personal responsibility for dismantling it. The individual may seek to distance him or herself from other Whites and actively seek relationships with people of color as a way of reducing the social isolation experienced earlier.

These cross-racial interactions may heighten the individual's awareness of the need to actively examine and redefine the meaning of his or her own whiteness. Though she does not use Helms's language, Becky Thompson's narrative (chapter 4) provides rich examples of this and later statuses. For example, the Psuedoindependent desire to distance from White people is vividly described. Thompson writes:

During the period—my "I don't want to be white stage"—I had great difficulty accepting myself as a white woman as I shifted from denying the realities of racism to wanting to dissociate from white people entirely. At this point, close connections with white people felt threatening. I felt as if I'd had more than enough of white people and that I needed to spend all my energy catching up—learning from and being with people of color.

As Helms (1995) describes, eventually this denial of one's own racial group evolves into a process of redefinition which is central to the fifth status, Immersion/Emersion. Actively seeking answers to such questions as "Who am I racially? What does it really mean to be White in this society?" the individual often begins to seek support from other White people who are engaged in a similar process. Gaining access to information about White allies, those Whites who have worked against racism, as role models and guides for a new way of thinking about White identity becomes especially important (Tatum, 1994). Again Thompson illustrates this process in her narrative: use Helms's language, Becky Thompson's narrative (chapter 4) provides rich examples of this and later statuses. For example, the Pseudoindependent desire to distance from White people is vividly described. Thompson writes:

I began to actively seek scholarship by white people who have historically stood up against racism—Elly Bulkin, Lillian Smith, Sara Evans, Angelina Grimke, Ruth Frankenberg, Helen Joseph, Melanie Kaye/Kantrowitz, Tillie Olsen, Minnie Bruce Pratt, Ruth Seid, Joe Slovo, Mag Segrest, David Wellman, and others. I also realized I needed antiracist white people in my daily life with whom I could share stories, talk abt complex "racialized" interactions (in the classroom, for example), and brainstorm about strategies. Most importantly I needed White friends whom I could trust to give me honest feedback.

The last status Helms describes, Autonomy, represents the internalization of a positive White racial identity and is evidenced by a lived commitment to antiracist activity, ongoing self-examination, and increased interpersonal effectiveness in multiracial settings, characteristics again evident in Thompson's self-description.

It is important to note that an individual may operate from more than one status at a time which status predominates may vary with particular situations. However, as one's cross-racial experiences increase and understanding about racism deepens, the later statuses are more likely to be the ones shaping an individual's behavior. Because the ideology of White racial superiority is so deeply embedded in our culture, the process of "unlearning racism" is a journey we need to continue throughout our lives.

THE COMPLEXITY OF IDENTITY

Helms's model is sometimes critiqued as being too linear and static to describe what is a very dynamic process of development, I find the problem lies mostly in its misapplication. Too often used as rigid diagnostic categories, the statuses might be better described as habits of mind, each representing a way of thinking about one's own racial identity and that of others. In any given situation, there is more than one way to respond. The question here is which way does an individual usually respond to racial stimuli? Is the usual response one of denying racial difference, perhaps claiming a "color-blind" position? Is it one of zealously interrupting every ethnic joke or racist comment, or one of collapsing into guilty silence? Is it one of "blaming the victim," resentful of even having to deal with racial issues? Is it one of distancing oneself from other Whites, preferring to associate with people of color? Or is it one of actively seeking other Whites for support in the effort to become an antiracist ally? While shifts from one way of thinking to another do seem to follow a predictable pattern, Becky Thompson's (chapter 4) observation that the models are generally presented in an ahistorical and sometimes simplistic way is an important point.

The concept of identity is a complex one, shaped by individual characteristics, family dynamics, historical factors, and social and political contexts. Though psychological perspectives on identity are sometimes assumed to be limited to the intrapsychic, it was Erik Erikson, the psychoanalytic theorist who first coined the term "identity crisis," and who introduced the notion that the social, cultural, and historical context is the ground in which individual identity is embedded. Erikson writes:

We deal with a process "located" *in the core of the individual* and yet also *in the core of his communal culture* in psychological terms, identity formation employs a process of simultaneous reflection and observation, a process taking place on all levels of mental functioning, by which the individual judges himself in the light of what he perceives to be the way in which others judge him in comparison to themselves and to a typology significant to them; while he judges their way of judging him in the light of how he perceives himself in comparison to them and to types that have become relevant to him. This process is, luckily, and necessarily, for the most part unconscious except where inner conditions and outer circumstances combine to aggravate a painful, or elated, "identity-consciousness."(1968, p.22)

How those inner conditions and outer circumstances combine is a clearly a social process, one in which who we are and how we identify is very much tied to how we see ourselves reflected in the eyes of others. The social context of which we are a part very much shapes those reflections. We all have multiple identities, but some dimensions of our identities are reflected more saliently than others—a distinction made apparent by the energy we invest in their examination. For example, I have spent much more time thinking about what it means to be Black and female (in that order), than I have about what it means to be heterosexual or able-bodied or middle-class. My life experience has certainly been shaped by my physical ability, my sexuality, and my economic status, but it is my blackness and femaleness that are most often reflected back to me as significant in the eyes of others. Like whiteness in a White community, being able-bodied or heterosexual or middle-class often goes unnoticed, reflected only as "normal" in a context where such characteristics are part of the dominant paradigm. Change the context and the reflection is also likely to change.

The complexity of identity and the significance of changing contexts is nowhere more apparent in these chapters than in David Wellman's narrative (chpater 5). Being a "cool" White boy in a Black neighborhood, the son of Communists targeted by the government, Wellman's reflected identity was quite different than that of the other White people he encountered at Berkeley. Yet even his story can be understood in a framework of racial identity development theory if we recognize that it was his targeted identity as a Communist (and later as working class) that was most saliently reflected back to him, rather than his dominant identity as White. In the tension between the competing perspectives of being targeted and recognizing privilege, familiar patterns can be seen.

The search for a name, a positive self-definition, is one piece of that familiar pattern. What do we call a White person who has rejected White supremacy, who has lived/is living a multicultural life, who is seeking to subvert racism in an ongoing way? Wellman calls himself a border person. I call such a person a White ally.

Whether we use the language of racial identity development theory or not, whether we see ourselves as border crossers or as allies, I share Becky Thompson's concern for the question How do we, whether White or of color, move ourselves forward to a place of empowerment? As educators, how do we facilitate other people's forward movement on this journey? A close examination of these and other autobiographical narratives deepens our understanding of the process.

MOVING FORWARD AS AGENTS OF CHANGE

Regardless of the names we choose, we all must be able to embrace who we are in terms of our racial and cultural heritage, not in terms of assumed superiority or inferiority, but as an integral part of our daily experience in which we can take pride. Educators, especially, need to be able to do this, because it is only when we have affirmed our own identities that we are truly able to affirm those of our students, both White and of color.

As many of the narratives in this book illustrate, for White people the journey toward acknowledging and affirming one's whiteness often means rejecting a culture of domination and silence about racism. But what shall take its place? That is the question my White students ask me.

For them, the choices seem so bleak. There is the option of the actively racist White supremacist, embodied in the media by Klan members and neo-Nazis. Though some may have grown up in homes with parents who actively embraced the notion of the superiority of Whites and the inferiority of people of color, the choice of "White supremacist" is one that is easily rejected by most.

The second model of whiteness might be described as the "what whiteness?" view, embodied by Whites who simply do not acknowledge their racial category as personally significant. Once racism has been acknowledged as an institutionalized system that advantages Whites and penalizes people of color, however, this choice loses its viability as a personal option. The individual can no longer ignore the fact that whiteness matters.

The third major model of whiteness might be described as the "guilty White" model. This choice is characterized by the heightened awareness of racism and the accompanying shame and embarrassment about being White that so many of my students (and several of these authors) describe. Experiencing oneself as guilty is an uncomfortable state of being and is also an unsatisfactory resolution of the question "What does it mean to be White?" Such guilt immobilizes rather than empowers and too often becomes self-indulgent while the racial *status quo* goes unchallenged.

Yet there is another potentially attractive choice. Another model of whiteness does exist. It is the model of the "White ally," the actively antiracist White person who is intentional in his or her ongoing efforts to interrupt the cycle of racism. As Becky Thompson was excited to discover, there is a legacy of White protest against racism, a history of Whites who have resisted the role of oppressor and who have been allies to people of color. Unfortunately these Whites are often invisible to us, their names are unknown or unrecognized.

Ironically, when asked, my students can easily recall the names of White people they consider actively racist, yet they are often unable to name even one well-known public figure that they consider to be a White ally without prompting from me. Those who do recall the names of public figures like Morris Dees or Gloria Steinem often see these people as living in a very different set of circumstances than their own. They do not see the process, only the result, and do not know how to replicate it for themselves. Too often the paths to claiming a personal identity as a White ally remain uncharted.

What does it mean to be actively antiracist on a daily basis? "Will I lose friends if I start to speak up about racism?" "My boyfriend makes a lot of racist comments. What can I do?" "What do you say to your father at Thanksgiving when he tells those jokes?" These are not just the questions of late adolescents. The mature White educators I teach in professional development courses ask the same things. One White teacher I interviewed described the early phase of her exploration of racism as "hell," a state of constant dissonance. Another commented, "I get really scared at some of the things that come up. And I've never been so nervous in my life as I have been facilitating that antiracist study group." As though groping their way through a dark tunnel, they struggle for direction. One young White man articulates this feeling eloquently: "I seem to have an idea and feel myself understanding what I need to do and why and then something presents itself that throws me into mass confusion. I feel that I need some resources that will help me through the process of finding White identity." For these and other Whites searching for a way out of the tunnel, the autobiographical essays in this volume are a glimmer of hope, a gift of light.

As a Black woman reading these stories, I have to confess it felt a little bit like being a spy at a White caucus meeting. I found myself impressed with the commitment to struggle with the discomfort that comes with acknowledging one's own privilege. At other points, I felt impatient with what seemed like the painfully slow process of moving from a dawning awareness to constructive action. Yet, I reminded myself that the writers are, as we all are, still "works in progress." In that spirit, we need to honor each other's struggles. And I, too, appreciate the gift of light.

How do I imagine that other readers of color, my students perhaps, might respond to these narratives? Will they read them as just more White angst that takes the focus away from the pain of people of color, recentering whiteness, and further marginalizing their voices? There is certainly a risk of that, but my own experience is that offering the stories of White antiracist activists to students of color serves an important purpose. They need to know that it is possible to have White allies.

I am reminded of the value of this knowledge whenever I invite a local White activist to my class to speak about her own personal journey toward an identity as an antiracist White. For some people of color, her presence challenges previously held assumptions about Whites. Particularly for those students of color born after the Civil Rights era, the idea that there are White people who have moved beyond guilt to a position of claiming responsibility for the dismantling of institutional racism is a novel one. They find hope in the possibility. Writing in response to an activist's visit, a Latina student commented: "I don't know when I have been more impressed by anyone. She filled me with hope for the future. She made me believe that there are good people in the world and that Whites suffer too and want to change things." For this reason, too, these narratives are a gift of light, illuminating the possibility of coalitions and cross-racial partnerships in the journey to justice for both White people and people of color alike.

When I talk about the need for racial dialogue, as I often do, I am sometimes challenged by other people of color who have experienced talking about racism, particularly with Whites, as a waste of time. Too often they have shared painful personal experiences with racism only to have those words fall on deaf ears, invalidated by Whites who are not yet ready to acknowledge the reality they represent. It is a burden to be asked so often to educate Whites about racism without clearly seeing the payoff. Yet for me, these essays offer an antidote to that frustration. They allow me and other readers of color to see the possibility that one well-timed truth-telling sentence from a person of color to a White-person-in-progress can make a tremendous impact, as when T. J. Johnson said to G. Pritchy Smith, "If you're not standing in this line, you're standing in the wrong line." That moment, when Smith, then a White college student, was challenged by Johnson, a Black friend to stop colluding with the racial segregation of that era, was a turning point for both of them.

Whether we are White or of color, we need to know the stories of change agents. They are a renewable source of energy and courage for the long haul of interrupting oppression. In them we find the turning points, the critical incidents, the ordinary moments that have an extraordinary impact. We are reminded that even small choices make a difference. Peter McLaren (chapter 2) wrote in his essay, "As critical citizens we need to act as if the elimination of the needless suffering of all others depended upon the day-to-day choices that we make." It takes courage to choose transformative actions. In telling each other the stories of our day-to-day choices, we light candles in otherwise dark spaces and give each other the courage to move forward. We need to do that as often as we can.

NOTE

1. The model of racial identity development theory I use has been articulated by Janet Helms (1990a, 1995). Several of the authors have made reference to models of identity development, some referring to the work of Bailey Jackson and Rita Hardiman (see Clark, chapter 6), others referring to Helms (see O'Donnell, chapter 9). While there is certainly some similarity between these models, they are not identical. In particular, Helms (1995) and her colleague Thomas Parham (1989) have provided clarifications of the identity development process that address the question of linearity.

———————4———————

Subverting Racism from Within: Linking White Identity to Activism

Becky Thompson

INTRODUCTION

I recently returned from South Africa, where, among other gifts, I was graced with experiencing myself as a White person in a way I have not in the United States.[1] For the first time in my life, I perceived being White as a flexible identity that was neither suspect nor dismissed, considered primary or essential. It was not that people were attempting to uphold the color-blind ideology— pretending that color did not matter or, worse, that White racism does not exist. Rather, I felt a level of relaxation about being a White woman I have never felt in the United States—that I was not seen or treated as if there was one monolithic White identity. Since I have been home, I have spoken at length with a White antiracist South African who recently visited her home country after many years living in the United States. She, too, experienced some of that relaxation and flexibility while she was there.

Some of this experience could have been because wherever I traveled, the Black South Africans I was staying with introduced me—I wasn't seen as an anonymous tourist. Second, even though apartheid has been officially abolished, it is still rare for White people to be in Soweto and outlying townships. When a White person who is not in a uniform does visit, warmth and respect is automatically offered. Third, and most important, while there is a long history of White people who helped to mastermind and uphold apartheid, there is also history of White people who have stood up against, and sometimes lost their lives resisting, racial injustice. The stories of Ruth First, Joe Slovo, Helen Susman, and others are part of the public iconography in South Africa. In other words, there is a known history of White antiracist activism—a history that, I believe, is at the core of why being White for me felt so different in South Africa than in the United States. Here, public imagery around whiteness might lead one to believe there are only two types of White people: those who have moved to or already live in Montana and those who would like to but are too apathetic to do so. As White people spearheaded the referendum to eliminate

affirmative action throughout California, and as Pat Buchanan won the 1996
Republican primary in New Hampshire on a platform that pivoted on White
supremacy, we do not need to look far to see why it is hard to claim "whiteness"
when it is so often associated with bigotry and domination. Yet, there is
contemporary psychological, autobiographical, and historical writing that shows
links between White identity and activism. Ultimately my interest is in a radical
race-conscious political agenda that would fundamentally change the cultural
representations of what it means to be White.

AS WHITENESS GAINS NEW SALIENCY

As a teacher of African American studies, American studies, and sociology
during the last decade, I have seen (and lived through) many scenes that illustrate
difficulties in claiming a subversive White identity. Some of the most recent are
as follows:

- A light, coffee colored Jewish student comes to my office to talk about a
  course, "Social Movements in the Americas," that she is taking with me
  and her ambivalence about racial identity. In a soft and shaky voice, she
  confides that a big reason she took the course was its focus on Latino
  politics and identity. She has often been mistaken as Hispanic and has felt
  both complimented by this association and ashamed that she does not speak
  up that she is a Sephardic Jew, not Hispanic. As she talked, she revealed
  how taboo it felt for her to be admitting her reactions and I was struck by
  her deep sense of wanting to belong. The pressures of assimilation aimed at
  Jews historically and her ambivalence about being a Jew made it hard to see
  Jewish identity as a source of belonging or resistance. For her, feeling a part
  of a culture of resistance required being seen as Latina. She knew nothing of
  White resistance to racism—including the history of Jewish activism—in
  the United States.

- During an early meeting with a group of White antiracist activists I belong
  to in Boston, we went around the room as each woman talked about the
  history of antiracism to which she considered herself connected. A few of us
  named the Grimke sisters, Lillian Smith, Mag Segrest, and Jessie Daniel
  Ames. Three of the Jewish women in the group had more of a sense of a
  legacy (e.g., Bulkin, 1984; Kaye/Kantrowitz, 1996). Most of us said that
  our role models had been women around us whose stories have never been
  written about. We all felt that our hold on a history of White antiracist
  activism was tentative at best. We all were troubled by why we knew so
  little. What taboos must we face down to chronicle a history that does not
  valorize, romanticize, or inflate White activism, but that allows us to take
  stock of the work that has been and still needs to be done? The scene also
  underscored how much of the day-to-day work of antiracism will not reach
  the written page. This goes for progressive activism in general and is a
  perennial reason why a history of subversive political work in the United
  States remains scant.

- A radio reporter contacted me about speaking on one of her programs. She was aware of my writing on multicultural education and she wanted to talk about the volume on racial identity I recently co-edited with Sangeeta Tyagi (Thompson & Tyagi, 1996). As we were talking, I made some reference to being White, and she stopped the conversation to say she had been assuming all along that I am African American. This is not the first time this has happened. In reviews of *A Hunger So Wide and So Deep*, a multiracial study of eating problems and recovery, I have alternately been referred to as a Black psychologist, an African American writer, or sometimes, an African Americanist (with my race left ambiguous). My reactions to this misnaming are contradictory and complicated. I think to myself that these assumptions must mean the work is good. If people think I am African American, then that suggests that they think I wrote about Black theory and Black women's lives well. So, I feel proud. At the same time, I feel like a fraud. Then, it dawns on me that most of the people who have mistaken my identity are White. What does that say about White people's faith in ourselves, our faith in each other? What does it say about the state of race-conscious feminist theory if multiracial work by a White woman is not even considered as a possibility?

These scenes highlight multiple vexing issues about White identity in the 1990s: the guilt and confusion many people feel about being White; a largely unwritten history of antiracist White activism; and a sense of rootlessness many White people are experiencing as the generational separation between them and their ethnic European roots increases (Alba, 1990). The scenes underscore the complexities of dealing with White identity in the 1990s, at a point in U.S. history when, as Howard Winant (1994) has explained, whiteness has gained a new saliency. The fact that White people are no longer a majority in many contexts makes it increasingly difficult for them to see themselves as raceless. The emergence of whiteness as a color, rather than a transparency, has made more obvious the ambivalence, fear, avoidance, and dismissal so often associated with what being White means in the post-civil rights period.

I come to these issues as someone who has been struggling for the past fifteen plus years to understand whiteness and my complicity in racism, and as someone who has been going through a process of racial identity development which has been neither neat nor pretty. Over time, I have come to characterize my development in four phases (Thompson, 1996b). In my initial way of proceeding—in the "I am not a racist stage"—I exhibited various intensities of denial, guilt, shame, and defensiveness. As a student in a 1977 college course titled "The Black Experience," I routinely chirped in with naive abandon that "I am not racist because my mother taught in integrated schools," and "I don't understand why we can't all get along. Slavery is in the past." While outwardly resisting an examination of my own racism, internally I felt that, as a White person, I did not deserve to be in that class and that I was morally inferior to the Black students. Looking back on my behavior, chances are several students—as well as the teacher—might have liked to show me the door during the first week of class.

Through my continued exposure to community activism and scholarship of people of color in the early 1980s, I eventually made a transition to a period when I felt I needed to do everything I could to overcome racism—mine and everyone else's. During this period—my "I don't want to be White stage"—I had great difficulty accepting myself as a White woman as I shifted from denying the realities of racism to wanting to dissociate from White people entirely. At this point, close connections with other White people felt threatening. I felt as if I had had more than enough of White culture and that I needed to spend all my energy catching up—learning from and being with people of color. I felt unworthy of being friends with people of color—afraid that at any moment I would reveal my racist self and alienate them forever. Yet I thought that if I could not break through this fear, my intentions to stand up against racism would be fraudulent. I felt extremely self-conscious about being in all-White crowds and proud if I was one of the only White people at an event primarily attended by people of color. I believed I needed to take my direction from them and distrust most everything White people said. In my attempts to break away from living a segregated life, I was still measuring my credentials as an antiracist White woman through my association with people of color. Looking back on these scenes, I see the distortions in my thinking glaring back at me and it still feels risky to admit them. When I congratulated myself as one of the only White people in a social or political context, I was still seeing antiracism as some sort of competition—with only a few spaces at the table for antiracist White people.

The next stage of my identity—what I would not label the "grappling for a steady position"—I think that I and many other White women were fumbling to find ways to proceed given the complexities of identity politics. By the late 1970s and early 1980s, identity politics emerged to shape feminist political organizing in significant ways. In 1979, the now classic position paper on identity politics written by the Boston-based feminist group Combahee River Collective was first published. The promise of this politic was the assertion that those who had been subjugated historically need to be in charge of creating strategies for change. One consequence of this foundational politic—and perhaps an inevitable one—was an increased jockeying for authority based on one's belonging to a subordinated group. In this distorted arithmetic, a White straight woman was "outflanked" by a woman of color, or a White lesbian had more "credentials" than a White straight woman. With this scenario, identity politics had been twisted into an essentialism that assumed that those from subordinated communities had "biological" or "natural" access to knowledge or ideas that people from dominant groups could never have. This essentialism fed what Elly Bulkin calls "oppression privilege" which assumes that certain criticisms can only be made by those who share a given identity. Within this construct, it is unacceptable, for instance, for a non-Jewish woman to criticize a Jewish woman or for a White woman to take issue with a woman of color (Bulkin, 1984).

A subsequent stage in my racial identity evolved as I began to understand the distinctions between identity politics and an informed consciousness—a stance based on one's political affiliations and relation to subordinated communities regardless of biology (Thompson & Tyagi, 1993). Some of this came about as I became more comfortable confronting racism, regardless of whether or not it was confirmed by a person of color. In this stage, those whom I could consider authorities and role models for understanding race and racism also broadened to include White people. My earlier competitive approach had been replaced by understanding that I did not have to recreate the wheel in my own life. I began to actively seek scholarship by White people who have historically stood up against racism—Elly Bulkin, Lillian Smith, Sara Evans, Angelina Grimke, Ruth Frankenberg, Helen Joseph, Melanie Kaye/Kantrowitz, Tillie Olsen, Minnie Bruce Pratt, Ruth Seid, Joe Slovo, Mag Segrest, David Wellman, and others. I also realized I needed antiracist White people in my daily life with whom I could share stories, talk about complex "racialized" interactions (in the classroom, for example), and brainstorm about strategies. Most importantly, I needed White friends whom I could trust to give me honest feedback.

If I were to describe what my life feels and looks like now, in terms of race and racism—a task that is much more difficult to do in relation to the present than retrospectively—I would say that antiracism and multiculturalism have become the centerpiece of my life. That reality plays itself out in all areas of my life: at home, in the neighborhood, in my writing, and in my teaching. One of the most obvious ways that I deal with my whiteness is as a teacher of African American studies. People's varied receptions to my disciplinary affiliation with African American studies is but one example of these dynamics.[2] By and large, people of color and White people judge my work by the quality of my labor—my writing and teaching. But, there are some people who, in racialized ways, question me. For students of color at predominantly White schools, it makes sense that they would scrutinize me and/or express disappointment that I am White. They have lived through a long history of having to look primarily to White faculty as their role models and authorities. It is one thing to have to do that in government or biology classes. It is another to have White faculty in African American studies as well. As a White teacher, I try to be receptive to their varied reactions and to help put their understandable responses in a historical context.

The most scrutiny I have received about teaching African American studies, however, has come from White faculty, whose responses have ranged from genuine interest to outright hostility. For those who are interested, I have tried to share the formative influences that led me to see African American studies as a vibrant and comprehensive way of understanding people's longings, struggles, and cultures in the United States. As an interdisciplinary field of study with activist roots, African American studies offers unparalleled and innovative methodologies, sophisticated ethical standpoints, and rich philosophical traditions that have served to document, celebrate, and scrutinize Black culture and politics. Through the prism of African American life, I have also learned much about myself and White culture. I have found African American studies to be a way to unearth much of what has been blocked at the level of the individual and body politic. As William Pinar (1993, p. 66) explains, "The repression of memory and history is accompanied by vigorous distortions of various kinds— political, social, racial and psychological. These distortions undermine intelligence in its various modes, including technical, psychosocial and aesthetic intelligences." Studying and teaching African American studies has been an antidote to these multiple distortions.

My interpretation of White people whose inquiries have been hostile has been different, however, largely because their responses reflect an academic form of racism. In effect, their hostility reveals a patronizing attempt to maintain an academic border patrol—in the form of monitoring disciplinary boundaries—as White people continue to decide who should and should not have rights to whole bodies of knowledge (Wellman, 1996). Typically, they muse about how difficult African Americans must make it for me to do my writing and teaching. It is on these occasions that I reinforce the tremendous support I have received over the years from African American scholars—as colleagues, comrades, and friends. At a point when I want to dismiss the critics' comments or become hostile myself, it becomes important to remind myself when, in my life, I have fallen into the same traps—of considering African American studies off limits, of seeing anger and discomfort in others that is really my own, of projecting a racial politic onto others that I myself have upheld. When I am successful at not making resistant White people somehow "other" than me, I then have an opportunity to speak my mind without losing a chance to shift the conversational frame of reference.

COMPLICATING THE FRAMEWORK

What I have learned from my own experience and that of other White antiracist activists has led me to see consciousness about whiteness and unearned privileges as a core process in psychic development. For this reason, I have appreciated the emerging psychological research on White identity development. During the past fifteen years, a number of models have been developed that trace White identity as a developmental process (e.g., Hardiman, 1982; Helms, 1990b). While there is some variation across models, in general, the stages are described sequentially as acceptance of White supremacy and stereotypes of people of color; dissonance or conflict with dominant cultural norms about racial hierarchies; immersion with people of color and resistance to racism; and the development of an integrated and positive White identity. This psychological research has helped interpret complicated racial dynamics in the classroom, in organizations, and in counseling (Tatum, 1992; Sue & Sue, 1990).

One trouble with the psychological models of racial identity development, however, is that they tend to outline stages that are ahistorical. Ahistoricity leaves little room for understanding how social movements and political activism shape racial identity. This limitation is particularly unfortunate since Black identity models—which were the precursors to White identity theories—initially evolved as a means of explaining the influence of the civil rights movement on racial identity development. The psychological models also tend to see racial identity as somehow separate from gender, sexuality, and class.[3] With such compartmentalization, there has been little room to consider, for example, how the feminist movement has pushed some White lesbians to deal with race in ways not often afforded to White gay men. A third limitation of most White identity models is their focus on whiteness as an identity constructed in opposition to Black people. This duality has its limits in a multiracial society, where many White people form their identities in relation to Asian Americans, Latinos, Native Americans as well as African Americans (Rowe, Bennett & Atkinson, 1994).

While psychological models help account for individual motivations and psychic transformations, I see racial identity in sociological terms: as intimately tied to history, as informed by multiple identities, as overlapping and often nonsequential. For me, the interesting question about racial identity is how individual development and social movements interface: What engenders what psychologists might identify as the final stage of White identity development and how that process can be mass produced? While we do not yet have sufficient sociological or psychological data to develop a theory that links whiteness to contemporary activism, autobiographical narratives written in the last fifteen years by White antiracist activists provide an initial window into understanding this link. Fueled by the civil rights, Black Power, gay and lesbian and feminist movement, this writing has begun to tease out the turning points in people's lives that allow them to question and oppose the dominant racial order. It is this literature that I turned to for help in developing a conceptual framework that I have subsequently been using for a current book project on White antiracist activism from the 1950s to the present.

David Wellman (1996), a White man who grew up working class in Detroit in the 1950s and who is now a scholar on race and racism, never went through a period in his life when his whiteness was unmarked. He never took his whiteness for granted or experienced it as normal, invisible. Raised by parents who were Communists, Wellman grew up being treated as red, not White, and found his support—politically and culturally—from Black people in his neighborhood. Blackness was never a devalued identity in his house, nor did he see White society as a place of comfort or acceptance (his father was imprisoned for his political beliefs and his mother faced the threat of deportation). It was not until Wellman was in graduate school that whiteness was the norm—a reality that was quite uncomfortable for him, since he shared little with his White classmates in terms of politics, class background or language. Wellman's story underscores how class, family politics, geography, and historical time period shape identity development. His life also shows why it is impossible to talk about racial identity development as a singular or linear process. (See also, chapter 5).

Wellman's (1996) story departs dramatically from that of Mab Segrest, who, in *My Mama's Dead Squirrel* and *Memoir of a Race Traitor*, chronicles how, as the granddaughter of a Klansman, she came to be the director of Carolinians Against the Klan (Segrest, 1984; 1994). Segrest's experience is a particularly southern story. She writes about "lying on [her stomach] beneath some bushes across from the public high school" as 200 Alabama highway patrol troopers escorted twelve Black children to their first day of "integrated" school. She knew from then on that "everything people have told her was right needed to be reexamined" (Segrest, 1984, p. 20). From the title of her first book, *My Mama's Dead Squirrel,* she tells a hilarious story about how her less than fastidious housekeeper mother, upon preparing for a card party at her house, had forgotten to remove a dead squirrel that was lying next to the card table. As her guests' eyes at the party trained on the dead animal, Segrest's mother had to decide how to proceed. She deftly grabbed the squirrel by its tail and swung it around as she proclaimed, "Ain't he pretty" (p. 57). Segrest uses this as a metaphor about how racism is smack in the middle of social relations in this country—under the carpet or not, everyone knows it is there. It is from this vantage point that Segrest traces her coming to race consciousness: how being a lesbian facilitated her willingness to question racial domination, how her mother's contradictory relations with Black women taught her that knowing Black women was not itself a form of antiracism, and why she came to organize against the Klan.

Narratives by antiracist activists also underscore how social movements (and the music, art, political meetings, friendships, and alliances that frequently develop) can catapult people into whole new levels of consciousness. Involvement in social movements often forever change people's political priorities, work choices, and even who they call family. This is beautifully portrayed in Joan Nestle's (1987) essay "This Huge Light of Yours," in which she describes traveling to Selma, Alabama, in 1965 to participate in freedom marches, boycotts, and voter registration drives. It was there that she learned for the first time that "fear had a taste, that terror could make you clench your ass muscles, to keep from soiling yourself" (p. 57). It was there that she saw and felt the "sunlight and hope and courage, and the dryness of brutality."

Along with class and sexuality, religion and ethnicity also inform how people see themselves racially. Writings by Elly Bulkin, Melanie Kaye/Kantrowitz, and Adrienne Rich, among others, explore the relationship between being Jewish and opposing racism (Bulkin, 1984; Rich, 1979). These writings demonstrate why it is impossible for these women to see themselves as White outside of being Jewish. Their commitment to racial justice is so informed by the legacy of Jewish justice work and their understanding of oppression is so shaped by their experience of anti-Semitism, that attempting to identify themselves as White in a way that is separate from being Jewish makes little sense. At the same time, as Ashkenazi Jews who are light skinned, all three believe that it is crucial to recognize White privilege in order to be effective allies with people of color.

Chronicling links between people's activism and their racial identities can help us avoid reinventing some political wheels. Creating a critical mass of activists requires that people recognize each other, network, and consider these ties crucial for further political work. Identity development is, in fact, a profoundly communal affair. It will take collective recognition and organizing for White people to break out of the racial scripts we have gotten stuck in. In her important article, Susan Stanford Friedman (1995) explains three of these scripts. The first and most well known is the "I am not racist" script of denial. The second script is one of accusation: "You are a racist," followed by "You are not like me." The third script is one of confession,"I am a racist, please forgive me." Friedman cautions against these three scripts, saying that they hinder the development of a multi-issue, antiracist feminist agenda. My interest is in how White people can work together to create new scripts in the future.

THE WORK AHEAD: ORGANIZING IN A CAMPUS CONTEXT

The work ahead for White people organizing against racism on college campuses is substantial. Of course, that is not the only—nor even the main—location for antiracist organizing, but I focus on it here since I am most familiar with that context. One challenge currently facing White people is the need to develop collective identities that are not rooted in denial and avoidance—that say as much about what we are against as what we are for. This requires grappling with a number of complicated questions. What does a White identity and politic look like that is based on undermining itself? Once domination, exploitation, and unearned privileges are accounted for, is there anything left to whiteness? What, outside of some one's class, ethnicity, sexuality, or religion, constitutes whiteness? Does standing against the racial order for White people require self-annihilation? If whiteness is nothing outside of an invented system of domination, then where does the power come to undermine it from the inside?

Based on my reading of recent writing on whiteness, there are at least two distinct perspectives on these issues. For some theorists, well represented in the work of legal theorist Barbara Flagg (1993), for example, becoming antiracist depends upon developing what she calls a "positive white identity." She does not mean "positive" in any kind of glorified or romanticized way. She does assert, however, that dealing with race in this country requires that all people understand that they are raced—including people. For Flagg, race is not, itself, the problem. Racism is. So the task is to develop a White identity that is not based on subjugating others.

Ian Haney López (1996), a critical race theorist, disagrees with Flagg, positing that any attempt to find goodness or acceptance of whiteness in this country is problematic. He writes, "Given the inextricable relationships of meaning binding white and Black, it is impossible to separate an assertion of White goodness from the implication of Black badness . . . . For Whites even to mention their racial identity puts notions of racial supremacy into play, even when they merely attempt to foreground their Whiteness" (p. 173). For this reason, López asserts that the only acceptable White identity in the United States is one bent on destroying whiteness, on becoming what has increasingly been called a "race traitor." For López, an example of this approach is seen in the Boston-based periodical *Race Traitor: A Journal of the New Abolitionism*, published with the slogan "Treason to Whiteness is Loyalty to Humanity" (Ignatiev & Garvey, 1996). The basic ethic of this periodical is that a race traitor is someone who "is nominally classified as White, but who defies the rules of whiteness so flagrantly as to jeopardize his or her ability to draw upon the privileges of white skin" (Haney López, 1996, p. 189). The editors of this journal, Noel Ignatiev and John Garvey, explain the logic behind this approach through analogy. They ask this question: How many counterfeit bills does it take to ruin the money system? Just as the presence of only a few counterfeit bills can undermine the integrity of the money system, White people who refuse to act and be White can undermine the integrity of whiteness as a whole. López sees race traitors as "potentially racially revolutionary." López reasons, "If enough seemingly white people were to reject such differentiation by claiming to be among the "them," the "us" at the base of white identity would collapse" (p. 189).

I first heard the term "race traitor" through antiracist activist Mab Segrest (1994) in her book *Memoir of a Race Traitor*. I have to admit that my first thought was one of relief. I finally found a term that described what I was trying to do. Likewise, López's analysis of the need to overturn White identity as it now stands makes sense to me. I also like the term "race traitor" because it captures how my life often feels. Like Wellman (1996), I often feel like a spy, listening in on conversations I plan on undermining in whatever ways I can. I am drawn to the radical connotations of the term "traitor." I see racism as something so large and all encompassing that nothing short of a national revolution will suffice.

On the other hand, I still find myself wary about this notion that whiteness has to be annihilated, in part because it took me so many years to stop denying my whiteness. I had to work through shame, doubt, and guilt to describe myself as White without feeling like I was choking. During the ten years that I have been teaching, I have watched many White students struggle through a process of identifying themselves as White without feeling the need to apologize. Flagg's (1993) understanding of gaining a positive White identity might be part of a process people go through on their way to becoming a "race traitor." But I worry about the ways in which the idea of becoming a race traitor can be a stand-in for continuing to hate ourselves, for continuing to look to people of color for cues, and for continuing to distrust our abilities to identify and stand against racism. None of the White activists I know of (or have read about) have come to their activism without accepting themselves as White people. The two go hand in hand. In other words, it may not be possible to do antiracist work as White people in this country and not see oneself as White. This reality requires getting past—or at least trying to confront—the denial, avoidance and fear that many people experience about being identified as White. White people's abilities to talk with each other about racism and activism depends upon dealing with the daily realities of our lives, the formative influences in our understanding of race, as well as the trials and tribulations that most of us have been taught never to share with each other.

My final concern about the writing on "race traitors" is the tendency to conflate race and racism, as if the two were one in the same. In the introduction to *Race Traitor*, the editors write, "Our intention . . . is to focus on whiteness and the struggle to abolish the white race from within" (Ignatiev & Garvey, 1996, p. 2). I agree with their first goal—to focus on whiteness—particularly as a means of countering the academic history of diverting attention away from White supremacy by focusing on Black "pathology." But I would amend the second part of the editors' assertion. To me, the task is not to eliminate the White race from within but rather to eliminate racism from within. Although the analogy is imprecise, I would argue in a parallel way that eliminating patriarchy need not mean destroying men. I am intent upon recognizing the fluidity between genders (and that there may well be more than two genders) and resisting sexism. I do not want boy children to grow up thinking it is wrong to be a man nor am I willing to reject all forms of masculinity as oppressive.

Ultimately, I agree with Winant (1994) that race, as a central organizing principle in the world, is here to stay. He convincingly argues against the dominant notion that the significance of race is on the decline. He sees attempts to get rid of race as unrealistic and a way of feeding the debilitating ideology of color blindness. His proposal is not to eliminate racial categorizing, but rather to democratize it. As a way of organizing the world, race is not inherently oppressive. The problem is the ranking of racial categories as a means to uphold inequality.

Unfortunately, I think the continuing vacillation about labels and the search for names that effectively describe White antiracists are not simply issues of semantics. Rather, the lack of terminology that is precise and subversive speaks to the reality that White people who challenge racism have not yet created the critical mass needed to name ourselves collectively. History has shown repeatedly that names that capture the essence of a political movement come out of struggle and collectivity. Such slogans as "Black is Beautiful," and "the personal is political" and such terms as "African American," and "womanist" come out of organized political struggle. So will terms that accurately describe what it means to be a White person who both acknowledges whiteness and rejects the ideology of supremacy it sustains.

DOING WORK TOGETHER AS WHITE PEOPLE

To facilitate this naming, White people need to find ways to open conceptual doors for each other. Rarely, however, in academic contexts, do I hear about White antiracist organizing as a method of political activism. Yet, without these political spaces, we are not afforded the chance to ask each other some of the hard questions about antiracist work. For example, why do White antiracist people often have such a hard time seeing each other eye to eye? A few years ago, a White friend of mine noted that when she and her partner, who is South Asian, attend an event that includes only a few other South Asians, the South Asian women make an effort to acknowledge each other—if not by talking then at least through eye contact. But, my White friend noticed that no such comraderie typically exists between White people when there tends to be just a few White people in a multiracial context. The contrast I am making may be a bit reductionist because what my White friend perceives as comraderie from the outside may well not feel like that between South-Asian women, given differences in class, religion, nationality and political relations to one's country of origin (Women, 1993). But my White friend's perceptions do trigger questions about why White antiracists often maintain physical and emotional distance between each other.

My guess is that a complicated combination of fear of competition and a fear of intimacy keep us away from each other. White people who are attempting to confront racism are often so hard on each other. When I have been honest, I have seen myself apply standards of conduct and communication for other White people that leave little room for a process of growing. Sometimes, my anger at other White people has really been anger at myself that I have deflected elsewhere. Subconsciously I have been quick to point fingers at other White people as a way to deflect possible critique aimed my direction. White people need to somehow learn how to give each other and ourselves a break. Demonizing White people is a frequent trap many of us fall into that only backfires. If I think I am better than other people, there is no way I can work with them as equals. The task for me, then, is to try to see every White person as a potential ally—even when they act in ways that do not even vaguely approximate such a politic. Ultimately, the biggest trouble I have with the concept "race traitor" is, as Lisa Hall has said, "its implied refusal to see other white people as kin."[4] Being "kin" does not mean that we have to like, never mind love, each other. But it does mean we are in this thing together—this way of organizing life based on the invention of racism—and we need to collectively refuse to participate in it in small and big ways throughout our lives.

Such alliance building requires understanding that lessons about race often take years to integrate. We need to take race and racism seriously enough to not believe that it is something that students, teachers and administrators can understand through a crash course. In analyzing a specific essay she once wrote Audre Lorde explained,

The piece I wrote . . . was useful, but limited, because I didn't ask some essential question. And not having asked myself that question, not having realized that it was a question, I was deflecting a lot of energy in that piece . . . It was a question of how much I could bear and of not realizing I could bear more than I thought I could at the time. It was also a question of how I could use that perception other than just in rage or destruction. (1984, p. 106)

This quote has tremendous relevance for racial identity development. In my own life, there have been many questions that I have not known how to ask about race that only years later I found the resources or courage to raise. For example, for the longest time, I was hesitant to explore how my lover and friendship relationships with women of color have influenced my activism. Looking back, I unconsciously dodged that question out of fear that I would be accused of having these relationships solely to facilitate my activism. I feared that teasing out connections between my personal life and public commitments might expose me as a wanna-be. It was only through working with other White antiracist activists, many of whom are in primary relationships with people of color, that I began to explore possible connections with less judgment, with more affection, with a possibility for insight I never allowed myself before.

Finding ways to look each other in the eye will help us to identify what motivates people to question and oppose racism. Many White people see the exclusions they faced growing up—on the basis of sexuality, class, and religion—as the springboards that spurred them to question racial exclusions. We need to identify what those springboards are and figure out ways to work with them. My own experience suggests that dealing with childhood trauma may be a necessary part of racial reorientation for many White people. Surviving abuse is no guarantee of political consciousness. All that abuse promises is scars. The rest is left up to fate, resources, and the healing that may come from collectively naming and organizing to stop abuse. A radicalizing force in my life did come from understanding the origins of my own "outsider's lens" and beginning to see how that lens enabled me to question other injustices.

It is tricky, however, for White people to explore the initial reasons for an outsider's vision if they then make simple equations between being an "outsider" and understanding racism. As Sally Lee, a self-identified African American, Norwegian, and German student in one of my courses recently wrote, "Anything which puts a distance between white people and privilege is a dissociation of whiteness."[5] This dissociation can lead to an unwillingness to recognize unearned privileges. The challenge is to recognize what has motivated us to question authority without using it as a way to imply that the injustices we have faced are worse or more long-standing than racism. In the process, White people need to acknowledge what we have been through without appropriating the writing and art by people of color to express it. There has been such vivid and creative work by people of color about processes of exclusion and their psychological effects that it makes sense why White people might want to latch onto their artistic creations. But we have to find our own language and our own imagery to describe our lives and struggles.

White students, faculty, and administrators also need to intervene when we try to out-Black, out-Latina or out-Asian people. As Lee explains, this can be seen among White students when they attempt to adopt non-White symbols—rap, styles of dance, dress, talk—as ways of showing they are "free," or "loose," or "cool." This appropriation can severely hinder cross-cultural communication. It treats culture as some kind of commodity rather than a way of life. As Lorde has written, "You don't have to be me in order for us to fight along side of each other. I do not have to be you to recognize that our wars are the same" (1984, p. 142). Cherokee critic Geary Hobson coined the term "white shamanism" to describe a historical pattern whereby non-Indian people "appropriate indigenous cultures and distort them for their own purposes" (Rose, 1992, p. 404). White shamanism occurs when non-Indian poets "assume the persona of the shaman, usually in the guise of an American Indian medicine man" (p. 403). The critique of White shamanism in relation to non-Indian appropriation of Indian culture can be generalized to include White appropriation of Black culture. White hair that is not combed for years on end is not the same as dreadlocks. How bad White uncombed straight hair looks is symbolic for how foolish it is to try to out-Black or out-Latina someone.

This pattern is what antiracist educator Patti DeRosa (1996; see also, chapter 12) calls "racism as tourism"—stopping along the road of life to learn bits and pieces of other cultures but not understanding the political implications of misappropriation, cultural intrusion, and seeing the "other" as "exotic." "Racism as tourism" occurs among White faculty when we assume that it is possible to incorporate one or two Black or Latino authors into a course syllabus without examining the course framework to begin with. "Racism as tourism" occurs when faculty assume that African American studies should be "mainstreamed" into a discipline without affording it an autonomous and stable base of its own. "Racism as tourism" flourishes when White faculty allow students of color to be their teachers because that is less threatening than developing peer relationships with faculty of color. I give these examples not as a means of castigating others, since many come from mistakes I have made myself, but rather to flesh out daily ways that racial tourism gets played out and supported within the academy.

The fact that White people have been racialized in the post-civil rights era will inevitably spur more work on the meaning of whiteness. My hope is that this work will usher in more attention to the links between White identity development and activism. Faculty need to find ways to reach out to White students—as racialized beings—and talk with them about our own processes of racial development. People from my generation can learn much from what students are now negotiating. Recently, I spent a few hours with a group of White students as they talked about what whiteness means to them and why they have become antiracist activists. They offered a level of sophisticated analysis I never could have mustered as an undergraduate. This sharp contrast gives me hope.

NOTES

1. I want to thank Elly Bulkin for her substantial contributions to this article and Lisa Hall who pushed me to put my ideas down on paper. Thanks as well to the Virginia Women's Studies Association for supporting this work.

2. Other racialized dynamics involve classroom politics, curriculum decisions, and negotiations among faculty. Unfortunately space limits my ability to analyze these issues in this chapter.

3. For important essays that do consider multiple identities see Connie S. Chan, "Issues of Identity Development Among Asian American Lesbians and Gay Men," *Journal of Counseling and Development* 68(September/October 1989): 16–20; Darryl K. Loiacano, "Gay Identity Issues Among Black Americans: Racism, Homophobia and the Need for Validation," *Journal of Counseling and Development* 68 (September/October 1989): 21–25.

4. Personal conversation, April 1996.

5. Paper written for "National, Transnational and Diasporic Feminist Theories," at Wesleyan University Spring 1996. Quoted with permission.

Transforming Received Categories: Discovering Cross-Border Identities and Other Subversive Activities

David Wellman

Until recently, my racial identity had no name I would answer to. Whiteness was never an unmarked category for me. I have not taken my whiteness for granted or experienced it as normal and invisible. My racial self-conception has been in a permanent state of war with the socially constructed version of who I am supposed to be.

My family members were always outsiders. We stood out in my neighborhood. When we moved to Clairmount Street on the northwest side of Detroit in 1950, our block was already "in transition." That meant liberal Jewish people were fleeing to the suburbs. By 1953, we were one of the only White families on the block.

But people didn't talk about our whiteness. Neighbors did not say much about race. They were, however, fascinated by my parents' communist politics. We were the Reds on my block.

My parents were openly and publicly Communists. When the cold war got hot, their faces were splashed prominently on the front pages of all three Detroit newspapers. In September 1952, my father was arrested for violating the Smith Act. He was charged with conspiring to teach and advocate the violent overthrow of the government. Soon after, my mother was arrested under the Walter-McCarren Act. Accused of being an "undesirable alien," she was subsequently ordered deported to Canada.

Two years later, my father was convicted and sentenced to four years and eight months in the penitentiary. While his conviction was eventually overturned by the Supreme Court, he spent nearly a year in jail as funds were being raised to cover his bail. My mother was spared deportation at the last minute. Her attorney discovered conditions under which Canadian officials would not be obligated to accept her. When a Canadian diplomat committed suicide after Americans officials insinuated he was a Communist, the Canadian Minister of Immigration chose to exercise that option. Though permitted to remain in the

United States, she was placed on "supervisory parole." That meant she reported her activities and associations to the Immigration and Naturalization Service each month. As McCarthyism cooled, her monthly reporting was reduced to an annual event. But she was still on "supervisory parole" when she died in 1974.

Because they were Communists, my parents did not identify themselves ethnically. Even though they were both children of immigrants (my father's family came from Eastern Europe, my mother's from Canada), neither saw themselves as ethnic nor did they see themselves as religious. My father's people identified as Jewish; my mother's as Christian. But neither side practiced religion. Their identity was political. They were Communists. That was their ethnicity. The powerful categories in our lives were not ethnicity, religion, or race. The category that defined us was politics. We were seen as Red, not White.

Anyone who read a newspaper or watched television knew we were Reds. For those who managed to ignore the mass media, FBI agents marked our redness. The government's eyes, always at least two sets of them, were visible twenty-four hours a day, inside the FBI cars parked outside our house. Periodically we were followed to school by agents who made no effort to disguise themselves. My sister and I were the only two kids at Brady Elementary regularly tailed by the police. Looking back, and using today's language, we were raced as Red. We were not treated like White people. We were the Reds.

TAKING SIDES

Being Red meant White kids marginalized us. We were pariahs. Some of my White classmates were not allowed to play with us. If they did, it was an act of rebellion. When Whites hung out with us it was an incipient form of protest.

Being Red also meant that some Black kids held my parents in high esteem. Not for their politics, but because they were public outlaws. "Your old man must be some kind of bad dude," Maurice whispered the day after my father's bail had been set at a six-figure mark.

The White teachers treated me no differently than my Black classmates: suspiciously and sometimes with contempt. Whatever privileges whiteness conferred were canceled by my redness. So I did not have a particularly well-developed sense of self. I had been taught that I was not very smart. I could not do arithmetic or spell. I did not know the difference between articles of speech and articles of war. I certainly could not diagram sentences. I agreed with Mrs. Ross, my sixth grade homeroom teacher, when she told me I had been assigned to a "good" homeroom next fall in junior high school "by some mistake."

The mothers of my Black playmates looked out for us. If Vickie or I got locked out by mistake, they took us in. When I skipped school, they called my mother. Every time I left George's house bound for home, Mrs. Smith would call my mother to say I was on my way. Maurice's mother made a special effort to let my mother know we had a place to stay if things got worse. I felt comfortable and protected—safe—knowing there were adults looking out for me, people I could count on. I could not help but recognize that, except for the small circle of my parents' Communist comrades, the few friendly faces in an otherwise hostile world were Black.

I do not remember ever wishing I was Black. But I do recall taking the "Black side" when arguments erupted along racial fault lines. I would like to think I did that because it was the right side. I am not sure that is true, though. More likely, I did it because my Black friends supported me. How could I take the White side when they treated me like an outcast?

SOLIDARITY FOREVER

Being Red had some benefits. It meant growing up in a world of living color. The Red community was "integrated." Today we would say it was diverse and multicultural. Communists were "antiracists" long before racism was a word in the American political vocabulary. I discovered that dramatically one afternoon. I was maybe six or seven, sitting in the back seat of the family car carelessly rhyming words. I do not remember the particular rhyme. But I will never forget what happened when I used the word "nigger." Before I could utter another word, my mother turned around and slapped me. "Don't you *ever* use that word again!" she yelled. "If I hear it, I'll wash your mouth out with brown soap."

I never used the word again. At least not until years later, when a couple of my Black friends used it in a manner they considered affectionate. But my mother insisted they not use that word in her presence.

My parents did not use words like "antiracism." They talked about right and wrong. Discrimination against Negroes was wrong. Keeping Negro baseball players out of the big leagues was not right. One of my mother's lapel buttons from World War II says it best: "Score Against Hitler. Lift the Ban on Negro Players." So when Jackie Robinson broke the color barrier I became a dedicated Brooklyn Dodger fan. That was making a political statement in Detroit because the Tigers refused to hire Black players and did not until much later, holding out as one of the last all-White teams in the majors. There was no official civil rights movement at that time. Nevertheless, my parents and their friends were already doing work that would later be called antiracist politics. Annie Shore headed up an organization called the Civil Rights Congress. Coleman Young and Chris Alston worked with the National Negro Labor Council. We went to meetings where I heard slogans like "Save Willie McGee" (a young Black man in the deep South sentenced to die for allegedly raping a White woman. He was not saved.) I saw banners that read "Free Haywood Patterson" (one of the original "Scottsboro Boys" who had escaped from an Alabama chain gang and was arrested in Michigan. He was freed, but re-arrested on another charge and eventually died in a Michigan prison.)

Blackness was never a devalued identity in our house. Quite the contrary. Black people—or, to be true to the language of the 1950s, "Negroes"—were held in very high esteem. Langston Hughes was a family hero. We had a picture of him sitting with my father in civil war Spain. My mother loved Billie Holiday records. Lena Horne was another favorite. She listened to Count Basie and Duke Ellington. Many of my parents' closest friends and dearest comrades were Black people. When Communist Party leaders came to town, they often stayed with us. My sister and I were excited when Louis Burnham, James Jackson, Claudia Jones, Claude Lightfood, or Henry Winston (Black people who were nationally recognized leaders of the Communist Party) were house guests. Black people moved in and out of our lives routinely. An all-White gathering would have been noteworthy, an exceptional event-provoking comment. Mixed company was normal, taken for granted. Homogeneity was not.

BEING COOL

While we weren't treated as White, I was not comfortable with the Red identity being constructed for me by the government and the media. I did not identify "Red." My heroes were not Communists. Lenin and Stalin were not my role models. I thought the Communist kids who identified with Communists were conformists. "Squares," I called them. I identified with James Dean and Marlon Brando. I worked hard to affect the rebellious sneer both of them did so well. Brando's role in *The Wild One* was my favorite. He spoke for me when the locals asked him what he was rebelling against. "What d'ya got," he grunted. Miles (Miles Davis), "Bird" (Charlie "Yardbird" Parker), and "Mr. B." (Billy Eckstine) were my models for being male and masculine. I found them more complicated, mysterious, and rebellious than most of the White male Communists I knew. The White guys were so damn linear, predictable, and single-minded. They had very little sense of humor or irony. They did not know how to move, much less dance, and they clapped on the wrong beat. They were square like their kids. I, on the other hand, saw myself as "cool." I identified with the "cats" at my junior high school.

Hutchins Intermediate occupied strategic sociological territory. From the east side, it drew working class and poor Black students, many of them first-generation migrants from the deep South. From the west and a little bit north, came the remnants of a working-class Jewish community along with upwardly-mobile working-class Blacks. Immediately north of the school, an emerging Black bourgeoisie was moving next door to retreating White industrialists, and to the south, poor Whites—called "hillbillies," sometimes "hitwillies"—lived alongside poor Blacks.

Out of the Hutchins' experience blossomed an amazing set of cultural innovators—in Gramsci's terms, "organic intellectuals"—who eventually left a profound and distinctive impact on American popular culture. People such as actress-comedienne-writer Lily Tomlin; poet-essayist-novelist-screenwriter Al Young; Motown stars Smokey Robinson, Diana Ross, and Martha Reeves, along with songwriter, Barrett Strong, were all Hutchins students in the mid-1950s.

Hutchins enabled strangers to invent an inclusive common identity, language, and codes, while simultaneously acknowledging and valorizing the important differences between them. Without relinquishing their class, racial, or ethnic identities, a portion of these kids fashioned a collective outlook. They transformed elements of the hip jazz world, southern Black and White culture, American-Jewish traditions, and working class activities into an identity they called "cool." The Red kid fit in perfectly.

Being cool meant being conversant in a distinctive language; it meant being what today would be called multilingual, being able to talk a special kind of talk—what we called talking "that talk." That talk included its own vocabulary: music was "sounds," hair styles were "dos," glasses were "peepers," and when all was well, things were "copacetic." Using today's language, we could switch codes as well as modes.[1] In addition to being able to talk that talk, we had to be able to "walk that walk." We had our own dress code: white shirts, collars turned up, Levis—neatly pressed—with a handkerchief carefully folded over the right rear pocket, and highly shined, pointed shoes, preferably "Stacies."

We had to be able to recognize and use important distinctions, such as the difference between being "hip" and being "jive;" between being "jive" and being "lame;" between what was "happening" and what was "not happening." Jewish kids learned to distinguish between talking "shit," talking "jive," and talking "smack." Black, as well as hillbilly, kids talked about the differences between "schmucks" vs. "putzs," on the one hand, and "schlemiels" vs. "schlemazels" on the other. Being cool involved cultural sharing as well as cultural dexterity. Cool Black and hillbilly teenagers ate kosher deli. Cool Jewish kids learned to like grits, blackeyed peas, greens, ham-hocks, and chitterlings (and how to pronounce that as well).

Being cool provided us with more than the veneer of hipsterism. It also gave us the opportunity to participate effectively in what would now be called a multicultural world. We learned how to be bicultural, not just bilingual. We learned how to operate as competent actors in more than one cultural world. We became knowledgeable about what was appropriate and what was inappropriate, what was acceptable and unacceptable behavior, and talk in cultures that differed radically from our own.

While recognizing racial and ethnic differences, "being cool" did not refer to one's race. Rather, it referred to a way of being, a style, a language, a pose. Like the adult jazz world it transformed, being cool was an existential ethos, a complicated style of rebellion that contained the seeds of a new culture and a new identity in which it was possible to both transcend and valorize racial, class, political, and ethnic differences. Being cool was a negotiated achievement produced by the dialogue between racial, ethnic, and class cultures. It was an accomplishment, a construction, not an ascribed, primordial birthright. One was not born with this identity. It was both practice and practiced performance. The cool identity was inclusionary (at least among males), improvisational, participatory, and adaptable. It was the perfect combination for a Red boy who was White, but not treated so, who found security in the Black community and emulated hipster rebels.

By the time I graduated from high school, my folks had left the Communist Party. We were no longer "the Reds." Now we were the only White family on our block, and I was perfectly comfortable with the status. In fact, I took pride in it. I was proud that my parents had not capitulated to the fears and fantasies that drove our White neighbors to the suburbs. I felt reassured by the close connection between their principles and practice. I liked that kind of predictability and consistency.

I also felt special. Not very many White guys were comfortable on Clairmount. They did not know how to act, how to survive. They did not know the culture and could not speak the language. They did not know what was appropriate and what was inappropriate; what was acceptable and what was unacceptable. They did not know the rules: when to make eye contact and when not to; when to smile and when to be expressionless; when to be revealing and when to be opaque. They did not know how to be in the minority. They only knew one world and I knew two. I took pride in being able to function effectively in contexts my White high school classmates had only read about or seen on television. I was proud to know how to be "different" and feel comfortable about that; able to be an "insider" in one situation and "outsider" in another.

It felt good to be trusted by our Black neighbors, to know I had proven I was dependable. I was proud to be accepted and excepted. I took it as a compliment when my Black buddies confided that "you're not like most White people." I liked that kind of differentiation. I did not object to being that sort of exception. I feared the White police, not my Black neighbors. The cops were suspicious. What was a White guy doing in this neighborhood? They did not believe me when I said I lived there. So they frisked me and insisted I produce some identification. In contrast, the Black guys on my block protected me: "Don't fuck with him," an outsider would be told; "he's cool."

Other than that, there was no name for people like me. We did not have a concept, a label, or a special identity. On my block, I was "cool." That meant being part of the scene, competent, supposed to be there. My presence did not call for a theory or an explanation. I did not need to invent a reason for being there. My identity was "he's cool."

Everyone knew I was White, including me. But that was not the relevant category. On Clairmount that did not matter. The critical category was "he's cool." He belongs here. I know from today's vantage point that sounds extraordinary. But what is even more remarkable is how "normal" I felt.

Unfortunately, the experience was not symmetrical. My Black male partners were never "cool" in all-White neighborhoods. They would be "out of place," and rousted by Detroit's virtually all-White, all-male and notoriously brutal police force.

I did not consider myself a "White-Negro." I did read the Mailer essay "The White Negro" in college but it did not resonate with my experience. In fact, it disturbed me. I thought it too dichotomous, biological, and unnecessarily sexual. Because my racial identity had no name at the time, I identified more closely with the title of James Baldwin's book *Nobody Knows My Name*.

The farther I got from the neighborhood and the experience, the more exceptional and extraordinary the two became, and the more difficult it was to convince my White friends that I really did live on Clairmount near Linwood, and that I actually felt quite comfortable there. A couple of middle-class (White) Jewish students in college challenged my account. "Prove it!" insisted one of them. So I told him to drop me off at the corner of 12th Street and West Grand Boulevard. (Four years later 12th Street would be one of the sparks that ignited a bloody rebellion that convulsed through Detroit for a week.) "Pick me up at Clairmount and 12th Street in an hour," I told him. "I'll walk there." And I did. I knew there would be no problem. Twelfth Street was one of my stops on the way to Hutchins.

INTRODUCTIONS TO CLASS AND WHITENESS

When I entered graduate school, in the early 1960s, I was the only person in my class who had been raised in a predominantly Black neighborhood. That was my introduction to Whiteness as an unmarked category. It took place at the University of California in Berkeley. For the first time in my life, whiteness was normal. It was invisible and I was terribly uncomfortable.

Except for the color of my skin, I shared almost nothing with my classmates. I was completely unprepared for life in an exclusively White world. I did not know the rules these people followed. We used the same words but spoke radically different languages. I did not know how to act. I was as uncomfortable in this all-White environment as my White high school classmates were on Clairmount. I could not wait to go home.

I discovered the source of my alienation when classmates discussed college experiences. Except for two European American women, also from the midwest, the bulk of my cohort was educated at elite private schools, Ivy League colleges, or prestigious state universities. Very few came from land grant colleges, much less commuter schools like Wayne State in Detroit.

An old category, one my parents talked about a lot, took on new significance for me. The category was "class," not gender. Women were nearly a third of my graduate cohort. So class became the salient category in my life. To this point, the word had been a weapon in my parents' ideological vocabulary. It was a slogan, an outmoded idealization, I thought. It was part of their Marxist ideology, and I was not a Marxist. All of a sudden, class became a lived category, and it explained my alienation from people who only shared complexion.

The category was useful in another way. It contained a language of differentiation that enabled me to distinguish myself from people with whom I shared similar amounts of melanin, but who treated me like an "Other," and toward whom I felt enormous hostility. I did not have to be one of them. I could be "working-class." Ironic.

In Detroit, being working class was normal. Class was the unmarked category, the taken for granted. Race and ethnicity were the salient markers. But in Berkeley, the situation was reversed. As a result, I did not discover my class identity in working-class Detroit. I constructed it in bourgeois, all-White Berkeley.

I did not call myself "White" until 1966, when the Student Non-Violent Coordinating Committee (SNCC) put Black power on the American political agenda. White SNCC supporters were encouraged to organize against racism in the White community. For the first time, I was no longer "cool" in the Black community. Though that was a deep hurt for me personally, I thought the strategy was a wise one. But it did present me with a political problem: What community would I work with? Realizing I would not be a very good organizer in the White community, I decided to follow another path. Using my recently discovered identity as an unmarked category—my Whiteness—and my graduate training in sociology, I would spy on the White world. Passing for White, I would find out what liberal middle-class Whites really thought about Black people. I saw myself as an undercover agent for the civil rights movement.

Recording what White folks said when Black people were not around, I would expose them. And I did. My findings were published in a book I titled *Portraits of White Racism*.

I called myself "White" when I wrote the book. That identification was political. It was done to make the invisible visible; to force White Americans to recognize the reality of race in American life. So I called myself White for tactical political reasons. But I could not identify with the category. Except for certain morphological features, it did not really fit. Instead, it felt like an uncomfortable garment, and I did not wear it very well.

CONVERGENCE, TRANSFORMATION, AND THE DISCOVERY OF BORDERLANDS CONSCIOUSNESS

White did no fit because this social-political construction was at odds with my self-conception and my experience. On Clairmount, racial identity was never neatly and dichotomously packaged in Black and White. Identity was not a binary category, automatically produced by the color of one's skin. Nor was it fixed and static, the result of rules, roles, and obligations one is born into. Rather, it was constructed, negotiated, fluid, and dialogic. People were evaluated by their behavior, not their pigmentation. Melanin did not matter if one was cool. The civil rights movement reinforced my Clairmount experience. People who organized demonstrations, got arrested, did community organizing called themselves "movement people," "brother," and "sister." SNCC people thought of themselves as members of a "beloved community." While serious differences between races and genders were recognized and actively engaged, most of us actually believed that we would overcome.

When the civil rights movement was defeated, there was no language that spoke to my experience, that gave voice to my self-conception. Usually I was exceptionalized, constructed as different from other White people by my Black friends. No longer "cool," or a member of the beloved community, I knew who I was not: not-Black and not-White. I did not belong in either category. I was none-of-the-above; the one whose racial identity had no name. While proud of it, I have never been completely comfortable with that identity. An identity that has no name is not an identity. Being defined negatively, or not-someone else, is not a useful sense of self. It does not convey the depth and complexity of my experience; the richness and diversity of the self I have constructed.

Fortunately, times are changing. Languages are emerging that catch up with the racial identities forming in America during the past quarter century. Though nobody calls me by it, my racial identity finally has a name I can answer to. I realize now that I am a "border" person. Clairmount was a "borderland." So was SNCC. Unlike the borders that divide two countries, these borders are produced, to paraphrase Gloria Anzaldua (1987), when the life blood of two worlds merge and a third country emerges: a "border culture." Borderlands are those unintentional, multicultural spaces—sometimes called "common ground"— where disparate cultures meet; where the people living on these peripheries discover cultural parallels and construct new as well as variable identities, based on—although neither reducible nor limited to—the old ones. "From this racial,

ideological, cultural and biological cross-pollinization," writes Anzaldua, "an
'alien' consciousness is presently in the making. . . . It is the consciousness of
the Borderlands." "The border houses the power of the outrageous," adds Juan
Flores (1993), "the imagination needed to turn the historical and cultural tables.
"The border is not difference, Ian Angus (1990) comments, "it allows difference
to appear." Ruben Blades (1987) calls these borders "convergence." "Let's meet
half way," he says, "and then we can walk either way together." The people
occupying this space are, in Renato Rosaldo's words "border crossers" (1993).

As a kid, I thought the "border" was that imaginary line in the middle of the
Detroit River that marked the end of the United States and the beginning of
Canada. At the time, I did not know that Clairmount was another kind of border.
I did not realize that being cool was an "alien consciousness," part of a "border
culture." Looking back, Clairmount (as well as many other Detroit
neighborhoods) was a classic "borderland." Like Anzaldua's intellectual mestizas,
we learned to juggle cultures. We operated in a pluralistic world. We did not use
those words, of course. We said that was "getting down," and "making the
scene," or "getting with it." Intellectuals today would say we practiced a
"multicentric perspective." We called it being "hip." What Henry Giroux (1992a)
refers to as "new cartographies of identity and difference," we probably would
have talked about as finding ways to be different and "together." I doubt that we
would have described our talk as a "plurality of vernaculars." For us it was
"street talk." But we would have understood what Juan Flores means when he
writes that borderlands produce "multiple interminglings."

The new theoretical languages giving voice to the emerging visions of identity
being invented and discovered on America's borderlands contain a number of
concepts devised to explain the process of code switching, cultural mixing, and
linguistic sharing that I experienced in Detroit. George Lipsitz (1991) calls the
process cultural "bricolage." Lynell George (1993) refers to it as "cultural
fusion" and "recombinant culture." In Marshall Berman's words (1982), it is a
"unity of disunity." Stuart Hall's notion of "transformations," in my view,
nicely captures border cultural exchanges and productions. Transformations, in
Hall's words (1981, p. 228), are "the active work on existing traditions and
activities." Transformations actively rework traditions so that they come out a
different way. They are historically specific cultural elements "that allow for the
expression of collective popular memory and the reworking of tradition" (p.
228). Hall's notion of transformations is useful for understanding the ways in
which diverse groups create common ground, while continuing to acknowledge
important differences. The idea of transformations explains how diverse peoples
can construct identities experienced as a common heritage.

I find the possibility attractive. It makes sense out of my experience. It names
my identity. Sociologically speaking, it also makes my experience a lot less
exceptional. It turns out I am not alone, in a category of my own. I have a lot of
company on the border. My experience is not an isolated instance of one
individual who is out of place and therefore does not fit in. Rather, it is an
example of a larger process: a process of transformations on American borders
where inclusive, multidimensional identities have blossomed—unintentionally,
fleetingly, and not always where expected.

That process continues. Thus, I was excited to recently discover that my experience in 1950s Detroit is being duplicated today. Traditions are being invented, new codes, languages, and collective memories are being created and identities constructed in contemporary border towns around Los Angeles—places like Culver City, Echo Park, and Carson. Describing an identity currently emerging at the edges of these neighborhood boundaries, one that seriously resembles mine, journalist Lynell George (1993) hears a language she calls New Age patois. She calls the young people in this world "cultural hybrids." Cultural historian George Lipsitz notes that the mixing on these borders is not an exclusively class-based phenomenon. "When I see desegregated groups of graffiti writers," he reports (quoted in George, 1993, p. 15), "one of the things that strikes me is that they're also mixed by class." These class- and race-mixed groups do not, however, dilute the constituent cultures. They do not construct same-ness. "There is a group of graffiti writers," Lipsitz points out, "who call themselves 'ALZA'—which stands for African, Latino, Zulu, and Anglo" (p. 15). ALZA, Lipsitz says, is Chicano slang for "rise up." "They found each other," he reports. "Nobody set this up. Nobody put an ad in the paper. They look for spaces that are what we call 'multicultural.' I don't think that they ever think to look at it in those ways," he says, "but there's a sense of interest and excitement and delight in difference that makes them look for more complexity. It is their love of difference, danger and heterogeneity that brings them together" (p. 15).

In George's estimation, this free-form amalgamation goes deeper than learning a handy salutation in Tagalog, being conversant in street slang, or sporting hip-hop-inspired styles. This sort of cultural exchange, she suggests, requires active participation and demands that one press past the superficial toward a more meaningful discourse and understanding. Instead of demanding that people reject their own identifiers, the mixing allows them to slip in and out of multiple identities. Like being cool on Detroit's West Side, this kind of mixing wreaks havoc with stereotypes and old-fashioned ideas about what it means to be African American, Latina/o, Asian American, or Anglo in a rapidly changing metropolitan area.

The idea of borders, and the cultural possibilities they contain, do more than articulate a vision for what might be. They also constitute a critique of current sociological theorizing about identity. Social analysts typically construct ethnic identity in "primoridalist" terms. The primordialist approach views ethnicity as "genuine culture" rooted in similarities of physical appearance, a shared language, religion, a sense of common origin and history, and the perception of shared life chances. This approach, according to Clifford Geertz, following Edward Shils, looks for "primordial attachments" which, he writes, has its origins in "the assumed givens of social existence . . . congruities of blood, speech, custom and so on are seen to have ineffable and overpowering coerciveness in and of themselves" (1973, pp. 109–10). So conceived, ethnicity refers to a set of rules, roles, and traditions passed on from generation to generation, essentially unchanged. The emphasis is on group differentiation. In this construction, ethnicity is a matter of hyphenation. Ethnic identity, moreover, is assumed to be singular and static: Only one ethnic identity is allowed per customer. Assimilation, in this paradigm, is assumed to be a one-

way street along which new arrivals "give-up" one identity and "take-on" another
one. Old identities are "melted down" into "new" ones.

These constructions are useless when applied to America's borders. They
inhibit understanding. In border cultures, identities are not discrete and finite
entities. They are plastic and open-ended; as much dynamic constructs as
inherited facts, as much strategic responses to the present as an immutable series
of practices and beliefs derived from the past. Border cultures produce identities
that are neither singular nor static. In these locations, multiple cultural identities
are invented, and people slip in and out of them without being called upon to
renounce their initial identifiers. In this context, identity is achieved and
inclusive. It is learned through the process of taking on and shedding the roles
required to participate in complicated cultures.

Border peoples trying on new and different identities learn that identities can be
changed. They find out that one is not completely bound by bloodlines,
nationality, occupation, or biology. Sometimes one catches fleeting glimpses of
gender becoming a less binary, less consequential identity in border cultures.
Gloria Anzaldua's intellectual mestiza is bisexual as well as bicultural. My
students tell me that skill is a more important consideration for acceptance in
their hip-hop culture than gender. Ironically, binary constructions of gender are
also subverted in those popular spectacles on male borderlands: professional
sports. Affection is routinely expressed with hugs and pats on the behind.
Necklaces, earrings, and bracelets are prominently displayed on the playing field
and off. Kisses are exchanged before competition commences. Restraint is
exercised with hugs and whispers rather than brute force. Professional
basketball's most popular badboy, Dennis Rodman, not only dies his hair exotic
colors, he publicly hangs out in gay bars offending good-ol'-boy rednecks in
Texas.

The roles border peoples try on, the cultural practices they learn to perform,
teach them how to be multicultural. They learn how to be culturally competent
actors in multiple cultural contexts. Border cultures, therefore, contradict
conventional sociological wisdom. They fracture received categories. The
discovery of border cultures calls for the formulation of sociological theories of
cultural identity.

Michael Fischer's approach to ethnicity (1986) is a useful starting place for
that project. Ethnicity, he writes, is "something dynamic, something that
emerges in full . . . flower only through struggle" (pp. 195–96). "Ethnicity is a
process of inter-reference between two or more cultural traditions" (p. 201).
Fischer's construction makes pluralism a fundamental feature of identity. In his
words, ethnicity is "a matter of finding a voice or a style that does not violate
one's several components of identity. In part, such a process of assuming an
ethnic identity is an insistence on a pluralist, multidimensional, or multifaceted
concept of self" (p. 196). At the heart of borderlands consciousness is that
pluralist, multidimensional, multifaceted concept of self; that voice that does not
violate the many components of one's identity.

PRACTICING BORDERLANDS CONSCIOUSNESS: DUES, BLUES, AND FEARS

I have spent the last twenty-five years constructing a voice that does not violate the many components of my identity. When that voice is heard, I am reminded that I still live on the border. That border is no longer in Detroit. It is now located at the intersection of class and race in the academy. (And gender too. Although being a heterosexual male, I do not experience gender as a border.) I was reminded of my border status many years ago when a senior "colleague" called me "you-people" in a drunken tirade directed at "aggressive, working-class men" in the university. I discovered first-hand why my Black classmates in Detroit bristled at the term. I am routinely reminded of my border status by the inner circle that runs my university. Members of this club make it quite clear that, even though we share melanin and gender, I do not belong. Even when I am asked to sit on powerful committees, I am not permitted to forget that I am an outsider. I am reminded when I do not laugh at their jokes. Not out of principle, but because I do not know they are "jokes." Or, thinking they must be kidding, I laugh when no one else does.

I know I am a border person when I realize university culture practices an etiquette that only certain people are taught. It is a class etiquette, gendered as well, and as I discovered in graduate school, it is learned at the elite colleges where many university professors begin as undergraduates. The working knowledge of this culture is not shared with class outsiders. It is not discussed at career counseling meetings for junior faculty. Border academics glimpse it when they inadvertently violate these unwritten rules. Being too "passionate," we learn, is unacceptable. So is being committed to principles that university insiders call being "inflexible" or "unreasonable." We discover that survival in the academy depends upon learning that it is inappropriate to argue from the heart or from a position of principle. The appropriate method is to invoke "empirical evidence," or remain silent until sufficient "data" have been collected. Border academics find out that direct talk, "telling it like it is"—or "speaking truth to power"—is counterproductive. The delicate language of euphemism and indirectness is the *lingua franca*. One learns that behavior that would be severely sanctioned on the mean streets of Detroit is acceptable in university settings where it is permissible to destroy someone's career so long as procedures are followed and confidentiality is maintained. Outsiders soon discover that it is all right to impugn another's honor and integrity as long as it is done cleverly, confidentially, with humor, and in "good taste."

While I find it comforting to now have a name for the identity I experience in the university, the identity does not permit me comfort. Being White, male, heterosexual, and living on the academic border means being truly in-between; not belonging to any side; not fitting-in. There are no clearly identifiable borderlands where border crossers like me meet and share experiences. This kind of border crossing therefore demands heavy dues. It means never being completely accepted by any side; always being suspicious and suspected. It means being on the outside, a potential traitor; always an exception. An outsider to insiders. An insider to outsiders. Being a White, male, heterosexual border crosser also forces one to wonder whether the border category actually fits. I am not entirely comfortable applying the concept to my experience. I worry that it might be another version of cultural appropriation. Yvonne Yarbro-Bejarano (1994) is right: "It is one thing to choose to recognize the ways one inhabits the 'borderlands' and quite another to theorize a consciousness in the name of survival" (p. 8).

The borders I live on are porous. My crossings are opportunities as well as options. I can choose to live on borders or to avoid them. That choice is privilege, even when experienced as pain. My colleagues of color do not choose border identities. They cannot refuse them either, and they cannot move between them as easily as do I. The elements of choice and privilege in my life mean I cannot be otherized in the same way as people of color.

Still, the borders I cross are real ones, so are the consequences for crossing them. Thus, to borrow from Caren Kaplan (1990), I do not consider myself a theoretical "tourist," a "boarder in the borderlands." I think the search for borderlands, the effort to generate common ground among border crossers, disrupts the core social order in a positive direction.

That is why the sociological tariff or border crossing is so personally expensive. Because it undermines conventional constructions, border crossing is a profoundly subversive activity. Border academics are troublesome to university culture because their crossings reveal borders that are otherwise invisible. Border crossers expose borders that universities refuse to recognize and deny guarding.

Border academics are double-trouble for the university. When they are not revealing borders, they expose the conflated character of other categories. White, heterosexual male border academics are unique in this regard. Because they share melanin and gender with university insiders, their border status must be attributed to class. When these people are on the border, whiteness is revealed to be as much about class as race. In addition to being constructed as not-Black, university whiteness turns out to be not-working class as well.

In racialized America, where the culture assigns people to either one racial category or another, border crossers are threatening because they refuse the assignment. By refusing the assignment and inventing a new identity, border crossers subvert the American construction of race. "White" border crossers are especially subversive. They undermine the construction of whiteness as "not-Black." Because whiteness cannot be not-Black when "Whites" act "Black," the defining feature of the category is subverted. The conventional definition of normal is disturbed. As a result, the norm of whiteness, to paraphrase Henry Giroux, cannot secure its dominance by appearing to be invisible. Plagiarizing a local bumper sticker, White border crossers "subvert the dominant paradigm." Maybe that explains why White civil rights workers were beaten so savagely in the South. Perhaps that is why White teenage border crossers are called "wiggers" in contemporary America.

But border crossing is subversive in a more profound sense. It radically disrupts key elements of American culture: Conventional understandings of propriety, reason, rationality, and harmony are subverted by border crossers as they move between epistemological, cultural, political, and methodological boundaries. But the most important convention that gets disrupted is the American propensity to create dualisms, to manufacture dichotomies, to generate a binary, zero-sum (you win-I lose) culture. Border crossing identities assault the racial dualisms in American culture. It is no surprise, then, that racial border crossers are as threatening to White Americans as cross-dressers are to heterosexuals.

Because border crossing is so subversive, a cultural border patrol is being formed. Signs of it have been sighted in the university where border aliens are accused of practicing political correctness. While the border patrol does not yet come into classrooms (usually), it does carefully maintain borders. It also keeps the spaces between borders incredibly narrow and isolated. The border patrol is not always obvious. Officers do not wear uniforms. Sometimes it is invisible, working undercover inside our minds.

The border patrol acts strategically. It protects America's cultural borders through a containment policy. Border consciousness is acceptable in its written form. At the university, it is even rewarded when published. But it is also restricted, limited to specially designated territories such as "cultural studies." When border consciousness leads to subversive border practices, it is frowned upon and sometimes punished.

I worry about the fate of border consciousness in the academy. Not that it will be silenced, but that it will flourish and that the price for success will be the loss of practice. Especially in the academy, I fear that border consciousness stripped of border practice, will eventually undermine the multidimensional, subversive character of border identity. If that is allowed to happen, the border patrol will have succeeded. Diversity will be normalized, and border crossing co-opted. Thus, like Marxism, border consciousness will have become just another academic discipline, another canon, another hegemony. A new academic territory will have been created: one with its own borders to patrol.

NOTE

1. An important qualification is in order: I am not suggesting that this language was generated at Hutchins. Some examples are partly Detroit and local. But anyone familiar with the period knows this language was standard talk in 1950s hip Black culture throughout the United States.

----------6----------

The Secret: White Lies Are Never Little

Christine Clark

INTRODUCTION

It is hard to write about becoming an antiracist racist without coming across as self-congratulatory, sort of a "look what a good White person I am," testimony (Friedman, 1995). As an antiracist racist I believe that I should always feel conflicted, full of contradictions, never as though I have "arrived."

In struggling to resist the racist tendency to overemphasize self-importance because I am White, to, in essence, *fetishize* my whiteness, writing a chapter about myself, my life as it pertains to my becoming an antiracist racist, became a real exercise in contradictions. Impossibly, I am attempting to decenter whiteness while simultaneously perpetuating its centeredness.

In revising my first draft of this chapter, a colleague's feedback facilitated my discovery of a never-before acknowledged racist tendency in myself. When I initially wrote this chapter, I had written a great deal about what I had learned about becoming an antiracist racist from the mistakes I witnessed other Whites make. Certainly there is something to be said for lessons learned through vicarious associations with others. However, it is far more difficult to focus on the lessons learned from one's own mistakes. In the subsequent drafts of this chapter, I have struggled, painfully, to maintain the focus on myself.

THE SECRET: UNDER CONSTRUCTION, CONSTRUCTED, AND DECONSTRUCTED

I decided to title this chapter, "The Secret," for many reasons that are deeply entrenched with one another. Essentially, the secret is a metaphor for all of the covert ways I was taught about White supremacy by my family and friends. Summarizing the secret so succinctly in one sentence might create the false impression that coming to understand it was fairly simple. On the contrary, it was not.

I was raised to be an antiracist, not an antiracist racist. While these two things may look very similar at a superficial level, the difference between them is vast and significant. Both confront injustice, but antiracists avoid confronting their own privilege when such confrontation calls them into question, where they live so to speak, when it costs them something personally.

The "race traitor" philosophy postulated by Ignatiev and Garvey (1996) speaks to this problematic. Essentially, this philosophy argues that to end racism, whiteness as a sociopolitical construct must be abolished, even as it pertains to the antiracist struggle. This is because antiracists (much like racists) become so invested in their status as such that they reify both race and whiteness, simply perpetuating, not dismantling, racism and White privilege. I was taught to confront injustice but not if it caused me to lose White race privilege.

This, then, is part of the secret I sensed existed in my unconscious conscious[1] from a very early age, about three or four. This part of the secret had to do with a border that was constructed for me not to cross but with the explanation for not crossing never disclosed—a secret. Do not ask why, just do not do it. In essence, I was asked to participate in the keeping of a secret that I did not even know.

Antiracists do not own the inevitability of their racism. They believe that in confronting injustice to the degree that they do that they cannot be a racist, the practice of confrontation signifies the antithesis to racism.

Antiracist racists know that even in the practice of confrontation of injustice, they are still racist, and ownership of this inevitability is not sociopathic; it is not in the "Of course I'm a racist, everybody is so what's the big deal" vein. Rather, it embodies an honest experience of the complexities of the racism occupying one's psyche mediated with a profound commitment to the lifelong confrontation and attempted eradication of it from one's psyche. No matter the terms and context of the struggle, the antiracist racist is forever engaged.

Here then, is another part of the secret I sensed but did not know as a child: I was raised to be an antiracist but that that was not the whole story; there was more to be.

In some ways, I see my life from this young age until I was twenty-three as a quest to find out the "whole" secret. I used to think that the whole secret could be disclosed to me neatly and easily if I could just find someone willing to let me in on it. Today, I am sure that it is not possible to ever find out the whole secret. What I have learned of the secret has come to me in bits and pieces, almost like sound bytes; some arrive like the turning on of consciousness, in a moment, as a lightbulb. Others arrive like the putting together of a giant jigsaw puzzle, a mosaic, slowly over time with incremental changes in perspective, constantly revealing ever-so-subtle new nuances. To add insult to injury, I have also discovered that it is forever a struggle to remember the details of the secret which I have come to know. It is far too easy to be seduced into "forgetting" them by White privilege. For example, there is great facility in taking White privilege for granted; to forget to question whether a store clerk's kindness was genuine or predicated upon my whiteness, and so forth.

In this chapter I will focus on what I believe are the most important lessons that I learned about the secret and that in learning them had the greatest effect on encouraging me to become a multicultural educator. These lessons have to do with *seeing*, *choice*, and *responsibility*.

Seeing was my first lesson.

THE SECRET UNDER CONSTRUCTION

To grow up in Grosse Point, Michigan, was to grow up in one of the whitest places in the world. Had it not been for the Black woman that my mother hired as a maid, it is likely that I would not have seen, much less had, any significant contact with any person of color until I was almost six, by which time, I understand, my personality would have already been fundamentally established. Strangely, while I believe my mother's unacknowledged and deep-seated racism and classism led to this occurrence, I will be eternally grateful that it did, for I am certain that, as a result, I became more engaged in the struggle to become an antiracist racist than I ever would have been had this Black woman not come into my life.

I do not remember a time in my life before Mrs. A was a part of it. Mrs. A was originally from Tennessee. She moved to Detroit with her family at a later point. Part of the racism inherent in my relationship with Mrs. A is that she knew everything about me and my family and to this day I know virtually nothing about hers. What I do know, such as the fact that she was originally from Tennessee, I learned as an adult, long after the last time I ever saw her.

My mother hired Mrs. A as a maid, a cleaning woman, on the recommendation of some other White family in the area for whom she either worked or had worked in the past. Mrs. A came from inner-city Detroit by bus to a stop in the suburbs near where we lived and from where she walked to and from our house. On occasion, my mother or father picked her up at the stop in our car and brought her to our house and then took her back to the stop at the end of her work day. Usually this was when the weather was bad, when it was dark outside, or when she did not feel all that well. Perhaps on occasion they even did it just to be nice.

My parents' relationship with Mrs. A was very "kind" but still very racist. The distance between employer and employee, between White and Black, between colonialist and the object of colonialization was mediated in one very significant way. They called Mrs. A, a woman at least fifteen years their senior, "Mary," and she called them "Mr." and "Mrs." To add insult to injury, as a two- three- four- and five-year-old child, I, too, called this adult woman, at least fifty-five years my senior, "Mary." When my mother or father talked to my sisters and I about Mrs. A in her absence we all called her "Mary," so I know our behavior in this respect was sanctioned at the institutional level in the family. My mother has said that this was what Mrs. A was comfortable with (as if she could have honestly said otherwise without fear of some kind of reprisal). When challenged that she could still have called her "Mrs. A" and had us do so as well, my mother, like so many other typical antiracists, is quick to blame these relationships of power on "the times."

In retrospect, I am horrified by what I know this behavior perpetuated. When a Black colleague spoke to me about how important it was to his mother that he and his siblings refer to all Black people but *especially* older Black people as "Mr." or "Mrs.," "Sir" or "Ma'am," even as "Mr." or "Miss" plus their first name if they didn't know the person's last name to show respect. The history conveyed to his siblings and he by his mother underlying this non-negotiable request was that adult Black men and women have so often been referred to by White adults, even by White children, without a title, by first name, or worse by a diminuitive or racial epitath, that they were to be given the utmost respect by their own community, *especially* by children.

I remember Mrs. A as an extremely warm and loving woman who, when she scolded me, never made me feel humiliated in the way that I remembered feeling when my mother or father did. She was firm but kind and always seemed more comfortable expressing both sentiments with appropriate physical affection. I know that I romanticized the kind of mother I imagined Mrs. A was to her own children in wishing I could be one of them. And yet today, I know as a result of having this feeling about her that I learned that working-class parents (and parents of color) can be better parents than those with greater means (or who are White) who often substitute material things for interpersonal interaction and call it an expression of love.

My specific memories of Mrs. A are few: She taught me to tie my shoes; she begrudgingly played hide-and-seek with me, all the while complaining that I was wasting her time, keeping her from her work, not to mention making more work for her by messing other things up in an effort to hide. It is these general impressions of her that have meant the most. When we moved to Shaker Heights, as a going-away gift she gave me a Santa Claus type doll/stuffed animal that, of course, had a White face and blue eyes. It also had a music box inside. With all of the unfixed boundaries around race that existed in my five-year-old mind at the time, I named the doll, which I still have, after her. This, coupled with my desire to be her child, illustrates the luxury I enjoyed as a White child in thinking about race unconsciously or rather in not thinking about, not *seeing*, it at all; as a White child I had the luxury of not having become raced yet, of not knowing that I was raced and, for that matter, that she was raced, too, and what that meant.

This is one of the ways in which Jackson (1976) and Hardiman (1979) discuss that racial identity forms differently in Black and White children. Black children develop a consciousness of, *see*, their racial identity as "Black," before they develop a consciousness of, *see*, their individual identity as "Tyrone," for example. White children develop a consciousness of, *see*, their individual identity, as I did of myself as "Chris," before they develop a consciousness of, *see*, their racial identity (if they ever do) as "White." Ironically, around the same time that I was experiencing myself as unraced, or rather not experiencing myself as raced, a critical incident (actually there were two) occurred in my life that forced me to experience, *see*, myself as gendered. I remember the exact moment that I developed a consciousness of myself as a woman (a "girl") mediated with a consciousness of how men see women as "less than" men; even four- and five-year-old little boys somehow understand that they have institutional power and that this power legitimizes their actions against girls. The first time I was four; the second time, five. The first time, there were two boys; the second time there were five, all age peers, all upper middle-class and White, boys whom I considered my friends, playmates. In both instances, the boys *premeditated* isolating and cornering me, then pulled my pants down against my will to view my vagina. A week before the first incident, the same two boys tried to drop a brick on my head when I followed them behind a garage to play. This failing, they chained me to a tree, where I remained for three hours until one of my older sisters, who came looking for me at dinnertime, helped me to escape.

What is significant about these incidents with respect to my racial identity development is that they raised my awareness about being female, about being "Other." Before the first incident, the two boys involved in it were just playmates, and in some vague way, male. Afterwards, they were not only not playmates, but in a very confrontative fashion they were boys and I was a *girl*. While I did not immediately and consciously understand the parallel to race implied here, this incident set the groundwork for me to *see*, to grow race conscious, to become White, to become an antiracist racist, not just an antiracist.

Perhaps most significant about my relationship with Mrs. A was how important and unique it was for me and how likely unimportant and usual I imagine it was for her. I now think of myself as having been just one more spoiled White child who, in enjoying all the attention that I did from her and the benefit I derived from it, was taking time away from her with her own children. Because racism exists and is so congruently mediated with classism, she worked for my parents to provide basic support for her family. I imagine that had she and her husband had the same opportunities that my mother and father did she would rather have been home with her own children than with me. Ironically and despite the somewhat antifeminist contradiction, my mother could have been home with me instead of Mrs. A.

My oldest sister sent me the book *My Soul is Rested: The Story of the Civil Rights Movement in the Deep South* (Raines, 1977) a few years ago. It is an autobiography of a White man who grew up in the segregated South with, like us and so many other White children from slavery to the present (White, 1985), a Black maid. He subsequently became heavily involved in the civil rights movement and attributes his consciousness in becoming so involved to the presence of this Black woman in his life as a child. My sister and I agree that Mrs. A had a similar impact on our consciousnesses. This is what is so hard to reconcile: Out of some of the most racist historical circumstances, antiracist racist consciousness emerges.

Seeing

The first important lesson I learned about the secret was coming to realize on a conscious level, *seeing*, that I am White, that I am raced, and that I have a culture, several in fact, from which I derive and practice cultural norms. I am ethnic, too. The irony here is that because in some cosmological way I perceived the existence of the secret without fully knowing it, this perception led me to experience myself, as an "outsider," "Other," in many ways throughout my life. This sense of myself as an "Other" is pathological in some sense because, as a White, upper middle-class child, I was *never* "Other," at least not with respect to race or class, hence I understand this sense of myself as rooted in both the antiracist and the antiracist racist part of my consciousness. I knew this self-perception made me different from those whom I was around, presumably family members and White friends. At the same time, I knew that we were somehow also the same. In essence, I experienced myself as in opposition to the collusion in and maintenance of the boundaries of the secret, while simultaneously sensing I was inextricably involved in its perpetuation. By not searching for the revelation of the secret, by never owning my whiteness, the persistence of my racism, and the requirement to confront this even when it cost me what I was never supposed to allow it to, I would remain in the experience of myself as unraced, absenting culture, norms, and ethnicity, uncritically conscious, forever unengaged with the real not pathological "Other," forever patrolling borders, never deconstructing them, and thus eroding the institutionalization of discrimination they "protect."

Choice was my second lesson.

THE SECRET CONSTRUCTED

When my family moved to Shaker Heights, Ohio, our neighborhood was still predominantly White, but not all White. I remember Black families within a block, including the Leverts (of the musical groups *The O'Jays* and, later, *Levert*). The public elementary school that I attended was Black and White. It was 1968 and the civil rights movement was hot. The junior and senior high schools in our district abutted the elementary school play yard. As a result, we were heavily influenced by the actions of the "big kids." We saw them interracially dating, so we did to the degree that first through sixth graders date. Interracial relationships were at least as common as same-race dating. The first three age peers that I can remember as boyfriends were all Black. While my age peers and I experienced ourselves as *choosing* to cross borders around sexual taboos—to have sex—*choosing* to cross borders around racial taboos—to interracially date—and *choosing* to cross both kinds of borders in having interracial sex, the extent of our actual *choice* in doing these things must be juxtaposed with the influence of the "big kids." I do not ever remember thinking, "Why am I having sex?" "Why am I interracially dating?" and so forth. I only remember that these were the things to do, so it raises the question of how much *choice* was involved. Nonetheless, these borders were crossed, at least publicly, as never before in history.

Perhaps one of the most significant racist contradictions in White society is the characterization of an extremely attractive and desirable man as "tall, *dark*, and handsome." My father has always been considered such, especially the "dark" part because of his so-called "olive-complexioned" skin, which allowed him to "tan" so well. White people head to the beach and to tanning beds in droves to brown despite the real danger of skin cancer. We jokingly compare ourselves to Black people in measuring the progress of our "tans." We romanticize the virility of a darkly "tanned" White man, racistly sexualize the virility of an authentically brown Black man, but make taboo the establishment of relationships between White women and Black men whether constructed around simply "jungle fever" (sexual attraction based on racist sexual stereotypes), or something more significant. We say dark is handsome but we construct it as the opposite when it is taken to its logical conclusion in blackness.

Interracial platonic friendships were also common in grade school. The *choice* involved in the development of these relationships was, I believe, more genuine, predicated upon personality similarities and common interests rather than fad and superficiality. My best female friend, Sue, was also Black. Sue and I were inseparable and were best friends with another pair of interracial best friends, Robin, who was Black, and Cathy, who was White. The four of us were *the* girl athletes in the school and the gym teacher's pets. Robin, Cathy, and I all lived within ten houses of each other. Sue lived about three miles away in an area that I frequented when shopping with my mother. It was a "Blacker" section of town though still fairly middle-class. The four of us had sleepovers often but always at Robin's, Cathy's, or my house. Sue and I had sleepovers even more often but always at my house.

I remember going to Sue's house *once*. It was very nice, though I sensed in some unconsciously conscious way that it was decorated in a race- and class-related culturally different fashion, Black and middle-class. It had shag carpet, comfortable chrome and leather furniture in the living room, which we were actually allowed to use, unlike at my house where we were relegated to the basement or my bedroom. There were family pictures everywhere. I think Sue's mother might have been a single parent, which, as a colleague pointed out, speaks volumes about the racist construction of our friendship. As with Mrs. A, Sue's life outside of school was as much a mystery to me then as it is today.

I called my mother from Sue's house that day to ask to spend the night. I remember the call as if it were yesterday. My mother was unwavering in saying, "no," no matter how much I begged. It was as if a definitive steel door between me and *the* experience I perceived at the time might have facilitated my coming to, once and for all, know the secret, was slammed in my face. Here, the *choice* to not cross a border was made for me, I had no *choice*; still, I felt responsible. Of course, Sue could come to our house but I could not stay there—period, end of discussion, no explanation. In retrospect, I imagine that the reason I was not allowed to stay had something to do with racist class-based assumptions about parental permissiveness. The irony here is that Sue's mother was *strict*, far stricter than my own.

I remember Sue's mother was watching me on the phone to see what my mother would say when I asked, as if she was waiting to confirm a suspicion. I knew at the time by the most subtle and, considering the circumstances, extraordinarily polite innuendo that Sue and her mother took my mother's refusal to be evidence of her and, probably by association, my racism. Of course, they were right, in this instance we reeked of racism. I also knew, again by innuendo, that by not being able to cross this border at this time, whatever open invitation I theretofore enjoyed with Sue to do so in the future had been revoked. Our friendship was never quite the same after this incident and altogether disintegrated when we entered junior high school where the race borders among the girls were constructed in concrete.

In contradiction, I also remember two White friends that I had, Susan and Peggy. They both lived about three blocks away in opposite directions. They were more middle class (like Sue), and while the exterior of their houses were as nice as ours (and Sue's), inside was another story—they were always a mess. Furthermore, there was never *any* supervision when I went to either place—sex, drugs, you name it—not to mention the racial epitaphs that abounded from their parents' mouths when they occasionally made an appearance. These people were the epitome of racist "White trash." My mother always expressed strong disapproval when I went to visit, and especially sleepover, at these two friends' houses because, I believe, of the racist attitudes to which she suspected I would be exposed. But, she never took the *choice* of whether or not, or to what extent, to interact with these friends—to cross the class boundaries between us—away from me as she had in the case with Sue. I am not sure she knew the extent of the disarray or lack of supervision in Susan's or Peggy's homes, but what is interesting is that she did not assume anything in this regard one way or another. What is significant is that she did not know the extent of the order, cleanliness, and strict supervision at Sue's house either, but she assumed the contrary. Had Sue lived in a predominantly White middle-class neighborhood instead of a predominantly Black middle- or even upper middle-class one, I believe none of this would have ever emerged as an issue. Hence, I learned that my mother's standard of class approval was higher for people of color than it was for Whites and that my ability to border cross or not was predicated on this racist standard.

Learning to respect borders as an antiracist racist grew out of these experiences. The enduring pain of the racist betrayal I feel I perpetrated against Sue and her mother serves as a constant reminder to me of the complexities of border politics and has acted as a thermometer for me in all subsequent relationships in discerning whether or not, when, and in what way it is appropriate to cross the border.

Choice

The second important lesson I learned about the secret has to do with *choice*; choosing *to* cross borders or, as Rorty (1989) describes it, "making the 'Other' 'us' rather than 'they' " (Chávez Chávez, working paper, p. 11), as well as choosing *not* to cross them. My major critique of Ignatiev and Garvey's "race traitor" perspective (1996) has to do with its notion that in owning White privilege, even as an antiracist racist, one is serving only the interest of the racist state. To work at counterpurposes to this state, Whites must become "race traitors." Essentially, we have to engage in struggle to abolish whiteness in all the ways in which it is manifest to afford people assumed to be White privilege over "Other." Ignatiev and Garvey argue that all borders serve only the interest of the racist state. I disagree. Often, I think borders are a people's weapon *against* the racist state.

Certainly, the antiracist racist movement has its own set of contradictions. We argue that race as well as ethnicity, class, gender, and so forth, are reifications, but we go on to argue further why, at least at this historical moment, we must continue to reference them to frame our discussion of power imbalances. A good critical pedagogist then goes on to confound, deconstruct, problematize them toward the end Ignatiev and Garvey argue but with greater caution because of the contradictions of privilege inherent in them all. Ignatiev and Garvey seem to throw caution to the wind in encouraging border eradication. As a multiculturalist, I want to become endeared to difference and functionally eclectic as a result of my border crossing. I also want to be critical in how I come to understand difference as good, bad, "exotic," and so forth, and in how I practice ecclecticism, especially avoiding the tendency toward appropriation. I want to be respectful of the border in and of itself. What is the function of each and every border? How does border construction, maintenance, and/or destruction serve the interest of the racist state?

For example, the introduction in *Race Traitor* (Ignatiev & Garvey, 1996) details the circumstances of White teenagers who have taken on so-called Black identities mostly through their attire. The teens call their association "Free To Be Me." Their town refers to them as "wiggers"—White niggers. Ignatiev and Garvey argue that the emergence of this conflict is a sign that the White race is beginning to disintegrate. This seems highly problematic to me. Neither Ignatiev, Garvey, or I know anything personally about the consciousness of these teenagers. Just because they dress "hip-hop" and appeared on a Black-hosted talk show denouncing their school for expelling them and their town for attacking their association does not mean that they did at the time nor will in the future think and/or act as abolitionists. They could still engage in actively racist behavior. The clothing could be an *appropriation* of Black culture in their minds, taking something from Blacks for themselves—an act of colonialism. Such culture cross-over is not necessarily to be seen as a sign of "unwhitening," but rather corporate marketing that may in fact have the effect of increasing the level of repression in communities of color. White parents, with access to institutional power based on skin color or the perception of skin color, displeased with the so-called Black influence in their community, make this displeasure known publicly, the media picks it up, and the Yusef Hawkins's story (a young Black man who was murdered for simply being in a White neighborhood) gets repeated over and over again.

I have come to understand, through experience, that I must *choose* to observe those specific borders that serve people of color against the racist state and, at least in this historical moment, that also require the continued reification of race and whiteness, but, in this instance, oriented, I believe, toward revolutionary not reactionary ends.

Responsibility was my third lesson.

THE SECRET DECONSTRUCTED

In the spring of 1987, as a part of my master's program at the University of Massachusetts at Amherst, I enrolled in the education course "Helping from a Racial Perspective." This course is now somewhat of a legacy because of the life-changing effect it has had on the lives of so many who have taken it. At the time that I enrolled in this course, I had been working at a private special education school for so-called emotionally disturbed adjudicated adolescents who had been kicked out of public school for "behavioral problems" for about six months. I say so-called emotionally disturbed because given what they had been through, at home, on the street, and, especially, in school (namely, the lack of a comprehensive sociopolitically grounded multicultural education), if they hadn't been acting out, then they would have been emotionally disturbed (Walsh, 1991). The fact that they were acting out—having a disturbed reaction to a disturbed reality—was, in my opinion, an indication that they were emotionally normal, and healthy.

It is most significant that I had this job when I enrolled in this course. Their convergence in my life, more than any other combination of experiences, created the context for my finally coming to know the secret. Ironically, this knowledge emerged in relationship to the analysis of the school's "behavioral management system" that I undertook while engaged in the course. The behavioral management system at this school was used to "correct" the behavior of its students. The system was based on privileges. The more "appropriately" a student behaved, the more privilege she or he was afforded. It mirrored society exactly. "Appropriateness" was predicated on "normalcy," a so-called God-fearing, law-abiding citizen's sense of what this was. But the contradiction was intense. How can a student labeled disturbed be expected to be normal? Also, so-called God-fearing, law abiding citizens are some of the most pathological. I liken this to our societal reward system: The more White you are or, at least, behave, the more privileges you are afforded. In this case, "behaving appropriately" can be substituted for "acting White," that is, adopting White cultural norms and values. The contradiction here is that no matter how White "Other" tries to be, they are still and always will be constructed as more "Other" than White, despite perhaps earning conditionally greater access to White privilege in being identified as less "Other" than most "Others." Also, the picture we have of so-called God-fearing, law-abiding citizens is of Whites, and the centering of whiteness, white privilege, Whites as norm-referenced, White as right is pathological. Ultimately, then, the students at this school, just as with "Other" in society, must trade the pathology they developed in response to injustice for one negating that this injustice ever existed if they want privileges or rewards—in short, if they ever want to be academically successful.

When I began the course, I had not yet developed this insight, but, I could see that virtually all of the students were Black, Latina/o, and male and that virtually all of the staff was White and female. I knew somehow that there was something racist about this, but I did not even know how to articulate it much less how to go about changing it. With this insight sitting in a hypnogogic, unconsciously conscious state within me, I entered my classroom at the University of Massachusetts. From that point forward, this insight awoke and jumped into my consciousness where it has resided aggressively ever since. What triggered this awakening was twofold.

First, at the onset of the course, the professor gave a homework exercise. To complete the exercise, students were not to consult any resources; we were only to reflect on our own life experiences. The exercise was simple: come to the next class prepared to discuss your race and ethnicity. The race question was not a difficult one for me. I knew I was White. I obsessed, however, over my answer to the ethnicity question. Over the course of the class, I came to understand that this was because as a mostly Anglo Saxon, my ethnicity, even to a greater degree than my race, was socially constructed in society as nonethnic, as "normal," the standard against which other ethnicities, even other White ethnicities, were measured and judged based on their proximity to it. I reflected on this and realized that I grew up with at least consciously unconscious stereotypes of the Polish as "dumb," the Irish as "hot-tempered" and prone to alcoholism, and Jews as "intelligent," but also "cheap" and "greedy."

As I wrestled to define my ethnicity, I decided for some reason, that it must have something to do with oppression or victimization. Given this, I reflected on my own experiences of oppression as a woman. In particular, I began to focus on my fairly recent battle with anorexia nervosa and my associated obsession with diet cola. While I drank Diet Pepsi, I decided that Diet Coke was a better symbol for me to use because of the Coca-Cola boycott vis-à-vis the struggle against apartheid in South Africa. Inside of this analysis I concluded that my ethnicity was Diet Coke. At the time I knew that my answer was wrong, but at least, I thought, it showed some intellectual effort to arrive at it. When I disclosed this answer in class, I got quite a laugh, even from the professor. As other White students answered the question I realized what in fact my ethnicity was. Later, I also realized that my answer illustrated my race and ethnic privilege. I did not know my ethnicity because I was not forced to by the sociopolitical conditions of my existence in society. I had come to *see* myself as raced because of my leftist political work, but *seeing* myself as raced and understanding the social construction of race were two different things—antiracist consciousness versus antiracist racist consciousness. My race consciousness, or rather unconsciousness, was superficial. I had been "trained" to acknowledge myself as White but never "educated" as to why I should do this. As with interracial dating in elementary school, it was just something done, not analyzed. Had I understood the concept of social construction, it would have been analytically simple to extrapolate from my race consciousness an ethnic one using deductive reasoning.

This experience has stayed with me. As a multicultural educator, I take from it the knowledge that true learning, "education," must be concept-based; anything else is simply "training." Training does not hold the promise of facilitating the undoing of the secret nor of building communities of learners in schools or society that think and act critically to bring about a more socially just, practicing democratic society for all; education does.

The second impact on my antiracist racist awakening in the course came through exposure to the Black Identity Development (Jackson, 1976b) and White Identity Development (Hardiman, 1979) models cited earlier. In particular, the White Identity Development model forever changed my life. This model suggests that there are four major stages in the racial identity development of White Americans: Stage One, Acceptance of Racism (where acceptance may be active, initiating a racist act, or passive, going along with a racist act); Stage Two, Resistance to Racism (where resistance may be passive, avoiding a racist act, or active, confronting a racist act); Stage Three, Redefinition; and Stage Four, Internalization.

The model argues that all White Americans, by virtue of their socialization in the institutionally racist United States, come, to some degree very early in life, to actively and passively *accept* racism. According to the model, one is born into this stage and may function within it for one's whole life (Hardiman, 1979).

Movement into subsequent stages is developmental and may occur in one of two ways: via informal experiences—circumstantial usually traumatic, highly emotionally charged events that have consciousness shattering impact—or via formal experiences—deliberate interaction designed to influence attitudes and/or behavior. Informal experiences are more likely the catalysts in engendering movement from stage one to stage two (someone in the acceptance of racism stage does not generally enroll in a racism awareness seminar unless they are mandated to do so), whereas formal experiences are more likely the catalysts in producing movement beyond stage two (Hardiman, 1979).

A circumstantial, traumatic event causes an individual, almost overnight, to rethink her or his whole existence. She or he sees how naive she or he has been and becomes angry at her or his own shortsightedness. In short, she or he moves into *resisting* racism, first passively and then later, if the rethinking and associated anger persist, perhaps more actively (Hardiman, 1979).

Once some of the anger subsides, *if* it does, the individual may begin to seek out ways to *redefine* racial identity not as only good (a characteristic of a person in the acceptance stage) or as only bad (a characteristic of a person at the resistance stage) but as an integration of both good and bad (Hardiman, 1979).

Movement into *internalization* occurs when the individual is able to integrate racial identity with all other identities vis-à-vis socioeconomic class background, gender, sexual preference or orientation, and so forth. At this stage, the individual is committed to facilitating other people's movement through the model (Hardiman, 1979).

The major critique of the models is that they are linear, modernistic, and positivistic (Kinchloe, Pinar, & Slattery, 1994; Hidalgo, Chávez Chávez, & Ramage, 1996). Despite their limitations, these models were liberating for me at the time I learned them. In particular, they gave me a conceptual framework for understanding race and racial identity; something to point to and say, "See, this is what I mean." They also helped me to think about my own antiracist racist consciousness in very specific ways. For example, once I understood the basic concepts of the models, I was able to manipulate them in ways that at least challenged their linear and developmental orientation. I would look at the models and ask whether or not an individual's consciousness can be at more than one stage simultaneously (can Nation of Islam membership occur at stage two and/or stage three depending on how this membership is viewed by the individual member?), or whether or not two people exhibiting similar behavior can be analyzed in terms of their consciousness in engaging in that behavior as at different stages (is interracial dating *always* "jungle fever" or can it be done with dignity?), and so forth.

Having learned at the outset of the course how to consciously *see* myself as raced and ethnic, White and Anglo Saxon, and hence, privileged, the pursuant learning of these models gave me the insight I needed to begin to make *choices* about how to develop myself as an antiracist racist and to understand the *responsibility* inherent in so becoming. While learning these models did not immediately enable me (nor motivate me) to move out of what I recognized in myself as active resistance through redefiniton and into internalization (I took refuge in my anger now that I understood it), it did enable me to give some structure to and put some signifiers on my autobiography as it related to race. In so doing, I was able to begin to make sense of racism as both a personal and political construct and, furthermore, to discern the ways in which I, as a multicultural educator, might make a contribution toward eradicating it.

Today, I think about these models differently. But no matter how my thinking about these models or anything having to do with this course evolves, I will always be eternally grateful that I had this educational experience. More than any other singular experience, this course solidified my desire to become a lifelong antiracist racist educator.

Responsibility

The last important lesson I learned about the secret is perhaps the most difficult to understand and actuate. A consequence of becoming an antiracist racist is that associations with Whites become difficult at the same time people of color do not always, nor in my opinion should they be expected to, embrace you. There is an element of longing to belong somewhere that goes with the commitment, the *responsibility* to antiracist racist struggle.

Clearly, the antiracist racist responsibility in borderwalking is phenomenally complex. Often, Whites trusted as allies by people of color are "let in," able to cross borders in ways that allow us to at least observe if not sometimes participate in, aspects of "Other" life that we would probably not come to know. I believe that sometimes we are trusted when we are not ready for, or do not yet fully understand, the responsibility this trust entails. I also believe that sometimes we are let in too far.

For example, perceived as both a nonally and an ally I have been called "White girl," "honky," "cracker," "white bread," "blanquita," "gringita," and so forth. As a nonally, I understand this naming to mean that I may not cross the border. As an ally, I understand this naming to mean that I may now, or already have been allowed to, cross the border. But, as an antiracist racist I also understand that in neither context may I use theoretically comparable names for people of color to insult or to embrace. This is part of the "power + prejudice = 'ism'" equation (Jackson, 1976b). While all people have prejudice, in this case race prejudice, not all people have access to power at the institutional level in society to enforce these prejudices—those who do create "isms," in this case racism. Racial prejudice and racism are distinguished by the institutional power associated with the latter but absent from association with the former. By virtue of being White and because Whites have and historically have had disproportionate access to institutional power in the United States, the racial prejudice toward people of color that all Whites are socialized, consciously and unconsciously, to essentially embrace is necessarily entrenched in and enforced via our political, economic, and social structures as racism. According to this equation, seemingly parallel actions on the part of a White person and a person of color have different impact because of the power issue. For me to be called a "honky" by a person of color is simply not the same thing as my calling a person of color a "nigger," or a "spic." My actions are reinforced exponentially by the racism of the superstructure, while those of a person of color toward me are not; hence, the latter carries less impact.

I have also been told that I am "Black by injection" or called, "negrita." Again, I understand this naming to mean that I have already been allowed to cross the border. I take such naming as an enormous compliment, an expression of support for my being an antiracist racist, which carries with it an enormous responsibility to never forget that I am White and never sell out my commitment to antiracist racist work.

In the last five years I have had an increasing number of White students who express a sense of being "let in" even further. They have Black friends who call them the theoretically reclaimed version of nigger, "niggah," or "my niggah," as in "my brutha'," "my homeboy," "my homie," "homecrunch," my good friend. I have students engage in discussion about what I call "in- and out-group naming," during which we debate if, even with in-group naming, terms, phrases, and/or symbols can be "reclaimed," or recovered, from their derogatory etiology and used instead to affirm pride in group membership. I believe that even in-group naming in the spirit of reclamation is evidence of some kind of internalized self-hatred. I know I feel this about myself when with other women I exchange the word "bitch" in a so-called affectionate fashion. At the same time, I do not presume to tell members of in-groups of which I am not a member how to refer to each other. I do point out to my students, however, that there are virtually no negative terms, phrases, or symbols aimed at insulting men as a group, nor have I ever heard White people greet each other with self-directed racially derogatory language like, "Howdy honky," though the converse is quite common, such as, "What'z Up, Niggah." Taken collectively, White male privilege absents White men from this phenomenon, which should make the rest of us think long and hard about why this is.

I have come to draw a line when these same White students go on to tell me that they are also allowed to use the term "niggah," and/or derivations thereof, toward their Black friends. Whites should never be let in this far nor should we want to be. Respect for "Other" must involve an understanding of the historical and present-day violence it references. If I am really someone's friend or ally; if I am really an antiracist racist, this is not a border I would ever cross.

FURTHER IMPLICATIONS FOR MULTICULTURAL EDUCATION

In May 1995, I accepted a faculty position at New Mexico State University in the College of Education, Department of Curriculum and Instruction, where I teach multicultural education at the undergraduate and graduate levels. In dialogue with students in several contexts about teaching and learning over the last two years, my thinking about and my attachment to the identity development models changed. For ten years, these models informed my everyday antiracist racist consciousness. Today, I see how they were limiting the further development of my antiracist racist consciousness and perhaps that of my students as well.

To begin with, I realized that I had previously ignored just how many students did not get anything out of them, not because they were in denial about racism or some aspect of their racial identity, but rather because these models, no matter how much I encouraged students to manipulate them, simply did not speak to these students' autobiographies.

Next, I noticed that in using the models I had unconsciously bought into an "approach" to the teaching of multicultural education. I had, to my horror, become a "methods fetishist" (Bartolomé, 1994). I realized that I had begun to believe that multicultural education had to be taught the way I taught it, namely with these models.

Lastly, I believe that my attachment to the models caused me to over identify people of color as victims in such a way that I took agency away from them and encouraged students to do the same. Because both White students and students of color so resist seeing the persistent, pervasive, and perilous nature of institutional racism (and other forms of institutional discrimination), I believe that I often used the models, especially examples from the resistance to racism stage, to practically assault them with the realities of institutional victimization of "Other," past and present. bell hooks sums up the downside of such practice in *Killing Rage: Ending Racism* (1995):

Those black folks who embrace victim identity do so because they find it mediates relations with whites, that it is easier to make appeals that call for sympathy rather than redress and reparations. As long as white Americans are more willing to extend concern and care to black folks who have a "victim-focused black identity," a shift in paradigms will not take place. (p. 58)

In considering the social reality of victim identification, I have come to believe that Whites are far better at claiming victim status than are people of color (I would make a parallel argument for all members of over-represented social membership groups, such as native speakers of English, the upper middle and upper class, men, and so forth). When I lived in Nicaragua during the U. S. orchestrated contra war, I saw more death than ever before in my life. People who I met and developed friendships with one week were dead the next. Funerals were an everyday occurrence. I noticed that few tears were shed at these funerals, and I asked a *compañera* about this. She said that the pain of loss was so persistent that people no longer cried on the outside at specified times, instead they cried on the inside incessantly. When she said this, I realized that White privilege (and many other kinds of privilege as well) had insulated me from having to develop the skill of crying inside.

About seven years ago, four years into my relationship with my husband and just about the time when I began to recognize the full weight of the injustices I would forever be forced to face as the White wife of a Black man in the United States, my former boss related to me his favorite mantra, "Black in America." At first I did not get it when he would say this to me every time I would complain about one incident or another that my husband encountered. After a while, though, I began to understand that in relating these incidents I was not telling him anything he had not heard before. I was simply relating the recurring details of what it was to be "Black in America." While this was news to me, it was old hat to him; like crying on the inside, he did his raging on the inside, too.

One last example was brought to my attention by a man who was a student in one of the classes I taught in the prisons in Massachusetts. We were discussing some aspect of women's oppression, and he asked the rhetorical question, "How come when something bad happens to a White woman she is shown crying about it all over the news, but when the same thing or even something worse happens to a Woman of Color we don't hear about it or if we do, we almost never see *her* cry?" These observations now lead me to ask myself and my students, "*Whose* playing the victim?"

Recently, my thinking about institutional racism (including the power plus prejudice equation), agency, victimization, and decentering whiteness was radically challenged. This challenge was launched by a participant in a session in which I was facilitating dialogue regarding this book and, more specifically, this chapter, at the University of New Mexico's conference, "A Celebration of Differences: Weaving Patterns of Respect and Appreciation."

The participant was a Chicano from South Central Los Angeles whose challenge was directed at the power plus prejudice equation and the way this equation referenced institutional racism. While he clearly understood the power relations these concepts were employed to describe for the audience, he believed that focusing the description of power relations around these concepts could, at least inadvertently, create the perception that when, for example, young Latino and Black males kill each other, it is somehow less important than when Whites kill people of color, or when agents of the state (cops) kill people of color. Certainly, the political right has made it clear that nothing is an epidemic until it negatively impacts the White middle class. But he was not framing his critique on the right, but rather on the left. In essence, he argued that when the left, especially the White left, employs these concepts in an attempt to advocate on behalf of people of color, we actually encourage the diminution of the source of greatest immediate destruction in of color communities—young men of color allied against each other in gangs. Clearly, when I work with Whites I have concerns about how easy it is for us to view the problems in of color communities as the fault of those who reside in these communities and disavow ourselves of any responsibility. Refocusing Whites on the root of the problem as institutional racism is an important part of getting us to invest ourselves in the change process. Typically, this process has focused on eroding the opportunity structures that prevent people of color from accessing positions of power—positions where the decisions about the prioritization and allocation of resources for education, housing, health care, and employment to of color communities are made. My challenger clearly understood all of these dynamics; still he felt that to focus efforts on addressing change at this level once again diverted attention away from the immediacy of the need for change at the grass-roots level in his community. He went on to articulate his sense that the focus of the White left on institutional, instead of individual, racism was but another way to recenter discussion around whiteness. In a deeply provocative way he is right about this. It puts us at the center again, not as the good guys but as the bad guys, which may be how the White left manifests it racist pathology to be at the center. I still have not come to any resolution regarding this man's challenge.

In January 1997, I radically revised my multicultural education course. Certainly, I still believe that the goal of the course should be to facilitate students' critical consciousness in three areas: (1) awareness, knowledge, and understanding of self in relationship to race; ethnicity; language; socioeconomic class background; gender; sexual preference or orientation; physical, developmental, and emotional ability; religious or spiritual affiliation; age and generation; size and appearance; geographic origin; and environmental concern;

(2) awareness, knowledge, and understanding of self (as delineated in #1) in relationship to others; and (3) awareness, knowledge, and understanding of self and others (as delineated in #1 and #2) as they impact multicultural education. However, I no longer believe that critical consciousness in these three areas emerges in a developmental fashion predicated on the identity development models. Rather, exposure to various perspectives on (1) issues of race, ethnicity, and so forth, (2) how they impact student learning, and (3) how they inform multicultural education, and then dialoging about them essentially brings about the same results and does so in a way that, pedagogically speaking, far more resembles the practice of democracy in my classroom. The same major questions, conflicts, and revelations emerge, though never, of course, in exactly the same way.

What has become most important to me now as an antiracist racist multicultural educator is that I practice democracy in my classroom. I use *all* the students' autobiographies as the point of reference for this practice, to focus students on the three areas of critical consciousness that I just listed—what a colleague calls, "to be" (the ontological), "to know" (the epistemological), and "to know how to do the right thing" (the axiological/ethical) (Chávez Chávez, working paper). This is what I now call *seeing, choice,* and *responsibility.* I want students to become critical thinkers especially with respect to seeing, choice, and responsibility, and I want them, as future educators, to want the same thing for their students.

The only thing I know for sure at this moment is that the practice of antiracist racist multicultural education is inextricably integrated with the practice of democracy in the classroom, not in telling students what to believe, think, feel, and do—not in *presenting* content—but in dialoguing, arguing, debating, *problem posing* with them about what they believe, think, feel, and do, how they see these ideas, emotions, and actions informing their pedagogy as teachers, and, more importantly, impacting *all* their students' abilities to access *full* participation in democracy through a process of achievement in critical multicultural education.

CONCLUSION

There are so many experiences in my life that I could have detailed in place of the ones that I have chosen. The process of discerning which ones to share was difficult as each is unique and offers its own piece of the race secret. The secret has many layers. Like the telephone game, the truth is so distorted by the time it reaches you, that rediscovering it without the distortion becomes a formidable and lifelong endeavor.

In teaching multicultural education, I focus on inclusivity and multiplicity by discussing race *and* ethnicity *and* language *and* socioeconomic class background *and* gender *and* sexual preference or orientation *and* physical, developmental, and emotional ability *and* religious or spiritual affiliation *and* age and generation *and* size and appearance *and* geographic origin *and* environmental concern as they pertain to student achievement. While I prioritize the issue of race and racism, I have found that student resistance to the overall subject of multicultural education is reduced when the discussion of race and racism is juxtaposed with the discussion of other issues. For example, a White female will become more engaged in the learning and ultimately supportive of multicultural education when, in the course of confronting her racism, she is affirmed in her struggle against patriarchy and sees that the men in the class are likewise being challenged to confront their sexism. Certainly, the essence of multicultural education (to the degree that *an* essence can be identified without turning the paradigm into something reductionistic) is in the inclusivities and multiplicities it stresses. If I were to address *only* race issues it would not truly be a multicultural education course but, rather, an antiracist (not an antiracist racist) education one.

In writing this chapter I have realized that another reason why I now prioritize *all* of these issues, instead of just one, two, or three of them, is because of how the recognition of the privilege embodied in each and every social membership group is a necessary part in the "coming out" or the race secret. It is clear to me that for the race secret to be completely revealed, so too must be the secrets of ethnicity, language, socioeconomic class background, gender, and so forth.

I had thought about discussing the race secret from the perspective of multiplicities. But, had I done this, I believe I would have fallen into another trap of *not* prioritizing the discussion on race and racism, which is the major purpose of this book. One of the most poignant critiques of multicultural education is that in prioritizing so many issues, the issues of race and racism get watered down. Racism is the seminal issue upon which our nation was founded. Five hundred years later, it is still the seminal issue in our nation's functioning, or better, its dysfunctioning. One of the ways that Whites in multicultural education perpetuate racism is in avoiding the discussion of race-related issues in favor of ones they feel more comfortable with that are also included under the multicultural umbrella. For example, as a woman, it is far easier for me to vehemently discuss issues of gender equity because it is obviously in my own self-interest. Whereas, as a White person, the vehement discussion of race equity issues is far more likely to make me uncomfortable because how it is in my self-interest in so doing is hidden. Antiracist racist consciousness *is* in the self-interest of Whites especially because it challenges our supremacist pathology. It is psychologically unhealthy to walk around with a distorted perception of ourselves as more important than "Others." We must frame the antiracist racist struggle in terms of White self-interest, otherwise, it becomes but another expression of colonialism, missionary zeal, rescuer pride, and so forth.

In fact, in discussing myself as an antiracist racist, I am often asked to explain why I am only talking about White people as racist. Certainly people of color are racist or, at least in light of the power plus prejudice equation, have race prejudice too? I find this argument to be at the crux of the "race problem." The history of race-related thought has always focused on people of color: how *they* are, what *they* do, what *they* do not do, and so forth. This serves to justify and reinforce the racist attitudes of Whites (Dennis, 1981). When people of color or an antiracist racist suggest that we refocus that thought onto White people—how *we* are, what *we* do, what *we* do not do that perpetuates racism—the White response is indignant. It is amazing just how uncomfortable Whites become when we are asked to look at ourselves and our behavior in relationship to this problem. With lightening speed, we preach to people of color to "take responsibility" for this and for that but fail to hold ourselves to the same standard. We don't practice what we preach. We don't take responsibility for interrupting the individual racist thoughts we have and for the individual and collective racist acts that we initiate and in which we participate, including, both inadvertently and deliberately, creating children in our racist image.

At least in a consciously unconscious way, I believe White people know we benefit from racism even if we are disadvantaged as poor, non-English speaking, female, physically differently abled, and so forth. We do not want to admit this benefit, however, because then we might have to go on to admit that it is unjust, at least in the context of a so-called democracy and certainly before a benevolent higher power, to enjoy this benefit at the expense of others. But this assumes that becoming an antiracist racist is worse than a zero sum game; that Whites must give up all benefit for people of color to gain any. This is why so many White people believe my ongoing struggle to be an antiracist racist must be, at best, a function of altruism gone awry. My profound commitment to this struggle does not permit me to belittle my colleagues in this struggle, both people of color and Whites, by engaging in it as nothing more than a glorified "do-gooder." While I benefit from racism, I benefit a whole lot more from being an antiracist racist. It is in my self-interest, the self-interest of all Whites as well as people of color, to engage in struggle against racism. If I work in cooperation with *all* people toward a common goal, we *all* benefit.

Finally, I have come to think about the reference to or the use of the race secret metaphorically as in and of itself a contradiction in some ways. I often struggle with how best to get students to *see* institutional discrimination so that they will make the *choice* to take *responsibility* for ending it. I am still shocked at how hard it is to illustrate, to facilitate their experience of something that today I take for granted as so "obvious." "Well," I have come to ask myself, "if it is *so* obvious then why do I both construct and deconstruct it herein as something hidden, a secret?" It is only obvious to the extent that the secret has been revealed. And that revelation continues.

NOTE

1. The notion of the unconscious conscious or the conscious unconscious (Chávez Chávez, 1998) as I employ it herein is a reference to the affirmation or denial of metacognition, respectively. As a child, I metacognitively affirmed the existence of the race secret in my unconscious consciousness, I knew it existed. As an adult, I might metacognitively deny that I benefit from racism. In my conscious unconscious, I refuse to acknowledge my privilege.

7

Becoming White: How I Got Over
Arnold Cooper

I was born in Philadelphia, Pennsylvania, in 1941. My world was sanitized and White. Every family in my neighborhood was White; every teacher, every playmate, every store, every church and synagogue, every aspect of my upbringing reinforced my whiteness. My parents bought a house in 1939 for $5,000 in a section of North Philly that resembled a suburb but was within the city limits. There were sixty attached houses on each side of my street; the city planted a tree for every two houses if owners agreed to water it.

I walked only one block to elementary school, about three blocks to a local library, and several more blocks to the movies on Saturdays. My environment was comfortable and safe. Neighborhood kids played baseball in the street, since there were no playgrounds. Occasionally, police mounted on horseback provided drama when they ambled down Mayland Street, but the appearance of any sort of law enforcement was rare.

When I was twelve years old (1953), I left my neighborhood and took a trolley car to Wagner Junior High School, a ride of about twenty-five minutes. On my very first day, a Black student pulled a knife and robbed me of my wallet. I was shocked and scared. I honestly do not remember any other reaction other than my parents' counsel "to be careful." My second experience meeting a person of color was more positive. Although I was defeated by Charles Dennis, an African American student, for homeroom president by one vote, he and I became friends. We would eat lunch together; we would talk about other students; we even said that we would visit each other's homes. We never did. Our worlds were so different that school became our only common meeting ground. Charles used to joke that his father was a "sanitation engineer" rather than a garbage man. I could not think of any other way to describe my father except that he worked as a buyer for a grocery cooperative.

My only other association with a person of color at junior high came when I asked Estell, a tall African American girl, to dance at a school social. I remember some White students telling me that we should not have danced together, but I do not remember their specific reasons, nor do I remember engaging in any lengthy debate about the matter.

What I do remember very vividly was asking my father to buy me a book on "Negroes" at the same time that Charles and Estell became my classmates. I do not know where he bought it, but one day my dad gave me a book entitled *Famous American Negroes* by Benjamin Brawley. At the time, I did not know that Brawley was an eminent African American educator. For the first time in my life I read about Booker T. Washington, the founder of Tuskegee Institute, an historically Black college in Alabama; about Harriet Tubman, who escaped slavery and returned nineteen times to bring other slaves to freedom; and about Frederick Douglass, a "Negro abolitionist."

I never knew about these figures, since my school books mentioned only White people. I find it ironic now that my introduction to African American history came at the same time that the Supreme Court decided in *Brown v Board of Education of Topeka, KS* (1954) that segregation in education as practiced under the doctrine of "separate but equal" was unconstitutional. My separate but equal education was not as dramatically altered, but my curiosity about people of color was piqued.

I do not know why my father agreed to buy me the Brawley book, since he was a man of prejudice. He was not an Archie Bunker, to be sure, but he was a man with decided uncomplimentary views about people of color. My mother and father never used racial epithets in front of my sister and I. Instead, they talked openly about their fear that "those people" were going to move into the neighborhood and that a prominent African American lawyer would become mayor of Philly. These things never happened in the mid-1950s, but my parents anticipated them and conveyed the message that people of color were a threat to the safety and sanctity of our neighborhood and our well-being.

At the same time that Brawley's book instructed me about the heroics of some African Americans, I was reveling in the TV episodes of Amos and Andy, a caricature of Black life on the radio during the 1930s by White actors and played by Black actors during the 1950s. Amos and Andy indulged in wholesale and blatant stereotyping of African Americans, from the slow and shuffling "Lightning" to the terrible tirades of "Sapphire," wife of the scheming "Kingfish," to an assembly of other ridiculous members of the Mystic Knights of the Sea Lodge Hall. My best friend, George, and I knew all the dialogues, and my imitation of the Kingfish was a masterpiece, at least in my own estimation. George and I parodied everything about Black life as a result of absorbing the negative cliches about how people of color were lazy or loud or indulgent. Nobody in our environment ever challenged us. Nobody ever told us that Amos and Andy propagated myths about people of color.

The media abetted my misconceptions of people of color. Never mind that my friends Charles and Estell hardly resembled the Kingfish and Sapphire or that the Brawley book highlighted African American achievement. The media proved more powerful than Brawley. Besides, there was no Bill Cosby show at the time to counter the portrayals of Amos and Andy.

When I entered high school in 1955, all of my teachers were still White and my textbooks sanitized. No mention of Harriet Tubman or Frederick Douglass or figures from any other cultures. No one talked about a young preacher in

Montgomery, Alabama, whose leadership of a bus boycott was about to revolutionize America. What I did talk about was the Brooklyn Dodgers. By now my small library contained a biography of Jackie Robinson. I was a Dodger fan in Philly land complete with a Dodger hat and a pennant on my wall. I avidly charted the homeruns of catcher Roy Campanella and the strike outs of pitcher Don Newcombe ("Newk"). My perceptions of the world were becoming less white through the medium of baseball.

I went to a state teacher's college not far from home, and I carried my lily whiteness with me. Although I do not believe that I had a coherent set of values very much different from my peers, I did write an editorial for the college newspaper supporting closer ties with a nearby historically Black college. I had met several African American students who transferred from that college and began to broaden my perspectives about interracial connections. I received no affirmation for my stance from peers or professors. In fact, one professor told me how disappointed he was with my viewpoint, since the Black college in question was not as good as "our" college. I did not forcefully challenge his critique.

The crucible for me came when I went south to study at Duke University for a graduate degree in history at the age of twenty-one. I had never been very far from home; no relative had ever left Philly. But, I was ready to leave with a sense of adventure and an avid interest in things historical. Duke was an exciting place to be in 1962 because of the civil rights movement. Several of my professors were northerners active in promoting awareness of racial inequities by encouraging students to participate in voter education campaigns or the picketing of a local Shoney's restaurant that refused to serve African Americans. I briefly joined a picket line and ducked rocks thrown by outraged Whites.

But, I was by no means an activist. Instead, I devoted my efforts to studying American History and for the first time began a more formal and systematic commitment to learning about the history of African Americans. The aura of civil rights activities, the proximity of a local historically Black college, and the broadmindedness of several of my professors probably contributed to my interest in expanding my intellectual horizons.

After graduation, I taught for two years (1966–1968) at a community college in Birmingham, Alabama, and experienced for the first time the absolute ugliness of southern White fury about people of color. Birmingham was then known as "Bombingham" because of the explosion of the Sixteenth Street Baptist Church that killed four young Black girls. The destruction of African American churches by arson that has been so rampant in the South the last few years is not a new phenomenon in America. Indeed, the militancy of southern resistance studied so succinctly by historian John Hope Franklin (1956) often included incendiary devices.

My colleagues were White southerners with the most virulent racist views I had ever encountered. There was no major university like Duke in the community to mediate such hostility. I was unprepared and still very naive about local outrage to any view or action that challenged accepted practice. For example, when I donated a number of books to a struggling Black college after reading an appeal in the paper, one colleague decried my action in the strongest and most profane terms.

As a stranger in a strange land, I searched for support from a local group affiliated with the Alabama Human Relations Council. For the first time in my life, I met White southerners concerned enough to speak publicly about local defiance of desegregation efforts. I learned an important lesson: not all Whites were "rednecks." I needed to know this because it was a little too easy for me to stereotype local Whites as renegades beyond hope or redemption.

I left Alabama in 1968 a more reflective and sobered individual. I still considered myself an educator rather than any sort of community activist. But I understood that if I were to remain in the South, I could not divorce myself from community resistance to segregation on the one hand or desegregation on the other. Subsequently, I taught high school English for a year in the Louisiana Delta. African Americans comprised 95 percent of the student body of the high school; the school board had only one Black member; the superintendent of schools and the high school principal were White.

I learned almost immediately that I had joined a school district significantly resistant to desegregation. Teachers were strictly segregated; only African American teachers could join the National Education Association (NEA) affiliate, while White teachers had to join a Whites-only teacher's group. When the principal conducted weekly faculty meetings, White teachers sat on one side of the room and Black teachers on the other side. Districtwide meetings replicated this segregated seating arrangement. The lesson here was obvious: We were desegregated in name only with little or no colleagueship expected or encouraged.

Since I was more interested in education than agitation, I took advantage of my students' interest in Black history. In the aftermath of the assassination of Dr. Martin Luther King, Jr., there was a renewed commitment to Black pride and heritage in this small Louisiana community. I accepted this challenge and infused themes about African American history and culture into my English classes. We read Frederick Douglass's autobiography and compared it to Benjamin Franklin's; we contrasted the writings of Black and White abolitionists; we debated the merits of accommodation versus militancy as advanced by Booker T. Washington and his nemesis, W.E.B. Dubois, an African American intellectual and civil rights strategist.

This was by no means a transformed curriculum. It had all the attributes of what the eminent scholar, James Banks (1994a) calls the "additive approach" where "content, concepts, themes, and perspectives are added to the curriculum without changing its structure (p. 25)."

I also witnessed attributes of what historian V. P. Franklin (1966) labeled a distinctive "core black culture," where education becomes linked with an aspiration for liberty. A number of parents participated with their children in an after-school tutoring program as a tangible commitment to their children's improvement in school. There was more at work here than remediation. These parents put the school on notice that education equaled freedom despite the strictures of a rigidly segregated community.

My education as a teacher was further enhanced because of a friendship with a wonderful couple who were leaders in the African American community. Our first meeting was accidental—we met in the local laundromat and talked about school and the community. After awhile, I was invited to stop and visit, which I did frequently. Mrs. D was a retired teacher, and her husband was self-employed.

He also became the first elected African American council member in the community. Mrs. D bristled at the fact that many of the local White teachers would not greet their African American colleagues outside of school. She counseled me not to "act White" like that. She also told me to talk carefully over the phone because of a possible lack of privacy.

This Louisiana experience, amidst the harsh realities of a segregated environment, helped me decide to become more active and expansive in community development beyond the confines of teaching. I decided to become a VISTA volunteer, a War on Poverty program started by President Lyndon Johnson as the domestic equivalent of the Peace Corps. I was assigned to a small community about sixty miles from Charleston, South Carolina, for six months and to a community about ten miles from Greenville, North Carolina.

These assignments affected me profoundly. First, I learned the vital distinction between a "come here" person and a "been here" person. I was the former, a stranger, a transitory figure with no roots in the community; a "been here" person knew his or her community intimately. As an outsider, it was up to me to bridge the gap, to prove myself because many Black folk were as suspicious of "do-gooder" Whites as they were of the local Whites they knew. Why, some asked, would any White person volunteer to live in a rural, poor, and isolated community? One Black resident in South Carolina continually taunted me and claimed that I must have an ulterior motive. I foolishly and naively tried to explain the purposes of VISTA. To no available, it finally dawned on me that I was taking the wrong stance, that all I was doing was trying, in the words of my nemesis, to "whip the game" on him. So, I admitted that he was right. Yes, I conceded, I was only in the community to make some money. He was so relieved with this admission that he became an ally. I had confirmed his suspicions about White people, that they only did things for their own benefit.

VISTA volunteers were sent to play supporting roles in a community and not usurp local leadership. I had to constantly remind myself of this mandate because sometimes community leaders, who were genuinely happy that we came to help, were very deferential. I remember that one individual constantly called me "Mr. Arnie." Such a salutation was common in the rural south where I lived, but it made me uncomfortable because it culturally defined my presence as a dominant one. After the individual and I got to know each other as friends, I asked him to call me something else. He seemed surprised but agreeable. I confronted what Powell (1996) terms "white hegemony," the notion that my whiteness was not perceived by others as neutral as I had hoped it would be.

As a VISTA volunteer, I discovered the role and relevance of the local African American church to the community. It was local ministers who worked with my sponsors, the South Carolina Commission for Farm Workers and the Wesley Foundation, to introduce me to their congregations. If these ministers had not sanctioned my presence, I would not have been able to function in any meaningful way. Their support provided credibility for my efforts as a community service worker.

As an example of African American enterprise and autonomy (Raboteau, 1992), the church played an important educational role. Students gathered after school for tutoring sessions; adults came at night for literacy lessons; information about community meetings received attention. Samuel DeWitt

Proctor, a distinguished African American cleric, describes the secular importance
of the black church that I witnessed: "If you attend no church at all, it was like
having no identity at all. Church was a social hour, a time to compare clothes,
exchange news, share a sad note, celebrate a new job, look for a partner in
romance . . . or pick up the name of a better doctor, tailor, or automobile
mechanic" (1995, p. 16).

My VISTA experience also gave me opportunity to view schools from the
outside rather than as a teacher in a classroom. Many of the African American
parents that I worked with distrusted the local schools because they were tightly
controlled by White principals, superintendents, and boards of education.
Compared to the institution of the church, schools were regarded by many
community residents as distant and foreboding places to visit, especially because
African American students were suspended from school in far greater numbers
than Whites and were placed more frequently in special education classes than
their White classmates.

Despite my best efforts to assist in community development projects such as
tutoring and adult literacy, my presence was not always welcomed. Once, when I
delivered some brochures to a family in the evening, the husband came home
from work and ordered me off of his property. We had never met. He told me that
he had worked hard all day, and he did not want to see any more White folks. I
had witnessed what bell hooks (1995) calls "White People Fatigue Syndrome"
(p. 49)—the sheer weariness of confronting racism and white people on a daily
basis felt by many people of color.

hooks is instructive here. She believes that African Americans have a "killing
rage," a fierce anger about their treatment in America and that the expression of
this anger constitutes resistance to White racism. Furthermore, such rage is
actually a "healing response to oppression and exploitation" (p. 12). Rage is
necessary because so many Whites deny their prejudice. There is a "harsh
absolutism" to White denial. Since racial hatred is so real in America, it is
"humanizing to be able to resist it with militant rage" (p. 17). Had I understood
hooks's perspective, I would not have been so surprised by the hostility of that
man who wanted me to disappear immediately.

Skepticism about my presence as a VISTA volunteer was not limited to an
incident of rage. Frequently, community residents would ask me if I was writing
a book. The implication was clear: The only motive for my presence was related
to some sort of investigation of the African American community. I never had
any intention of writing a book and politely said so. I made a conscious decision
not to formally study my surroundings because I believed that it would somehow
deter me from active involvement in community affairs. This resolution did not
mean that I refrained from reflection about what I was doing. In fact, I renewed
my efforts to read more widely in the field of African American history and
culture to buttress an understanding and appreciation of my surroundings. I was
still an academic at heart.

My service as a VISTA volunteer was a critical incident for me as a person and
as a professional educator. I now understand, better perhaps than I did twenty
years ago, that often "profound changes that take place within us during [the
most challenging periods of our lives] first test, then alter, and finally strengthen
the foundations upon which we build our beliefs and behaviors" (Mathison &

Young, 1995, p. 7). I knew then that I wanted to work in a rural, southern school district where education and community were closely aligned.

My opportunity came when I became an assistant principal for four years in the South Carolina low country, an historic area between Charleston, South Carolina, and Savannah, Georgia. A number of forces combined to keep the African American community traditional and somewhat isolated. Union forces captured the area early during the Civil War, permitting slaves to acquire property. Literacy education helped freed slaves to avoid losing their land through illegal means.

Segregation of people of color and Whites was the rule rather than the exception in this entrenched African American environment. Most of the local White students left the public schools to attend a segregated academy named after a signer of the Declaration of Independence. In the early 1970s, it was not unusual for many southern communities to declare their own liberty from integration by appropriating such names as Jefferson or Washington for private Whites-only schooling.

The school district exemplified African American enterprise. People of color controlled the school board; a man of color served as superintendent; all school principals were African American with one exception. A number of African Americans who had left the community a decade or so earlier for further education in the North returned to provide vigorous leadership. The local community also reflected an ethnic political clout. An African American was elected sheriff for the first time since Reconstruction, and a woman of color was selected for the state legislature.

These ecological features affected school life. Students supported Black History Month with vigor. A number of faculty refused to stand for the Star Spangled Banner at football games and informed me in private conversations that racism stained the American flag. Nobody that I knew of ever declined to stand for the singing of "Lift Every Voice and Sing," a stirring song of hope written early in this century by the noted African American writer James Weldon Johnson.

In Louisiana or as a VISTA volunteer, I had never experienced the heart-felt sense of alienation among educators and students as I did in this community. My study of history helped me understand that the estrangement many African Americans felt from this country because racism was deeply embedded and not a phenomenon of the 1970s. A pantheon of African American leaders from Frederick Douglass to Paul Robeson, a noted singer, athlete, and activist, and from Sojourner Truth to Fannie Lou Hamer, a civil rights leader from Mississippi during the 1960s, proclaimed a sense of outrage that America could never be what it claimed to be as long as racism pervaded this nation.

Neither my own study of African American history nor my prior experiences as a VISTA volunteer made me immune from student fury when I had to suspend a student for a serious infraction of school rules. Frequently, I was accused of being a racist. I rarely, if ever, debated the issue because I knew that it was foolhardy to claim that I was somehow different from other Whites. However, my reluctance to fully engage a hostile student over the matter of race stemmed as much from my whiteness as it did from a steely realism. Powell (1996) explains the matter very well: "As a person of European descent and a beneficiary of white privilege, I have often found it difficult to talk about racism. For one thing there is a certain legitimacy to the argument that Anglos cannot completely understand the ramifications of racism in our society . . . . [Our] cultural experiences do not allow us to comprehend fully the magnitude . . . of the problem" (p. 12).

Fortunately, my connection to the local community was not entirely determined by my role as an assistant principal. I had made a momentous personal decision to join an African American Baptist church attended by many of my students. I had attended a number of such churches as a VISTA volunteer but never formally affiliated with any. Then, in October 1975, I accepted Rev. James R. White's altar call to join his church. It was not a spur of the moment decision but rather a private and intimate recognition that something was missing in my life.

My membership in church was a living textbook. I experienced what a powerful training ground the church was for African American leadership. The deacon board controlled financial matters; young people had many role models, from the choir director to the women's auxiliary, to emulate; the congregation made key decisions about buying property, affiliating with other churches in annual associations, and holding fund raising events, among many others. A noted African American cleric, Bishop Daniel Payne, recorded a century ago what I witnessed in the 1970s: "[The autonomy of the black church benefited] people of color by giving them an independence of character which they could neither hope for nor attain . . . if they had remained . . . the vassal of their white brethren" (1969, p. 195).

I was welcomed by the senior deacon who instructed me in the ways of the church. Every Sunday evening for months I went to Deacon Pinckney's house where we talked about the gospel. Finally, I was baptized and extended the right hand of fellowship as a small group of congregants sang "Been to the Water and Been Baptized."

My church attendance had a residual benefit beyond the personal, since many high school students were also members. Frequently, students would come to my office to talk about a church-related rather than a school matter. We walked on common ground here. Every member was expected to contribute to the life of the church. I decided to join the adult choir not because of any musical ability but because I really enjoyed the music. The choir director understood that what I lacked in competency I was more than willing to make up in volume.

After two years of church attendance and active participation in Sunday School, the choir, and fund raising, I was asked to become deacon. I honestly believed that I was not worthy of such an honor or the responsibility the position entailed. I saw myself, in the words of a gospel song, as a "Soldier in the Army of the Lord" but not as a leader. Several deacons who had befriended me when I joined the church encouraged me to join their ranks, since a number of older church leaders had died and they needed assistance. I resolved my doubts because I was very comfortable in the church and saw an opportunity for service.

I did not become a deacon overnight. I had to study the Bible and pass an oral exam conducted by the minister and other deacons. I had to become more active in serving others by visiting the sick and learning church procedures at monthly meetings. When I completed my apprenticeship, I became Deacon Cooper at a

Sunday evening prayer service attended by deacons and ministers of other local churches as well as members from my congregation.

My church service and my career as an educator complimented each other. I had more credibility when I spoke with parents of errant students. Many students themselves were more accepting of me because we shared communion and church activities. Because the church was as important to the African American community as the schoolhouse, my participation in both institutions defined my role in the community. I was not just an assistant principal; the "deacon" in me was as important if not more so to many community residents as the "educator" in me.

I had much to learn about church protocol. Reverend White frequently reminded his deacons that he was the "major shepherd" and we were "minors" in his flock. Any disagreement with his leadership had to be settled in private. For example, one of the deacons raised the issue of whether or not church members should continue to use the segregated facilities of a White funeral home. Reverend White did not want this issue publicly discussed because he feared it would jeopardize the congenial relationship he had with the White funeral director.

The patriarchal hierarchy of my church treated women as second-class citizens. For example, if a young woman had a child but no husband she had to appear before the congregation and confess her sin. The father of the child was not expected to do the same. No one ever dissented from this policy, at least publicly. Women in the congregation did not teach Sunday School classes nor were they permitted to preach. The church was run with a firm hand by men. But, women made their views known on church matters during monthly meetings, through auxiliary groups, and quarterly conferences.

My active service in the church and as an assistant principal ended in that community when I decided to study for my doctorate at Iowa State University. I was ready to pursue serious scholarship and a career as a college professor. Many church members said they would pray for me on this new journey. One, Sister McDonald, expressed concern that too much education might cause me to become less involved with religion. She was very suspicious of "book learning." Once, she informed me that a certain minister had received his religion from school rather than personal experience, thus his inability to preach with fervor.

When I left South Carolina, I fully understood how my tenure in that community had affected my thinking about education. I knew first-hand the intimate and vital connections between the schoolhouse and the house of prayer. My students taught me how important it was to get to know them on their territory, in their neighborhoods. Their parents instructed me in the ways of group protocol, how to defer to the elders, and how to listen twice as much as I spoke because God gave us two ears and only one mouth.

When I arrived in Iowa, I read Pat Conroy's *The Water Is Wide* (1972) about his experiences in a neighboring South Carolina community and resonated with his reflection that when he left he had "lost a relationship of infinite and timeless value, and one that I would never know again (p. 298)." This much I knew: knowledge about a culture was not enough. Active engagement in the lives of others was imperative in order to propel learning into action. The fact that I was a student of African American history was not sufficient in South Carolina as a VISTA volunteer or in Louisiana. I had to learn to translate scholarship into action, and one way to do that was to treat others as "concrete" rather than "generic" individuals (Schwartz, 1993, p. 63). No amount of book knowledge could compensate for a lack of shared experiences with others. That is why my sojourn in the South remains a living memory after two decades.

As an academic, I have accepted the pedagogical challenge of designing a number of courses related to multicultural education. I wanted to devise an offering that would be more than a "sampler" of different cultures. My intent has been to provide genuine support to students in the basic tools of analysis, exposition, and structured thinking in order for them to grapple holistically with the concept of diversity. I selected Ronald Takaki's *From Different Shores: Perspectives on Race and Culture in America* (1987) as the main text for this effort because of his fundamental premise: *"From Different Shores* refers to the multiple origins of Americans—how our roots can be traced to Europe, Africa, Latin America, Asia and North America itself. Who we are and how we are perceived and treated in terms of race and ethnicity are conditioned by where we came from originally" (p. 9). I have embraced Takaki, no doubt, because I came to the South from a "different shore" and understand now better than I did twenty years ago how my origins conditioned my responses.

I also selected for required reading autobiographies representative of different cultural experiences in America. Examples include Richard Wright's *Black Boy*; Maya Angelou's *I Know Why the Caged Bird Sings*; N. Scott Momaday's *House Made of Dawn*, and Mary Doyle Curran's *The Parish and the Hill*. This literature contains perceived cultural realities of how individuals have validated and legitimized their lives in cultural terms.

These choices were not arbitrary ones. Rather, I tried to adhere to Banks's (1991) suggestion that "groups that vary in cultural characteristics, geographical location, socioeconomic status, racial characteristics, history and level of assimilation should be selected for study" (p. 489).

Many autobiographies do more than touch at the heart of diversity in America. They reinforce the important notion that "we are all culturally defined, and therefore, we are constrained by our own limited experiences. As cultural beings, we hold certain assumptions that have formed by who we are, both as individuals and as members of particular groups (race, class, religious affiliation, etc.)" (Powell, 1996, p. 12).

I recognize the constraints that I brought to my own experiences as a teacher in Louisiana, a VISTA volunteer, and an assistant principal in South Carolina. I was unprepared for the suspicion I encountered from some people of color. I should have known better. At times, I timidly accepted sexist thinking about the role of women. I should have been more vocal and less accommodating of unfair attitudes that I found in my church, for example. I became part of the chorus instead of creating my own cacophony of dissent.

But, cultural competence does not come easy. Such a facility means "knowing how to operate as a competent actor in more than one cultural world; knowing what's appropriate and what's inappropriate; what's acceptable and unacceptable in behavior and speech in cultures that differ quite radically from one's own" (Bensimon & Soto, 1997, 44). Cultural competence also requires "conversations of respect," where "participants expect to learn from each other and to be changed by the experience."

As I reflect upon my personal experiences and the beliefs that shaped my behavior, I know that what changed me was the common ground I shared with others in my journey from Philadelphia.

8

Seeing Things As They Are

Carolyn O'Grady

We see things not as they are, but as we are.
—the Talmud

When I was asked to write this chapter for a book on White antiracists, I was very excited. I hoped this book might be something I could use with my own predominantly White students, who look around and see a lack of role models for being antiracist. I felt confident that I could fairly quickly draft a chapter that explained my background and how it led me to the work I do today.

As I attempted to write, I discovered how wrong I had been to think that this was just about "background." Indeed, Ruth Frankenberg's (1993) term "racial social geography" is a much better description for the constellation of life influences and patterns that develop our beliefs about race. Although some of the stories you will read in this chapter are ones I use from time to time in my teaching, it was emotionally overwhelming to piece together in one place some of the insidious messages about race that I have absorbed in my life. Consequently, this has been one of the hardest pieces of writing I have ever had to do as I have struggled to both speak about and analyze the very personal.

Gail Griffin (1995) describes a world "positively cross-hatched with color lines" (p. 19), lines she only saw years after growing up in a White, progressive household near Detroit. These lines paint a picture with invisible ink on our minds and hearts of "us" and "them." We do not see this picture if we are white. The "us" is just us, but the other is most emphatically "them" in what Adrienne Rich (1993) describes as a "white silence that was utterly obsessional" (p. 181) in her own childhood. I cannot pinpoint exactly the moment I "saw" my own race, but I can examine other scenes in my life that describe my ongoing journey toward becoming an antiracist racist.[1]

ACT I: GROWING UP

Like many of my White students today, I had a subtly racist and ultimately segregated upbringing. My parents never used bigoted language, and I do not remember others using it either (though Pearl Rosenberg (1997) notes how easily we may misremember the past as we mediate our memories through our own prejudices). The residents of my home town probably would not consider themselves racist (or would not admit it if they did). My father certainly denies that he is racist, yet some years ago when hearing the term "people of color," he responded "I'm so glad we don't have any of those here." The irony of this is that we lived on an Indian reservation, but to my father these particular people of color were invisible (hooks, 1995). I grew up absorbing the unspoken attitudes of my well-intentioned parents as well as the overt and covert messages I was given in the community about those who were "Other." Joseph Feagin and Hernan Vera (1995) describe these as "sincere fictions"—personal mythologies that reproduce societal mythologies (pp. 14–15). Consequently, I developed attitudes about people of color and others who were different than I was both through their presence in my life and their absence.

I was born in July 1954, the same year as *Brown v. Board of Education.* Perhaps it is this synchronicity to which I owe the work I do today, as a multicultural educator and diversity trainer. But the ripples of *Brown v. Board of Education* did not even stir a leaf on a tree in my small town in Idaho. Segregation and racism seemed to be issues that caused problems somewhere else. It was assumed that we had no problems with race because in our community everyone was White (or *apparently* all were White, as both Frankenberg (1993) and Patricia Williams (1991) point out in noting that many Whites may be more racially mixed genetically than we realize). The civil rights movement of the 1960s might have happened on another planet, for all the impact it had in my town. This deafening silence about race sent a peculiar message to me as a young child, expecially given the proximity of the Nez Perce Indian Reservation.

Scene 1: I Spent the Summer Lying in the Sun

I knew a lot of American Indians when I was growing up. After my parents married, they lived in a house my father built on the reservation. As a child, I was often cared for by a traditional Nez Perce woman who was a leader in the native community. I played with her grandchildren when I went to visit her house at the other end of town. All the Indians lived at the other end of town, a stunning example of *de facto* segregation that I never questioned. In fact, had I known enough to ask about it, I expect I would have been told that the Indians preferred to live separated from the Whites; in fact, I was told by my parents that Indians preferred to live on reservations rather than off.

My family lived in this reservation community until it was time for me to go to school, when my father built a house off reservation in a slightly larger and completely White town. I do not know if this happened because he wanted me to go to Catholic school or because he did not want me going to school with Indians, or both. At any rate, we continued to return to our reservation home every weekend for the next ten years, and while I no longer thought of myself as a resident of the community, I never completely lost my ties with it either.

While I was growing up, I took dancing lessons, and the classes were held at the Indian community center. Many Nez Perce girls were in dance class with me. One year, early in my adolescence, the dance teachers decided to send a contingent of Nez Perce dancers to that year's pow wow. I was a good dancer, having taken tap and ballet classes since I was five, and I was included in the preparation for the pow wow. For weeks we practiced a traditional dance with the guidance of some of the Nez Perce mothers. I was the only White dancer. The steps were easy for me to learn, but the moves were not. This kind of dancing had a dipping and swaying and body language that was new to me. The mothers spent a great deal of time working with me. For the first time, I was no longer the dancer the other girls watched to get the moves "right," but the one who had to try to follow the others. I did not like not knowing how to do something that looked so easy.

One family lent me a decorated leather dress that had been in the family for three generations. No one mentioned I was the only non-Indian. No one questioned the appropriateness of my participation. On the advice of my (White) dance instructor, I spent the summer laying in the sun to get a deeper tan so I could "pass." When we drove onto the pow wow grounds and the gatekeeper asked for our tribal affiliation, my mother answered "Nez Perce" without hesitation. As we drove through the gate, she rolled up her window and said with relief, "Good thing he was drunk. He wouldn't have noticed what we were." Thus were two ideas reinforced: that White folks have the right to be part of everything and that Indians are drunks.

Scene 2: "The Girl Will Get It"

The first African American person I clearly remember having contact with was a blind man whom my mother befriended on a bus trip to California. She and I were traveling alone—perhaps I was five—and she was distressed when she realized that this man was being ignored by everyone in the bus depot. I do not know if she was bothered because he was African American, or in spite of it. She helped him find the bus he needed—which turned out to be ours—and then helped him again when he needed to transfer later. This is the one and only time I remember my mother showing any overt concern for someone of a different race (perhaps it was his disability rather than his race than inspired her). The image of my White mother holding the arm of a blind African American man as she led him through the bus depot remains fixed in my mind.

When I was twelve, I traveled by myself to visit my aunt and uncle in St. Louis. They had no children and lived in a wealthy suburb of the city. One day they and some of their neighborhood friends took me to lunch at their country club. I remember the details of the dining room perfectly. I was seated at the end of a long table with my uncle on my left and my aunt across from us. Everyone in our party was White; most were middle-aged. All of the servers were African American.

During lunch, I accidentally dropped my fork on the ground. When I leaned over to pick it up, my uncle hissed at me, "The girl will get it." The way I had been raised, proper etiquette was for people to pick up their own forks. My uncle was furious when I did so. I had clearly violated some code, but I was not sure what it was. After lunch he drove me through what he called the ghetto, saying, "See how these people live? See how they take care of what's given to them?" Years later, reading Kozol's *Savage Inequalities* (1991), I realized my uncle must have been driving along the perimeter of East St. Louis. At the time, all I knew was that there was something wrong and terribly upsetting about what my uncle was saying, but I did not know what it was.

This example of overt racism is no more powerful than the subtle racism that was more common in my childhood. For instance, during my early teens, a Job Corps facility was built in a neighboring community, and most of the residents were African American (there were no African Americans living in my town of 3,500 people or anywhere closer than a four-hour drive). We girls were warned (by whom I do not recall; it was just "in the air") that these "boys" were dangerous criminals, and we should avoid them if we encountered them because they might hurt us. We were never warned about the White boys in the Job Corps. It was only in writing this chapter that I realized how strongly I had received and retained the impression that African American men were sexually dangerous and needed to be controlled.

When I was a sophomore in high school, word got around that an older girl, who had graduated the year before and gone off to college in Seattle, was dating an African American guy and had stopped going to church. It was hard to know which was worse, but they certainly seemed connected. Many of us asked our parents what they would do if we came home with an African American boyfriend. The answers were predictable. To our parents, it was worse than an interfaith marriage.

Scene 3: As Children We Had Pulled on the Corners of Our Eyes

I spent the last two years of high school at an all-female, Catholic boarding school in another state. During part of that time, I roomed with Rosemary, an exchange student from Taiwan. I barely tolerated my new roommate. She shuffled around the dorm in slippers and played high pitched music that reminded me of fingernails scratching on a blackboard. She wore heavy framed glasses that always slid down her nose. She had the kind of eyes that we had seen as children in the occasional western that included "Oriental" laundry men, and as children we had pulled on the corners of our eyes and said "ah so" to each other and thought we were hilarious. Rosemary seemed to have no sense of humor, and she studied constantly. She seemed more different from me than anyone I had ever known until then. Everything about her made me uncomfortable. Before the end of the semester, I asked to be given a single room. I never once thought about the loneliness and isolation she experienced.

A few years later at college in Seattle, I dated a Chinese-Hawaiian man, an ethnic combination that at the time I described as "exotic." He was not like my stereotypes of the short, seemingly effeminate, geeky Asian students I knew from the university, and his English was perfect. He knew how to use chopsticks, and he could order food for us in Chinese when we went to Chinatown. He was just exotic enough, but not too much.

Scene 4: Was It His White Skin?

I did not meet a Jew until I went to college. Somehow I "knew" that the Jews, whoever they were, had been responsible for the death of Jesus. I was a very pious Catholic child and was prepared to hate anyone who had caused Jesus to suffer so for our sins. We were never told that Jesus himself was a Jew, much less that his skin was darker than our own. Although anti-Semitic phrases such as "jew me down" were not prevalent in my childhood, there was nonetheless a subtle anti-Semitism in my Christian upbringing that created an image in young minds of Jews as dirty, stingy, and anti-Christian.

At college my religious beliefs underwent some transformations, and I was thrilled to become friends with a Jewish classmate, Isaac, and felt very nervy to be doing it. (Perhaps this was easier for me because he was not observant, though these distinctions were unclear to me in those days.) He was the only Jew in the program I was in during my first two years of college, and among the other thirteen of us, all were White except Lorraine, an African American woman. Now I wonder why I became friends with Eli but did not with Lorraine. Was it his white skin?

I write about Jews here because the anti-Semitism of my childhood was as egregious as the racism, however, subtle. In my upbringing, Jews were so much the "other" that they might as well have been "colored."[2] Indeed, the prejudice I developed toward Jews was as insidious as that which I felt toward Asians or African Americans. In contrast, I was not aware of having any attitude at all toward Latinos, the group I had the least contact with or knowledge about until I was in my mid-twenties. Their absence in the circumstances of my early life had what can only be considered a negative consequence: they were "invisible" people. As far as I was concerned, they did not exist (in this I mimicked my father).

By the time I finished college, I had acquired a somewhat more expanded understanding of how much diversity was all around me, and I discovered that I liked urban living. This developing awareness was about to be tested and honed in one of the most interesting urban classrooms in the country: New York City.

ACT II: GROWN

When I was twenty-four I moved to the upper west side of Manhattan. Since then that area has become gentrified, but at the time it was racially and economically diverse. The day I moved in, I went to the Red Apple supermarket around the corner from my studio apartment. The clerk at the check-out was a very dark-skinned African American woman who seemed mad at me. My evidence was that she never once looked at me. She never smiled or said one word. She shoved my purchases down the chute, grabbed my money out of my hand, and thrust the change back in my general direction. I walked out of the store convinced she hated me because I was White. This, I was sure, was how African Americans felt about Whites. I wondered how long I would survive in this neighborhood.

It was several weeks before I had enough experience of the city for it to occur to me that most New Yorkers acted in this way. Her manner toward me may or may not have been related to race. Indeed, it might not have been any kind of "manner" at all except as I perceived it as such. Like a typical White (unintentional) racist, I saw everything through the lens of my own race without realizing I was doing so. As I continued to frequent that store and became known as a regular, this woman started greeting me.

Living in New York City was a key influence in my education about diversity. In New York, I was in a cultural milieu that bore little resemblance to where I had come from, and after my initial anxiety, I began to love it. I loved to walk down the streets of the city and see all the colors of the faces, all the different clothes, hear all the many languages. I loved the knowledge that not one person on the street knew who I was or anything about my family. In my neighborhood, I could hear Spanish spoken at any time, buy my newspaper from the African American man who owned the corner kiosk, eat *real* Chinese food at the Szechuan restaurant up the street (not the Chinese American "cuisine" of my hometown restaurant), and pay my rent to the Puerto Rican woman who lived downstairs. From my street, I could walk cross town to hear a talk at the 92nd Street Y (the "Jewish" Y), take a French class at the Alliance Française, get my hair cut by a gay man in a salon on Christopher Street, eat spicy Cuban food, and come home in a bus driven by an Arab American. It was amazing, and it slowly began to crack all my assumptions about what was "normal."

Yet I still had not learned to "see" my own race or to understand what it means to be White in a racist society. After several years in New York, I went to graduate school for a masters in education. I became a high school English teacher in western Massachusetts where I taught the traditional canon in traditional ways. My graduate education (like my prior twelve years in school) did little to prepare me either to live in or teach about a multicultural world. I did not find this odd. Knowledge was knowledge and life was life. They were two different things. One came from books and had been in place for hundreds of years, and who could question such time-tested certainty? I certainly did not, and I was considered a good teacher (by other White teachers).

Then one year, I chaperoned a group of high school students on a school trip to England and once again my life took a new turn. I was twenty-nine years old and had never been to Europe. I returned from this trip wanting only to return, scheming how to make that possible. Within months I had quit my teaching job, sold everything I had, and left the United States not knowing when I would return. I took only a back pack and a list of names friends had given me.

ACT III: GROWING

If living in New York was a key learning experience about diversity, traveling had an even greater impact. During the nearly two years I spent out of the United States, I literally became a different person. Because I traveled cheaply, I was forced to rely on strangers often and to learn to trust people who would have stood out like a sore thumb in my home town. Sometimes I was in places where I could fit in as long as I did not try to say anything, particularly in Europe (being dark-haired, I could pass for French, Italian, Spanish, or even German). But once I traveled beyond Western Europe, I was often in places where I stood out, a first in my experience. I got a small taste of what it feels like to be a minority at those times when I did not know the local language (or customs), or when I was ridiculed for being an American, or when I was the only female foreigner in a community. By this time I no longer considered myself Christian, and it was eye-opening to be surrounded by Muslims whose religious and cultural beliefs were so vastly different from mine. These experiences had a profound effect on me, shaking me out of the complacency that comes with considering oneself the "norm."

I was often lonely. More frequently, I felt I was living at so intense a pitch that every new encounter, each fresh experience, seemed to open up whole worlds to me. It was total culture shock; I was forced out of my comfort zone. I learned much about myself, and about others, in these several months. Feagin and Vera (1995) speculate that Whites who have some personal experience with discrimination or exploitation may be more likely to empathize with people of color who are oppressed. This may not be true in all cases (Frankenberg, 1993; Sleeter, 1996), but my limited exposure to what it feels like to be the "Other" made an important difference to me.

On the other hand, I did not intentionally seek experiences that would challenge my assumptions about race. I allowed chance to govern where I traveled. Chance did not take me to Africa, for instance, a country where I would have been forced to see myself as a racial minority. My emerging consciousness about my own racial identity remained incomplete. In France I lived for several months with a Black woman from Martinique. She told me of the racism she had personally experienced and introduced me to other people of color who described racial tensions in France. As I traveled throughout Europe and parts of Asia, I heard other stories of racial and ethnic tensions, but my education about my own whiteness was yet to come. It was several years before I read Peggy McIntosh's (1989) article on White race privilege. All I understood about privilege at this point was that I could charge my return plane ticket to my Visa card at any moment I chose, a privilege I was grateful for when I finally ran out of money.

ACT IV: SEEING

I returned to the United States during the Christmas season. I had come from Turkey, a Muslim country vastly poorer than the United States but also cleaner. I was appalled at the dirt I saw everywhere around me in New York—the trash, the smog, the excessive and rapacious consumerism. For a long time, I could hardly bear to walk into a supermarket and see the glut of food that filled the store. The price of one subway token was a fifth of my day's allowance of traveling money. Some kind of innocence had worn off. Little did I know that the maturing process was just getting started.

The spring after my return, I got a job as a secretary at the University of Massachusetts, and enrolled as a doctoral student in education to take advantage of the free tuition I received as a university employee. I had friends who had spent years working on dissertations, and I was not interested in doing this, but I wanted to find some way to make cognitive sense out of the experiences I had had during the months of traveling. One of the first classes I took was "Institutional Racism." The Somi, native Laplanders I had met in Finland, and the Kurds I had met in Turkey described government policies that at best threatened ethnic identity and at worst sounded like genocide. Their stories sounded too much like the ones I knew from growing up among American Indians in Idaho. I did not exactly know what "institutional racism" was, and I was pretty sure I was not racist, but I figured I would learn something about how past injustices created present conditions.

This course provided another turning point for me and a host of effects that still ripple through my life. To begin with, the class was multiracial. For the first time, I was part of a diverse group of people who wanted to intentionally talk about the effects of race in their lives, in fact, insisted on doing it. Lois Stalvey in *Education of a Wasp* (1988) describes her shock when she realizes that an African American woman she knows has had a very different experience in the local community than Stalvey has had. I was typical of Whites in assuming that my experience in the world was the norm for everyone. I had never thought before about whose skin color "flesh colored" Band-Aids were for. It had never crossed my mind that the "westward expansion" I'd learned about in history class was not called "eastern encroachment" for a reason. I learned the meaning of the word "stereotype" and, worse, got to see how many of them I had. From drunk Indians to brainy Asians to dangerous African American men, I had absorbed the subtle but powerful cultural messages about the inferiority of "non-Whites" and, by implication, White superiority.

Far from being overwhelming, this new awareness felt like a release. I felt I finally had language and concepts to describe the emotions and experiences I had had. Pieces of my past history took on a new meaning. As we talked in class about oppression, it was not a big leap to understand that the racism that was so systematically embedded in me not only was oppressive to people of color, but also limited and hurt me as well. Concepts such as "internalized oppression," "power," "domination," and "privilege" acquired real meaning for the first time as I examined my own social identities.

Another important effect of this class was that it forced me to think about how to create social change. As part of this class, all the group members participated in an anti-apartheid rally held in a nearby city. This was the first time I had ever rallied for anything more important than a basketball game. I was one of hundreds of other folks—of all colors—who came together as a group to protest an injustice. I got an inkling of how much power coalitions can have and also how far there was to go before there could be change.

I took more classes that focused on multicultural education and issues of social justice. I immersed myself in grappling with my own bigotry, not only my racism, but my discomfort with disabilities, my internalized sexism, and, perhaps the most insidious, my attitudes about social class. I was lucky to find wonderful mentors in Seth Kreisberg (1992) and Sonia Nieto (1996) and lucky to have friends and colleagues who confronted me, commiserated with me, and never let me give up. By the time I finished my dissertation, I knew that while I might not always know what job I would have, I certainly did know what my life's work was.[3]

INTERLUDE: LESSONS AND MEANING

Before describing the current act in my personal drama, it is important to pause and consider the meaning of the events that have shaped me. Michael Apple (1997) cautions us about the risk of focusing on autobiographical stories to the exclusion of taking real action for change. If we only tell our own story, we may fall into "possessive individualism" (p. 127), a pose that permeates Western culture and hampers critical analysis of systemic oppression. Moving between personal story and critical reflection helps me analyze the meaning of my life experiences in the context of a world "constructed along multiple axes of power" (p. 127).

As I have matured in my understanding of racism and racial identity, I have come to identify five key lessons about doing antiracism work. I do not consider these ideas particularly original, but they are how I make meaning of the personal experiences of my life and are the foundation upon which I attempt to work actively against racism.

1. *As a White antiracist, I must acknowledge my personal debt to people of color and seek to build coalitions with them.* Every White person who is honest must acknowledge the crucial role people of color have played in our understanding of racism. In my case, there have been those many individuals who took the time to answer questions or point out inaccuracies in my knowledge or confront and challenge my assumptions. Without this generosity, my education about race would have been much more limited. I consider these

experiences gifts. To take them for granted would be to perpetuate the racist perspective that people of color owe me something because I am White.

In addition, being part of multiracial groups both challenges and enhances my own perspective on the world and calls me to live out in practice what I preach in theory. The ability to work together in coalition requires of all members the willingness to engage in conflict. Seeing conflict as necessary for growth, and being willing to share power equally, models for the larger society the goal of a multiracial, multicultural organization. My experiences as a member of multiracial teams have taught me that when whites and people of color work together on a project, the quality of the outcome is enhanced by the differing perspectives that diverse individuals bring to the task. This does not mean that working in coalition is easy, but for me as an antiracist White woman, it is profoundly rewarding both personally and professionally.

Even as I write that, however, I know how easy it is for Whites—including myself—to assume that we should be part of everything. This sense of entitlement was reinforced for me as a child when my presence at a closed pow wow was taken for granted. I have had to learn not to assume that my presence is always productive or wanted and to deal with the feelings of hurt or rejection at not being included. I see this feeling of entitlement among Whites who are angry at being given limited access to fishing and hunting grounds that belong to American Indians through treaty. I see the entitlement when I hear my White students complain about how African American students always sit together in the dining commons. I especially note this entitlement when Whites (including my students) blast affirmative action as "reverse racism." Thus, while working together with people of color in coalitions is crucial for White antiracists, the second lesson I have learned about being an antiracist is equally as important.

2. *As a White antiracist, I must ally with other White antiracists for knowledge and support.* Being an antiracist white can be profoundly isolating. Once we begin to identify previously taken for granted assumptions and to analyze our own socialization in a racist society, we begin to see and hear the racism of our family members and friends and must confront our own collusion in perpetuating racist attitudes and beliefs. Do we challenge our father when he tells his racist joke, a joke we have heard thousands of times before and remained silent? Do we tell our classmate why we are uncomfortable when she uses a word we now know is racist? How do we deal with our own pain at realizing how often we ourselves have unconsciously (or deliberately) said or done something based on our bigotry? Later, if we continue to work actively to be a White ally to people of color, we may find our motives questioned by Whites and people of color alike. As Christine Sleeter (1996) writes, "No white person is exempt from pressures from other white people to 'fit in,' with the price of conformity to a racial norm very often being approval and friendship" (p. 151).

Making connections with other Whites who are working on their racism can ease our isolation and provide us with much needed knowledge. While I was in graduate school, I participated in a support group for Whites working on their own racism. Despite the group's right-wing-sounding name of "White Allies," we were a handful of individuals who were deeply troubled by the extent of our socialization into racism.[4] We all believed that we should not assume it was up to people of color to educate us about racism (though all of us at one time or another had asked a person of color to tell us what it "felt like" to be African American or American Indian or different, and how we as Whites could "make a difference"). That group helped me see that there were other Whites who cared about the same issues I was grappling with and gave me a safe place in which to talk about my own racism—and my feelings about racism—without inflicting these stories on people of color. As Whites become antiracist, we must grapple with the many emotions involved in this process, including fear, anger, and sadness. Sometimes we also have to cope with our belief that we, as Whites, have no "culture," the focus of my third lesson.

3. *As a White antiracist, I must explore my own ethnicity and cultural identity as a foundation from which to explore that of others.* For a long time, I was embarrassed about my primarily German ethnicity. When I traveled in Germany, I found myself liking that country less than any other I had been in, and I often ridiculed Germans I encountered outside of Germany as "tourists" who could not leave home without their own food. I was grateful that my mother's genes gave me some Irish and French influence, and for a long time, I repeated the family myth that there was "some Indian somewhere" on my mother's side. Leaving aside the likelihood that most Whites really are not that White genetically at all (Frankenberg, 1993; Williams, 1991), it is clear to me that while Whites do not really want to *be* anything but White, there is at the same time great envy of "exotic" otherness and "having culture" (hooks, 1990). Somehow American Indians (or African Americans, or Hmong, or Puerto Ricans) "have it" while Europeans do not.

Yet if Whites are really to be antiracist, then we must avoid appropriating the cultural history and values of people of color. I still do not feel strongly identified as a German American woman, and probably never will, but over time I have come to have a fuller understanding of the cultural attributes that my complex background offers me. As I have explored the genealogy of my own family, I have learned about the ways in which some of my ancestors took risks to try a new life, coping with fear and danger but nevertheless persisting because of their belief that change was necessary. These qualities of persistence and trust in change are part of my cultural inheritance that strengthen me in the challenging work of anti-racism. I have also learned about the ways in which my ancestors disenfranchised people of color and have had to grapple with the responsibility I therefore have not to perpetuate my family's injustice. The more I understand and accept my own ethnic and cultural background, the more I can honor that of others.

4. *As a White antiracist, I am not "fixed;" I am in process.* A lesson I learn over and over is that I still have a lot to learn. Here is how I see the way to become antiracist working. It is like peeling an onion with infinite layers. A layer gets peeled away, and new insight or understanding results. Then something happens and another layer of racism is exposed and must be grappled with. Sometimes I think I really "get it," and then I find myself thinking some

incredibly racist thought and I realize it is not over yet. I do not believe that one of these days I will be "fixed." I do not think of racism as an "illness" from which we can eventually recover. This metaphor implies a lack of willed participation on the part of the sick one. I recognize that there are ways every day that I as a white person collude with and benefit from a racist system. Sometimes I know I am doing it, as when I choose not to challenge an elderly friend who describes a kind man in town as having "a white heart." Other times I become aware of my collusion only when it is pointed out to me, as when I "forget" to question why all the applicants in the final candidate pool are White.

Lately, I have begun to realize that my racism toward Asians is probably as profound as it was when I roomed briefly with Rosemary at boarding school. I have spent a great deal of time in the last ten years working with or getting to know many Latinos, Native Americans, and African Americans, but I have avoided opportunities to become friendly with Asian Americans or involve myself in predominantly Asian groups. I do not know the exact cause of my discomfort, and I am certainly not proud of it. But the first step toward grappling with my bigotry is to acknowledge its presence and begin to educate myself. I have avoided confronting these attitudes in myself until recently, when I have been given the opportunity to work more closely with Asian American colleagues.

I am sure that throughout my life I will continue to find gaps in my ability to live up to being an antiracist and will have to continue reaffirming my commitment to being an ally to *all* people of color. Paradoxically, one of the most important lessons about being antiracist that I have learned is that race is not everything.

5. *As a White antiracist, I must not essentialize race or see everything in terms of race alone.* There is a paradox in this lesson, since the point of being an antiracist White person is to focus on race and one's own racism. Yet I have learned that all of us are composed of multiple social identities (Jackson & Hardiman, 1988; Hardiman & Jackson, 1992), only one of which is race. To ignore gender, sexual orientation, social class background, religious affiliation, ability, and other markers is to decontextualize an individual and assume—often inappropriately—that I know more about who they are than they do themselves. My experience with the African American woman in the Red Apple supermarket is an example of this kind of categorizing. I could only see her as African American and thus could only make assumptions based on what was important to me at the time, not what might have been important to her.

The work of Bailey Jackson and Rita Hardiman (1988; 1992) has been helpful for me in understanding the complex nature of social identities in a world defined by who has power and who does not. As a White person, I have White privilege and, therefore, have access to the opportunities and resources available to Whites in a White-centered culture (McIntosh, 1989). As a woman, however, I have often been the target of male sexism, both on an individual level and through institutionalized norms and values that privilege men. Thus, I have a perspective on privilege and oppression that varies depending on the particular lens I am

using. Am I female first or White? Is my middle-class upbringing more of a
marker of my identity than either my race or gender? Does it depend on the
situation and context?[5]

My students often avoid identifying someone by their race, believing that to
point out that someone is African American is in itself racist. This reminds me
of my inability before I lived in New York to describe someone as a Jew; I
assumed it was pejorative until I knew many different people who were Jews.
For Whites at this stage of their understanding of racism, it is crucial to be able
to name difference and see difference not as deficit but as a marker of individual
identity. Only in this way can Whites avoid the reassuring, but inaccurate, trap
of assuming that "we're all like," or "we should focus on similarities, not
differences." However, to focus solely on race, as I myself have done in my zeal
to acknowledge people of color (trying to make up for all those years in which
they were invisible to me), is to essentialize others and limit understanding of
the full complexity of who they are as individuals.

ACT V: DOING

Currently I teach in a predominantly White teacher education program in a
predominantly White college in a rural town in the Midwest. When I ask
students early in the semester how they think they as Whites have been hurt by
racism, few of them know what to say. When I ask them what being White
means to them, they have even less response. They have never thought about it
before. For them, being White is not a racial identity, it just is. They remind me
of myself when I was their age. Like I did, they conceive of race as something
external to themselves rather than a factor that shapes their daily experience
(Frankenberg, 1993).

Let me describe the best of what happens in our classroom. Through readings,
guest speakers, field experiences, and every other eye-opening experience we can
develop, students come to understand the toll that racism takes on people of
color and on Whites. As I did, my students begin to see that they have
sometimes been unintentionally lied to by people who love them and who are
unwitting vehicles for perpetuating injustice. They recognize that many of the
institutions they formerly took for granted as havens of justice for all—the
courtroom, the classroom, the operating room, the pulpit—are riddled with
systemically discriminatory policies and procedures. They start out, as I did, with
comments such as "I'm not racist," "I don't even see what color a person is," and
"I'm not to blame for racism." Slowly, painfully, they consciously begin to
discover their racial identity development as Whites. Hopefully, they leave with
a vastly richer, more complicated, and more weighty view of the world.
Hopefully, they continue to grow in their understanding of the roles power,
privilege, and oppression play in their lives, in their future classrooms, and in
the lives of others.

I take seriously my responsibility as a White person to educate other Whites about racism. Until White folks begin to examine what it means to them to be White, both in their present lives and in the way "whiteness" has been historically configured, we cannot begin to fully reach out to and for people of color. I long for the *beloved community* hooks (1995) describes, "formed not by the eradication of difference but by its affirmation, by each of us claiming the identities and cultural legacies that shape who we are and how we live in the world" (p. 265).

Of course, there is a risk for Whites who choose to be allies to people of color. Anyone who names injustice and attempts to change it can be targeted and isolated, even Whites. Sometimes we lose the support of our friends or family. I do not know whether that server in the country club in St. Louis cared one bit whether or not this White girl picked up her own fork, but my uncle has never forgiven me for the foolish notions he could not root out of me on that day. Sometimes I see him in some of my students. More often, I see young White people who desperately need allies and so begin tentatively to explore how to be a White ally to people of color. As a teacher, I believe that I cannot help anyone else make a journey I have not been on myself.

The bottom line is that I am an antiracist not so much for others as for myself. It is not altruism that guides me as much as pure self-interest. A life filled with diversity of all kinds is vastly more interesting to me than one which is not. Now I find that I am most comfortable in environments that are multiracial, not because they are easier (they are not), but because they offer more opportunity for rich dialogue and fruitful conflict, humbling experiences that deepen my understanding of the world and my place in it. I am White through an accident of birth and, for me, that privilege carries with it an ethical responsibility to challenge the "vast encircling presumption of whiteness" (Rich, 1993, p. 181). Ultimately I am an antiracist because now I do see some things as they really are, and I can never pretend again that I do not.

NOTES

1. As Thompson and White Women Challenging Racism (1997) point out, the term "antiracist racist" can be problematic in that it only says what I am *against*. Nevertheless, this term conveys my belief that as a White person I am thoroughly socialized to be racist, while at the same time, it conveys that I actively seek to challenge my own racism.

2. See Britzman (1997) and hooks (1995) for useful discussions of the relationship between anti-Semitism and racism and the question of whether or not Jews are (or consider themselves to be) White.

3. Thompson and White Women Challenging Racism (1997) note, "antiracism is often less about people's job titles than it is about how we use our power and expertise within and outside of our paid work" (p. 356).

4. Thompson and White Women Challenging Racism. (1997) note the difficulty of using language that has not already been co-opted by White supremacists. "Because there is no other language, we need to use the same words they do—with opposite meanings—and figure out how to organize amid this contrast" (p. 363).

5. See Connolly and Noumair (1997) and Sleeter (1996) for more discussion of the complexity of this issue.

-------------------------------------9-------------------------------------

The Recollections of a Recovering Racist
James O'Donnell

INTRODUCTION

The term "recovering" is used in two ways in this chapter. First, the idea of
recovering is related to the issues faced by a recovering alcoholic. Racism can be
seen as a disease such as alcoholism. As a social [chronic] disease, I am aware of
its presence in myself, in society, and its institutions. Much like a recovering
alcoholic, I am aware of my own racist inculcation and the daily and constant
struggle that I am participating in to remain antiracist. I continue to uncover
past actions and even new thoughts that emanate from the race ideology into
which I was socialized.

Second, the term "recovering" signifies how through this struggle to discover
how racism affected me, I may recover and reclaim my humanity. There is some
innocence and decency that one loses as one is socialized into and participates in
racism, consciously or unconsciously. I think of Paulo Freire's discussion of
how oppressive relations dehumanizes both the oppressor and the oppressed
(Freire, 1970). So I understand this work toward antiracism as a step toward the
recovery of my own humanity.

My story relates my experiences and perceptions of racism via Black and White
race relationships. Michael Omi and Howard Winant (1994) discuss how race
relations between Blacks and Whites are historically constructed as the national
"race issue" in the United States. Therefore, social issues related to race and the
political policies enacted to deal with racism are usually conceived in Black and
White race dynamics. Omi and Winant, however, argue that racism is also local
and regional. Thus, to understand race relations, it is important to understand the
local and regional dynamics of how race operates within a community. Though I
grew up in a midwestern city whose racial make-up was and is primarily Black
and White, I did learn how American Indians, Latinos/as and Asian Americans
were marked as the Other. My story and primary experiences, however, are about
my experiences with racism in the context of African Americans marked as the

Other. My race reasoning, that is, how I thought about race, race relations, and racism, revolved around my experiences of racism in reference to African Americans. In working through these experiences, I came to realize how racism informed my understanding and relations with American Indians, Latinos/as and Asian Americans, as well as similar oppressions related, for example, to class, gender, religion, and sexuality. For the record, I am a middle-aged, White, Irish-German, reared Catholic, heterosexual, reared working class, abled (body/mind) male.

As I began to construct this chapter, I started chronologically recalling an incident that happened when I was five years old. But I realized as I started to move forward, marking off the incidents, events, and moments related to racism in my life, that my consciousness of racism actually did not occur as a result of some passage through time as if wisdom unfolded as I became older. Rather these past experiences became clear and understandable to me much later. It was an incident that I had as an adult that made me confront my own racism and how I was socialized into a racist society.

THE INCIDENT

I went to West Africa in July 1980 to serve as a Peace Corps volunteer for two years. Even the idea of going to Africa was an incident that should have jarred my own awakening to the dynamics of race. But it did not. I remember that during my phone conversation with the Peace Corps recruiter when he mentioned that I would probably be going to Sierra Leone, my mind began to run through all of the countries in South America. While I was racing through my vast geographical construction of the world, the recruiter said to me that Sierra Leone was in West Africa. I replied as though I knew that. What I should have learned from that brief conversation was that Africa was a continent that was never part of my education or social geography.

Several volunteers were assigned to Sierra Leone, so after a six-week training session, each volunteer left for various parts of the country. I was stationed in an area approximately 280 miles from the capital and about 80 miles from the nearest large city. Though I lived in a large town of about 5,000 people, my little corner of the world consisted of six houses on the edge of the town. I became adept at moving through the town streets staying very much unto myself, in many ways avoiding contact with neighbors and townspeople. There were other volunteers from the United States, as well as from other European countries, living in this town. These Westerners served as my initial community. I knew that I was avoiding townspeople and, in fact, was in self-conversation about this problem on a Saturday in October 1980 when there was a knock on my front door.

The knock startled me because no one had ever knocked before, and I was not expecting anyone. There was no peephole on the door to survey who had knocked. Further, if I went to the window I would be seen. I did for a split second contemplate not answering the door. However, I opened the door and standing before me were three Black men.

When I saw these three men standing there, a rush of fear overcame my body. I discovered in this moment of fear a sense of clarity that allowed me to recognize on both an affective and cognitive level that racism deeply affected me. I knew this fear was irrational and came from somewhere within me that I did not fully understand. I knew, however, that this fear came from racism and emanated from my having lived in a racist society.

Prior to that moment, at the door, I would not have characterized myself as racist or even as having racist thoughts. I would have described myself very much like many of my students do today: "I'm not racist, I don't see color. I treat each person as an individual." Therefore, I would have described myself in the classic, liberal, colorblind fashion (O'Donnell, 1995). To me, racists were individuals such as those who belonged to the Klan or Nazis. Further, racists were those individuals who sat at social gatherings and used the n-word and denounced integration. Since I was none of these, I could not be a racist.

Fear would also not have been a characteristic that I would have used to describe my experience and understanding of race relations. Prior to coming to Africa I had lived in an integrated neighborhood; I taught in an inner-city school and I was"liberal" in my social and political outlook. Furthermore, the fear was not from the prospect of living in a different country. I had lived and worked in Bogota, Colombia, for a year in the mid-seventies. But I realized in that moment of opening the door that I was racist. This particular incident did not put everything into place. What I learned from this incident was that I was affected by racism. Further, I knew that I wanted to understand what racism was and how to change.

RE-EDUCATION

While in the Peace Corps during my training phase, I met an African American professor who came to teach the volunteers about the principles and strategies of non-formal education. During one of his presentations he mentioned the name of Paulo Freire and Freire's educational theories for the oppressed. I had read Freire's *Pedagogy of the Oppressed* (1970) earlier as an undergraduate in education but several of my education professors at that time in the early 1970s felt that Freire's work held very little relevance for the United States. This professor, however, did understand Freire's relevance. I asked him where he had done his graduate work and if he had a contact for me. He replied that he attended the University of Massachusetts at Amherst and told me of a professor to contact. On my return to the United States after two years in West Africa, I pursued a doctorate in education at the University of Massachusetts at Amherst. In essence, I started my formal re-education in January 1983.

I took courses from many thoughtful professors and engaged in many insightful conversations with fellow graduate students. But the most significant experience in relation to my theoretical understanding of oppression and its manifestations, especially racism, was my involvement in the Social Issues Training Project under the direction of Professor Bailey Jackson. The Social Issues Training Project was an organization of committed faculty and graduate students who were trying to understand: what oppression is, how it operates, and who the players are in it.

As a player in this process, I had to come to some understanding of how I learned racism. The theoretical background that I gained through readings and discussions, as well as the actual experience of teaching and engaging undergraduates in weekend workshops on racism, were experiences that enabled me to acquire a clearer understanding of oppression and racism.

One activity that I recall being asked to do in a four-day intensive course called "Helping from a Racial Perspective" was to create a timeline from birth to my then present age and indicate on this timeline incidents and events that I could describe as racial. The first time I did this activity I was able to go back to an incident that occurred when I was twelve years old. In this particular incident, several Black children threw stones at me and my friends as we crossed through their neighborhood. Two days later, when I revisited the timeline, I was able to go back to an incident that occurred when I was five years old.

In this incident, my younger brother and I were traveling on a bus with my grandmother to spend the weekend with her. The sheer excitement of being on a city bus with my grandmother was too much to handle. I can still remember the joy and the excitement of seeing the skyline of the city, its tall buildings, and even the smell of the bus fumes that made this journey memorable.

On this trip, we crossed through the downtown part of the city. I can recall looking at all the people walking the sidewalks and waiting to cross the street while stopped at a traffic light. As I peered through the window at the people standing on the corner, I remember excitedly telling my brother "to look at those people, they're . . . ." (I think that I was going to say "Black" or "colored." I cannot recall. All I know is that this is my first conscious recollection of seeing Black people and I was excited. But I never did say anything.) At that moment, my grandmother brushed my hand from the window and said, "Don't point at those people." Her tone and her manner signified to me that something was "different" about those people. In my effort to make sense of her response and reaction, I later related these feelings of fear, avoidance, and intrigue that I felt to the little girl who lived three doors down from my apartment door. I was told not to go near her and not to bother her. I learned years later that she had Down Syndrome.

The point of this exercise was to recognize that racism is often taught to us by the people we most love and trust. They are our parents, grandparents, aunts and uncles, brothers and sisters, peers and family friends. Therefore, I learned that racism operates within an individual context where individuals share and help perpetuate racist ideology. But I also learned in this course and in subsequent course work and readings that racism also operates within the institutional and cultural context. Institutions such as schools, places of worship, workplaces, the media, especially television, participate in enacting policies and presenting stereotypes (or no representation, which leads to invisibility) that perpetuate and maintain racist ideology. In addition, on a cultural level, the dominant White culture in the United States participates in perpetuating a racist ideology through its values (e.g., competition, individualism), role models (e.g., school textbooks' legacy of White men), expectations (e.g. hard work, "middle class" and corporate world) and language (e.g., "standard" English). Each of these contexts operates in conjunction with each other to form a system in which we are socialized as children.

FEAR

I remember when I opened that door in West Africa several years ago that my first thought in the moment was that this fear that I felt was not normal given how I identified myself. We are taught this fear, however, in many subtle and not-so-subtle ways.

As I look back and reflect on my grandmother's reaction to my curiosity and wonder of the world, this fear that I sensed must have always been operating on a subconscious level. If I look back at family gatherings and think about the tone of the conversations, fear must have been expressed in the false bravado of the adult males as they echoed how they would fight and protect their families from rioters. (In the wake of the urban riots in the mid-sixties, I can recall such conversations at social gatherings.) Fear must have lingered beneath the surface when I was informed by parents and others about which routes to drive home in order to avoid certain neighborhoods.

But as I learned about racism through classes and readings, I realized that fear is a necessary component of race hegemony. It is necessary because the fear helps to maintain and rationalize the need for separation. The fear, for example, that was/is promulgated and "legitimated" regarding the sexuality and criminality of the African American has a long history in this counry (e.g., Thomas & Sillen, 1972; Hutchinson, 1994). But that fear is not a historical anomaly. It remains present, though often coded, so as not to recall or make mention of our historical blemish. Through textual representation, especially the mass media in its selection, distribution and representation of the Other on television shows, for example, *America's Most Wanted* and on film, for example, *Mona Lisa* (e.g., Young, 1990), such media portray and display stereotypical constructs that help to engender an image of the Other as criminal and sexual predator. There is also the political manipulation of race in presidential elections, the Willie Horton affair during the Bush campaign and in state elections the bashing of immigrants and the misinformation campaign on affirmative action, for example, that brought California Propositions 187 and 209. Educational reforms of the 1980s and those suggested to bring us to the year 2000 are infested with coded language (Haymes, 1995a) that defines the crisis of education and the downfall of the United States in terms of the deprivation of the home life of the "not-two-parent-household-drug-addicted-child-living-in-a-crime-ridden-urban-area." These words and images are not harmless. They enable our aggression toward the Other and eventually toward our self (our self-destruction) (Fromm, 1973).

Fear is an integral part of racism. It is socially constructed through a systematic process of adult-to-child socialization and a social campaign of misinformation (e.g. Allport, 1954; Dennis, 1981; Karp, 1981; Frankenberg, 1993). This fear, however, is irrational and, as Ruth Frankenberg (1993), explains, "an inversion of reality."

In her study of White women and their understanding of racism, Frankenberg notes that fear was a common element among several of her participants. In her analysis, she indicates that this feeling of fear is

an inversion of reality. In general, people of color have far more to fear from White people than vice versa, given, for example, the on-going incidence of White supremacist terrorism around the United States, which targets African and Asian Americans, Latinos, Native Americans . . . and the problematic relationship with the police that leaves many communities of color with, at the very least, a sense that they lack legal and physical protection (1993, p. 60).

Frankenberg goes on to explain how this fear is part of a racist discourse that perceives racism as an essentialist construct. She argues that an essentialist racism describes the Other as different in a "fundamentally" distinct manner. One example that she shares and that other writers have also discussed (e.g., Hutchinson, 1994; Thomas & Sillen, 1972) is the idea of the Black male as sexual predator. Citing Angela Davis (1981), Frankenberg explains that this myth was promulgated during the aftermath of the Civil War in order to maintain and protect White economic and political power. "The lynching of Black people was a means of social and political repression; accusations of rape were used as alibis for what were in effect politically motivated death squads" (1993, p. 61). In addition, Frankenberg discusses how earlier "nativist" movements depicted Chinese, Japanese, and Filipino male immigrants as violent sexual predators.

Today, immigrant bashing and the criminalization of persons of color, especially males, continues. Direct accusations and naming of persons of color as predator and criminal, however, are perhaps not necessary. A history of racialism and a campaign of promulgated fear and terror seems to have resulted in a coded language of racist discourse. Descriptors appear to no longer be needed to name and mark the Other. In a recent newspaper commentary, columnist Suzanne Fields (1996), for example, describes the emergence of a new type of predator, the "superpredator." It is interesting to note in her description of this "superpredator," no racial words are used. Instead, a coded language is employed to depict this new "superpredator." Through three-quarters of the article Fields uses terms such as drugs, gangs, guns and terror. She never uses a racial term or the name of a city to isolate this growing problem, until she introduces the "name of a Bloods gang member Body Count". Further, Fields, in reference to Body Count comments, "When the boy was asked how he came to be called Body Count he answered in the cadence of a rapper: When da shootin's ova', das what I do, I coun' da bodies." Dwight Conquergood (1994), quoted in Peter McLaren (1995), states that "[g]angs are constructed in public discourse as the cause, effect, and aberrant response to social disorder and urban decay. The demonized figure of the violent gangbanger is the sensational centerpiece in a self-righteous morality play called 'the urban underclass' playing currently in mainstream media and social-policy institutions," (1994, pp. 53–54; McLaren (1995), p. 12). Such coded-language is receiving more use today because of the need to shield one's racist intentions (Omi & Winant, 1994). It is not in good taste to be an overt racist today.

Rutledge Dennis (1981) talks about an irrationality that guides the racist's psychic. I think when I first read this several years ago, I thought of my Southerner-as-racist construct and pictured the White people in Little Rock, Arkansas and Selma, Alabama who stood on the sidewalk and made racist jeers at the Black students and marchers. Thus, I believed and hoped that somewhere outside of me, racism reigned. I realized after much thought that this fear and its irrationality not only affects and pervades the human psyche but this irrationality also affects and infects society's social and institutional sites. A brief historical review of the legal and scientific manipulations enacted in the name of white race supremacy exposes the irrational and demonic nature of racism (e.g., Gould, 1996; Thomas & Sillen, 1972; Lazarus, 1991). The irrational lies in the energy used to hide and to distort the truth.

In an essay from bell hook's *Talking back* (1989), hooks makes reference to a book detailing the African presence in pre-Columbian America. I became intrigued by the notion and found the book, *They Came Before Columbus*s by Ivan Van Sertima (1975). In addition, I read a more recent book edited by the same author (Van Sertima, 1992). As I read these books, I had to struggle to overcome a gnawing sense that I was reading fiction; that somehow the thesis and supporting facts outlined could not be true. The presentation of this thesis and facts juxtaposed my sense of "history" and reality of the world such that intially I could not imagine their veracity. I recall similiar feelings when I first read Dee Brown's *Bury My Heart at Wounded Knee* (1971). I felt that this must be some sort of fabrication and deliberate hyperbole of minor incidents. But after reading and understanding more of the workings of the ideological hegemony of White racism, I am less susceptible to the manipulations.

Working with many students to demystify their history of the United States, I often come face-to-face with students' responses challenging the perspectives presented by the historians and the scholars that I share in my courses. Some students put forth a concerted effort to scrutinize each of the facts and sources of the facts that are presented. In an exercise, for example, on Columbus, adapted from Ira Shor (1992), I have my students write a short paragraph on what they know about Columbus. The majority of the written responses usually describe the purpose of his voyage (to find a passage to India), name the three ships, and identify for whom Columbus sailed and his ethnicity. After we read several of the entries and students exhaust their knowledge of Columbus, which for the most part does not go beyond what I just presented, I ask students to read the first chapter of Howard Zinn's (1980) book, *A People's History of the United States*. His first chapter is titled "Columbus, Indians and Human Progress."

In this chapter, Zinn details the slaughter of Indians, their enslavement to mine for gold and portrays an avarice and cruel Columbus. Some student responses to this new information range from outrage and disbelief to questioning Zinn's "selected sources" and his political allegiance and agenda. But I understand these responses because of the distorted image and notion that the United States is a pristine, honorable, democratic, and just society. This belief in an ideal United States often times can get in the way of working on issues of race (Dennis, 1981; Tatum, 1992).

This fear that I speak of is not just race and gender specific, it is also classed. It is the myth of the working class as poor and poverty stricken and, thus, depraved, deprived, deficient, and most covetous of the status quo. When I began to deconstruct this fear that at the time I described as irrational, I realized that I needed to return to my childhood in an attempt to capture where, when, and how this sense of fear emerged.

CATHOLIC SCHOOLING

In order to understand how the school contributed to my understanding and knowledge of the Other, it is important to recognize that my early schooling from grades one through seven occurred in the context of a Catholic school. Each school day began with a mass, and each class began with a prayer. The religious presence of the Catholic Church was obvious. Feast days of the saints were celebrated. The lives of the saints were told, and their selfless sacrifices, undying love for the poor and downtrodden, and their inevitable martyrdom for the glory of the Church were shared. As a young boy, these saints, many of which were portrayed in carved and sculpted figures on the church and classroom walls, filled my imagination and became models to emulate.

The ideas of martyrdom and missionary work were captivating concepts and images that formed my understanding and knowledge of the Other. Often the idea of martyrdom in the lives of the saints occurred when many served as missionaries who traveled to "exotic" places to share and extol the virtues of Christianity to the "pagans, heathens and savages." Not only "pagans, heathens and savages" were targeted for redemption but also the politically "savaged," that was (is) the Communists. I recall an incident in the late 1950s when three missionaries recently released from a Chinese prison came and talked to the school children. I was perhaps eight to ten at the time. They were from the Passionate order. On their cassocks, they wore an emblem of a red bleeding heart, encircled by thorns and in the center was the imprint of a crucifix. In their talk, they described how they were forced to march many miles while yoked as "cattle." I felt sympathy and passion. I was witnessing courage. I wanted to go forth and strike down the "commies" and, most importantly, protect those poor, innocent Chinese peasant people.

I had this same emotional experience several years later when I was introduced to the work of a young naval doctor, Tom Dooley, who worked in Vietnam. He was bringing medicine and comfort to the poor and the innocent. The moment I recalled from this talk was how the enemy, the Communists would chop off the arms of the young children who Dr. Dooley and his companions recently inoculated.

While these talks and descriptions of lives filled my imagination, "pagan" children on pint milk cartons sat on my desk collecting pennies for food and clothing. None of these children was White nor did any appear to be from the United States I did learn of missionaries who worked in the United States These were the Glenmary Missionaries. Their work, however, was with the poor Whites and Blacks who lived in Appalachia, that is, in the "country," and in the South. (In my home and community, "hillbillies" and "poor White trash"[1] were terms used to denigrate people who lived in rural areas, especially from Appalachia. In addition, the idea of "country" and its people were depicted as backward, slow, lazy, and dull-minded.)

What I gained from these spirited talks and representations was a construct of the Other. The Other was (1) a person who did not look like me, that is, White, blond, and blue eyed; (2) a person who did not live in the United States except for the "poor White trash" and Blacks who lived in the "country"; and (3) a person who could not help or take care of themselves, that is, they were powerless. They were helpless, and they needed me. I could pray for them. I could send them money. I could go out and "mission" among them. These images and feelings guided my cognitive and affective understanding and knowledge of who the Other was and how the Other acted within the world. They were not me and most importantly, they were less than me. They needed me. I was a sympathizer and pitied their condition. I was ready to do battle. But battle whom?

The South, the Negro, and Slavery

The construction of the White southerner and slave master as the embodiment of evil emerged early in my childhood. I cannot recall when the idea of slavery was introduced to me in school. I am not even sure if I heard of the term "abolitionists" in grade school or if that idea came in high school. I think and know that television also served to play a role in how I constructed the idea of the South, the Negro, and slavery.

I lived in a northern state. Images of the Civil War, always defined in terms of fighting slavery, were represented in contradictions of the good and righteous North and the evil and treacherous South; the Blue and the Gray; the Yankee and the rebel; the good and the bad; the free-ers of slaves and the holders of slaves. I recall old television movies depicting the war between the states. The good soldiers were the Yankees doing and winning battles against the rebels. These old melodramas had their usual damsels in distress and, almost as an aside, Negroes as slaves.

What I learned from these tales was that Lincoln, the Union troops, and, especially, the North set the slave free. Further, I constructed from these types of shows the "passive Negro." This construction meant that the slaves did not do anything to eradicate slavery. In addition, the slaves were happy and grateful to the North and those who fought for their freedom.

Besides TV tales of the Civil War, I had a large dosage of *Tarzan*, the *Three Stooges*, and *Our Gang*. Each of these shows portrayed the African American in demeaning ways. The superstitious, cruel, and savage natives of the jungle who were always overran and outsmarted by a White man, woman, boy, and chimp. The buffoon parodied as an African native who was crafted by three fools indicated the backwardness of the African. I can still see Buckwheat's frightened expression as he accidently runs across one of the "gang" dressed as a ghost.

Each of these images contributed to my understanding of the Other in this case, the African American. This "passive Negro" appreciated and liked the North. The "real" problem was in the evil and backward South where "hillbillies" and former slaveholders resided. What I was able to do as a young child of eight or nine, and perhaps for many years after, was to conceive of the African American in an image of passivity. Passivity such that the African American was freed by good people who saw the evil of slavery. These good people were President Lincoln and those in the North. By living in the North, I was good because by proxy I had freed the slaves. As such, former slaves should be good to me.

The Civil Rights Movement and Me

I was twelve years old in August 1963 when the march on Washington, D.C., occurred. I do not remember the march, and I cannot recall my parents, my parents' friends, or my relatives speaking about it. (And this topic definitely was not discussed in school.)

Much of my early understanding and interest of the civil rights movement came in bits and pieces. I usually gathered these tidbits when, for example, my folks would have or take us to a family gathering. While running to the picnic table to grab a bunch of pretzels or chips or get a soda, I would hear adult conversations and hear words such as "marchers," "the Negroes," "freedom rider," "bombings," as well as the phrases "It's sad;" "They been wait'ng long enough;" "Hell, can you blame them;" "Blame 'em. Bullshit, send them &@#* back to Africa."

The n-word was often used in these conversations. I remember saying the n-word when I was a young boy. I was punished for saying it and threatened with having to eat a piece of soap. But neither of my parents, who punished me, ever protested to their friends for using such language. Subsequently, it took me many years to learn how to interrupt and to challenge other adults' racist comments.

The word that seemed to catch everyone's attention was "riot." In 1965, when I was fourteen and while Detroit and Los Angeles burned, I was able to sit down at the picnic and dining room tables and listen to the adults talk. It appeared as though the conversation did not change much from the previous years. But there was urgency and concern in their voices, more pronounced anger, disgust, and dismay. The sentiment to send Blacks packing and talk about shooting "them before they shot us" was much in the conversations. But my mother stood her ground in presenting her view that rioting seemed like a rational response given "what has happened to those people." Maybe she could share her bravado easily, since we had moved out of the city and to the country in the summer of 1964. But still, I was very proud of her stance. It made me think deeply about the contradictions in this country and to read about what was happening.

In 1967, I watched in disbelief and in fear as the National Guard drove down the interstate to stop the riots in the city. I was not sure of what the meaning of this conflict held for me. I did not really feel connected to it. On one level, I was not aware of who the conflicting parties were. There was conflict, yes, but between whom?

Television had convinced me through its images and use of the words "riot" and "looting" that the conflict was self-inflamed and inflicted. It was a battle among and within the Black community. Though we had friends and relatives who lived in the city and who announced that they were buying guns and affirmed their right to protect their neighborhoods, no one that I recall had any direct contact with the riots. It did not affect the neighborhoods in which we lived or visited.

It was at this juncture in the late 1960s that my own image of African Americans began to shift from that of "passivity" to that of the "Black Panther."[2] I place the term "Black Panther" in quotes because the image portrayed to me in the media at the time was not the Black Panthers. The image of the

"Black Panther" was of a violent, aggressive, and indiscriminate killer. "He" was doing harm to the struggle for Black freedom. "He" hated "Whitey." But I also hated "Whitey."

This "Whitey" that I hated was the White man of the South,[3] the bigot; the racist who clubbed, who maimed, who lynched, and who unleashed dogs on marchers. This "Whitey" image that I hated represented for a long time the image of the racist. It was this image and type of active racist from whom I was able to protect myself and in the process name myself not a racist.

I remember with excitement and with trepidation this new image of the African American as "Black Panther" that was being formed. My representation of the African American was shifting from a perspective of passivity to one of aggression. (I would today use the term "resistance" instead of "aggression." I understand resistance as a political and social act that counters race hegemony and political oppression [e.g., hooks, 1989; Giroux, 1983]. Further, I would add that resistance has been a continual characteristic of all oppressed groups in this country.) I was very supportive of the struggles for freedom, equality, and social justice. What eventually evolved for me during this period was an image of myself as an antiracist. The civil rights movement and other social movements of the late 1960s helped to formulate my liberal politics and an awakening to the need for social justice in this country. But at the same time, I was able to shield and to feign any references to me as racist. My sense of racism was Jim Crow and the accompanying laws and attitudes that blocked, harmed, and denigrated people. Further, the image of the racist was "Whitey," and this image ensured that I was not a racist. Once I went to West Africa, however, this construct fell apart.

CONCLUSION

In understanding the development and process of my own racism and unfolding critical race consciousness, I see three epistemic experiences that needed to occur for me to further liberate myself from race hegemony. The first experience was a movement away from an individualistic construct of racism revolving around an image of an individual or groups of individuals as racist, for example, the KKK or other similar neo-Nazi groups. Such individuals and groups do exist and need to be dealt with in an appropriate manner. But I needed to realize for myself that I was a racist and that I had been affected by my upbringing in a race conscious society (Omi & Winant, 1994). With this realization, I was open to learning about how racism as a social, cultural, political, and ideological construct permeates the entire society. The epiphany for me occurred when I opened that door in West Africa. There was no other reason for my reaction except for my prior experience of living in a racist society.

The second epistemic issue is an understanding of myself as a member of a social group and, in this case acknowledging, a racial identity as a White person. I was always capable of seeing the differences in physicality and color of the Other. But I never saw or described myself as White, especially with an understanding of what that White racial description meant. I could mark myself in my ethnicity and distinguish myself from other Whites who occupied their own ethnic category. Through course work, readings and workshops, I came to acknowledge and accept my own raceness. Therefore, I am a White person and being a White person I have privilege.

I have had a hard time accepting this notion of privilege. This is the third epistemic construct that I needed to struggle with and realize. My Whiteness my skin pigment has gained me privileges. This is not an easy fact to acknowledge especially living in a society whose central cultural motif is the individual, who by his [sic] own wits and willpower pulls himself [sic] up by his [sic] boot-straps to achieve the "American dream."

I see that the issue of privilege for myself operates on an individual level and institutional level. As White, I have always been given the privilege of seeing myself as an individual. I never had to see myself as a member of a social group unless I wanted to see myself as such, therefore, I claimed my Irishness. I never felt that I was named, marked, or perceived as a member of a group. Further, I never had to worry about how another member of my group might act because that member's action had nothing to do with how people saw me, the individual. My White individualality has gained me access to places. It has gained me mobility. As a White person, I could live in an integrated neighborhood without suspect or alarm. I could teach in a predominantly African American school and neighborhood and my credibility and professionalism as a teacher would not be questioned or second-guessed.

Living and teaching in an integrated neighborhood and school were my first border crossings. But I crossed those borders as a tourist; I did not really "live" there. I lived on the fringe of the community. I could sample what I wanted to sample. I could use where I lived to show myself and other Whites and Blacks that I was "cool," "hip," but especially that I was not a racist. As a tourist, I could leave when I wanted to leave. My passport was my whiteness, and I did not realize this until recently.

I came to an understanding of how my whiteness provided me privilege when I acknowledged my being a beneficiary of a White society and its institutions. The public school's curriculum, as Pinar et. al. (1995) discuss, participates in an identification process that permits Whites to seeing themselves as active agents in society. Though John Paul Jones, Andrew Jackson, and Teddy Roosevelt and the Rough Riders were given little academic currency, I as a White student had the privilege of the possibility to participate in their adventures and conquests. Walt Whitman, Henry David Thoreau, Ralph Waldo Emerson, Thomas Jefferson, and Edgar Allen Poe provided me with a world where the White man played and ruled and the possibility to achieve was marked by their own achievements. In addition, the great electronic campfire where tales are spun to inculcate the young into society, TV, gave me endless characters for whom I could play and dream. I have come to realize that my privilege emanates from the fact that images and tales describe and represent the White man that I am. Growing up, I did not have to search for heroes. They were in my school books and on my TV screen, as well as the movie screen. For White children today, those representations of self within a world much like themselves continues. Yes, there are exceptions. But the exceptions are always paraded out to somehow excuse ourselves from the real work and change that needs to occur.

Another issue that I have come to accept as part of my privilege is how past historical injustices benefited my forebears and myself. I'm a White, Irish-

German American most of whose great-grandparents emigrated to the United States in the 1880s. By this time slavery had ended. Though my great-grandparents did not own slaves, they and many other Whites, then and into the present, have benefited from the inherent (and continual) racism of such formal legal practices as slavery and segregation. Slavery and segregation of African Americans and subsequent legal exclusion policies regulating work, property ownership, and citizenry, for example, enacted toward Native Americans, Latinas/os, Asian Americans, and others have been the Whites' affirmative action policy (e.g., Haney Lopez, 1996; Wilson, 1980). By these exclusionary policies, Whites have been able to secure for themselves a place in the economy, in the workplace, and in the polity. With this revelation, I came to understand the need to support and to work for continued affirmative action measures and for equal opportunity.

NOTES

1. I heard the term "poor white trash" for many years while growing up. It is the only time that I can recall the racial descriptor "White" being applied to White people. In this context, in reference to the people of Appalachia, saying "poor white trash" did not indicate a racial category, rather, it implied a nonethnicity, therefore, no culture. Culture in this context means "high culture." This "high culture" was something that my family and I aspired to obtain. The term "White" was used as a descriptor to distinguish them from their perceived counterpart, that is, the poor rural Black who also lacked this "high culture."

2. In my mind, there was a distinction between Martin Luther King, Jr., his work, and those associated with him. This image was cloaked with the cloth of pacifism. It is with the introduction of the "Black Panther" via the media that this shift in imagery occurs. Further, I am aware of the absence of African American women in this construction. Their absence is and was part of the problem. But when I look back and recall how African American women were portrayed in the media, two images emerge, the nanny or maid and the lascivious woman.

3. This Southerner-as-racist construct that I learned overshadows a history of White Southern antiracist activism. Myles Horton's Highlander Center and Morris Dees's Southern Poverty Law Center are examples of White Southern opposition and resistance to racism. See, in this volume, chapter 4 and chapter 11 for a discussion on the research of the history of White antiracism.

What Could a White Girl from South Boston Possibly Know about Racism? Reflections of a Social Justice Educator

Mary M. Gannon

As I entered the residence hall where my classroom was located, a twinge of nervousness ran through my stomach. Surprised at this, I laughed and thought, "Even after four semesters of teaching this course, I'm still nervous?" I hesitated before I entered the room. I was beginning another chapter of discovery about myself as an educator, and unknowingly, I walked into the room, looked around, and smiled at the group that was gathering. There was not the unbearable silence that often permeates the room on the first day of class; in fact, students were laughing and standing in small groups, sharing stories about a difficult roommate or a course they were about to drop. Right away, I noticed that the standard racial lines were drawn: students of color on one side; White students on the other, with minimal intergroup mingling. This was not unusual—I observed this behavior in most of my classrooms. But something was different. What was it? My eyes scanned the room again. It occurred to me that this was not the usual classroom population that one sees at this large, northeastern, public university. The racial balance appeared to be different. There were visibly more students of color than there were White students. *How could this be? This never happens; these students must be in the wrong section.* I told myself to wait another five minutes, since it was not quite 2:30 yet. *More students will arrive, and they will probably be White.* As I reassured myself, I simultaneously wondered what was fueling my anxiety. Why was the possibility of having a classroom that was more than 50% students of color such a frightening prospect? Of course, I knew the answer but did not dare give it too much thought for fear that someone in the room could read my mind.

More students filed into the room, and I counted off in my head: 10, 11, 12, 13, 14 . . . 17, 18. Thirty students total, eighteen students of color, twelve White students. *What am I going to do? I can't teach this group; I don't know how to manage this many students of color with White students in the room. What if they don't like me? What if these students of color do not want a White teacher for a class on social diversity?* All of these conversations went running through my head as I stood in front of this group, terrified, and wanting the first one hour and fifteen minute class session of the semester to be over.

This experience is still with me as if it happened yesterday—a "teachable moment" for myself as I witnessed my own racism come alive! It was a critical incident that led the way to a profound transformation in my own racial identity development. It is often described in the field of multicultural and social justice education as moving from a racist consciousness to more of an antiracist consciousness, where we are able to acknowledge ourselves as both racist and antiracist (Jackson, 1976b; Hardiman, 1979). As I began the process of owning my White racial identity, it also became evident that I needed to explore what the implications of this identity were for me as a White educator and for my racially and ethnically diverse classrooms. It was not possible for me to make a distinction between the personal and the professional aspects of this discovery process. If I was going to face myself as a White person, it was imperative that I critically examine how my White identity was directly implicated in my role as an educator.

My identity as a White person had been, up until the incident described earlier, an aspect of myself that I never had to consider in any authentic or critical fashion. Living in what I have come to understand as a White-centered culture, I had the privilege of never having to think about my identity as a White person. In addition, the amount of terror and fear I would have to face in acknowledging my whiteness kept me from participating in activities focused on race-related issues. Attending racism workshops and participating in discussions with other colleagues and peers, particularly people of color, were avoided at all costs. *What if they think I am a racist?* At the time, I was unable to articulate my feelings and thoughts to anyone and this resulted in what felt like an excruciating silence. But I continued to keep a comfortable distance from my feelings about what it meant to be White, particularly as an educator in the fields of social justice education and multicultural education.

My teaching continued, and I began to feel like an impostor. *What a hypocrite you are. Preaching to other White people about owning their White skin privilege, and you have not acknowledged this yourself yet!* These internal conversations would bring me to the edge of my fear, and it was moments like these when I needed other White people to talk to and get support from about my experience. Of course, this kind of resource was not easily available, since most of my White colleagues were likely having an experience similar to mine and were not discussing it either. This denial of our whiteness and associated race privilege was insidious, yet we each played a convincing role as conscious social justice educators. I have always found this particular contradiction overwhelming but yet so easy to collude with. The tension, however, that this paradox creates within myself as a White educator who claims to embrace an antiracist pedagogy has, at times, created a certain amount of internal conflict. At one point, this conflict became too great for me to continue reconciling, and I began to search for a way out of it. The shift in my racial identity development from a racist consciousness, moving toward an antiracist consciousness, began when I chose to no longer perpetuate the contradiction that had existed about myself as a White educator. In these pages, I will share some of my experiences of this process and, more importantly, reflect on how owning my White racial identity continues to impact my work as a social justice educator, whose practice is informed by an antiracist pedagogy.

The story of my formative years is somewhat atypical, considering geographical location, among other factors. Growing up on the borders of South Boston and Dorchester, located just outside of Boston, I was familiar with racist attitudes and beliefs—racism was all around me. The White, Irish-Catholic, working-class community that I grew up in had a strong sense of pride and righteousness about who they were and how they worked hard for what they had attained. Comments such as, "If you work hard enough in this country, you can have anything you want—the minorities out there are lazy, that's why they have no work. Hey, look at the Asians, now they work hard and they're making a place for themselves" were a part of dinner conversations among my relatives and friends' parents. These were some of the more benign sentiments that I would hear frequently but never spoken by my own liberal-minded parents. This type of racist thinking was not condoned in our household; instead, we engaged in a more pervasive manifestation of racism that I call "silence."

My parents both came from strong Irish-Catholic backgrounds but were asked to leave their respective churches when they married in 1963. My father was married and divorced prior to marrying my mother and she married a divorcee, resulting in the local parish considering them not "Catholic enough" for the Church, and certainly not "Irish-Catholic" enough for the neighborhood. This action resulted in a significant consciousness-raising experience, primarily for my father. In our home, he talked to all of his children about accepting and understanding differences. He would explain what his understanding of racism was and what his expectations were for us in regard to this social issue. This was quite different from the experience of my peers, who were being fed a healthy serving of racist jokes at the dinner table and were repeatedly told to stay away from certain parts of town because it was not "safe." It was a confusing time for me, as I tried to make sense of the conflicting messages I was hearing from influential people in my life.

At the age of twelve, I was introduced to the "silence of racism." My parents, fueled by my father's liberal leanings, adopted a three-year-old African American boy. Philip came to our home and lived with us for sixteen months, and for those sixteen months, we never discussed the fact that a young boy of African heritage was living in our White household, in our White community, in one of the most racist cities in the United States. This silence proved to be one of the most powerful sources of information for me and my siblings. This silence said that it was not appropriate to notice that Philip's skin was darker than mine, and it also said that we were supposed to ignore his rich cultural heritage and expect that he would assimilate into our cultural norms and values. This silence spoke so loudly that it became impossible for me to get any of my questions answered. It resulted in an internalized fear of talking about racial issues that would haunt me until my late twenties. My parents believed they were doing the right thing by not calling attention to Philip's differences, but unfortunately, it resulted in some of the most racist behavior my family ever engaged in.

Eventually, my parents realized they could not manage Philip's emotional health and the Department of Social Services annulled the adoption and moved

Philip to another family who lived in a more racially heterogeneous community. Our family moved on from that experience and, to this day, has never talked about Philip's presence in the family. It was not until my late twenties that I began to reflect on that time in my life and how it impacted my understanding of myself as a White person, then and now. Having a brother of African heritage could have been a positive learning experience, but my White parents lacked the consciousness and the skills necessary to make Philip's presence in our family less invisible. This resulted in my inability to get answers to my questions about racial differences and the loss of this young boy as a member of my family.

The fear, anxiety, and sense of ignorance that all people experience from a lack of accurate information about racial differences has become clearly evident to me in the process of the transformation of my own racial consciousness. Target group members (people of color) and perpetrators of racism (Whites) have been socialized in a system that reinforces notions of a racial hierarchy, resulting in people of color not feeling affirmed or worthy in a society where Whites benefit from the privilege of White skin. Whites may also experience a lack of awareness and celebration of one's ethnic identity, a consequence of seeing ourselves only as White people, the perpetrators of racism. Although this phenomenon is not particular to only White people, this is another example of how racism impacts White people in the United States, particularly those of Western European ancestry.

As a young child, I somewhat identified with my Irish heritage, but it was limited and often misinformed. It was important to be included in the circle of my Irish peers, who wore green on St. Patrick's Day and had stories of alcohol abuse in their families. I, too, could laugh about my Uncle Sullivan, whose beer cooler was always full and who was drunk at most family gatherings. There was also stories about my mother, who was consuming more than her fair share of alcohol on the weekends. At the age of twelve, I believed that identifying with Irish heritage included drinking a great deal of alcohol, telling racist jokes, and being suspicious of anyone who was not Irish. Needless to say, my understanding of what it meant to be Irish came from limited sources, and what I did witness was inaccurate and eventually became a source of humiliation for me.

Leaving South Boston and my Irish roots to attend college was not a sad parting. I was ready to embark on this new journey with the hope that I could leave my past behind. During my college years, I went through a period of my own consciousness-raising. I was introduced to the notion of feminism and became involved in different women's groups on campus. Eventually, I co-founded The Women's Resource Center and dedicated a great deal of my time to education on sexual harassment and domestic violence. Working on social justice issues became a focus for me, and I also began to educate myself about homophobia and the gay, lesbian, and bisexual community. Many of my co-workers and peers were gay and lesbian, and it was a comfortable and safe transition to consider one of my dominant social group memberships, as I had developed friendships with people in the community who trusted me as an ally. I worked extensively on this issue, examining what it meant to have heterosexual privilege and eventually began speaking on the campus Speaker's Bureau for Gay, Lesbian, and Bisexual Students as a heterosexual ally. This became important work for me as it was a stepping stone to a similar journey I would need to embark on regarding the issue of race. During this time, I knew there was something missing, a piece of the puzzle that was lost and trying to find its place in the bigger picture. No one had challenged me yet on my White skin privilege, and I was certainly too scared to face that demon. I continued to actively challenge heterosexism and sexism, hoping no one was noticing my White skin.

I entered graduate school with the "demon" pulling the hair at the back of my neck. I ignored it and continued on with "business as usual." At the time, I was working as a child care provider for a Black man and as the issue of my Whiteness began to enter the forefront of my consciousness, I hoped and prayed that he did not notice I was White or discover that I was born and raised in South Boston. I worked very hard that year, trying to be a "good White girl."

As I continued on in my racial identity development, I spent a considerable amount of time immersing myself in other cultures or as Terry (1975) calls it "going native." This term defines a White person who "abandons Whiteness in favor of overidentifying with Blacks. The person tries to gain personal recognition from Blacks for being 'almost Black.'" My own need to identify with people of color was not something I was consciously aware of about myself at the time, but it was clearly part of my identity development. Wanting so desperately to be included and accepted in the African American community, I enrolled in African dance lessons at the local dance studio. I would braid my hair, pull it up high on my head, wrap it in a brightly colored cloth and arrive at class, hoping that no one would notice I was one of two White women in the studio. The other White woman seemed to be more accepted; she kept her hair in dreadlocks and spoke with what I perceived, a certain inauthentic accent. Eventually, I stopped going, as the looks sent my way made me feel uncomfortable, but I did not understand why I was not welcome in that community. I left wondering, *What did I do wrong?* Still the demon poked at my consciousness and still I remained resistant.

Story after story, experience after experience, I struggled with my need to feel accepted by the people of color that I interacted with and remained fearful of having to confront my White identity—or worse, be confronted! This time of my life created a great deal of unnecessary anxiety and internal turmoil. But, slowly, with the help of a mentor, other White senior graduate students, and Peggy McIntosh (1989), this started to change. I began to critically examine my identity as a White, Irish American woman from South Boston and how certain life experiences had impacted the formation of this identity. The critical incident that I opened this chapter with spurred this process significantly. As the White teacher in that classroom, I was forced to consider the issues that were raised in the classroom because of the racial and ethnic diversity of the students. It was also at this time that I began to confront my fears and recognize more clearly the connection between the personal and the professional aspects of this issue—they were not separate. My teaching became more informed by pedagogy that was antiracist and as a White instructor, I felt more authentic and more capable of teaching about racism and other multicultural issues because I had faced the demon—my own racism.

As the semester progressed, my students were in their own process of dealing with the racial demographics in the class, especially the White students. Most of them were experiencing for the first time what it was like to be in the racial minority in a college classroom and as evidenced by their journals and their comments in class, they were uncomfortable with the situation. At one point in the semester, when the tension level was high, a few White students accused me, in their journals, of playing favorites with certain students of color. This accusation did not surprise me, since the class preceding these journal entries had focused on a dialogue between White student and student of color caucus groups, which was difficult for everyone. These particular White students were most likely feeling betrayed by me as the White teacher because, during the discussion, I had challenged the White students to consider the notion of race privilege, which they responded to with some resistance. Hence, the journals came back to me, expressing their anger and confusion about my role in the classroom as a White person. Their accusations were difficult for me to hear because I was appalled with the possibility that my own racism may have become evident in my classroom. The familiar tapes played over in my mind: *Maybe I am paying too much attention to the students of color. I have been trying to connect with them and build trust but isn't that what I am supposed to do? How should I make sense of this tension—are the White students' observations accurate or is something else happening for them?*

In my feedback to these students who had written about this issue in their journals, I remained as "objective" as I could, despite my own discomfort with the situation. I wrote that I appreciated their courage in sharing their concerns with me, and it was important that as White people, we look truthfully at what manifests for us because of the issue of racism, particularly in this classroom. I also gently encouraged these students to think about their comments to me and what they were feeling at the time. This was the first time I had experienced this kind of reaction from a student, and it was important that I respond in an undefensive fashion, since this could decide if these White students labeled me as a race traitor or believed that I was supportive of them in their process. The weeks following this critical incident were incredibly challenging for me. I was conscious of every word that came out of my mouth, fearing how I would be interpreted. I kept a watchful eye on the White students and was overly aware of my interactions with all of the students. It was exhausting! At this point, I did not know what to do next, and I was very uncomfortable with myself.

Looking back at this experience, I realize that it never occurred to me to consider the behavior and actions of these particular White students. Up until that point, my role in the situation was the only aspect that seemed relevant to think about. It was not until recently, with the helpful insights of another White colleague who struggles with these issues, that I was able to ponder other possibilities of understanding the experience of these White students in my class.

I have come to examine this situation in two ways. Both are critical to developing a deep understanding of how racism pervades a classroom. First, as the White educator in this multiracial classroom, it is very important for me to be conscious of the multiple identities I bring as a teacher into the classroom, specifically, the racial identities I bring. However, what I have often wondered is if my heightened awareness of this identity is motivated by a need to prove my authenticity as a White teacher and a White person in an effort to gain validation and acceptance by students of color—in essence, overcompensating. If I am overcompensating, a lack of authenticity with all of my students results. This was the analysis I employed in reading their journal comments. I was not genuine and they had figured it out—I was caught!

But, another aspect of the situation that needs to be considered is the behavior of the White students in this multiracial learning environment. A crucial point in understanding how racism operates in this society is acknowledging that this culture is White-centered. Most White people have been socialized, whether consciously or unconsciously, with the belief that whiteness is the norm. As I attempted to create an inclusive learning environment, where all of my students could feel they were equal members of the classroom and that their issues were equally relevant, I may have caused some discomfort for the White students—the decentering of whiteness is uncomfortable for Whites. My White students were being challenged in this process and, without a framework for understanding whiteness, it was not possible for them to respond in any other manner except with anger and fear. This fear, I believe, is a result of their belief that their issues were not going to be heard if the White teacher was not on their side of the issue of racism.

This experience has allowed me to deepen my understanding of what it means to embrace and practice an antiracist pedagogy in my classroom, but it has left me with many questions as well. One particular question that I will continue to struggle with is this notion of decentering whiteness. What does this mean? How do I approach this overwhelming task in my classroom and in my own life? How do I teach my White students about the complexities of racism if I am not sure that I understand my own whiteness? I may not have all of the answers to these questions, but I am certain of this: Whiteness is a notion that needs to be raised in my classrooms. One of my tasks as a White educator is to provide White students with an opportunity to see how our culture is White-centered. If we are to get to the core of our humanity, Whites first need to acknowledge White privilege, which is the result of a White-centered culture. My intention is to support students in ultimately reclaiming their humanness, which would support all of us in our work to eradicate racism.

This experience was an important growth opportunity for me as a White educator teaching about race. I certainly was lacking a deeper understanding of what dynamics were occurring in my classroom, but I believe that getting uncomfortable is a key component to change. We must be willing to move out of our own comfort zones if we want change to happen in our classrooms. This is an essential element to an antiracist pedagogy. Change happens with critical questions, open dialogue, and a willingness to leave our comfort zones as students and as educators.

I have been involved as an educator and trainer in the field of social justice education for over ten years. My work has brought me to many diverse groups of people in many different settings. However, the questions I have been posing to myself for the last few years regarding my role as an educator and the impact of my White identity on classroom dynamics were not questions I had asked in the earlier years of my work. I recognize now that certain factors were operating at the time that hindered my ability to consider some of these issues, mostly the fear of facing my own bias and prejudice. Having spent the earlier years working in the field without critically examining my identity as a White person and as a White educator, I know I believe that if an educator does not consider who she or he is and how these identities impact the classroom environment, students will not have a positive learning experience, where they feel included and acknowledged. Weinstein and Obear (1992) refer to an educator's self-awareness as "self-monitoring" (p. 42). Weinstein shares a personal perspective: "Even though I come into the classroom as a professional teacher, I do not leave my identities at the door. I am a blend of such identities, for example, white, male, heterosexual, Jewish, beyond middle-age, working-class background, now middle-class" (p. 42). He goes on to say that although this process can be uncomfortable for educators, revealing this awareness of identity to oneself and to students supports the students' ability to have a positive learning experience, where they feel included and have a voice.

The decision to "self-monitor" as a White educator has become a "have to" for me. It is a process that needs to happen if all of my students—White, Asian/Pacific Islander, African heritage, Jewish, Native American, Latina/os— are going to feel included and affirmed in my classroom. Wilkerson (1992) articulates well the fears of so many educators who are confronted with this decision of self-monitoring:

To bring these cultures into the classroom is to confront the ignominious as well as the glorious side of our history. Some faculty fear they will be unable to handle the inevitable conflict, anger, frustration, and confusion of their students, as well as their own fear, anger, or feelings of guilt. "I am not prepared to be a social worker," they cry: "I am a scholar and teacher!" This fear is very real and is, in fact, symptomatic of the profound challenge educators face in our times. It is the "self" that is really at stake here, the very notion of "personal identity" around which liberal education has evolved. (p. 59)

Historically, educators have not been trained and supported in raising issues of difference in the classroom or managing these discussions if the students bring the topic to the table. It is not possible, however, to continue resisting this pedagogical challenge. Not only are issues of personal identity presently a critical aspect of the social fabric of this country, but they are of great importance to the young people who are in our classrooms everyday across this country. Youth of this generation, particularly those of non-White racial and ethnic identities, are exploring who they are and are identifying strongly with their ancestral roots. As a White educator, it is imperative that I inform myself about who is in my classroom and consider the implications of these diverse racial identities and my own for the learning environment. In order to do this, I need to engage in self-discovery, owning my whiteness and acknowledging my White skin privilege.

As an educator of White, Irish American heritage, I have had the privilege of not having to consider these aspects of myself. In the last two years, however, I have been working in settings where I, as a White person, have been in the minority. This has increased my awareness dramatically about my relationships with other educators, administrators, and students who are racially different from me. As a White educator in the field of multicultural and social justice education, it is critical for me to acknowledge my privileged racial identity and to ask myself everyday, "Have I done something today to combat racist attitudes, beliefs, and history in my classroom today?" It no longer becomes a choice of whether to confront racism at any level; it becomes a "have to."

I have come into contact with many different teachers of varied subjects and levels, mostly through teacher training sessions and education courses. Most of these educators, not to my surprise, had never once considered the implications of their racial, ethnic, religious, or any other identity as the educator in that classroom. In *White Teacher* (1979), Vivian Gussin Paley tells the story of her struggle to come to terms with her White identity and her own racism as a White, Jewish school teacher teaching kindergarten in the ghettos of Chicago and New York.

The child has already learned which of his characteristics are seen as weaknesses by those who take care of him at home . . . . Suddenly a stranger called 'teacher' is trying to find out not *who* he is, but *what* he knows . . . . The further away the teacher is from the child's cultural . . . background, the more likely it is that the wrong questions will be asked. The child . . . soon figures out that *he* must be the one who is inappropriate. Thus he begins the energy-consuming task of trying to cover up his differences. (p. 42)

This teacher's experience with her Black students reflects the damaging cycle that is created when educators, particularly White educators, do not consider the implications of identity and life experience that each student brings to the class environment. When I am working with teachers, I share with them what I believe to be the consequences of not having this awareness of our students:

• The student is not valued and acknowledged for her or his differences and therefore is treated as if she or he has the same life experiences as the rest of the group.

• There is an expectation that all students learn the same way no matter who they are.

• The students do not experience an inclusive or holistic way of seeing the world.

• Relationships do not develop among members of different groups because there is no support or modeling of this by the teacher.

Knowing that elements of consequences take place in classrooms everyday, including mine, I am more compelled than ever to continue noticing my position in the classroom, particularly as I pursue the development of intergroup dialogues in my classrooms and continue to build relationships with students who have different social identities and diverse life experiences that I can learn from.

As I continue to examine and think critically about my identity as a White educator, I am also excited to explore more fully my Irish heritage. Just recently, I have become more interested in reclaiming the ethnic part of who I am and learning about my ancestors and their struggles in Ireland and here in the United States. I look forward to integrating this information about myself into my curriculum and encouraging other White students to explore their ethnic heritage.

This process of discovery about ourselves as White educators is lifelong. We may confront the fear, the terror about our identity as White people and being seen only as racists, but it is a lifelong process, personally and professionally. We will not figure it all out in that lifetime, but embarking on the journey of becoming more authentic and genuine with ourselves and with our students is a profound contribution to combating social oppression and making our classrooms and school systems more inclusive for all students.

As I work to create valuable learning experiences for my students around issues of social justice education, it is important for me to continue to examine the intersections of my role as the teacher and my social and cultural identities. This process continues to challenge and support me in becoming a conscientious educator, as I become more aware of how these identities impact how I am perceived, how I interpret what is happening in the classroom situation, and how I use my identity as an instrument of education in the classroom. This awareness of who I am and what I bring to the classroom is vitally important in creating a more socially just classroom, as well as strengthening my role as a White educator.

When I dare to be powerful—
to use my strength in the service of my vision,
then it becomes less and less important
whether I am afraid.
     —Audre Lorde (1984, p. 113)

11

If You're Not Standing in This Line, You're Standing in the Wrong Line

G. Pritchy Smith

> That which we are, we are
> One equal temper of heroic hearts
> Made weak by time and fate, but strong in will
> To strive, to seek, to find, and not to yield.
> —Alfred Lord Tennyson, "Ulysses"

T. J.'S CHALLENGE

One of the most important critical incidents that helped me clarify my role as a White person in a racist society occurred during the summer of 1959 when I was an undergraduate at the University of Texas. I was enrolled that summer in a Foundations of Education course. In that class was Thomas Jefferson Johnson, who preferred to be called "T. J." for short. For the most part, schools were still segregated in Texas. In fact, in all the 15 years of schooling that I had prior to that class, T. J. was my first African American classmate. In the beginning, perhaps T. J. was only a curiosity to me, but something told me that I wanted to know this young man better. One day on the way to class, T. J. called out to me from where he was sitting under one of those grand spreading oak trees on the University of Texas campus. "Hey, Smith, you want a cup of coffee?" The idea sounded good to me. T. J. pulled from his briefcase a thermos and poured me a cup of coffee. We began to have coffee together under that oak tree almost like a ritual, sometimes before and sometimes after class.

At these meetings, I learned that T. J. was a French teacher in a segregated Black high school in Abilene, Texas. He was at the University of Texas to complete a degree and get a teaching certificate. I began comparing myself to T. J. I was chagrined that his vocabulary of English words far exceeded mine and that his pronunciation in French seemed flawless to me, a White boy, who even though I had had fourteen credit hours of college level French, still pronounced such phrases as "MUR-SEA BOW-COOO, MAY-MWA-ZELLE" with those long, flat, dipthonged Texas vowel sounds. I could see that T. J. seemed more sophisticated and more intelligent than I did. Sometimes T. J. talked about becoming "a great teacher," as if teaching were a special calling. I had never before heard anyone talk about teaching as T. J. did. He also said things that frightened me sometimes. He used phrases I had never heard before such as "the movement" and "freedom for the People."

In order to understand the importance of my encounter with T. J., one has to remember what it was like in 1959. Neither T. J. nor I were really supposed to be at the University of Texas—T. J. because he was Black and me because I was what some of the White fraternity boys called "White-trash." After all, I was not the son of a banker, a doctor, a lawyer, or some well-to-do business man. I was straight off the farm. I was so politically naive that it had not even occurred to me that the reason T. J. and I were drinking coffee from a thermos bottle was that there were no integrated cafes or lunch-counters where the two of us could sit down together in the Austin, Texas, of 1959.

One Friday night about midway through the semester, I was strolling by myself down Gaudelupe Street, known as "the drag" to college students in those days. As I passed the Longhorn Theater, a movie house, I noticed a strange phenomenon. The line of people in front of the Longhorn Theater stretched the entire length of the block, and I noticed the line was really a double line of partners, one Black and one White. Then I heard someone call out, "Pritchy, over here, over here!" I looked around to see T. J. standing in this unusual line of people. I walked over, and he asked, "Why don't you join us, Pritchy?" I asked in return, "What in the world are you doin'?" He retorted, "We're trying to integrate the theater, fool. This is how it works. You see, we stand in line in tandem, a Black and White, and tie up the line so that people who really want to see the movie give up and go on home instead of standing in line all night to get their tickets. When we get to the ticket window my White partner here asks if he and I can buy a ticket. Of course, the ticket seller always says no and we go back to the end of the line and start over. It's a kind of boycott. The theater owner is either going to have to integrate the theater or go broke."

T. J. asked again, "Pritchy, why don't you join us?" I faltered as I tried to speak. I stammered "I, uh, uh, I don't know. I don't think so. I uh." After all, at twenty-years old I had never in my life taken a public action against anything. I had never even stood up for myself when I had been done a wrong, much less ever stood up to or against authority that had done someone else a wrong. I remember clearly that in less than a second the expression on T. J.'s face changed. His smiling face became stoic and hard. His eyes transformed suddenly from the happy twinkle I had known to a piercing, cold, steely stare. With eyes of ice, he looked straight into my eyes and said, "Pritchy, if you are not in this line, you are in the wrong line." Then he looked away from me. I felt my scalp tighten. I felt chills run up my spine. I began to back away, almost stumbling from the impact of his words on me as I continued walking down the street. As I walked, his words kept ringing in my ears. I kept hearing over and over in my head, "Pritchy, if you are not in this line, you are in the wrong line." I thought about those words all weekend, again and again. I tried to understand what was happening inside me. I had no prior social context within which to place this experience. You have to remember that this was prior to Dr. Martin Luther King, Jr., and Montgomery and Selma.

On Monday, I started to class early. I had to see T. J. I went to the oak tree, but T. J. was not there. I went to class. T. J. was not in class. The next class day, T. J. was neither at the oak tree nor in class. A week passed. Then the following week, T. J. was seated in the classroom. Acting like nothing had happened the week before, I said "Hi, T. J. Let's have coffee after class." T. J. did not look at me. He did not speak. He looked past me with the same icy eyes I had seen on that Friday night in front of the theater. After class, without a word he walked past me and out the door. T. J. had cut me out of his world.

Another week passed, then I joined the boycott, an experience that was to affect me forever. Some bad things happened before the protest ended. For example, one night policemen leaped from trucks, swinging their nightsticks. I had never seen policemen swing nightsticks as they plunged into a panicked crowd, hitting men and women in their stomachs and heads. I was terrified by the shrieks and cries from the panicked crowd of protesters and even more terrified by the blood that was being splattered on me as the police hit people coming closer and closer to me where I was pinned by the crowd against the building. I could see that these uniformed men were not just trying to break-up a protest. They wanted to kill us. I was lucky that night. I survived without injury, but it was that night that I realized, for the first time, that police in those days were there to preserve a racist social order, not to protect protesters who were exercising their constitutional right to assemble peacefully.

T. J. and I worked hard that summer mimeographing and passing out flyers and always making certain we took our turn at the boycott down at the Longhorn Theater. At the end of that hot summer, in August, T. J. and I parted ways. T. J. had to return to Abilene to start a new school year, even though, as T. J. said, "Most of the kids at the Negro School will be picking cotton until the end of September." We met one last time under the oak tree. The Longhorn Theater was still segregated. We felt surrounded by the kind of sadness a person experiences when he tries as hard as he can but does not win, the sadness of an unachieved triumph. It was the feeling I think Langston Hughes must have been trying to capture when he wrote about "a dream deferred." As hard as we had tried, we felt like we had failed. We did not know at that moment that it would be nearly another year before the owner of the Longhorn Theater would stand before the crowd of protesters to announce that henceforth the doors of the theater would be open to all. It would be a great moment of triumph with the crowd cheering and tossing their caps and signs into the air—a moment of joy that T. J. would not be there to experience.

We had met at the oak tree to have one last cup of coffee and say good-bye, but we did not know how. When it became time for T. J. to leave, there was an awkward uneasy moment, as if both of us were groping for some words that would sound right—like so often happens when men "just don't know how to act." Then, T. J. broke the silence and said, "Smith, you're O.K. for a White boy. You're gonna be all right."

I stood there a good long while, watching T. J. grow smaller as he walked down the street toward the bus station. I remember feeling like something in the world had changed that summer—like I was not ever going to be the same again, like maybe I knew for the first time that people have a choice. They can stand in the wrong line. Or they can stand in the right line.

On that last day, there was no way I could have known that T. J., just five years later, would be killed in the Vietnam War. It was just a few years ago, in fact, that I found myself standing before the Vietnam Memorial in Washington, D.C., weeping almost uncontrollably as I touched my fingers to the letters of his name carved into the stone. The only words I could whisper aloud were "T. J., you did become a great teacher."

I learned many things from T. J. and our experience with the boycott. The most important thing, however, I learned was about myself. I learned that "I could not stand up as a man until I stood up, first, for someone else"; that "I would not become a man until I stood against injustice." It was this single lesson that would enable me later on in life to understand the full meaning of Martin Niemöller's passage about his inaction in Nazi Germany when he said:

First they came for the Jews and I did not speak out because I was not a Jew. Then they came for the communists and I did not speak out because I was not a communist. Then they came for the trade unionists and I did not speak out because I was not a trade unionist. Then they came for me, and there was nobody left to speak out for me.

The boycott experience taught me also to question this society. It also enabled me to begin to understand what James Baldwin (1963) was saying in his famous 1963 speech, "A Talk to Teachers," about empowering students not to settle for society as it is, and what Lerone Bennett, the African American historian, meant when he wrote that "an educator in a system of oppression is either a revolutionary or an oppressor" (as cited in Hale, 1978, p.7). It was my experience at the University of Texas that enabled me not to respond to James Baldwin and Lerone Bennett by calling them "radical" or "militant," but to respond, instead, by beginning to question the injustices in this society.

CULTURAL REJECTION

Upon completing my doctorate at North Texas State University, I took my first tenure-track teaching job at California State College in Pennsylvania in the midst of national turbulence. California State College was nestled in the Monongahela River valley in Southwestern Pennsylvania about fifty miles south of Pittsburgh. I was twenty-nine years old and it was 1969. America was in turmoil, caught in the throes of the civil right's era, an unpopular war in Southeast Asia, and perhaps the greatest youth rebellion America has ever experienced. If you were young, you could feel the excitement of change and hope in the air. The young were going to make America fulfill its promise of democracy! But America was divided—young versus old, liberal versus conservative, Black versus White, pacifists versus supporters of the Vietnam War.

The unrest in the larger society was beginning to be felt at California State College. I was one of about sixty new faculty members with doctorates that the college had recruited nationwide to prepare for a Middle-States accreditation review. A good many of the previously hired faculty had attended California State as undergraduates and earned only a master's degree or a doctorate at either the University of Pittsburgh or the University of West Virginia, both within fifty miles. Almost immediately a rift grew between the new and old faculty members. Prior to the arrival of the new faculty members, the campus had been a relatively quiet place. Many of the new faculty members had just earned their doctorates at institutions where campus protests were commonplace. Developing allies among a few faculty of the old guard who had similar views, the new faculty began to try to change policies and organize protests almost immediately.

My own conflicts with the community and the college began almost immediately. One conflict after another began to form what later became one long chain of cultural clashes over the seven years I worked at California State College. Upon arrival, I telephoned a realtor in Uniontown to help me locate a house to rent. At the end of an unsuccessful day of looking at rental properties, the realtor advised me to continue my search in person rather than by telephone. He said, "With that Southern accent of yours, I thought you were a nigger." Within the first week of arrival, the Uniontown School District was threatening to expel my six-year-old son for violating the dress code. His cowboy boots were "unorthodox dress."

Before I had completed the first academic year, I was evicted from the house I had rented. Located across the street from the Uniontown Hospital, the house was an older, charming two-story structure that had been the home of a prominent Uniontown family. The only son of the family, a local attorney, was leasing out his boyhood home for the first time since his parents had passed away. Across an alley that ran behind the backyard was a federally subsidized housing project where a number of children lived who became my son's friends. I built a treehouse in the backyard for my son and his friends. When we returned one weekend from our first trip to explore the countryside, the tree house lay on the ground in a pile of broken boards. I did not think much about the destroyed playhouse at the time. I assumed that perhaps some neighborhood vandals were responsible. I rebuilt the treehouse. The next weekend that my family and I were away, it was torn down again. When I asked the mother of one of my son's friends if she had seen any kids tearing down the treehouse, she said, "It wasn't kids. It was your landlord." I telephoned the landlord to ask why he had destroyed the treehouse. He said, "My family spent our entire lives keeping the nigger kids on their side of the fence. I'm not about to let them start playing in the yard now." The next week I received a notice of eviction in the mail.

Racism was at the heart of some of my conflicts on campus, too. I was extremely naive about racism in the North. One reason why I had chosen to teach in Pennsylvannia was that everything I had read in school textbooks and elsewhere had implied that racism was a Southern phenomenon and that racial attitudes were better in the mid-Atlantic and Northern states. I had looked forward to raising my family in a better racial environment than where I had been raised. How wrong I was.

I was naive enough to believe that all professors of education believed that teachers ought to be prepared to teach in inner-city schools. After all, the inner-city public schools of Pittsburgh were only an hour away from the California State College campus, and many of our students were already taking jobs there when they graduated. I wrote a proposal for an urban education program that consisted of six additional credit hours of course work on teaching in urban schools and a full-semester student teaching internship in the Pittsburgh inner city schools. The director of student teaching, who was well-respected among his peers nationally, made his objections known by screaming in my face, "I'll be damned if we are going to send our students over to Pittsburgh to teach those jungle bunnies!" I was shocked. I found it incredible that a man who enjoyed so much respect locally and nationally would make such a racist remark. I was dismayed again when I presented my proposal to the Teacher Education Curriculum Council. There was heated debate. When the anger subsided and votes were cast, my inner-city program hung in the grip of a tie vote. A tie vote required the chair of the council, the dean, to vote to break the tie. The room was silent as all eyes turned to the dean. He looked over his glasses down the long polished surface of the conference table with a stare that spoke, without a word, the message: "I dare anyone to question my decision." Without batting an eyelash, he said, "I vote yes." To this day, I admire him for courageously voting for his convictions.

The student population at California State College was extremely diverse compared to student populations I had taught elsewhere and enabled me to see whiteness in a different light. I was extremely provincial. I had not seen much of the world outside my birthplace. Diversity at San Angelo High School had been defined triculturally—White, Black, and Mexican American. As a teaching fellow and part-time instructor at North Texas State University, I had taught a primarily privileged middle-class White population, largely from the suburbs of Fort Worth and Dallas, although a few of my students had been African American and Mexican American who, more often than not, were also from middle-class backgrounds. Generally, except for the students of color, the students at North Texas State University identified themselves as White or Caucasian with moderately conservative values. Among the White students was a sizable minority with liberal social and political values. At California State College, however, I found a much more complex cultural diversity. The students were from over eighteen different ethnic groups, but the majority were from Southern and Eastern European heritages. Most were Italian, Greek, Polish, Yugoslavian, Croatian, and Serbian. A small percentage of students were English, French, or German. African American students constituted less than one percent of the students. Although most of the European American students saw themselves as White, most identified themselves by ethnic group. Generally, the students at California State College were from blue collar, working-class or lower middle-class backgrounds.

Teaching at California State College was an experience of mixed successes and failures. At times, I felt I was having almost no impact on changing the attitudes of White students toward diversity. Despite small triumphs here and there, I felt as if I were trying to bail the ocean dry with a bucket. For the first time in my life success did not seem proportional to effort. The harder I worked, the more attitudes seemed to remain the same. I had had no formal training in prejudice reduction and human relations theory throughout my master's and doctoral programs, but I had read and studied the theory and research in these fields on my own. I experimented with various approaches to prejudice reduction. I experimented with various ways to structure and sequence activities that were congruent with the principles of contact theory developed by Allport (1954). I tried an excellent new program designed specifically to prepare teachers to teach in inner-city schools. Designed by Scientific Research Associates, the program consisted of videos, a text, a series of activities and case studies, and a kit of cumulative folders on each student in an inner city classroom. Yet, at the end of each term, I felt that if I placed most of my students in a inner-city school they would have done more harm than good. In my eyes, most of the White students simply did not have the prerequisite attitudes and beliefs that would enable them to be successful in the all-Black schools in Pittsburgh.

With each new semester, a new group of primarily White students declared their interest in volunteering for the inner-city teacher education program I had designed. I began to doubt the extent to which a semester-length or even a two-year program could change students' negative attitudes toward children and adults of different races and ethnic groups. After all, I was asking people to re-create themselves and their belief systems in deep and fundamental ways that I had never before seen accomplished in a two-year program. In my own case, I knew that the small measure of progress I had made toward antiracism had taken my whole lifetime. I knew deep down from personal experience that attitude changes did not occur rapidly and that my expectations might be too high.

At the time, I felt more successful in my work with the African American students than with the White students. When I first arrived at California State in 1969, there were only about 50 African American students among the total population of almost 6,000 students. There were only two African American faculty members; seven years later there would be only four. As a result of the courses I was teaching, a group of African American students, including Ida Bell Minnie-Frizell, asked me to be the faculty sponsor of the Black League, a social and political student organization. Ida Bell, president of the organization, said that they needed help to plan activities that would retain Black students who were leaving at a faster rate than they were being recruited.

Knowing that I and the African American students had some reservations about a White faculty sponsor of the Black League, I accepted the invitation and began writing proposals. A proposal I wrote to the Kaufman Foundation resulted in funds to establish an African American Cultural Center in an off-campus house owned by the college and donated by the college president. The grant money enabled us to build a considerable library of Black literature, operate some recruitment activities, and host some speakers and seminars at the center. Members of the Black League helped me write a proposal for a series of mini-courses to be offered at the center, including one that enabled me to train recruitment teams who visited area high schools to encourage African American students to attend California State College. The president applauded our efforts and worked directly with me on a plan to staff the African American Cultural Center with graduate and workstudy students and to provide a college vehicle and gasoline expenses for the student recruitment teams. A third proposal written with the help of the Black faculty members was funded by the

Pennsylvania Department of Education to establish a counseling program that addressed Black students' problems in adjusting to the predominantly White campus. A fourth proposal for a summer Upward Bound program was also funded. At the end of a three-year period, we had increased the African American student population from 50 to 250.

Despite my growing sense of failure in my efforts to prepare teachers for inner-city schools, I did experience instances of success at California State College. Some students believed that my courses had made a difference in their lives. But they taught me far better than I taught them. I developed a deeper empathy for White students and their resistance to attitude changes and the ideas of multicultural education. My tolerance for White students who had racist attitudes grew. I began to understand their prejudices as the product of a larger local and national cultural context. I also began to see that the transformation from racism to antiracism was not a process likely to occur overnight. Like me, my White students who had internalized racism through a complex process of socialization were masters of their own journeys to becoming better people. Like me, some would transcend their present biases. Some would not.

By the sixth year of my tenure at California State College, growing resentment from some of my conservative colleagues, both faculty and mid-level administrators, became more than I could bear, particularly in combination with a growing sense that my failure with students seemed to far outweigh my successes. Although I did not perceive myself as such, some of these colleagues began to refer to me as "militant" and "radical." It seemed that some of the resentment was caused by success in my work with the African American students. Small acts of subterfuge began to occur. The fiscal officer let purchase orders on the grant monies accumulate, unprocessed for months. Anonymous letters sent to me from faculty members blamed me personally for inciting Black student protests and sit-ins, as if the Black students did not have minds of their own. A letter signed by "concerned faculty" was circulated on campus to complain that the African American students we were recruiting "were not college material." This comment was strange to me in light of the fact that large numbers of White students were enrolled in remedial English and mathematics courses at the college. Some of the language of these letters was racist and was meant to ridicule me as a White person who was working with Black students. One letter was addressed to "B'wana Smith." Another referred to me as "Doktari," the title of a television program in the 1970s about a medical doctor working in Africa.

In the beginning, small acts of harassment only strengthened my resolve to continue the work that I was enjoying. In fact, one of the things I learned during this period of my life is that resistance is important to the growth process. Eventually, the harassment intensified. Attacks on me and my work became more public, more personal, and more frequent. In the midst of a predominantly White student sit-in in the Administration Building, the dean of students, a person I counted among my friends, glared at me and said, "Smith, you're responsible for this demonstration." In truth, I hardly knew any of the students who occupied the building. Some of the multicultural education courses I taught were open as electives to non-teacher education students. In the building where the social sciences were housed, some unidentified faculty members began placing signs in the hallway warning students not to take "Smith's courses." The signs declared that my courses lacked substance and would not be counted even as electives in specified degree programs. Ironically, these signs were posted in the World Cultures Building.

During my sixth year, harassment peaked when a coalition of conservative faculty members brought before the Faculty Senate charges of "violating academic policy" against me, an art professor, and the dean of arts and sciences. We had allegedly violated a policy that stated that no student could register for courses after a specified date each semester. The art professor was accused of permitting a student to enroll in a one-credit hour independent study course. I was accused of signing a permission slip that enabled the same student to enroll after the deadline in a one-credit hour, three-week mini-course. The dean of arts and sciences was charged with violating the registration policy because he had approved both of the transactions. The Faculty Senate spent two of its monthly meetings discussing the charges, then requested we appear before the senate to explain our actions. I knew that there was more to this situation than appeared on the surface. After all, registering students after the deadline was a fairly common practice, particularly in situations where advisors discovered that a senior was short of the credit hours required for graduation.

After meeting with the dean of arts and sciences, the art professor and I decided to answer the charges against us at the next Faculty Senate meeting. I welcomed the chance to learn the names of the faculty members who had been hiding behind their anonymity until now. The dean of arts and sciences warned that we should understand that the charges were every bit as much an attack on us as an attempt to punish the student. This student had disrupted the dedication of the student union building by parading around the ceremony holding a sign that read "Fuck Censorship." He was protesting the admministration's removal of an art exhibit that contained nude paintings. At the Senate meeting, the art professor gave his explanation for enrolling the student in a course. I gave my explanation last. I declared that the real issue had little to do with a policy violation and that the real issue at hand was a witch hunt led by a small group of disgruntled conservative faculty members who wanted to punish the student, the art professor, and myself. To prove my point, I read a list of twenty-six cases of similar policy violations that term in which even some of the faculty members who had filed charges had enrolled students in courses after the enrollment deadline. I also read a letter of petition that had been signed by one of the leaders of the conservative faction to request the president to permit a student to graduate without the required number of hours. Afterwards, the senate was faced with either dealing with all of the other policy violations or dropping the charges. Instead, they did neither. They voted "not to accept our explanations."

For the first time, I realized that a group of my faculty colleagues did not merely disagree with my ideology. They despised me. I had seen the anger and hate in their eyes that night. I had witnessed their red-blotched faces trembling and heard the undertones of their words as they had tried to contain their anger in the public forum. After the senate adjourned, one of the faculty members whispered to me in the hallway, "Smith, we'll get you yet." I knew at that moment I would either have to work among colleagues who hated me or find an institution with a more hospitable environment.

My experiences at California State College for six academic years were an important part of my evolution as an antiracist, multicultural educator. At the end, I felt rejected by my own cultural group, particularly by conservative and racist Whites. In turn, I rejected them. I wanted no part of them. I did not want to be like them, nor did I want anyone else to think I was like them, particularly my friends and students of color. To me, my conservative and racist White colleagues at California State College were simply modern-day counterparts to those White ancestors who had established an elite, exclusive meritocracy that was founded on racism and privilege rather than on true democratic principles. I equated my colleagues with the same conservative mentality of those who, historically, had opposed teaching slaves to read and write, who had opposed and lobbied against Horace Mann's efforts to make free tax-supported elementary and secondary education a reality in the United States, and who had opposed the 19th Amendment and higher education for women. In my mind, my racist colleagues represented the modern-day thinking that paralleled the White racism that had enabled our ancestors to enslave Africans, to adopt a policy of genocide to rid the United States of Native Americans, and to incarcerate Japanese Americans during World War II. I saw them as the extension of the same conservatism that opposed racially integrated schools, PL 94–142, and the 1972 Title IX Education Amendment outlawing sex discrimination. In truth, my association of whiteness with conservatism and racism caused me to reject my European American cultural heritage. I knew that if I were to accept and resolve that aspect of my heritage that concerned the atrocities European Americans had committed against people of color, I would have to do so at some future time in my life.

CULTURAL IMMERSION

From 1975 to 1985, I worked as an administrator and professor at two historically Black colleges (HBCs). Three years were spent at Paul Quinn College, a liberal arts college affiliated with the African Methodist Episcopal (AME) Church. Seven years were spent at Jarvis Christian College, another liberal arts Black institution located in Hawkins, Texas. It is impossible to summarize in this brief treatise all of the significant aspects of this decade. Someday I hope to write the full story of this period of my life. It was not a period during which any one powerful critical incident occurred; instead, it was a period of time in which many less dramatic experiences merged to have as powerful an influence as did any of the previously described critical incidents. First, the decade I worked at HBCs was a period of almost complete immersion in African American culture, a culture very different from my own. Beyond the African American influences, the social and academic culture was different from any other that I had previously known. Never before had I found myself in the social position of "Other" to the extent I now found myself. Although I had experienced being an outsider in my own culture and although I had experienced the process of earning the respect from members of another culture, particularly of the African American students and faculty members of California State College, I had never before been "a minority" day in and day out. This experience was not like being the only White person at an African American social gathering for a single evening or day. Total immersion over time in another culture is a different experience altogether and is probably the closest that a White person can ever come to having life experiences similar to those that people of color have always had in the White-dominated society of the United States. It would be arrogant to suggest that my experiences were the same as those experienced by people of color, but total cultural immersion forced me to earn respect on my merits alone without the benefit of the unearned privilege of White skin. For the first time, affirmative action phrases such as "even playing field" and "uneven playing field" began to have real meaning at a deeper level of understanding. I can only describe this level of understanding as something somewhere in "my soul and bones." It is an understanding felt deep in consciousness rather than at some abstract level of intellectual understanding.

Working at HBCs provided an experience where I worked daily with individuals from other races and cultures who had talents, skills, and abilities that exceeded mine. At times, I was humbled by the vast array of talent and wisdom that surrounded me. I had long before accepted intellectually that talents, skills, and abilities were distributed widely across races and cultures on the planet, but I now believe it takes first-hand experience for some of us White folks to put asunder forever deeply conscious and unconscious notions of White superiority. I worked with a vast array of people who were greater orators, better speakers of other languages, better writers, better leaders, and better teachers than I could ever hope to be.

I learned at HBCs that it really is possible to have a truly multicultural faculty. At both HBCs where I worked, about half the faculty was African American and the other half was non-Black. Of the non-Black faculty, about half was European American and the other half Native American, Hispanic American, Asian American, and other cultural heritages. HBCs provided me with a model of what the faculty at predominantly White institutions ought to be. Later on when I would work again at a predominantly White institution, I would take the model of the ideal multicultural faculty with me as a guide to whatever influence I would have in selecting and hiring new faculty members and administrators.

Like T. J., my colleagues and my African American students were great teachers. I learned much from them. I learned from the students about their aspirations and dreams. I learned about what their parents expected from them. I learned enough to shatter forever the myth that "African American students are unmotivated and their parents don't value education," a myth believed by so many White educators I had known.

For the first time, too, I found that my ideas seemed to be accepted. The philosophical tenants and goals of multicultural education seemed to be accepted readily by my African American students and colleagues. Unlike most of the White students I had taught at California State College in Pennsylvania, my African American students did not argue against multicultural education. Instead of bracing myself daily for assaults on the ideas of multicultural education, I found myself looking forward to teaching and engaging in conversation about multicultural education at higher, more positive levels of dialogue than I had experienced with most of my White students at California State College. Unlike my White students, my African American students did not consider the ideas of multicultural education "radical" or "militant." To most of my African

American students, multicultural education was simply common sense, merely a set of self-evident truths. The existence of a system of White oppression was a given, documented by experience, to my African American students. Almost no one argued against the creation of a more fair, just society as the primary goal of education. Indeed, most of my African American students had witnessed firsthand the devastating effects of poverty on children. After the previous six years at California State College, where some of my colleagues resented and despised me and where most of my White students expended enormous amounts of bitter energy arguing against mulicultural education, teaching at HBCs felt like coming home. It was in the safe haven of HBCs that I was given a much needed reprieve from feeling hated by other White folks and from feeling the battle fatigue of what had seemed like six years of an exhausting, unwinnable war against the White power structure.

More importantly, the HBCs were places in which I was nurtured and re-educated by African American colleagues and students. For these privileges I remain thankful today. Much of the decade spent at HBCs was spent in self-reflection, synthesizing, and trying to make sense of what I had learned from experience. It was during this period that I came to the realization that I was well on my way toward a White multicultural identity. Of course, I knew that I was not and likely never would be a finished product. I understood that developing a multicultural identity and becoming a multicultural educator were processes without a known point of arrival. I also realized that no matter how comfortable I felt in the nurturing arms of Jarvis Christian College, the real problem of the larger society remained White racism. I knew I was ready to re-engage myself in the re-education of my fellow White Americans.

RE-ENTRY INTO THE WHITE WORLD

Since 1985, I have worked in the Division of Curriculum and Instruction at the University of North Florida in Jacksonville, Florida. Except for the first four years that I spent as division chair, my work at the university has consisted almost entirely of teaching courses in multicultural education to undergraduate, master's, and doctoral students. My work in scholarship and service has consisted primarily of publishing in the field of multicultural education, delivering keynote addresses at conferences, conducting in-service sessions and workshops in multicultural education at schools across the nation, and helping to found and develop the National Association for Multicultural Education (NAME). Like California State College, the University of North Florida is a predominantly White institution. In some ways, the university is progressive; in other ways, it is conservative and traditional. About 90% of my administrative and faculty colleagues are White, yet the university is the first of the predominantly White public institutions in Florida to have an African American president. A great deal of lip service is given to "diversity," but most faculty search committees result in the hiring of another White colleague.

Most of the students enrolled in my teacher education courses at the University of North Florida are White. Only three or four, about 10 to 15%, of every class of thirty are students of color. Most of my students are White females from low-middle or middle-class suburban or small town backgrounds who would prefer not to teach in inner-city schools. From my perspective as a multicultural educator, I do not believe most of my White students have the prerequisite attitudes or lifestyle patterns that would enable them to teach children who are different from themselves. Most of my students were socialized by their parents to live monolingual, monoracial, and monocultural lifestyles as the preferred norm. Not all of my students are racists, but too many are. My own harsh assessment is that about one-third of my White students are hard-core *intractable racists*. Another third of them I would classify as *moderate racists*, young people who are relatively unaware of their racism, who, in fact, are blind to their own racism and have not given much thought to their racial attitudes. Another 20% I would classify as *nonracists*, young people who might be described "as good kids who want to do the right thing" but are rather passive and quiet about their thoughts on race. Another 10 to 12%, perhaps three or four in every class, arrive in my classes as *antiracists*, young people who have the prerequisite belief system to become social reconstructionists. In short, my White students are very much like my generation was at their age. The most racist of my students, however, seem more outspoken than their counterparts of my generation, and they are much more sophisticated in describing their racism as "not being racism at all" but merely some form of beneficent conservatism.

I am happy in my current setting. My successes seem to outweigh my failures. My successes are seldom dramatic, but I do help some of my students clarify their cultural and racial identities. There exists no organized subterfuge or resentment from my colleagues to divert my psychic energy from the work I enjoy. The development of my own White racial identity has reached a sufficient level of maturity that I am better at translating other cultures to both White students and students of color than I was as a younger man. I still experience periods of frustration, but the sting of frustration is not as strong as it was years ago. I have noticed that these periods of frustration occur when I begin to assume that my students ought to be less racist than they are and more advanced in their development toward a multicultural lifestyle but having traveled a good portion of my own journey now, I am more empathetic than I used to be.

THE MEANING OF IT ALL

When I look back over my life to analyze my own progression toward becoming an antiracist, multicultural educator, I can see some distinct factors and critical incidents that had a profound impact on my development. I can also see some recurring patterns. Cutting across critical incidents and special periods of time and sequences of experiences are four recurring patterns that seem to characterize my development as an antiracist, multicultural educator: (1) establishing interracial and intercultural relationships, (2) experiencing a constructive form of guilt, (3) confronting resistance, and (4) having no White role models who were antiracists.

Throughout my entire life, I have had a tendency toward reaching out to establish interracial and intercultural relationships. I suppose this pattern began with the Johnson family, a Black neighbor, during my infancy and early childhood years. There must be some significance in the fact that I ran from my mother on a busy sidewalk to wrap myself around the leg of a Black man, a total stranger, when I was a small child. Despite the fact that there were few peers of a culture different from mine throughout the elementary and high school years, I befriended José, a Mexican American classmate, and at the University of Texas, T. J. and I became friends.

During the ten years I worked at HBCs, my closest male friends have been African Americans. Curious White people have often asked what these friendships were like in a tone of voice that implied they suspected we must have had nothing in common upon which to base a close friendship. My answer must have been disappointing because all I could say then and now is that we did "the things men do when they hang out together." We went fishing together, raked leaves together, barbecued, watched ball games, swapped lies and secrets, and watched out for each other, particularly in times of crises. We also introduced each other to our wider group of friends. Such occasions often meant that I was the only White person among a party of five or six African American men on a deep sea fishing trip or that my friend was the only African American at an otherwise all-White backyard barbecue.

These friendships led me eventually into experiences characteristic of the stage of development Banks (1992) refers to as biethnicity. Although I cannot pinpoint the precise moment, at some point in time when I was teaching at Paul Quinn College I became aware that I no longer felt like the "Other." I learned to play Bullshit, a verbal game often played at African American parties. I attended Black church services and functions and funerals. I met aunts and uncles, godparents, and other extended family members. My closest male friend at the time was Lester Clark. He enabled me to become as much of an insider in the Black community as perhaps a White person can become. He took me to places in Waco, Texas, where few White men were invited, or ever seen—backroom gambling parlors on Elm Street, soul food cafes, pool halls, and barbecue huts in No Man's Land. Wherever Lester took me, I met other African American men. In the beginning, my White presence caused tension. Sometimes Lester would ease the tension by saying, "Don't mind the White boy, he Black anyway." As I think back on these times, we were always aware of race. More often than not, Lester addressed me as "White boy." He would drop by my office and say, "Come on, White boy, let's go eat." One time I asked Lester what he thought it meant when he called me "White boy." Lester was taken aback for a minute and said, "I hadn't thought about it before but that's some heavy stuff." After thinking in silence for a moment, he said, "It means you are a White boy who thinks Black."

It is difficult to synthesize precisely what I think I have learned about myself and others from interracial relationships. I am convinced, however, that a person who has loved a person from a different race has lived a different kind of multicultural lifestyle and has had his or her world view shaped by different factors than the person who has not. First, I am convinced that honest interracial love can be a door to some kinds and levels of interracial knowledge that can never be understood or known by those who have not experienced it. Second, since interracial romantic relationships and marriages remain largely taboo in the United States, people involved in such relationships tend to experience both the best and the worst aspects of tolerance and bigotry in their own and their partners' cultural groups. These types of experiences are somewhat unique to interracial couples and often have a powerful influence on their perceptions. My own interracial relationships, no doubt, influenced my youngest son who is married to an African American woman. The prospect of having grandchildren who will be called "mixed race" children in this society has clarified more clearly for me my expectations regarding a more fair, just, and bigotry-free world. I am adamant that my grandchildren shall not be mistreated or relegated to second-class citizenship; thus, my resolve to continue as an antiracist, multicultural educator has been strengthened. If anything, the prospect of having biracial grandchildren has made me even more inflexible regarding bigoted and racist preservice teachers who are in my teacher education courses.

A second recurring pattern throughout my development has been the experience of a constructive form of guilt. I am not writing here about the counterproductive, neurotic form of guilt that becomes an unnecessary obsession. The kind of guilt to which I am referring motivates individuals to become better people than they perceive themselves to be. This form of guilt is somewhat akin to the guilt described by Maslow (1970) that is experienced when one feels remorseful about personal shortcomings related to humankind's inhumanity to each other. Simply put, my conscience bothered me when I fell short of doing the right thing. I remember experiencing this feeling of guilt when I did not speak out on behalf of José to my racist friends in high school and when I did not have the courage to accept T. J.'s invitation to stand in the line to boycott the segregated Longhorn Theatre. Furthermore, not only have I experienced this feeling of guilt periodically over my lifetime, I continue today to rely on it to guide my behavior. With respect to racism and other forms of bigotry, I have learned that I will feel much better about myself if I follow my conscience rather than conform to the dictates of my peers. From my own experience, I presently believe that constructive guilt is a necessary motivational factor in the process of changing racist attitudes. A racist who feels no remorse about his or her attitudes and behaviors is not likely to be reformed through human relations and diversity training or university courses. To my knowledge, the research literature on the role of conscience and guilt in changing racist attitudes is almost nonexistent and, therefore, should be a fertile area of research.

A third recurring pattern evident in my growth toward becoming an antiracist and multicultural educator has been confronting almost continuous resistance. Actually, there seemed to be an ebb and flow to this pattern that often involved, first, my working toward a less racist society and, second, coping with reactions against my efforts by pulling back. Resistance constituted a challenge against which I would press. On the positive side, resistance seems necessary to the growth of a social activist. That is, resistance constitutes a challenge to the boundaries of one's ego strength. The social activist presses progressively forward inch by inch against resistance, stretching the elastic boundaries of his or her ego strength. Even when forced to retreat, the boundaries of ego strength seldom snap back to where they were before. The boundaries of ego strength seem to stretch and enlarge slightly with each effort. Of course, there are times that resistance can be too extreme, as was the case when I was teaching at California State College, but even so, it seemed a necessary prelude to the period of reflection that followed while I was working at HBCs. Turning inward during this period of reflection contributed to my growth.

A fourth pattern characteristic of my development has been the almost complete absence of White antiracist mentors and role models in my immediate environment. There were, of course, White individuals whom I would classify as nonracists and White individuals who were supportive of my efforts, but none were antiracist activists. This absence of White antiracist role models has had several consequences for my generation. Without much help from members of our own race and culture, we had to chart our own journey. For some of us, it was a lonely journey. The most serious consequence, however, was a delayed acceptance of our own cultural heritage. (See chapter 4, in this volume, for a discussion of the history of White antiracist activism.)

If I am honest, I suspect that there are a good many contemporary European Americans who have achieved a reasonably high level of antiracist activism without ever coming to terms with the worst aspects of their cultural heritage. I believe I am such a person. I am of a generation that studied during their formative public school years a curriculum that suppressed any information about the crimes against humanity committed by our forebearers. The curriculum enabled us blissfully to believe European Americans were the good folks that all the rest of the world should emulate. Not until the 1960s and 1970s, when we saw people on television who looked like us beating African American civil rights workers and napalming women and children during the Vietnam war were we forced to confront the inhumane side of our heritage. This dramatic period of history enabled many of us to reject rather than embrace our European American culture and identify with cultural groups and individuals who opposed and even fought oppression in the streets. Some of our new identification figures were people of color. A few were European Americans. The important point I am trying to make here is that many of us were enabled rather easily to become antiracists without ever coming to terms with the negative dimensions of our cultural heritage by simply rejecting our cultural heritage. Many of us, in fact, believed that we *should* reject our cultural heritage and that our true purpose was to create a new culture, one that was multicultural, multiracial, and free of bigotry. Once again, my generation of European Americans were able to "forget about the past" by denying, suppressing, or rejecting it. To some extent, we robbed ourselves of the rich opportunities for growth that could have resulted from coming to terms with the distasteful aspects of our cultural roots.

Theoreticians suggest that there are loosely sequenced stages characteristic of the healthiest path toward developing an integrated ethnic, cultural, or racial identity that ultimately leads to becoming multicultural and committed to social justice activism. For example, in the six stages of ethnicity developed by Banks (1992), Stage 3, Ethnic Identity Clarification, is described as one in which "the individual is able to accept and understand both the positive and negative attributes of his or her ethnic group" (p. 96). Similarly, to reach the stage of Autonomy, the highest, healthiest stage of White racial identity development, Helms (1994) emphasizes that White children must have opportunities to grapple with the moral issues and dilemmas imbedded in European American culture and must become aware not only that they can choose the kind of White person they will be, but also that they can construct a personal White identity from those aspects of White culture that feel morally right. I know of no theoretical model of healthy identity development that advocates avoidance of confronting the negative aspects of one's own culture, yet, I believe many of us, particularly myself, somehow arrived at an antiracist stage of commitment to social justice without appropriately dealing with the most vile, hateful aspects of our cultural history. Some of us either worked through the process of coming to terms with our negative cultural history later on, or we are still engaged in this complex process.

THE FUTURE

Because I teach courses in multicultural education to educators, I see the development of my own identity as being intertwined with that of my students. With respect to my own development, I have gone back to work through coming to terms with the negative aspects of White history and culture, particularly the ancestral legacy of European American violence against people of color. Part of this process has been to re-educate myself by reading almost everything I can that presents a more authentic heritage than the propagandized history I studied in my formal education. This process has been painful at times but also liberating. It has been painful to learn that European American dominance, racism, discrimination, and violence were actually worse than I had imagined. It has also been painful to learn the extent of the lies taught to me in school about my White heritage, but it has been liberating to discover that there were European Americans in every period of history who fought against the mistreatment of fellow human beings. What is sad about my personal journey is that it took so many years, most of a lifetime, for me to discover that to be White does not have to mean that one is a racist. There is an alternative White identity one can have. I understand now that an antiracist, multicultural White identity is an authentic identity also, one that has been legitimized by historical precedent. It very well may be that an antiracist, multicultural White identity is the only authentic, psychologically healthy identity that White people can have. Other forms of White racial identity may simply be pathological.

I see my role in the future as continuing on the same path I began many years ago. The pace is different, however. I am no longer racing down the path to find myself or to change others overnight. The pace is slower, more rhythmic. I no longer believe that a healthy racial identity can be taught in the classroom. The development of a healthy racial or ethnic identity is a long-term process of self-discovery. Classroom instruction can only provide some experiences that may help White students and students of color clarify the differences between a healthy and a pathological racial/ethnic identity, but students must construct their own identities. They must live their lives and make their own choices.

It is not easy for a young person to develop an antiracist, multicultural perspective in a racist society. One of the almost universally difficult things with which European American students must cope on their journey toward antiracism is the historical record of atrocities Europeans and European Americans committed against people of color. Some cope by directing their anger toward the curriculum or the teachers who reveal the truth about historical and present-day atrocities. Some use denial. Some exclaim that they "are not responsible for the past." Some want to forget about the past and "move on." Others choose not to identify with those European American "heroes and heroines" who committed acts of hatred against others. Unfortunately, most history and other school textbooks do not provide alternative European American role models. Thus, the next frontier of historical scholarship must be to uncover the forgotten European Americans who fought alongside people of color and other oppressed groups to achieve higher levels of democracy and equality in the U.S. society. To work through the most immoral aspects of ancestral history, European American students will need to be able to identify with same-race heroes and heroines like Andrew Goodman, Mickey Schwerner, James Reeb, and Viola Liuzzo. After all, European Americans who search for nobility in their cultural heritage find it difficult to admire either the individuals or cultural group who were responsible for the U.S. government policy of genocide in the treatment of the First Americans, the enslavement of people of African descent, the Chinese Exclusion Act, the internment of Japanese Americans and seizure of their property during World War II, and an almost continuous resistance to civil rights for people of color in the United States. Although there were always some European Americans who fought against racism and the maltreatment of fellow human beings, we know little about them as individuals or as a group. This missing part of White history and culture must be found and taught to future generations. Young European Americans in particular will need a new set of historical role models to admire if they are to cope and come to terms with the historical atrocities committed by so many of their ancestral heroes and heroines.

In addition to presenting a more authentic, truthful history of our multicultural heritage, I see my most important instructional role as that of modeling an antiracist lifestyle. I believe that what I teach may not be nearly as powerful as what I model. Long after my teacher education students have forgotten the specific facts, the formal theories, and the bodies of research on racism and multicultural education, what they are likely to remember most of all is how I lived my life. I must model a multicultural and multiracial lifestyle. It is important for my students to see me engaged in interracial friendships. It is important for my students to see that I not only believe that a racially integrated education is superior to a segregated education but that I actually sent my children to integrated schools. I do not want my students to see me merely as a nonracist, but I want them to see me as antiracist, actively engaged in my community fighting racism and other forms of bigotry. Modeling moral courage is the only way I know that I can make an authentic contribution to the development of my students.

12

Building Blocks: My Journey Toward White Racial Awareness

Patti DeRosa

When the call came, in 1996, it was hard for me to contain my excitement. A student from my alma mater had heard about my antiracism work and called to invite me to be part of the "Forming Cross-Cultural Alliances" weekend at the State University of New York in Oneonta, where I had graduated from in 1979.[1] This young Latina woman was instrumental in organizing a weekend of events, with the goal of opening a dialogue about racism on campus in this small, mostly White town in upstate New York where tensions had been building since the infamous "Blacklist Incident" of 1992.[2] I eagerly accepted the invitation and anxiously looked forward to the opportunity to return to the undergraduate school that had been the site of some of my most profound learning about racism.

Although racism has an alarming capacity to mutate to new forms and new circumstances, it tends to retain its core elements, basically remaining the same poison but packaged in new bottles (Seldon, 1992; Batts, 1989). Students today may have more inter-racial contact than I did; they may have more friends from different racial backgrounds; see more people of color on TV; listen to more music from a variety of cultural styles; and see more people of color in positions of power and influence. Yet, most of that is illusion, a smokescreen that hides the continuing realities of racism in America. Angela Davis (1996) has observed that "The vast changes mask the reality of the continuity of racism . . . The fact that we can witness the end of racism in mass popular culture does not alter the reality of racism in the real world . . . We tend to recognize racism only when it rears its head in old forms . . . Racism still wears the old garb but has learned to clothe itself in more contemporary apparel" (p. 127). The superficial multiculturalism of popular culture has a direct relationship to the resistance to antiracism activism, affirmative action, and multicultural education that we see among some White people today. Swayed by the current hype, many White people believe not only that the fight against racism has been won, but that it is white people who are now at a racial disadvantage. For example, a 1995 survey found that 58% of Whites think that most Black people have better jobs than most White people. Fifty-six percent think that Black people are better off in education and 41% think that Black people make more money that White people. The reality is that only 17% of Black women are officials, managers, professionals, and technicians, compared with 32% of White women; Black college graduates make only 76% of the money of White male college graduates; and the average Black family makes only 59% of the money the average White family makes (Brodie, 1995; Jackson, 1995).

The need for accurate information about racism is urgent and immediate, and the task is huge. White people often have very strong feelings about issues of race. At the same time, they have very little accurate information that informs those feelings, yet they think of themselves as well informed. With little accurate knowledge of the history of oppression in the United States, no concept of institutional racism, minimal contact with the realities faced by most people of color, and no insight into White racial advantage, it is understandably difficult for many White people to make sense of the need for the continued struggle for racial justice. The recent trend of manipulating the language of the civil rights struggle in order to dismantle and undermine racial justice, such as the attacks on affirmative action, create even greater confusion, for example, California's Proposition 209.

GROWING UP

I am a forty-one-year-old White, Italian American woman, who was raised Catholic, middle class, and heterosexual. I grew up in New York and Florida and currently live, at this writing, in Randolph, Massachusetts, a suburb south of Boston. I was born in 1957, which means that my formative years were the 1960s and 1970s. These were times filled with enormous pressures for social change: the civil rights movement, the Vietnam War, women's liberation, the sit-ins, the demonstrations, the "riots." Social change was everywhere, and while some may have remained untouched, my worldview was profoundly changed by it all. Yet I was still in elementary school when the mass marches of the civil rights movement occurred. I was too young to participate in many ways but not too young to be deeply and permanently affected. I am also aware that most of my recollections of and early learnings about racism are based on racism as it relates to African Americans and Whites. In the 1960s and 1970s, the experiences of Latinos, Asians, and Native Americans were not yet a part of my consciousness in any substantial way. This was the background from which I began to think about what racism means to me as a White person in a racist society.

I grew up in a fairly "typical" middle class family on Long Island, New York, for the first fourteen years of my life. That's not totally accurate—I actually was born in Brooklyn, in Bensonhurst to be exact, and my parents were part of the exodus of White folks who were new entrants to the middle class. We moved to the suburbs in the 1950s chasing the "American Dream." When I shared an earlier draft of this chapter with my mother, she was able to fill in a significant piece of family history. She told me that she and my father did not initially want to move to Long Island. They first looked in Bensonhurst but quickly discovered that the homes there were more expensive than they could afford. It was only then that they decided to explore Long Island, which was aggressively marketing to young White couples to fuel the housing boom of the 1950s (many developments included restrictive covenants that excluded Blacks and Jews). Prior to purchasing my childhood home, she and my father had seen a house in another Long Island town that she loved. Seeing her enthusiasm, the real estate agent spoke with my father privately and warned, "Are you aware that there are Blacks living on either side of that house? You better reconsider, because I see your wife is really set on this house." When my father shared this conversation with my mother, she remembers her response, "So what?" My father then got quiet and said, "Maybe we ought to keep looking." She said that she does not recall fighting him on the issue, and that was the end of the discussion. They eventually purchased a house in Franklin Square, where I grew up.

It is significant that I almost forgot to include this, for in many ways, that simple act was the beginning of my "White education." One of the ways that White racism works is by inducing a kind of historical amnesia, conveniently forgetting the ways we get access to privilege and benefits and denying what our motivations were to begin with.

I rarely heard overtly racist statements in my home, although I have no doubt that I received a million implicit messages. The few times I did hear the overt variety, they came during occasional visits of particular relatives or friends of the family or from my father who would from time to time throw out a flippant comment to provoke me to respond with righteous outrage, which I did with predictable consistency. I learned racism in much more subtle, hidden, and indirect ways. Lillian Smith highlights this in her classic book, *Killers of the Dream* (1961), when she says: "This process of learning was different for each child as were his parents' vocabulary and emotional needs. We cannot wisely forget this. And we learned more from acts than words, more from a raised eyebrow, a joke, a shocked voice, a withdrawing movement of the body, a long silence, than from long sentences" (p. 90).

It seemed to me that the adults around me never gave me accurate information about race and racism, although I now understand that they did the best that they could given the misinformation they too had received. Questions about these topics seemed to generate nervousness and tension, similar to the way many adults act when children ask about sex—full of caution and anxiety. Other times, the answers were simplistic: They said things such as, "Everyone is the same" and "All people are equal." These kinds of answers did not explain the madness that I saw happening all around me, and I started to feel that if the grown folks were not telling me something, then it must be *very* important indeed. I made it my business to find out what it was—but that comes a bit later.

My Long Island neighborhood was multicultural but not multiracial. There were a variety of White Europeans in my community but no people of color. Italians and Jews were the two largest groups, and I thought that was true for most other places as well. I now realize that this experience was regionally limited and not reflective of the reality of the rest of the country. There were few White Anglo Saxon Protestants in my environment, and I thought of them as a small minority group. I most certainly did not think of them as a powerful majority running society. Although I consciously remember conversations with an Italian girlfriend in which we said we thought the Anglo kids were kind of "boring," I also recall how we were already becoming aware of the benefits and privileges accrued to this group.

As early as elementary school, my dark-haired girlfriends and I discussed how the boys seemed to think any girl with blonde hair was pretty, just because she *was* blonde. Like Whoopi Goldberg in one of her famous skits, I, too, used to play "make-believe" by putting a long white slip on my head pretending to have long silky blonde hair rather than the coarse, curly dark hair that I did have. The pressures for assimilation were clearly not the same for me and young African American girls. Yet at the same time, there are enough similarities in the process for Goldberg's portrayal to resonate with me. The similarities and differences of these two experiences hold much potential for exploration between African American and Italian American women. At six years old, I remember wanting to change my name to "Alice," as in "Alice in Wonderland," so I could be more like that idealized image of Nordic beauty—blonde, blue-eyed, small-nosed. I was already beginning to internalize standards of White supremacist beauty that had little room for even my Italian American self.

I remember being aware of race from a very young age. My earliest recollection is of going shopping with my mother in a department store in Hempstead, the county seat and a town with a large Black population, when I was four or five years old. I was carrying my favorite Thumbalina doll, when a little Black girl about the same age as myself approached me and pulled on my doll's arm. I recoiled and hid behind my mother. I am not sure if I was afraid because she was Black, because she was some strange kid grabbing my doll, or both. What I do remember is my mother's response. She said calmly, gently, and immediately, "Don't worry, Patti. The little girl just wants to play with you." That was all the encouragement I needed, and the little girl and I went off to play, hiding under the clothes racks until our mothers had to pull us away from each other. My mother's response was echoed years later when I first dated a Black man. All she said was, "I'm not sure how I feel about this, but I guess I'm going to find out if I really believe everything I tried to teach you." Her modeling of owning her feelings and holding herself accountable for her own racism has been an inspiration to me.

When I was around eleven years old, a business colleague of my father's was invited to our home for dinner. Mr. Fox was from the South, and my father warned us that he might say some things that were "upsetting." I am sure he never mentioned the word "racist," but like all good white folks, he was talking in racial code and we knew how to decipher it. I'll never forget that night at dinner when Mr. Fox said with a big smile on his face, "There's nothing cuter than a little pickaninny. The only problem is that they grow up to be Nigras!" Then he laughed out loud. My face flushed, and I opened my mouth to speak, but my mother firmly squeezed my hand under the table and gave me a pained but instructional look to keep quiet. I hated that man at that moment, and I was disappointed in my parents. Why did they let him come here? Why didn't they stop him? Why did I have to be quiet? Was a business deal that important? I am reminded of another passage from *Killers of the Dream* (1961) in which Smith describes her reaction as a child witnessing her parents' collusion with racism: "I knew my father and mother whom I passionately admired had betrayed something which they held dear. And they could not help doing it. And I was ashamed by their failure and frightened, for I felt they were no longer as powerful as I had thought. There was something Out There that was stronger than they and I could not bear to believe it" (p. 96). Facing the contradictions between values and behavior was to become a driving force for me.

My internal struggles with prejudice and racism spilled over onto my elementary school playground. A little boy insisted on telling me that his father told him about "all those Black people in the city" and how terrible they were. I intuitively fought back, saying that was unfair and wrong. He then challenged me by saying, "What makes you think you're right? How do you know? Do you know any Black people?" I had to admit that I did not know any Black people at all, and for a moment I remember thinking, "Well, maybe he *is* right. How *do* I know I'm right? I never really met any Black people." Still, something deep inside me rejected his logic. I went home and wrote in my journal "Prejudice is stupid. Anyone with half a brain can see that it doesn't make any sense!" A year or so later, my seventh grade English teacher gave us an assignment to write a poem in fable form, with a moral. I wrote this poem in 1969; it is the only piece of school work I kept from my elementary and high school years:

The Mutt and the Pedigree

One day walking down the street a pedigree and a mutt did meet
And as they walked they began to talk about their masters and things.
"My master," said the pedigree, "likes civil rights and being free.
He never speaks directly to me, but I listen in, of course."
Then as the mutt began to speak,
The pedigree's master came down the street
He pushed the little mutt away and said,
"Go away now and stay away!"
The little mutt was now confused,
The master's behavior could not be excused.
"If his master is so much for being free,
Why must I be a pedigree?"
Moral: People can accept change until it affects them.

I include this poem because I feel that its child's voice speaks to something that was gnawing deep inside of me: the hypocrisy of espousing one set of racial values while living by another. Is this not the classic American dilemma (see L. Thompson, 1996)? Bold pronouncements of liberty and justice for all, while simultaneously engaging in slavery, genocide, oppression, and "crimes that would disgrace a nation of savages" (Douglas, 1972, p. 104)—these contradictions never made sense to me. I never enjoyed *Tarzan*, war, or "cowboy" movies as a kid, though I could not have articulated what made me feel so uncomfortable about them at the time. It was a *feeling* that I viscerally felt but could not yet name. By the time I was in seventh grade, I recited the Pledge of Allegiance with the final line altered to "with liberty and justice for *some*."

Virtually all of my contact with people of color was via the media. I was aware that African American, Latino, Asian, and Native American people existed, but for some reason that I did not understand, they did not live in my neighborhood or go to my school (except for the occasional Black, Latina/o, or Asian family that would move in for a year or so and then suddenly disappear). I believe that this is still true for many White suburban young people. My junior high school Social Studies teacher told us that the Ku Klux Klan had burned a cross in the next town a few years back when a Black family tried to move in, and I wondered how that could have happened here in the North, in New York. After all, were not all those racists supposed to be down South?

It would be easy to say that I did not know anything about racism until I met people of color but that would be a lie. I now understand that my all-White neighborhood was one of my first lessons about racism. It wasn't an accident that there were so few people of color in my school, and none in my neighborhood. There was very purposeful segregation going on: Real estate agencies steering Black people away from the neighborhood; school boards dividing up our school districts to keep them all White or all Black; and a school curriculum that taught me about the world through European eyes, even as it spoke about concepts of brotherhood and civil rights. All this was happening, but I remained unaware and thought of myself as open-minded and unprejudiced. My racial isolation allowed me to believe this myth about myself.

Going South

I soon had a chance to check out my theory about Southern racism when, in 1971, my father's job moved my family south to Hollywood, Florida. My new community was mostly transplanted Northeasterners, many of whom I suspect left to avoid not only the cold but the increasing racial diversity of the Northern cities. My neighborhood was still all White, but we were now one of only a few Italian families in a predominately Jewish community.

My new school in Florida had been recently desegregated. This was a new experience for me and my family, but if my parents had any anxieties about it, they never expressed them to me. Since it is likely that they did indeed have some anxieties, I have to wonder about their silence and our inability to communicate about it. I remember approaching the situation as an adventure and being excited about meeting so many new and different kids. I was an outgoing adolescent, extremely verbal, mature for my age both physically and socially, and I made friends easily. Many of my new White friends were from places like New York City and Brooklyn. They had had a lot of inter-racial contact, and much of it had not been positive. They were somewhat jaded, cynical, and fearful, and they warned me not to walk down the school hallways where Black students congregated. I thought they were paranoid.

My racial naiveté may have worked to my advantage in my new environment, as racial isolation can work in strange ways. For better or worse, I had very limited contact with people of color, and I was less fearful than curious about people different from myself. I just ventured out boldly into the unknown. I quickly found out that I was breaking some unwritten rules that I did not understand, from both Blacks and Whites. White folks told me to "be careful" (of what they never said directly) and scolded me for being "too friendly" with "them." Black folks introduced me to their inner circle by saying I was "different" from the other White kids. Everyone was so new to me that I found it hard to keep names and faces straight. When I continually confused the names and faces of White kids who in reality looked nothing alike at all, I remember consciously realizing that the old racist saying "they all look alike" was actually a statement about social distance, unfamiliarity, and fear of the unknown.

Florida was no racial utopia by any means. Friendship groups were by and large rigidly segregated, as were the neighborhoods and the job market. I observed that the White school administrators clearly came down harder on Black students, and one of the deans actively lived up to her name—"Dixie." I experienced inter-racial friendship for the first time, yet those friendships rarely crossed the line outside of school time. In this environment, I experienced more challenges to racism than I ever had before through the Black adults and young people I built relationships with, but I was also privy to more blatant racism than I had ever witnessed before either, such as the White man in my neighborhood who proudly told my mother and I that he trained his dogs to attack Black people. My mom told him he was disgusting and promptly changed the subject.

It was in this environment that I began to see the rituals of racial oppression firsthand. In biology class, a young Black girl offered me some of her "Screaming Yellow Zonkers," a popcorn-like snack food, but before I could respond, she lowered her eyes and said softly, "Oh! I'm sorry . . . you might not want to eat from my box." My favorite teacher was an African American man who was the first Black adult role model in my life. He gave me a ride home from school one day, only to stop his car a block from my house to ask if it was all right to drive me to my door, or if I preferred that he drop me off a block away. My racial consciousness at the time was extremely limited, yet intuitively, I knew that there was something very wrong in these interactions. I ate the popcorn and asked my teacher to drop me off at my home to demonstrate my alliance, as well as to reaffirm my own self-image as "nonracist." Other experiences, however, severely tested that image of myself.

I learned about Black pride and my own racism from a Black male friend who was the first person who befriended me on my first day in my new school. I once used the term "boy" in referring to him in a conversation—not in the racist usage, but descriptively, as we were, after all, only fifteen years old. He cut me off mid-sentence and in a tone of voice that demanded attention and respect said, "I'm not a boy, I'm a man." An awkward silence followed, and I learned an important lesson about the assertion of racial dignity. This incident taught me the power of how words can wound and that we bear the weight of their history and legacy regardless of our intent. My relationship with this young man was the first time I remember having to seriously confront the hypocrisy of my own racism. Although we were crazy about each other and secretly admitted our feelings, it was I, not he, who did not yet have the courage to publicly acknowledge them.

This is another example of how the recurring theme of anger, pain, and shame at collusion with racism—my own, as well as those of other White people—has pushed me in my own growth. My professed values and my actual behaviors were out of sinc and seeing myself betray my own ideals, and betray my friend, was unbearable.

"ANYWHERE SOUTH OF THE CANADIAN BORDER"[3]

Due to my parents separation, my stay in Florida was a brief two and a half years, but it was transformational in many ways. In 1973, my mother and I returned to the same community in New York that we had left. I returned to the same school and the same friends, but I was not the same person. I had a new set of eyes and ears, and everything seemed different. When I left in 1971, my primary interests were cheerleading and football games. When I returned, I was focused on playing guitar, writing songs, and working for social justice. My social studies teacher even approached me one day and asked me if I was on drugs because I did not seem interested in the same old things anymore! I remember thinking, "He's got to be kidding! There's racism and poverty and war, and he's worried about the football team?"

Here I was back in "liberal" New York where I heard endless platitudes about "racial tolerance" and "those racists" who were always other people but not "us" (even as my schoolmates mocked the all-Black basketball team who came to our school with racist insults). My racial identity at this point was in that "I'm not a racist" stage (B. Thompson, 1996b; see also, Hardiman, 1982; Helms, 1990a). My racism was of the "color blind" variety. I pretended not to notice color, while simultaneously being extremely aware of it. I used to say, "The only people I'm prejudiced against are people who are prejudiced." I carried feelings of guilt and shame, and I had little insight into my own biases and prejudices and no understanding of institutional racism. Yet, something kept pushing me on to explore further.

I gradually began to have the realization that overt prejudice and bigotry were only one part of the picture—and not quite enough to explain the gross inequalities that I saw in this country. Something bigger was going on that I needed to understand. By the time I got to the State University of New York at Oneonta in September 1975, I was more than ready. I was hungry for new information and explanations to help me make sense of the nonsense.

THE LESSONS

It was amazing to me how many memories came flooding back to me as I tried to prepare my campus talk. I could write a volume on just the isolated stories that came to mind, seemingly unrelated, but deeply tied together in my racial consciousness. I share some of them here to try to create a picture of the early years of my racial development. So often it is assumed that White antiracist activists are all children of activists who were brought from demonstration to demonstration in infancy and learned to talk by debating the revolution. That just was not the case for me. What stands out to me more is how "ordinary," in that White "Ozzie and Harriet-with-an-Italian-flair" kind of way, that my upbringing was in regards to racism. Most profound is the recurring theme of my preoccupation with unraveling the continual contradictions—the verbal messages about equality contrasted with the overwhelming whiteness of my world.

After hours of reflecting on my early experiences, I realized I had not written a word of my speech. There was so much on my mind and limited time. How could I frame this in a talk to the students? How could I take the most significant learnings and concisely share them in a way that was meaningful? I decided to present my thoughts as a series of lessons I had learned right there on that campus by weaving together personal stories and relating them to the political realities of racism in America. It is only in hindsight that I have come to understand the lessons of these stories. I could not make sense of them or know their power at the time I first experienced them. The lessons that crystallized at Oneonta became fundamental to my later antiracist activism and have become the focus and passion of my life's work. I hoped that in sharing my lessons they might help others, as well as reaffirm that learning for myself. These are the lessons I shared with my audience that evening.

Lesson #1: The Invisible Power of Privilege and Institutional Racism

My first lesson became apparent to me as I focused on my feelings about returning to Oneonta. Oneonta is a place of wonderful memories for me, of learning about life, and love, and sexuality, and friendship, and music, and growing up, and oh yes, academic learning too! It feels familiar, comfortable, friendly, inviting, a home. My identity as a White, middle-class, Catholic-raised, heterosexual female from Long Island informed and structured my sense of belonging there in the 1970s, as well as when I returned in 1996. My whiteness had everything to do with why I felt Oneonta was my space and why I could claim it so easily. Therefore, my first lesson is about the invisible power of privilege.

As these thoughts came to mind, I remembered a talk I heard in 1995 by Lani Guinier, who President Bill Clinton nominated for a top civil rights position and then withdrew the nomination, caving into pressure from conservatives who dubbed her "the Quota Queen." She spoke of returning to speak at her law school alma mater of Yale and hearing her male colleagues, who shared the panel with her, speak of how they felt to return "home," with fondly remembered stories about their law school years. She, however, had a different experience. She went right in to her formal remarks, sharing no personal stories. She said "a profound sense of alienation and isolation caught in my throat every time I opened my mouth." The huge portraits of White men that adorned the walls of the room and her recollection of a professor who opened his class each day with a greeting of "Good morning, gentlemen," despite the women present in the class, reminded her that this place was not home and was not safe (Guinier, 1994). The stark contrast between her experience and mine highlighted my privilege for me in a new way.

What do I mean by privilege? I am thinking of all the things we never have to think about if we are members of dominant or "preferred" groups in society. The privileges of this status remain invisible because we are seen as the norm; we are held to be the standard; we are affirmed, and our identity and experience is reflected back to us in a myriad of ways. For example, if when describing the color of a Band-aid, the first impulse is to say "flesh-tone," then we must consider that the flesh the term "flesh-tone" refers to is White flesh by implication. In this way, a simple piece of pinkish plastic reflects back to White people that we are the norm and demonstrates one way that White privilege manifests itself (see McIntosh, 1989).

This was a critical lesson for me to understand because it moved me from thinking of racism as only a set of hateful ideas about people who may be different from me to include the concept of White privilege and institutional power. When I made this shift, I began to see how oppression is not solely personal attitudes and behaviors, but also an institutionalized system of privilege, advantage, and power that was operating all around me and structured my life in innumerable ways. Examining the systemic nature of institutional racism helped me move past my feelings of guilt and shame because I saw that the system operated even as I personally rejected that system and struggled against it . In other words, even as I commit my life to fighting racism, I still benefit every day as a White person from a system of White privilege that was established for White people, even though my ancestors were not even in the country when those systems were set up.

For example, in 1979, a Black family tried to purchase a home in my New York neighborhood. My neighbors, who prior to this had had their share of ethnic conflicts, immediately bonded together as "White folks." They formed a "civic association" that tried to block the sale by colluding with a local real estate agency. My mother and I attended one of the association meetings to challenge the racism and were both bodily evicted. I went public about what was occurring by writing a letter that was published in the main Long Island newspaper, and immediately, we began to be harassed and threatened by our White neighbors. During this period, I was driving home alone late one night, when I noticed I was being followed by another car. I zig-zagged erratically to try to lose him, but the driver continued to follow me. Frightened, I drove to the local police station and asked them to follow me home. They easily obliged and gave me an escort to my door. I have since realized that even though I was being harassed because of my antiracism activities, it was my White privilege that allowed me to feel safe enough to ask the police for protection. A person of color in a similar situation might be less likely to see that as a viable option.

Another example occurred when my husband, Arnold, and I took a trip to London a few years ago. I had filled out my declaration card on the plane so I went through the line first, while Arnold stayed behind to complete his form. The immigration agent was friendly and courteous, and asked me if I was there for business or pleasure (my answer: both), and how long I would be in England (two weeks). He said "Thank you," and I was on my way. I stood on the other side of the counter and waited for Arnold to come through the line. The agent was equally friendly and courteous, but a strange thing happened. In addition to the questions he had asked me, he asked Arnold how long he was staying more than once, and asked him to produce his return ticket. Arnold complied, the agent said a cheery "Thank you," and that was it. I asked Arnold if he had noticed anything unusual in the interaction. He said no, and then I proceeded to tell him what I had witnessed. What explained the different treatment? I am White and American, and Arnold is Black and an Antiguan citizen. The British government was closely monitoring all Afro-Caribbean people entering the country and carefully checking to make sure that all who entered had tickets to leave. White privilege and institutional racism had operated right in front of us with a polite and nonintrusive face. It was only in contrasting our experiences that we were even able to figure out what had happened.

When we lose sight of the concept of privilege, those of us who are White can easily become defensive when we are told that we are racist. When we define *racism* only in individual terms, it becomes easy to distance ourselves from racism by saying, "Well, I don't believe those hateful things, so I'm not racist." Yet, what we fail to see when we fall into this trap of faulty logic is the extent of the ways privilege and advantage influence our experiences on a daily basis, just by virtue of our whiteness (or maleness, or heterosexualness). This happens with or without our cooperation. Even our resistance to racism bears witness to its existence and power in our lives.

Lesson #2: Liberal Racism

When I was a student at Oneonta, I was part of a group that was then called the Concert Committee. We planned musical events and selected the artists that would perform at the college. As best as I remember it, the Concert Committee was a multiracial group, which probably means there were a few, though not many, people of color in the group. At one meeting, an intense conflict arose about the selection of performers. The Black students stated that there were very few Black acts booked on campus, that the few that were booked were cross-over artists defined by White musical tastes, and that they, the Black students, were always out-voted anyway.

An intense argument ensued, with the White students going on about how the Concert Committee was for the whole campus, and how we had to do what was in the best interests of the majority. One particularly vocal White male student was a senior and chair of the committee, and often ran meetings in a very controlling way. He argued and argued with several Black students. Finally, I decided to speak up and intervene. I remember talking about how we had to remain calm and listen to all sides and that the Black students had a point—after all, weren't we trying to book Stevie Wonder? Would enough students, meaning White students, of course, show up to see Confunksion or Tavares? What happened next I have conveniently forgotten, probably because it likely entailed some polite rolling of the eyes and frustrated shaking of the head by the Black students. As I recall, the Black groups that were requested never did come to Oneonta.

The lesson here is that of liberal racism. I thought I was helping, but my help not only didn't help, it made things worse (Batts, 1989). I thought that I understood an experience that I had no insight into whatsoever. I thought I was being antiracist, when, in fact, I played the classic role of the color-blind liberal. In *Killing Rage: Ending Racism* (1995), bell hooks states:

It is the very small but highly visible liberal movement away from the perpetuation of overtly racist discrimination, exploitation, and oppression of black people which often masks how all-pervasive white supremacy is in this society, both as ideology and as behavior. When liberal whites fail to understand how they can and/or do embody white supremacist values and beliefs even though they may not embrace racism as prejudice or domination (especially domination that involves coercive control), they cannot recognize the ways their actions support and affirm the very structure of racist domination and oppression that they profess to wish to see eradicated. (p. 185)

I was seduced by the myth of "fairness," but what I was really perpetuating was the "tyranny of the majority." Majority rule is very convenient when you *are* the majority. A liberal racist, I colluded in the illusion of participatory democracy, even though mine, and other White students' desires and choices were virtually guaranteed success at every turn. Liberal racism entails being able to mouth the rhetoric of democracy and equality without having to give up anything or make any changes. An essential element of liberation is not only sharing power, but also sharing discomfort.[4] In that meeting, I, along with the other white students there, was unwilling, or unable, to share either.

Liberal racism is the trap that I most frequently still get caught in and about which I must remain most vigilant. In the days leading up to the 1996 presidential election, I engaged, on two separate occasions, in heated conversations with two African American friends, championing all the reasons we needed to support Bill Clinton, despite his rather uneven record on progressive issues. Although we all agreed that the threat from the right wing was real and serious, my "lesser of two evils" argument seemed to ring hollow for my friends. I had to sit back and think about why I was so willing to defend traditional liberalism in this context, especially when I am usually the one critiquing it when I am among my more middle-of-the-road liberal friends—both White and of color. Liberal reforms may have given some comfort and legal protection to many, but they did not necessarily address the realities of people of color nor did they fundamentally transform the racial landscape of the United States. In fact, the superficiality of these changes may have entrenched the power imbalances even deeper. I think my middle-class whiteness made it easier to defend, and harder to turn my back on, token liberal changes (Hardisty, 1996).

Lesson #3: Racism as Tourist

While an undergraduate student at Oneonta, I was an anthropology major, with a focus on the cultural aspects of the discipline. It was through my anthropology classes that I was exposed to the writings of Paulo Freire and Franz Fanon— none of which I understood when I read them the first time. I was also a music minor, which I transformed from a study of Western classical music into a minor of "non-Western music," as it was called at the time. I took courses in Javanese Gamelan, Indian Raga music, West Indian and Latino music, and African Drumming and Dance.

African Drumming and Dance was not a class for observers—you basically joined the drumming and dance troupe that was lead by a man from Ghana. I was excited and thrilled by the music and the class. I remember feeling self-conscious about being the only White person in the class, and this is probably because I rarely had other occasions that made me have to think about being White. I am also aware that I never considered how the African American and African students felt about my being there. In retrospect, I recall that several African students actively befriended me, but that the African American students eyed me cautiously. What a sight I must have been at our final dance presentation dressed in full African traditional dress and dancing up a storm. It might have been a more difficult experience if I had not been a pretty good dancer and a quick study! While I gained a great deal from this experience, it is telling that I never paused to consider the impact on Black students of my presence in this class—this class which provided rare African-centered space on the very White campus of Oneonta. Though my naiveté allowed me to be open to new cultural learning and to explore new ways of knowing, and I tremendously value the experiences I had in that class, I am not sure of the cost of that to others.

In the 1980s, I joined a Caribbean steel drum band in Boston. By that time, I had learned enough to have a candid discussion with the band leader about the racial implications of my being the only White person, and non-West Indian, in the band. I played with the band for five years and was awkwardly aware of the status that gave me as a "cool White woman" in some people's eyes, and to a certain degree my own. As the years went on, I no longer had the time or energy to commit to the band, and I think I may have stayed on longer than I should have in order to protect that image in some regards. When I finally did make the decision to leave, I was conscious of the fact that I no longer felt the need to be a band member to legitimize me. This was an important step in the development of my own healthy White antiracist identity.

The lesson here has to do with racism as tourist: stopping along the road of life to learn bits and pieces of other cultures, but not understanding the political implications of misappropriation, cultural intrusion, and the seeing "the other" as "exotic." Racism as tourist often manifests itself in the form of cultural theft, with White people taking credit for or inappropriately identifying or using traditions and cultures of people of color to suit their own purposes. Sometimes this is done for financial gain (as in the case of the theft of Black music by White musicians). At other times, it may start as an honest attempt at spiritual evolution (as in the case of White explorations into Native American spirituality). Ironically, this kind of searching for "the other" is in many ways a reaction against the ugliness of White supremacy and the oppressive and sterile value system that it represents. Yet, deep ethical questions about the line between celebration of other cultures, and the exploitation of them, remain (Johnson, 1995).

Lesson #4: The Loss of the Joy of Living

The musical theme of Lesson #3 reminded me of a story about a dance club that was once in downtown Oneonta called The Fleetwood. The Fleetwood was the only disco in town, and the one place you could dance to something other than the Grateful Dead. The Fleetwood was also the only club in town that had a multiracial clientele, with the other exception being the Black Oak, which tended to pull in the arts and theater crowd (but even that was still overwhelmingly White). The Oneonta bar scene was quite segregated. The crowd at the Fleetwood tended to attract a lot of international students, both male and female, and a fair number of White women.

A friend and I rather spontaneously, without much discussion, started going to the Fleetwood on occasion to dance the night away. Immediately, our friends cautiously whispered questions: "Why are you going there?" "Aren't there a lot of Black people there?" "Does anyone who goes there speak English?" "Are you trying to pick up Black men?" The racism in this is self-evident. The lesson I draw from this has to do with the way racism has distorted White people to the point that they cannot even enjoy dancing, enjoy music and movement, without racializing the experience, either by engaging in "wanna-be" pretensions of trying to look or act Black (whatever that means) or by sexualizing any interracial contact. Several years ago, a White male student in a graduate course I teach on racism disclosed to me that he had great difficulty being sexual or dancing unless he fantasized that he was a Black man. This speaks volumes about the loss of true self and distorted White identity and the way that White racism causes White people to project feared aspects of that self onto others in racist ways. I call this lesson the Loss of the Joy of Living.

Lesson #5: Hypervisibility and Hyperinvisibility

I lived in a dormitory on campus during my freshman and sophomore years. My dorm director during that time was a Black man who had a reputation for being rather tough, and we also had two Black RAs (resident advisors). This was pretty unusual on campus in those days. The fact that I even remember it is significant because I have little recollections about the White RAs in my dorm. The only racial comments I recall being made about our dorm director are vague and involve someone saying they felt he thought he had to be tougher on us than the other dorm directors because he was Black. We were also aware of the relationship between the Black male and Black female RA, and speculated about their romantic involvement. I recall no conversations about what it might have felt like to be one of so few Black people on campus in general, and in our dorm in particular. This lesson is about visibility—the paradox of the hypervisibility of people of color—living under the microscope, your every move noticed coupled with hyperinvisibility—despite being keenly aware of the presence of people of color, as a White student I never really saw beyond the superficial nor made efforts to get to know students of color as individual people. I unconsciously made assumptions that their experiences were "just like mine" in color-blind fashion.

I see this hypervisibility-hyperinvisibility paradox dramatically play out in many of the organizations where I work as a diversity consultant today. When the people of color in these organizations succeed, they are perceived as individual "exceptions" and treated to comments such as, "I don't even think of you as Black," which not only insult, but which also de-race them and render them invisible. Yet, if they exhibit any real or perceived performance problems, their visibility is heightened as a group, with comments on the office grapevine reflecting the more familiar racial stereotypes generalized to all members of the group. In other words, if you're a person of color, you're perceived to succeed as an *individual* but fail as a *group*. Another example is how racism is kept largely invisible by the media until a major "incident" occurs, such as the Rodney King beating, the O. J. Simpson trial, or the Texaco tapes, at which point the issue is discussed repeatedly, albeit in distorted ways that reinforce the dominant mythologies.

Lesson #6: The Impact of Transformative Education

Some of the most profound learning that I gained from my college days have to do with what I learned in the classroom.[5] I took several courses in psychology, history, and anthropology during my junior and senior years that fundamentally altered the way I view the world. It is funny how I even decided to take these courses. For a few weeks at the start of my freshman year, we had seven people living in our suite instead of the usual six, because of overcrowding. One woman, named Karen, who was notably different from the rest of the women I lived with, eventually moved out. She was a free spirit, into nature and New Age things, and she meditated and chanted. We were not close, but I was intrigued by her, and we had several long and interesting conversations. Karen and I parted ways when she moved out, but we periodically ran into each other on campus, and it was through her that I heard about "The Dynamics of Racism" class. She was aware of my interest in racism from our talks about national and global politics, and she told me she had taken this incredible course that I just *had* to take.

This course and a few others transformed the path of my life. It was through these classes that I came to understand the concept of institutional racism and began to understand that racism is more than a set of attitudes that one group of people has toward another. I learned about the role of power to impose those beliefs in far-reaching ways. I learned about parts of U.S. history that no one had ever really told me about before. I began to develop a framework for understanding oppression that continues to evolve. I was like a sponge in those classes, soaking up all the professors had to offer. I took notes like a "human typewriter" (computers were not on the scene yet), and I still refer to those notebooks to this day. I began to read everything about racism that I could get my hands on. I became enraged about how I had been miseducated, lied to, misled, brainwashed, and confused by racist conditioning, and my anger propelled me into activism.

In one of these classes, I remember several White women who often argued with the African American professor about sexism, women's issues, and homophobia. At the time, I did not have a clue as to what they were talking about. I thought of myself as a feminist, yet I had never taken a women's studies course and had never read feminist books nor attended any women's meetings. But I was a strong, independent, and self-confident woman, who believed in equal rights, and so I thought I "got it"—I did not! As for heterosexism and homophobia, I was, in a word, clueless. But I still thought I was enlightened, yet here were these women battling with my beloved teacher.

I have since come to realize that although this man was brilliant when it came to racism, he had yet to explore his own sexism and homophobia, and that came across in the classroom. I am still forever grateful for the knowledge about racism he gave me, for the foundation of understanding oppression that I received from his classes exposed me to a new mode of analysis that led me to question other "isms" and to see the connections between all forms of oppression. Just as I have continued to grow and learn in the intervening years, I trust that this professor has done the same.

It was in one of these classes that I first read *The Autobiography of Malcolm X* (Haley, 1986), which I still think should be required reading for everyone. One part of this book in particular gave my life direction. There is a story that Malcolm tells of a young White woman who approached him on a college campus and asked him what she could do to help the Black struggle. Malcolm turned to her and abruptly said, "Nothing," and walked away, leaving the bewildered White woman to ponder what happened. Later in his life, Malcolm said he wished he could tell that White woman that there was something she could do. She could take responsibility by working with other White people in White communities to challenge racism, and then work in alliance with people of color to end White supremacy. In Spike Lee's movie version of Malcolm X's life, he used only the first part of this story when Malcolm told the White woman there was nothing she could do. I have always felt that the omission of Malcolm's later reflections on the matter were a lost opportunity to inspire and educate more antiracist White activists. In any event, Malcolm's words were a wake-up call for me, and it guided me in the direction of my life's work. Malcolm's vision also helped me to reframe my racial questions from the paternalistic ("What can White people do for people of color?") to those that expose White privilege ("What can Whites do to dismantle White supremacy?"), thereby helping me to take responsibility for racism as a White problem.

It was transformative education that encouraged me to push the limits, receive the gifts of learning offered to me, be open to my own growth, and helped me recognize the importance of being in the right place at the right time for my own learning. For me, pushing the limits involved taking the courses, reading the books, going to the lectures, meeting the people, visiting the places, doing all the things that I never thought I would or could do, and that I did not perceive to be "about me." I came to find out how much our lives are interdependent and how what I thought was someone else's history was really part of my own.

Receiving the gifts of learning meant that I accepted the new concepts and information that were offered to me, even while I rejected certain aspects of that learning that was problematic to me. Had I refused to learn because of sexism and homophobia, I never would have done the intensive learning I did about racism. In fact to do so might have colluded in my own denial about racism. Still, we must be vigilant to raise the contradictions as we see them, and not privilege one form of oppression over another.

Being open to my own growth meant learning how to push through my own defensiveness and denial. I thought of myself at the time as a feminist and an antiracist, but it is clear to me now that I had minimal understanding of the depth of what both of those things truly meant. Learning to let go of my defensiveness and self-righteousness is an ongoing challenge.

I have come to realize that being in the right place at the right time for my own learning was a critical element of why that learning was so powerful for me at that moment of my development. If I had taken those courses five years earlier, I might not have been ready to hear so clearly and the information might have gone over my head. If I had taken them five years later, when I was working through issues of sexism and homophobia, I might have resisted the lessons on racism that I also needed to learn. Ideally, I believe that this learning can, and should, be done together, and Black feminist scholars and activists, including Angela Davis, bell hooks, and Audre Lourde, have shown us the way.

Years later when I was in graduate school in Boston, I met a White man at a party who went to Oneonta at the same time I did. As we talked, we realized that we were in a racism class together. He then proceeded to say, "Wasn't that the worst class you ever took! That professor was so anti-White!" I was stunned. How could he have had such a different experience from me? This class had transformed me, forced me to look deep within myself, my history, and my identity as a White person—it was the best class of my life! I try to remember this now when I am teaching and keep in mind that what makes a classroom safe or exciting for one student may have the opposite effect on another.

LOOKING FORWARD

The 1980s and 1990s have provided me with a wealth of experiences that continue to challenge me to understand oppression at deeper, more complex, and ever more personal levels. I am not sure where the next part of my life will lead me or what form my work will take, but I know that antiracism and social justice will be at its core. My hope is that other White people will join me and that there "is a generation of kids who are tired of racism and White supremacy, who are less willing to engage in denial, a generation that may be willing to launch organized collective resistance" (hooks, 1995, p. 226).

For lessons to be truly meaningful, the learning must be put into action. So, I pose these challenges to myself: What will I do to further develop my understanding of racism? What will I do with the insights I continue to gain? How, and to whom, will I be accountable? What actions will I take? How much am I willing to risk? What will anchor and support me in this journey?

The more I learn to acknowledge, value, and love all parts of who I am, the more open I find myself becoming to other people. This helps me to lessen my defensiveness when confronted with my own racism and allows me to find allies in faces and places where I least expect. I am working on claiming all aspects of my multifaceted identity and wearing them proudly, while not letting them restrict or define me. I am a woman but that is not all I am. I am White, but that is not all I am, either. I am Italian American, but as I embrace that culture, I can expand its boundaries without betraying my roots. Our identities are essential, but we are more than essentially our identities. We need to work apart at times to heal and grow strong, but we need coalition work to thrive and succeed. My personal desire is to find ways to work together to challenge injustice, reclaim all aspects of our own fragmented and destroyed humanity, and begin to heal from the nightmare of oppression.

My trip to Oneonta felt like a homecoming of sorts, like I had come full circle, though I realize now that the circle never ends. The imagery of a series of mountains and valleys helps me conceptualize the journey that I am on. Just when I think I have climbed to the top and "got it," I look over the peak to see another range of mountains that I could not have envisioned from my earlier vantage points. I have chosen to gather my energies and keep on moving.

NOTES

I would like to thank Donna Bivens, Valaree Crawford, Norma DeRosa, Angela Giudice, Ulric Johnson, Joyce King, Mel King, Fran Smith, Becky Thompson, and Cooper Thompson for their thoughtful review and feedback on this chapter.

1. I would like to acknowledge Roberta Caban of the Student of Color Coalition and the Center for Multicultural Experiences, and faculty Ralph Watkins and Caridad Souza (now at Rutgers University) for their commitment to antiracist activism on the Oneonta campus and for their role in inviting me to participate in this event. This paper had it's origins in the talk I delivered on campus on March 22, 1996.

2. "The Blacklist Incident," as it has become known, refers to an incident in September 1992 in which an elderly White woman was attacked in Oneonta by an assailant she said was a Black male. In response to a request from the police, the State University of New York at Oneonta gave the police a list of the 125 Latino and Black male students registered at the college. The other college in town, Hartwick College, and the local Job Corps refused to comply with the request. The state, local, and campus police used the list to track down, harass, and question the young men in their dormitories, in their classes, and in their jobs, violating their right to be presumed innocent until proven guilty, violating the Family Educational Rights and Privacy Act of 1974 (the Buckley Amendment), and violating their civil rights. The response from students on campus and alumni was swift and intense in condemning the actions. Yet, the vice-president who authorized the release of the list was suspended for only one month without pay and demoted. He was reinstated to his prior position in December 1995, and students learned of his reinstatement just prior to my visit to the campus in 1996. A class-action lawsuit has been filed on behalf of the students. For a more detailed discussion of the incident see Ruth Sidel, *Battling Bias: The Struggle for Identity and Community on College Campuses* (New York: Penguin Books, 1994) pp. 82–84.

3. This refers to Malcolm X's well-known statement about racism existing not only south of the Mason-Dixon line, but anywhere south of the Canadian border.

4. I thank Nancy Richardson of the Harvard Divinity School in Cambridge, MA for this insight.

5. I would especially like to thank Professors Ena Campbell, Rashid Hamid, Don Hill, Jim Preston, Bill Starna, Ralph Watkins, and George Young.

13

"Justice, Justice Shalt Thou Do!"

Elizabeth Aaronsohn

CONTEXT FOR REFLECTION

The moment in which I am writing feels like a moment of hope in the essentially apartheid state of Connecticut in which I live. In midsummer 1996, the state supreme court ruled against the state in the landmark school desegregation case, *Sheff v. O'Neill*. The suit was initiated almost a decade ago by families who live in the inner city of Hartford, whose experience of life in the wealthiest state in the union could be a chapter from Jonathan Kozol's *Savage Inequalities* (1991). The 4–3 decision overturned the previous year's narrow ruling that the state has no responsibility for de facto segregation. As a teacher educator at a state university, trying to prepare monocultural teachers for a multicultural world, I am one of a minority of White persons thrilled rather than terrified to see the local headlines "Court Orders Desegregation." I join the moment of jubilation with the 95% African American and Latino parents and children of the city who were forced to argue, yet again in America, that separate is inherently unequal.

My feeling of hope may seem naive in light of persistent institutional racism. The governor of Connecticut, who rewarded the state's attorney general with a bottle of champagne when the lower court judge originally ruled for the state the year before, responded to the new decision with adamant resistance. His immediate reaction—"no busing!"—effectively captured the headlines away from the court decision, narrowing the public perspective on remedies. However, I cannot dismiss this governor as merely an individual racist. Looking for some institutional commitment to action for genuine equity as early in this case as 1993, I joined an ad hoc delegation from inner city schools in a meeting we requested with a liberal legislator on the Education Committee. We were sobered when, candidly and without shame, she spoke about feeling pressured by the imminent judgment in the *Sheff v. O'Neill* case. But instead of acknowledging the complexity of the issues or considering what actions might rectify the injustices, she said of the legislature, "We have to look like we're doing something."

Such cynical disregard serves the racism that has been growing openly, over the years since *Sheff* first went to trial, throughout the nation. From Reagan's presidency on, permission has been given to be outright racist. Certain talk radio rhetoric appears frequently in the conversation and writing of many of my White students. They repeat uncritically the stereotyping of Black mothers on AFDC, immigrants whose first language is not English, and all Black men. Black churches have been burned again. Perhaps because I am aware of it now, the language of racism and stereotyping seems even worse than when I heard it from my own father, my aunt (his sister), and my neighbors, as I was growing up.

PART I: STORY

Recognizing the Concept of Race in Cincinnati

Where I grew up was not really the Midwest, as I assumed, but "the upper South," just across the Ohio River from Kentucky. One of the very first stops on the Underground Railroad, Cincinnati was a haven for people trying to escape oppression or desperate poverty, or both: slaves, then Jewish refugees from Nazi Germany and landless White people from Appalachia. The city of Cincinnati must have always had fascinating layers of deep racism and conservatism on the one hand and radical abolitionism and socialism on the other.

In my home, the focus on race was double and inherently contradictory. I was brought up to be fiercely, proudly patriotic as an American, anti-"Jap" as much as anti-Nazi. As Jews, however, we knew we were a despised race in Europe and only marginally tolerated in the United States. I recognized at a very young age that I was part of a race that historically suffered oppression. In the 1940s, I pored over and am still haunted by eerie pictures from the concentration camps. I grew up afraid of all Germans, even German Jews: Their accent sounded like the Nazi voices in the movies. Similarly, the anti-Asian feelings I absorbed at such a young age have taken years of consciousness to undo.

While being so self-consciously "American," keeping the religious traditions was the natural expression of my parents' beliefs and feelings and their deliberate attempt to maintain our ancient culture by living it. I went to Sunday School and to synagogue with my father on Saturday mornings and the holidays. Now, I am grateful that I grew up immersed in the Hebrew language and music of prayer, as well as in the Bible stories, worldview, foods, and rituals of Judaism. But as an adolescent, I longed for the straight hair, straight nose, and Christian calendar schedule that would make me normal within the dominant culture.

At first, our Jewish race was the only "Other" of which I was conscious. My direct experience of people of color in those early years involved noticing that on weekday mornings, silent and isolated, African American women got off the bus and walked down our street. They carried their small packages of clothes to change into, to work in "White ladies" houses for the day. Then, still silent and alone, tired, they walked back up the street to the bus stop at the end of the day, carrying their work clothes. One of those women was "Ella" (as we called her—even we children did not call her "Mrs. Ella."). I must have been very young, because I remember being home and hanging around Ella, enjoying her company as she silently, deliberately, expertly pressed our clothes. I remember asking to have my lunch with Ella and being told—I am not sure by whom—that sitting at the table with her was not acceptable. Maybe that is where my rebellion began.

In my unaware childhood, the range of my friendships was circumscribed. Like Connecticut towns and cities now, neighborhoods in Cincinnati when I grew up there (1936–54) were clearly segregated by race, though the class, religious, and ethnic lines were somewhat more blurred. We lived on my father's military disability pension and part of my aunt's income, next door to a working-class family on one side and a doctor's family on the other, both "non-Jewish." People having a variety of jobs, some professional or managerial and some working class, and both Christian and Jewish, lived on our block. But everyone was White, and the neighbors, including my family, seemed to have an understanding that they would all keep it that way. Though hardly anyone ever moved, and though we were by no means a coherent community, many times I heard in my home and others that they "would never sell (their) house to Negroes." This was so even of the Jewish families, whose heritage taught us that because we had been "strangers in a strange land," we must treat all human beings as kin.

The population of my elementary school, both students and teachers, as I remember, was entirely White, except for one Japanese child. I took a bus to that school in the 1940s, as I did to my high school (grades 7–12), a college preparatory public school for admission to which one had to take a citywide test. Walnut Hills High School then had only token integration; the number of students of color was not nearly proportionate to their population in the city. My memory of my graduating class recalls only three African American faces and names. Though I knew and respected Elizabeth, Gwen, and Ralph, from homeroom, classes, the yearbook, the newspaper, and sports, our social circles did not intersect. My ignorance about a world other than the White world was complete. When Gwen brought in the social pages of a newspaper from her African American community, it shocked me to see wedding and engagement pictures. I realized only then that people of color never appeared on such pages in the mainstream Cincinnati newspapers.

From as early as I can remember, whenever my aunt drove us through our old neighborhood to go to synagogue, she and my father talked about how that neighborhood was "changing." They casually referred to the newest residents of Avondale, just beyond downtown, as "schvartzas" (the Yiddish equivalent of "niggers"). Ironically, it was from my father's words I learned the Biblical rhetoric "Justice, justice shalt thou do!"

Smith and Yale, 1954–59

Escaping to college, I found my political attitudes (carry overs from my father and aunt) very much in the minority. Embarrassed that I had no ideas of my own and seeing that Senator Joseph R. McCarthy was not as revered at Smith as he had been at my father's table (my mother was always in the kitchen), I began to listen more than talk.

Two other challenges to my identity confronted me there. First, I was one of very few students on scholarship (and on what would now be called "work study"). Second, I was Jewish. Although I was not aware of it at the time, Jews had been admitted under a strict quota. I attended the small Hillel services, mostly to please my father, but I was strongly attracted to the White New England Congregational chapel to which the majority of the girls went every Sunday morning. Reverend Unsworth's sermons were stunning, political as well as religious in their moral fervor. I may well have learned the very same lessons from the scholarly, gentle Rabbi Ruchames, but I was ashamed of him: He was a Jew.

Through Reverend Unsworth, I first heard about the Montgomery bus boycott, which was then in process. Through his urging and mentoring, as newly elected president of the Interfaith Association in 1957, I invited representatives of the boycotters to come to speak at Smith. Their coming was a turning point in my life, though I took in few of the facts, and very little of the historical context of their bold movement. I was deeply inspired by their clear, sure presence, their solidarity, and the faith and conviction in their singing: "My feet are tired but my soul is resting."

I emerged from Smith and then one graduate year at Yale with a high school teaching certificate, a graduate degree in English, a job for the fall, and a completely transformed personal and political agenda. I had become friends with some members of the Yale Russian Chorus, with whom I began listening to and singing folk music from all over the world. The songs from the United States taught a history I had never learned in school. I was especially drawn to the music of Pete Seeger and Odetta but found that music not welcome at home. When I played an Odetta album in the family living room at the end of that year at Yale, my father stormed out of his upstairs study, furiously demanding: "Is that African music?" From our increasingly strained conversations during four years of vacations, he and my aunt had already decided that I had been hopelessly tainted by all the "pinko" professors at the two Eastern colleges.

My new friends and I at Yale—all White, as Yale essentially was then and still is—created and put enormous energy into an ambitious extracurricular program, which we called "Challenge*." (The asterisk was part of the name, which included this definition, written in what we thought was perfect iambic pentameter: "*A student program at Yale University to confront, with realistic concern and responsible action, the crucial issues of today's world.") We made ourselves as knowledgeable as we could about the two issues we had chosen: nuclear testing and racism. By the end of the school year, and through the summer of 1960, my New Haven apartment had become the first headquarters of the program's activities. Full of ourselves, thinking we had broken the silence of the 1950s, we were oblivious to the simultaneous direct action and organizing that was going on in the South among Black students and communities. But it was an exhilarating time on a northern White campus. For the first time in my life, I turned in academic papers late. When I wrote about the English poet Shelley, I concentrated on the politics rather than the form of his poetry. The feelings of the people from the Montgomery bus boycott, who had inspired me the year before, had turned me around.

"Three Negro Honors" North of Chicago, 1959–62

My first teaching job was at the high school in Evanston, Illinois, a town in which I soon became involved in peace movement activism. As I recall, all of the members of the peace group in Evanston and the surrounding towns were White. Perhaps 95–99% of my students were White. By my third year at Evanston, assigned to teach a junior English honors course, (3 English H), free to choose my own approaches and some of my own texts, I boldly engaged the issue of racism. I taught the standard *Huckleberry Finn* from the radical perspective I had begun to cultivate since leaving home, a perspective heightened by a summer in Israel where I witnessed and recognized Jewish anti-Arab racism. To be sure, the students noticed a persistent theme in our readings and discussions. After the South African novel *Cry, the Beloved Country*, some Langston Hughes poetry, and *Raisin in the Sun*, some of my students began calling the course "3 Negro H." When I left teaching to join the Peace Corps at the end of that year, the rumor in Evanston was that I had married a Negro.

"Selected Out" of Peace Corps Training, 1962–63

Peace Corps training felt like student activism at Yale. It seemed to be a place to express, and test, the heady idealism of John F. Kennedy's America in the early 1960s. Recklessly, according to my friends, I insisted out loud that I would not have servants in Ethiopia, even if all native teachers had them. I asked too many questions of our government trainers, once I learned more about the world than they had wanted us to know—more than most Americans knew then about U. S. involvement in the French colonial war against the people of Vietnam. Though I avidly studied Amharic, the Ethiopian language, and the culture and history of the country, I resisted what the trainers told us we were supposed to say and not say about America. In our free time, I played my four chords on the guitar and taught the protest songs I had learned in Challenge* and in the peace movement. Clearly, I was not a good risk for representing the United States in Ethiopia. When Peace Corps "selected me out" at the end of training, all they told me was, "Maybe it's the way you wear your hair." Devastated, I began to rethink what I thought I knew about America and about myself.

Activism in Seattle, 1963–64

Being pushed out to the margins allowed me a clearer perspective than I had ever had. I joined CORE (Congress of Racial Equality); I attended meetings and demonstrations for equal housing and job opportunities in Seattle, where I found myself in the summer of 1963. When the famous March on Washington occurred, we mounted an impressive simultaneous march, in solidarity, for the great numbers of people who wanted to be involved but could not make it all the way across the country. It was a time of high activism in Seattle, in which

Black and White people were really working together for change. I learned many more freedom songs and sometimes played them with my four chords to back up our singing at demonstrations. I recognized the Old Testament in the lyrics. It felt familiar. Freedom. Justice. I was loud, active, and alive again.

I had been avidly reading an alternative newspaper, *The Guardian* (at that time called *The National Guardian*), since my ill-fated Peace Corps training. Its perspective matched mine, helped me analyze my new experiences, and greatly extended my knowledge and range of concern. In *The Guardian's* pages, I found a call for volunteers for the Mississippi Summer Project of 1964, to work in voter registration and Freedom Schools. Needing to leave an unhealthy marriage, encouraged and sponsored by Seattle CORE, and remembering the people from the Montgomery bus boycott, I went.

The Movement, Mississippi, 1964–66

In Mississippi, as a Freedom School teacher and then as co-coordinator of the Freedom Schools, I soon learned that I knew nothing of real value. Until CORE, I had never questioned or recognized my own White privilege. My upper class education at two Ivy League schools had reinforced deeply absorbed feelings of both White supremacy and academic superiority. I had to unlearn it all. My inflated academic language and my pace were inappropriate for dealing with both SNCC (Student Nonviolent Coordinating Committee) workers and local people. I had to learn to "break it down"—to talk in ordinary language. More important, I had to learn to listen. It took me the two years I was there, after doing damage with my egocentric interrupting, rushing, violating, and stepping in front of people, to finally see my own arrogance. It was hard but transforming for me to hear a local friend finally tell me, "Liz, you walk around here as if you think you're better than us." At twenty-eight years old, with all my study and activism, I had not really undone my own racism at all.

I was one of many White volunteers who came down assuming that we knew something that disenfranchised Black people needed to learn, that we were leaders, that our job was to take over. What a terrible arrogance that was. The only thing that really served me in that situation was my knowledge of the Bible and my passion for justice. I cannot claim to have given much of value to the civil rights movement in those two years. But I learned a great deal about African and African American history and about politics. I learned firsthand what is real and profoundly disturbing about America. I witnessed the faith and the community that continue to keep an incredibly courageous, resourceful people alive and determined to move forward. I learned to value struggle. In contrast with the community orientation of the people with whom I was living and working, I discovered in Mississippi how individualistic I had been trained to be.

New York City, 1966–71

Regretting deeply the psychological damage my ignorance must have caused some people in Mississippi, I came out of the South even clearer about America. I had seen it from the inside. Ready to teach formally again, I chose

New York City, where a teacher shortage gave me an immediate provisional certificate. Having been so immersed in Mississippi Black culture, I felt solidarity with my students and their families, a richly wonderful mix of African American, Caribbean, Haitian, and Latino cultures, and a very few European Americans.

I also felt clarity about what was important to teach, and it was not the standard canon. I had learned plenty of other literature—Black literature—in Mississippi. I had also learned there that teaching is not telling. Although I did not realize it until twenty years later, SNCC and CORE had been developing and practicing in our meetings and our Freedom Schools what liberatory educator Paulo Freire was doing in Brazil, at great risk to his life, at exactly the same revolutionary time. In encouraging people to ask questions about the structures that oppressed them, our teaching was dangerous in both Mississippi and the inner cities of the North.

My approach within a high school classroom was radically different after Mississippi. This time, I taught writing by encouraging the students to talk and write freely, honestly, without shame, in their own languages, about their own lives. I asked them to examine the lyrics of the songs they listened to and treat it as poetry. I urged students to talk and listen to each other. I listened. My aim was to work with two languages—their own home languages and standard English. I was starting out with them as Sylvia Ashton-Warner had done with her very young Maori students in New Zealand: letting them first trust the process of writing and their own voices. For those nontraditional approaches, within two months of that first year in New York City, I was fired.

As a humbled day-to-day substitute for the rest of that year, I found my way to many different New York City neighborhoods and kinds of schools. Again, with the double consciousness I had developed in Mississippi, I learned much more than I taught, exploring the dimensions of the city's incredible diversity. I saw firsthand the extent to which the public schools were populated by children of color, and I witnessed and dealt with the tragic inadequacy of facilities, materials, and approaches for them.

Hired fulltime again as a long-term substitute in the fall of 1967, I faced the New York City teachers' strike—the rebellion of the overwhelmingly White teachers' union against the experiment in control over their own schools by four communities of color. Though I was a union member, I was ready to scab on this one. I had joined a splinter group from the union, Teachers Against Racism, so when I decided to set up a Freedom School in a nearby church, I did not feel alone. We kept learning going, Movement style, while the strike kept schools shut. Again, my students were predominantly of color, and again, even when we were back in our buildings, I encouraged them to write from their own experiences. This time, however, I tried not to let any papers escape from the classroom before spellings and other mechanics had been turned into standard English.

On the day Dr. Martin Luther King, Jr. was assassinated, I urged the principal to close the school out of respect for Dr. King and for the students' grief and anger. She refused, then blamed me for causing the riot I had predicted. Forever after that, I understood Malcolm X's words: "I come to report a fire and you blame me for setting it."

The next fall, a longer strike occurred in which I scabbed again, choosing to teach at one of the community-control districts. Ocean Hill-Brownsville is in Bedford Stuyvesant, one of the oldest, most neglected low-income areas of the city. As I had experienced before, the residents were African American and Puerto Rican. Because there was no high school, I was assigned to an elementary school. Having to teach first grade with no training was baptism by fire! Once again, I learned vastly more than I taught. As I had done with some of my high school students the previous year, I visited the children's homes. Again I found that going deep inside to make a personal connection quickly undoes stereotypes triggered by having to pick one's way along the sidewalks around broken bottle glass and the rubble from burned buildings.

The promise of a real voice in their children's schools, and of teachers who cared and believed in the children, was a brief, short-lived moment of hope for these families. The mayor of New York betrayed the people, aligning his power with the mostly White teacher's union in opposition to the communities of color. Stunned by that betrayal, siding with the parents against the union, some of us tried to stay and keep at least the quality of teaching and commitment for the children and their families. But within three years at Ocean Hill, we saw the experiment defeated by money, power, politics, and racism. Feeling overwhelmed by the defeat, by the contradiction between poverty and wealth in the city, I returned to western Massachusetts, looking for the fresh green world of my college days. I have never gotten over feeling guilty for the White and class privilege of being able to choose to do that while my students' families could not.

A Dying Mill Town, 1971–76

The shift back to an all-White world was a terrible shock for me. I went to live and make a garden in a small rural border town in southern Vermont, a few minutes from where I found a first grade teaching job in North Adams, Massachusetts. At my first town meeting, my neighbors looked to me like the Mississippi KKK members—tough, Anglo, cold, White. It turned out I had moved into a town that had only one other Jew, and no one of color. In the school, all my students were White; all the other teachers were White. It was a lonely and confusing time: for seven years I had learned to be more comfortable with Black people than with White people. It took a while to relate warmly even to the children.

Though I had left the South accepting intellectually that the task of White people in the Movement was to work in White communities, my New York experience was still mostly in communities of color. Besides, North Adams, a dying mill town, did not feel like a community. I had come back to wary, narrow, isolated individualism along with despairing poverty. So I began to do the kind of work I had done in the South, and the teaching I had done in New York. I listened to the children. I helped them validate their voices and their lives in writing, art, and discovery and then to stretch beyond what they thought they knew. I visited them and their parents in their modest, working-class homes. Once I began to see the nature of their oppression, the families became people to me, and I could teach again.

School of Education, 1986–89

Some fifteen years later, working as an adjunct in the English departments of two colleges while cleaning houses for a living (as a single mother after a divorce), I heard Peggy McIntosh speak from her "Interactive Phases of Curricular Development." Inspired, I returned to graduate school for a doctoral degree, at the University of Massachusetts in Amherst, determined to find a way to balance the curriculum not only in terms of gender, as McIntosh had outlined, but also in terms of race and class. I assumed my field would be English, especially after one stimulating summer-long seminar, "Ethnic and Immigrant Literature," and then two graduate English courses, all of which introduced me to Black women writers. The reading was wonderful, but I was disappointed with the text-bound "literary criticism" focus of English classroom conversations, often wrapped in obscure deconstructionist jargon.

Concerned since Challenge* with the politics of text much more than with its form, I decided instead to work for my degree at the School of Education. Each course and independent study stimulated my thinking about teaching, politics, and their interconnection. We read Paulo Freire's *Pedagogy of the Oppressed* (1970), and heard him speak. In Sonia Nieto's Introduction to Multicultural Education course, we read James Banks, Howard Zinn, research on bilingual education, and the Council on Interracial Books for Children. Sometimes the energy at the School of Education was like being back in the civil rights movement. I re-established contact with people I had known in Mississippi and met others from all over the world. It was wonderful again to work alongside colleagues who were as eager as I was to ask of textbooks, "Whose story is left out here?" But for all the connections I was able to make, Sonia Nieto herself had to gently challenge my use of the term "non-White"; she had to teach me that it sets up White as the norm. I still had so much to learn!

Connecticut, 1989–Present

Multicultural Education is not really popular right now. I hear the Connecticut governor's thinking among my predominantly White students, many of whom are teachers in the public schools. Most rely on TV news and mainstream talk radio shows for their opinions about race, as do my otherwise decent White neighbors, and, unfortunately, some of my highly educated White colleagues. Over the past eight years of teaching in Connecticut, I have been experiencing a marked increase in outspoken White student resistance to considering the perspectives of people who live in inner cities. As discouraging as this is I remind myself that the White people I am dealing with were raised essentially as I was: by second-generation immigrant families, in segregated small towns and suburbs, insulated, deprived of contact with people of color, yet full of superior and fearful assumptions about them.

PART II: ANALYSIS

The Role of a University Teacher Educator

As my story indicates, nothing in my home, my neighborhood, the movies or newspapers, or my seventeen years of formal schooling in the 1940s and 1950s invited my peers or me to question our arrogant assumption of White superiority. As I observe in schools and work with practicing teachers, I realize that is still the norm for the raising and educating of White children. It should not surprise me, therefore, that all but a very few of the White students I have taught, the White faculty I have taught with, and the formal institutions I have taught within still participate fully, if unconsciously, in those same expectations, self-concepts, and attitudes of privilege that define White racism (Scheurich, 1993a).

I take as my task the work of encouraging preservice and inservice teachers to challenge all of their assumptions: about teaching and learning, and about the structures of oppression in our society. In doing so, I still struggle to confront and dislodge residual racism in myself, even after more than thirty years of consciousness. In certain ways, my own ongoing struggle helps me in my work to create conditions that force the issue for White students (and sometimes White colleagues), and then to support them as they deal with their realizations.

Privilege Requires Responsibility

I have come to believe that White faculty who have long been actively and consciously working against their own racism can be crucially important to the process of White students' recognizing, naming, facing, and beginning to work on theirs. Taking very seriously Paulo Freire's assertion that all education is political (1970), I see my position on a university faculty as an opportunity to address institutional and personal racism: in my classes and with student teachers in the field, on committees, in informal interactions on campus, and in the community. Not that I always do address it. But I can, and that, it seems to me, is the responsibility that accompanies the privilege of my position. Certification courses have specific other agendas besides personal consciousness, to be sure. But even in those courses, I choose and assign certain readings, for example, Howard Zinn's *A People's History of the United States*, Rethinking Schools' newspapers and its *Rethinking Columbus*, Jonathan Kozol's books, and others, experiences, and reflections as a way of engaging students in reflective dialogue, hoping for and often witnessing deep shifts in attitude and behavior as students see structures of racism for the first time.

In addition, I have discovered a few interventions that help develop perspective. One is a simple Piagetian task: "Draw the chair you see in the center of our circle. Now make eye contact with a person across the circle from you, and draw it as that person sees it." Once in a while, a student will get up and go across the circle to see from the other person's perspective before drawing. The others, conditioned by all their schooling, stay stuck in their chairs. Students routinely refer to that activity when they describe the need to put themselves in another person's shoes.

In another, more sustained and direct intervention designed to help students "see" White privilege, an African American colleague and I do "our salt and pepper routine." This interactive exercise, using the content of Peggy McIntosh's "White Privilege" article (1989), was adapted from a suggestion by Sandra Lawrence at Mt. Holyoke (personal conversation, 1994). Each item on McIntosh's long list of privileges is written on a stack of file cards, which we pass out to students. For example, "I can be sure that if I need legal or medical help my race will not be held against me," or "I can do well in a challenging situation without being called 'a credit to my race'." Each student must read hers or his aloud and say whether it is accurate for her or him. All the European Americans say, with their body language and tone, as well as with their "eyes," that they take all of these "privileges" for granted. Then my colleague, or a student of color in the class, reads hers, and says "no" to even the most obvious one "I can choose blemish cover or bandages in 'flesh' color and more or less have them match my skin." European American students then begin to realize that, without their consciousness or consent, as White people they enjoy many unearned privileges that are denied to people of color in America.

Seeing "the Other," but not oneself, as having an ethnicity is one aspect of dominant culture privilege. At age fifty-two, in the last stages of a doctoral program, after years of what I had thought was paying my dues in antiracism work, I had to be taught not to use the term "non-White." Likewise, students I have dealt with really do not see oppression that does not victimize them. Peggy McIntosh's article comparing racism to sexism is instructive here (McIntosh, 1989; Sleeter, 1993). At least once a semester in my classes, men will laugh off sexist remarks or images, saying that we women should "lighten up." These men do not see the insult. Of course not. They cannot. They are not the objects of the insult; its very existence privileges them. In the same way, White students report honest confusion when students of color report injustices. "I don't see any racism," they say. Of course not. They would not see it. It is not directly affecting them; in fact, its very existence privileges them. Not having to see is privilege.

Even faculty and administrators seem to have these places of blocked vision. I know I did and sometimes realize with alarm, shame, and recommitment that I still do. This no longer surprises me: My very privilege keeps me from seeing. For example, like many of my shocked and unbelieving students reading from the Native American perspective, more than one of my colleagues was ready to let Christopher Columbus off the hook. They insisted that his behavior as invader, oppressor, land-grabber, and slave-catcher, cannot be judged in terms of "our" standards. Highly esteemed educators resisted the rethinking I posed. They deny, or honestly do not know, that Columbus's own contemporary, the priest Bartholome de las Casas, severely judged the behaviors of Columbus and his followers. From that standpoint, those educators put themselves comfortably in position to deny that we, as a postmodern nation, despite high rhetoric about supposedly superior "values," conduct foreign and domestic policy that continues to be deeply racist and imperialistic. Even for some of the most highly educated, the dreamy conquistador Columbus is indeed the cherished hero image of European America.

In the privilege list activity, my presence makes it relatively safe for White students, who come in insisting they are "not prejudiced." The activity gently urges them honestly to face the fact that their freedom from a long list of daily insults faced by people of color in the United States privileges them. By gradually redefining racism in this way, and by uncovering the extent to which racism poisons all of us, the issue becomes de-individualized, and White students can let go of feeling personally accused. With both professors representing the continual learning that comes from lifelong struggle, students can hear and engage in intensive honest discussion about the structures, as well as the pervasiveness, of racism. A White antiracist activist's perspective may help students begin to overcome the powerlessness to which they have been socialized. Assured by the example of an active, hopeful White ally against racism that it is possible to move beyond paralyzing guilt and self-protection, students can focus on constructing positive attitudes and taking positive action.

One such activity is only a start. A full semester-long class, with plenty of simulations, visits, readings, writings, and discussions is really the minium that is necessary for a student to understand and move through stages of consciousness. Without that focused and intensive work, I am not convinced that any teacher can really get White students to transform the attitudes and behaviors that result from racism. All we can do so far in our classes is get some students to begin to uncover, recognize, and rethink some of their own unexamined assumptions. For myself, it probably took the entire two years as a civil rights worker in Mississippi (1964–66), and now the full three decades since, to begin to uncover, understand, and undo all aspects of the racism I had unconsciously took South with me. But I would not send a person such as me again, without the preparation I try to do with my own students. My own learning, on site, was too damaging to SNCC staff and local people.

Certification and University Agendas

I cannot say I know for sure how to help students develop antiracist attitudes. But I do not trust institutional policies or priorities to take care of it. I hear universities, and even high schools, being shaped by the demand of business "leaders," economists, and politicians for graduates who will be "competent"—well-trained technologically—and "responsible"—show up every day, neat and respectable, on time. The products of our university expect to emerge with skills they hope will serve them in the marketplace. In the Teacher Education department, we spend time revising programs so they will prepare students to meet the Connecticut Teaching Competencies and help graduates update and upgrade for career enhancement. Their administrators will expect them to produce high student scores on standardized tests. I have seen what the pressure of that agenda does to teacher tolerance for children's legitimate needs, interests, and differences. That narrow focus becomes a kind of subtle oppression.

Faced with fiscal uncertainty, our university has recently undertaken what promised to be honest self-evaluation. Perhaps inevitably, however, given American society, the focus of that self-evaluation seems narrowly to define itself as doing the best job we can of making sure our individual graduates will be "competitive" in the world as it is. Missing from that dialogue is a commitment to send our students out to be passionately involved in and empowered to change that world. As an antiracist White faculty member involved in that dialogue, I have continued to say that I believe our real responsibility is to make the world, or at least a student's/teacher's part of it, more inclusive, more habitable, more just, more caring, less competitive, less destructive. I think we can work toward that in our teaching.

I am learning to speak out in the least threatening way that I can, understanding that some of my colleagues may not have ever had the chance to examine the dimensions and politics of their own White identities. On the other hand, the need is urgent: Children in inner city schools are being subjected to yet more teachers who do not believe that inner city kids can learn or that their parents care. Children in White schools are still essentially growing up as I did. My commitment, as an antiracist White faculty member, is to present to my colleagues, and name as an unacceptable reality, evidence that our racist and ethnocentric students graduate still racist and ethnocentric, full of unexamined assumptions (Aaronsohn, Carter & Howell, 1995; McCall, 1995; Bollin & Finkel, 1995; Manning, 1995; Yon, 1995). Once we have seen the research, the task is to look honestly at all the reasons why that happens and correct them all.

One clear reason White students remain stuck in racist assumptions is that curricular offerings in the university continue to privilege the dominant culture. While most still rely on "the canon" of traditionally acceptable literature, some English department members at this university are using the new *Heath Anthology* for their text in American Literature, beginning with early Native American chants, songs, and stories rather than with colonial English sermons and other published pieces. Students from those English professors come to teacher education classes with a new awareness that American literature was made by women, African Americans, Latinas/Latinos, and Asian Americans as well as by White men of property. Some history professors, as well, are including the perspectives of marginalized peoples in their survey courses. Course catalogues also include elective programs and courses in African American studies, women's studies, and Latin American and Caribbean studies.

I know this about other departments because once in awhile a teacher education student will bring some surprising prior knowledge to my assignments of unit lesson plans based on research in multicultural projects. I feel that such colleagues and I have succeeded when White students express anger at their earlier schooling; some even decide they have been "culturally deprived." However, I worry about how well prepared they will be to do critical reading of the standard textbooks from which they will be expected to teach, once they get into their own elementary and secondary classrooms. While attempting to be more inclusive of heroes, literature, and pictures from cultures other than the dominant culture, even the newer elementary and secondary textbooks still conveniently evade the hardest issues. So we must take those very textbooks as a location in which to learn to use textbooks critically.

Process is as important as content in this regard. As long as we teach content as material to be tested on, multicultural or monocultural, we cannot expect transformation of attitudes and behaviors. Traditional pedagogies such as lecture and competitive debate are even harder to transform than content; they continue to privilege European American middle-class male students. Such pedagogies reinforce dominant culture assumptions that their values are universal values, that their points of view are the only possible ways of seeing. As these traditional methods effectively exclude or alienate students and perspectives of other cultures and ways of knowing, distancing pedagogies such as lecture, answer-pulling (Holt, 1967), argument, and debate reward the ways of learning and habits of interacting which made me so ineffective in Mississippi. Within these structures, women, Latino, Native American, Asian American, some African American, and most White working-class college students in particular tend to be silenced (Culley & Portuges, 1983; Belenky, et.al., 1986). Many "core" subjects still view "received wisdom" as the norm, so that in most academic subjects preteachers are socialized to accept it without questioning and to expect themselves to teach in the same manner. As with all anti-oppression work, directly bringing all of these issues to consciousness while modeling inclusive structures and processes is the only way I know of to counter the situation.

With all of that work, the results are long range, not immediate. In Mississippi, I learned that education is much slower, but also longer lasting, than demonstrations. Though education is not as dramatic as high energy public action, both are necessary to bring about change (Aaronsohn, 1990).

Seeing from a Standpoint Other than Our Own

Recent graduates now teaching in inner city schools routinely report feeling unprepared for the issues they find themselves experiencing and surrounded by faculty with negative attitudes toward the children. Beyond the inner city, as families of color begin to move into previously all-White towns and suburbs, or as voluntary (or soon court-mandated) integration is attempted, children of cultures other than the dominant culture are increasingly appearing in those classrooms. Frequently, schools are resegregated by tracking, or by labeling inner-city children as special education, or "troublemakers." Will our graduates, as teachers and citizens, contest those racist and classist practices?

Our university does not require a multicultural education course for either teacher certification or graduation, nor does the department have a course in urban education available for undergraduates. The state determines how many credits we can require, and other courses with other content have been determined to be more important for students seeking certification and facing a formidable standardized test. But even if one is teaching in a predominantly or totally White school, the time for educational apartheid is over. It would help if the university would focus on the communities it should serve. Institutional commitment to professional development schools, especially in inner cities, would be one way for enlightened teacher educators to be on site where our graduates, as well as undergraduates, are practicing (we hope) what we have taught them. Presently, many of the professional development schools from our university are being established primarily in suburbs, where faculty live and are comfortable.

But before we go out into inner-city schools, it seems we need to work on ourselves as faculty. At least one direction for beginning to overcome White racism among faculty on a university campus was a Race/Culture Seminar at Eastern Connecticut State University in 1990–91. A handful of faculty, staff, and administrators attempted to unlock, examine, and address those blocked places of their own. To be sure, one intensive weekend of talk, simulation, readings, and activities, and one follow-up half-day were not enough to dislodge the dominant paradigm. For example, one professor could not hear his own attitude of ethnocentrism in the remark, "I'm not prejudiced against Puerto Ricans, but why can't they come on time?" His statement reminded me of a graduate student who looked at a list of European American cultural values and insisted, "But these are human values!"

I have found some resources that help to get both students and faculty to consider standpoints other than their own. Nancy Schniedewind's and Ellen Davidson's game, "With the Odds Against Them" (1987) enables participants to "get it" about who has the privilege of individual choice and who does not. The decks are stacked, and the obstacle cards give clear messages. It is a powerful simulation, in which students feel for themselves how trapped people can become by circumstances that society constructs. My only caution is that some university students, caught up in trying to win, can at first miss the point of the game. Racing through the reading of their obstacle cards, impatient with the obligation to lose points or wait seconds before resuming play, they seem oblivious to the clear messages about institutionalized oppression that the cards convey. In freewriting immediately after final scores are tallied, still distressingly many do not easily make the larger societal connections. Processing their experience of the game, therefore, has become the most important aspect of it. With plenty of talk, students reflect on how important we in the United States have made it to be dominant, how much contempt we have for "losers." They also see that being comfortably situated in the "top" groups insulates people from the despair of those on the bottom.

In the freedom of one graduate course—"Education in the Inner City"—a specifically focused elective not packed with requirements for certification, I can do much more directly antiracist work. In one sustained activity, I invite students into the world and the consciousness of an African American single working mother in Harlem through a semester-long intensive reading of Ann Petry's compelling 1946 novel, *The Street*. Over time, most students become so drawn in by the story, the characters, and the imagery that they begin to identify with the hero, Mrs. Lutie Johnson. The power of Petry's writing is such that even the most resistant students feel Lutie's strength and integrity within the complexity, blocked possibilities, pain, and reality of her life. By the end of a semester of that novel and the other activities described here, even the most reluctant students have begun to do less judging. They start understanding. Taking their consciousness beyond the novel, some students report hearing comments from colleagues, family members, and even TV news stories differently. Many report daring to interrupt racist statements from those same sources. Most have at least briefly become aware.

The Opportunity

Antiracist White faculty members have the responsibility to lobby within departments for meaningful multicultural education, which at the very least welcomes other paradigms and people of other perspectives (Sleeter 1993). Our task is to keep departments from getting lost in the logistics and structures of a semester, or budgets, or partnerships, or juggling our course work with our research, supervision of student teachers, advising, searches, meetings, and committees. To be sure, the politics of peer evaluation can make such lobbying dangerous, as all antiracist work can be. Therefore we must build coalitions, to support other antiracist faculty in the struggle to make our work, and our workplaces, fully inclusive in content, process, and spirit.

The day after the *Sheff v. O'Neill* decision was handed down by the Connecticut Supreme Court, I went to the Hartford Courant to buy multiple copies of the newspaper, the African American woman at the counter of the customer service department was at first cooly professional, but once she recognized my excitement about the outcome of the case, she opened up, sharing her own thrill. She told me that although her son was only nine and could not really understand the full meaning of the news, it was important to her to let him know that somehow this was a victory for him. Her trusting that I would understand felt like a genuine moment of connection. It increased my courage to educate myself, my students, and some of my colleagues, starting in the fall.

14

White Man Dancing: A Story of Personal Transformation

Gary R. Howard

It is time for a redefinition of White America. As our percentage of the population, declines, our commitment to the future must, change . . . . The future calls each of us to become partners in the dance of diversity, a dance in which everyone shares the lead. And because we have been separated by race and ethnicity for so long, we may feel awkward at first with the new moves . . . . But with a little help from our friends in other cultures, even White folks can learn to dance, again, as we once did among the great stone circles of ancient Europe (Howard, 1993. p. 41).

Since I first penned these words for a special multicultural issue of the *Phi Delta Kappan*, edited by James A. Banks, many people have asked me about the dance of White America. Twenty years ago, when I started the REACH Center for Multicultural Education, some people challenged whether a White person ought to be involved in this work. Now that the movement has matured, and REACH has a diverse corps of trainers who work with schools all across the country, the inclusion of Whites is more accepted and usually actively encouraged. The question remains, though: Why would any White person choose to become involved?

As I travel throughout the United States and Australia, people continue to ask how I became committed to multicultural education. What experiences brought me to this place? What lessons can be learned for other White Americans? In the reflections that follow, I have tried to deal with these questions in a personal way, piecing together the strains of my own life's song, looking for the lessons that have drawn me into the dance.

THE LUXURY OF IGNORANCE

I was born White and have been that way for over fifty years. The first eighteen of those can best be described as a period of "cultural encapsulation" (Banks,

1994b). Since I had never met a person who was not White, had never experienced the "Other," race for me was a nonrelevant concept. In my youth, I had no conscious awareness of anything that might be called "racial identity." Like water to a fish, whiteness to me was the centerpiece of a constant and undifferentiated milieu, unnoticed in its normalcy.

It was not until my senior year in high school that I discovered my whiteness. A White male friend, who was going out with an African American student from another school, asked if I wanted to join them on a double date with one of her friends, also Black. This was the first time I had ever been invited to dip my toes in the river of racial consciousness. It was the first intrusion into my whitewashed world. I was afraid. I was confused. I was curious.

Like most of my fellow White Americans growing up in suburbia in the 1950s, people of color had existed only on the distant periphery of my social reality. "Amos and Andy," "Tonto," and clips of civil rights activities on the evening news were my only tenuous connections with the other America. Even these limited images were, of course, coming through several layers of White media filtering, with all the inevitable prejudice and racism intact.

This simple invitation to meet a new person, to go on a date with an African American woman, shook loose one of the basic linchpins of my social isolation. It is interesting that my initial response was fear. Fear is the classic White American reaction to any intrusion into our cultural capsule. What will happen to me? Will I be safe? What will other White people think of me? What will "the Other" think of me? How do I act? What do I say? Will I survive? I was overwhelmed by an emotional flood of narcissistic and xenophobic trivia.

I did go on the date, and I had a good time. This young woman enabled me to make a human connection across the barrier of race that had been constructed around both of our lives. With neither our awareness nor our consent, we had both been born into a society that had already decided that our lives should not touch. In the simple act of coming together to share a good time, we broke through that wall, creating one small crack in the artificial barrier of racial isolation.

Reflecting back on this experience, I realize that members of the dominant group in any society do not necessarily have to know anything about those people who are not like them. For our survival and the carrying on of the day-to-day activities of our lives, most White Americans do not have to engage in any meaningful personal connection with people who are different. This is not a luxury available to people who live outside of dominance and must, for their survival, understand the essential, social nuances of those in power. The luxury of ignorance reinforces and perpetuates White isolation.

This one connection I made in high school with a person outside my own race symbolizes an essential step for any dominant culture person who wishes to grow beyond the limits of encapsulation. We must become aware of both our differentness from, and our relatedness to, other people and their cultural realities. Whether we deepen in our awareness and continue to grow through such experiences, or merely shrink back into the safety of isolation, is determined by our reaction to the inevitable fear of stepping outside the boundary of ignorance.

BAPTISM BY FIRE

My second major lesson about whiteness came with a move from Seattle to attend Yale in 1964. This happened not because Yale was particularly diverse at that time, but because New Haven was such a hotbed of racial conflict and civil rights activity. I came to Yale with the Bible in one hand and a copy of Barry Goldwater's platform in the other, foreshadowing what we were to see emerge thirty years later in the Ralph Reed and Christian Coalition version of numbing religiosity. I was not at that time a likely candidate for radical shifts in racial consciousness.

However, it was these same adolescent spiritual stirrings, coupled with the starched and ironed Presbyterian doctrine of salvation through works, that led me in my freshman year to begin working with young inner-city Black and Hispanic kids through a YMCA program. One afternoon a week, I walked six blocks and several light years of social reality away from Yale to spend a few hours with my group of pre-teen males. My job was to be a big brother for them, create fun activities, go to the gym together, and help keep the guys off the streets and out of trouble. Their job, as it turned out, was to teach me more and deeper lessons than I learned in four years at Yale.

These young men lived in "the Hill," one of New Haven's most impoverished neighborhoods and an area that had been targeted for the mixed blessings of urban renewal. From the perspective of most Yalies, the Hill was a place you did not go, a dangerous and dark world, festering with crime and social disintegration. For the social scientists and Great Society bureaucrats, it was a treasure trove of study and grant opportunities. All the demographics of race and poverty pointed in the right direction to make a strong case for "cultural deprivation," that most unfortunate and inaccurate of terms that was so popular in the 1960s.

For me, the Hill was where Tyrone, Ruben, Charlie, Bruce, and the other guys in the group lived. I was naive and idealistic, full of missionary zeal, wanting to help in some way. I did not understand the larger social realities that had created this neighborhood as a "ghetto." I was invited into the homes of my group members, met their extended families, and came to see the Hill as a place where concerned and worried parents, often working against great odds, were trying to give their kids a decent chance for a good life.

It was only gradually that I came to understand the larger American reality that the Hill represented. I met other Yalies who had dedicated their undergraduate years to civil rights organizing in the South and in New Haven. I met Black and Hispanic community leaders who extended and deepened the re-education I was receiving from my young group members. I began to steer my academic program toward courses that would give me the intellectual tools to understand racism, poverty, and the historical, political, and economic manipulations that had led to the creation of the Hill neighborhoods of our nation.

In the middle of my Yale career I got married, and Lotus and I moved into an apartment on Howard Avenue, in the heart of the Hill. The lessons deepened as we lived there and as the urban struggle of the 1960s intensified. During three consecutive "long hot summers," our neighborhood was racked with riots and burning. National Guard troops, with their heavy weapons and armored vehicles, became a regular sight on the streets of the Hill, as was true in hundreds of other neighborhoods across the country. Lotus and I worked together with our neighbors in programs for kids, trying to give them some sense of a normal summer, safe from the violence, the burning, and the military occupation of their streets.

The last fires came in spring 1968, just after the assassination of Dr. Martin Luther King, Jr., when several blocks around our apartment burned to the ground. I remember my former Yale roommates calling from campus that night to ask how we were doing. They had heard about the riots on the news and were worried about us. "We're fine," I said. "Just watching the burning out our back fire escape, and it looks like our apartment will be okay."

Over thirty years later, these memories of fire and frightened children and the vast social and psychological distance between Yale and the Hill remain as some of the most powerful images of my life. How would I be different today if I had never ventured into the Hill? Who would I have become had I not been baptized in the fires of that particular time? My reality was fundamentally and unalterably changed during those years. My politics shifted from far right to far left. My religious beliefs were challenged and transformed. The single-truth simplicities of my Christian fundamentalism were melted down in the heat of that reality. I lost the faith of my childhood and found the direction for my life. I could no longer be the self-righteous missionary with the answers for others. I could only hope to be one small part of a seemingly overwhelming struggle for healing and social justice.

How can White Americans, those who have never been touched viscerally by the realities of race, break out of their cultural isolation and ignorance? It was fire that burned away the walls of my encapsulation. It was engagement with real people in a context totally different from my former life in the suburbs. Yet, even the deep changes of this intense time were only the beginning of my personal transformation.

BRINGING IT ALL BACK HOME

I did not realize it at the time, but this naive missionary period was merely the tentative beginning of a long journey toward multicultural awareness. The missionary phase began to dissipate as I gradually realized I was receiving more than I was giving. I was amazed that I was welcomed and treated so well by my neighbors in the Hill, considering their painful history with most of the White world. I was invited into the life of the community and given incredible opportunities to grow beyond the limits of White ignorance. I do not know how conscious my Black and Hispanic colleagues were in their efforts, but it was as if they had decided together, "Here's one we can perhaps educate. Let's allow him in and see how much he can take. Then we can help him move on to the real work he has to do."

One of the culminating experiences of my New Haven period was to work as the only White staff person in a Black Identity and Leadership summer camp for inner-city high school students. A close friend, who was a social worker and a leader in the Black community, asked me to take on the assignment of "being a White person for the kids to react to as they work out the issues of their Black identity." I thought this would perhaps be the most intense experience I could

possibly add to the riots and other stresses of life in the Hill, so, in the true
spirit of the 1960s, I took the job.

It was here that I was introduced to the issues of White privilege and
complicity, which were not academic concepts to be argued about in the
antiseptic pages of professional journals, but a matter of daily pain and
awareness for the students and the staff in that summer program. They put the
truth in my face, and they taught me well. In a sense, I was placed in the role of
representing all of White America for that summer, and it was not a pretty job.
They taught me about the 500-year history that exponentially increased the
likelihood that I would be a student at Yale and they would not. They confronted
me with the fact that even though my family was hanging by a toenail to the
lower rungs of the middle class, our limited success had been achieved through
the land we stole from the Indians and the labor we stole from Blacks, Asians,
and Hispanics. This is part of the standard multicultural mantra today, but thirty
years ago, it was a new and powerful awareness for me. Indeed, our family farm
in Minnesota, which has been one of the cornerstones of my personal history
and connection to culture, is built on land stolen from the Ojibway people only
thirty years before my great-grandparents acquired it.

The students also reminded me that "You may live in the Hill now, and hang
out with Black people, but you're at Yale and you can go back there whenever
you want. We were born in the Hill and don't have any other place to go. It's not
an option for us not to be Black, that's what we are twenty-four hours a day for
our whole lives. If you wanted to, if things got too heavy for you here, or when
you graduate, you can walk away from this thing and never look back. We can't
do that." None of my Yale professors taught me these realities of White
privilege, yet young Black students in the late 1960s were quite articulate on the
subject. They were my allies and my most influential teachers. White Americans
desperately need this kind of re-education, and it is indeed a blessing when
someone takes the time to provide it, as these young Black leaders did for me.

My missionary mentality was further eroded and essentially obliterated by the
arrival in New Haven of Black Power politics and the growing presence of the
Black Panthers. It was exciting to be in the middle of these historic
developments. The passion for change was palpable on the streets. The struggle
was real, and many people were willing to risk everything for it. In the midst of
the pain and the fear, there was profound hope, and both the Panthers and the
ideology of Black Power embodied this rejuvenation of energy and spirit. The
line was drawn and there was no going back.

Most White Americans were frightened and confused at this time in the history
of our nation. The Black Panthers reversed the formula on who had the right to
bear arms in the ghetto, and the Black Power politicians rejected the legitimacy
of the do-gooders and Great Society gurus who thought they knew what was best
for Black folks in America. It was instructive for me to observe how White
people in power dealt with this threat to their assumed dominance. The
crackdown was swift, ruthless, and mostly illegal. One by one the strong voices
in the Black community were silenced through drug set-ups, illegal busts,
trumped-up charges, intimidation, and official violence. Following the
unfortunate conclusion of the Bobby Seale–Black Panther trial in New Haven,
the renaissance of hope was essentially terminated. The lives of many of my

neighbors had been damaged or destroyed along the way, and the Hill neighborhood is in more disarray and danger today than it was thirty years ago.

Involvement in these events of the late 1960s stimulated an important step in the evolution of my White identity development. Before my immersion in the urban revolution at that time, I had no way of perceiving the power and willingness of White America to maintain its own dominance. I did not know the extent to which Whites in power would subvert their own expressed values of justice and liberty in order to destroy those outside their group who justly claimed access to those same values. This was not the America I had read about in my high school textbooks, that idealized and just nation that too many White folks still trust to be real. It was only through living with people outside my particular fishbowl that I was able to finally perceive the true nature of my previously invisible milieu. Through their eyes, I came to see the water of White dominance as a highly selective poison that continually steals the life blood from those people who have not been marked with the genetic code of whiteness.

ADVENTURES OF AN ANTIRACIST RACIST

These experiences in New Haven led me to a profound shift in consciousness that has guided my career for over thirty years. Helped along by some strong feedback from Black Power leaders and friends in the Black Panthers, I came to see that my real work was not in the Hill neighborhood, but back home with my own folks. The core of the problem was in White America, and if I wanted to help excise the cancer of racism, I had to go to the source of the tumor. In the spring of 1969, my Black colleagues and neighbors challenged me to take what I had learned from them and find a way to teach those lessons within the context of the White community. Together we buried the missionary and gave birth to the subversive.

I was not enthusiastic about this new assignment. For me, the action was in the inner city. That was where I had come of age and where the most profound experiences of my young adulthood had taken place. The Black community had been the laboratory where young people and community leaders had performed the alchemy of my personal transformation. The Hill had been the altar of fiery baptism that forever changed the way I saw the world. I did not want to go back home and deal with my racist Uncle John, the Brady Bunch, and the rest of Ozzie and Harriet America.

I had entered the period of rejecting my racial identity. I had learned what it meant to be White in America, and I did not want to have anything to do with it. I had broken the seal on my own cultural encapsulation, blown away many of the old images, and did not want to be identified with White folks anymore. I had opened the door on understanding my own complicity, privilege, and racism and wanted to put this in the face of other White folks who had not yet paid their dues. I wanted to be different, not one of them.

I did accept the challenge, however, and went back home to work within the White community. Needless to say, my early attempts at sharing these new insights were not often warmly received by the unknowing White people who were the unfortunate recipients of my wrath. It was clear to them I had a chip on my shoulder. Working in my first career, which was as an assistant minister in a large White church, my basic pedagogical approach to parishioners was, "What you need to know is that you're a racist." This was the typical strategy for most "White Racism Awareness Training" workshops in the early 1970s, and I was among the more energetic practitioners of that particular style.

It is no mystery that my career in the church was short lived. The passions that fueled my ministry ran upstream against the safe liberal theology and politics of the senior ministers and most of the congregation. In the community of White affluence to which I had been called, I was allowed three short years to spread my particularly caustic version of the social gospel. I concluded at the time that many White Americans were quite content with "Father Knows Best" and the other programmed myths of their cultural encapsulation. They did not want to switch channels to see the world through my eyes. The realities of the Hill were once again light years away, and I felt wounded and alone in my first attempts to penetrate the dominant reality of my own people.

By the time I entered my second career, that of education, I had begun to mature in my understanding of both the message and the messenger. My work in the church could be characterized as a period of rejecting my own whiteness and confronting other White people with theirs. The next period, which has continued in some aspects even to the present, can best be described as a time of working on "the re-education of White America." I came to see that the awareness and growth I had gained in the concentrated, high voltage context of New Haven from 1964–1969, could not be transmitted directly to other White folks who had not lived similar realities. They needed to be engaged in an educational process that would help mediate the transition to a different perspective, a different way of being White.

Still in keeping with my 1960s commitment to mind-altering intensity, I began my education career by teaching U. S. history to thirteen and fourteen year olds in a White rural community. In a seemingly idyllic setting nestled among the foothills of the Cascade Mountains of western Washington, Black families had been burned out of their homes when they tried to move into the area. There were murmurings of the Klan's presence down the road a few miles. My students were much like I had been at their age, totally oblivious to the larger multicultural story of their country. In them I saw reflected the same cultural isolation that had dominated my youth. Teaching in that middle school was a full turning of the circle of my life, a homecoming of sorts, and I wanted desperately to find a way to reach my students with the lessons I had learned.

This was a pivotal time for me and perhaps instructive for a larger view of White multicultural identity development. Following the church experience, I had moved to this rural setting in the hills and invested five years of my life turning inward, living simply with my wife on the land, having children, building a home, earning a subsistence living through physical labor that had nothing to do with either my academic preparation or my commitment to ending racism. It was a time of incubation, softening, and consolidation of all that I had experienced in the firestorm of the New Haven years and the frigid climate of the church. I needed this time to heal from the harshness of what I had seen.

After five years on the land, I emerged ready to be engaged again. Having gained some measure of rest and renewal, I could not avoid the inner voice that called me to be involved in change. I went back to school and wrote a master's degree thesis on "Multicultural Education in Monocultural Schools," which made a case for teaching about diversity even in schools where diversity was not evident. Next, I procured funding to develop classroom strategies and materials aimed at multiculturalizing the teaching of U.S. history for predominantly White populations. Following this came the design of a teacher training program to help White educators reconceptualize their curriculum and their pedagogy from a multicultural perspective. All of this developmental activity formed the prototype for what was later to become the REACH Center approach to multicultural education, which has now been implemented in all fifty states, as well as Australia.

In relation to White multicultural identity development, I had now moved into a time of positive activity. I was searching for a method and a focus for sharing the experiences and learnings gained during my immersion in New Haven. The bitterness about my whiteness and the harshness in my approach to other White people were beginning to dissipate. I wanted to invite other White folks into the worldview that had been given to me. Rather than beating my students and colleagues over the head with their whiteness and their ignorance, I wanted to find ways to help them break out of their own encapsulation. This positive engagement with other White people in a process of mutual growth provided a healing balance to my earlier strategy of frontal assault. I was beginning to realize that the appropriate response to learning about the realities of White racism in America is not rejection, guilt, denial, or distancing from ourselves as White people, but rather direct action with others for positive change.

It is important to point out that none of the multicultural growth I had been able to achieve up to this point would have been possible without the support and honesty of many friends and colleagues of color. Our current diversity jargon makes much of the need for White folks to become allies for people of color in the battle for equity and social justice. This is an important issue and essential for systemic change, but I have discovered that the road of allyship must run both ways. Without my allies from other cultures, I would still be swimming in the suburban fishbowl of White ignorance. The young people in New Haven, my neighbors and friends there, the community leaders who challenged me, the highly diverse staff and trainers at the REACH Center in Seattle, my colleagues across the United States and around the world — all of these diverse people have contributed to my education and transformation as a White person. White identity development is intrinsically tied to direct engagement across the cultural and racial divide.

SHAPING AN AUTHENTIC WHITE IDENTITY

In recent years, as I have entered my fifties, the rhythms of my journey have been shifting, and the music has been changing in subtle ways, calling for new steps in the dance of White identity. Several experiences have been catalysts for this new time. At a National Service Learning Conference in Minneapolis, where I participated in a panel discussion on diversity issues, a White high school student in our group told a story that has continued to echo in my heart. She described her involvement in a summer multicultural leadership camp, where each evening students from a different ethnic group were asked to share a creative presentation of their cultural and historical perspectives. First, there was African American night, followed by Hispanic night, then Asian American night, Native American night, and finally, on the last evening of the camp, it was White night. She talked about how emotionally draining it had been for her to observe each of the previous presentations, repeatedly being exposed to the painful experiences with racism, oppression, and genocide that these other groups had endured, all at the hands of White people. When the time came for the White students to present their story, she could not participate. "I felt like ripping off my White skin," she said.

After hearing her story, I was not able to free myself from the image of this young woman's painful revulsion in the face of her ethnic identity. I thought about my own teaching, and the multicultural materials I had developed for teachers and students over the years. Even though my approach had softened from the "up against the wall" style of my church career, I saw that nothing I had done could adequately respond to this young woman's troubled emotions. In fact, as I realized later, I had probably placed untold numbers of White students and teachers in exactly the same position. Through the REACH Center, we had distributed thousands of copies of our *Ethnic Perspectives Series* of student books, including *An African American Perspective*, *An Asian American Perspective*, *An Hispanic/Latino Perspective*, and *An American Indian Perspective*. Like those ethnic evenings at the summer camp, these books tell the story of racism and oppression perpetrated by the dominant culture, including much of the information that has not been included in the commercial texts. I wondered how many of the White students in REACH classrooms all across the country had wanted to rip away their ethnic identity after being exposed to our books.

From this and similar stories from other White Americans, I have come to realize that our efforts to "re-educate White America" must go beyond the mere recitation of other groups' suffering at the hands of White people. It must also go beyond "appreciating other cultures," and it must go beyond acknowledging our own racism, complicity, and privilege. Confronting the realities of my collective history has been a necessary step in the evolution of my White multicultural identity, but it has not been sufficient. Embracing the negative aspects of whiteness does not suffice as a cultural identity. Oppression has been a part of my history, but it does not fully define me. For myself, my children, and my White students and colleagues, I want to provide more than mere acknowledgment of our legacy of hate. I want to provide more than valuing and appreciating other peoples' culture. And more than working to overcome the realities of racism and oppression. These are necessary aspects of an emerging White identity, but they do not create a whole and authentic person.

The broader and beginning strokes of a larger picture have begun to come into focus for me only in the past few years. After a year-long sabbatical, during which I was immersed in different cultures around the world, I found myself alone one night on a moonlit beach at Byron Bay, on the east coast of Australia. I had just completed a whirlwind tour of Aboriginal Australia, the guest of a friend who is an emerging elder and caretaker of the land in the spiritual tradition of her people on the North Coast of New South Wales. She had taken me to many of the important places, the prominent physical features of the land that are central to the stories and song lines of her tradition. I had met one of her teachers, a woman in her ninities, who told me stories as old as the land itself. As I was drawn into their world, the stories came to life in the spirit of the landscape. Myth and magic merged with my own reality, and the borders grew fuzzy. Each night I awoke with vivid dreams dancing in the quietest predawn hours, the time when my friend had told me the spirit messengers were most active. I seemed to be getting more than the standard tourist excursion

It was after three weeks of this intensity that I stood alone under the full moon on the beach at Byron Bay. I had said goodbye to my friend and was flying out the next morning. As I watched the playful mutual caress of moonlight and sea foam in the surf, I thought of home 8,000 miles across the Pacific. I wondered how I might translate my Aboriginal immersion experience over that immense distance. More importantly, I pondered how I might apply it to the home within myself. The lesson that came to me then, and has been deepening since, is the realization that for over thirty years, ever since my New Haven days, I had been relying on other people's cultures to provide me with a sense of meaning. Life had been most real and vital for me when I was engaged in intense multicultural experiences. I felt most alive when I was immersed in a cultural reality different from my own. Much of my sense of identity had been forged in diverse cultural contexts separate from White America.

I did not see this as negative, merely incomplete. My experience was not what we normally think of as the "wannabe" phenomenon, which is a typical pitfall for many White folks who have a longing for culture. My motivation had not been to become an Aboriginal person, or a Black American, or a Native American. My particular issue, as it came to me at Byron Bay, was that I had centered much of my sense of self on my experiences with people outside my own cultural group. This had worked well for the formation of multicultural awareness, but it left a large void in terms of understanding my own culture as a White person. I saw that my intense identification with the "Other" had been part of a continuing effort to distance myself from the distasteful aspects of being White. I had spent my adult life looking for meaning in other people's culture, and now it was time to find it in my own.

Not so coincidentally, the last stop on my sabbatical world journey was the British Isles, ancestral homeland for my father's side of the family. Here my wife and I joined a small band of fellow travelers in a pilgrimage to many of the ancient sacred sites of the old Celts, including Glastonbury, Stonehenge, and Iona. Led by a wonderful young man, who is a storyteller, dancer, and contemporary Scottish bard, we danced and sang and storied our way across the countryside. Through his passion, and the power of the places we visited, I was able to get a feel for the magic of the Isles in the time before the Romans and the Church came to do what the British and the rest of Europe later did to indigenous people around the world. The Celtic tradition, like that of Native Americans and countless other groups, was nearly decimated by the invaders, and Christian churches were superimposed on many of the old places of Celtic worship and wonder. In spite of these acts of desecration, however, I found that many of the stone circles remain today as living testimonials to the earthy vibrance and mystical vision of my cultural ancestors.

Upon arriving at Stonehenge, we found the central attraction had been fenced off, inaccessible to the tourists who had proved too disrespectful in past visits. Fortunately for us, our bard-in-residence had some ancestral pull with the guards, and we were able to enter after closing time to spend the entire night with the giant stones. We played our instruments and performed our folk dances for this august audience of silent, watchful witnesses. The wind was strong that night, and blackened clouds ran across the Salisbury hills, mirroring above the flow of our dancing below.

This was a magic night for me. I felt the presence of the ancient Celts who had chanted here their prayers to earth and sky and performed their rituals through the sacred geometry of these same stones. The circle was drawn, and we were inside the space created for us, the place designed to teach us about ourselves, our relationship to each other, and our connection to everything else outside the ring of stone. This is the function of culture, to provide a context, a circle of meaning, and a sense of relationship to all of life.

This night in Stonehenge seemed to answer the question posed for me earlier, half a world away at Byron Bay: "How do I incorporate into my own identity these intense experiences with other cultures?" I discovered that I do so by finding a deep connection with personal culture that is indigenous to my own heritage. At Stonehenge, I embraced my whiteness, all aspects of it. I found my rhythm, danced through the night, and felt at home.

Only recently have I thought more about the fence around Stonehenge. I was shocked when I first saw it and thought we could not get in to be among the stones. Our history as White people has been like that. Barriers of dominance and racism and the pressures of assimilation have neutralized our connection to culture. We have collectively destroyed other cultures, buried our own, and denied the histories of both. My whole life, since I was eighteen, had been an effort to rebuild the bridges to other people's cultures. At Stonehenge, I penetrated the fence that had separated me from my own.

Subsequent to my sabbatical tour, we have now written *A European American Perspective* book to compliment our REACH *Ethnic Perspectives Series*. This student text acknowledges the history of White dominance, but goes beyond that to highlight the many White men and women who have fought, in all times and places, to limit and resist the legacy of racism. The book validates the fact that White people have culture, and it explores the highly diverse ethnic roots of White Americans. In addition, we now include a White American presentation in our training events, to reinforce the understanding that we are all part of the multicultural agenda. We find these efforts have rekindled a fire in the minds and hearts of White participants and students, who feel included at last in the circle of culture and change, not isolated in the dance hall of dominance and blame.

THE DANCE CONTINUES

Learning the dance of diversity is not easy for White Americans. There are complex moves and many ways to lose the step. Before my lessons could begin, I first had to break out of cultural encapsulation and isolation, which entailed much initial shock in the New Haven years, followed by continuing waves of seismic dislocation of my former reality. I began to see myself as Blacks,

Hispanics and others outside my group saw me, both collectively and personally. I had to face the history of White dominance. I had to confront my own ignorance and often tripped over my own and others' feet as I felt my way into the choreography of the larger dance.

In order to continue the lessons and learn the more difficult steps, I had to acknowledge my own complicity and privilege and the racism in myself and my family. I had to learn to move with some degree of grace and style to these new rhythms, without stumbling over guilt, denial, or the rejection of my own whiteness. Then, as the tempo heated up, and I began to feel the groove, I wanted to get other White folks into the dance. To do this, I had to learn to be an instructor myself, finding a way to share what I had learned and help heal the pain of the past.

Today, as the dance of diversity continues for me, I want to take more time to think about the music. Where is it coming from? Am I dancing to my own rhythm or merely moving to someone else's tune echoing in my heart? I find myself listening more now for my own inner music. In my work with other people, I am slowing down the pace and inviting them to go deeper in their understanding of themselves and their relationship to realities outside their own. I am less patient with our diversity jargon and the surface strains of the old multicultural tunes, which sometimes push us to impose our own assumptions rather than waiting for the larger truths to emerge. I want to explore the more subtle tones of the music now, the nuances and complexities created by our vast differences and similarities as human beings. The lines we have drawn around race and culture seem too simplistic to speak to the incredible diversity of our actual lives.

I know the dance of White identity will continue to change and deepen for me. The choreography is a work in progress. Each new step I learn brings me closer to my unique place on the dance floor, helps me find my personal harmony, and guides the creation of a new way of being White, one that is both authentically connected to my own history, as well as finely tuned to the rich mixture of sound and beat that is multicultural America. It is this new dance that sustains me in my work and inspires me to search for new avenues to healing that will transcend the limitations of our past rhetoric and best intentions.

15

Rewriting the Discourse of Racial Identity: Toward a Pedagogy and Politics of Whiteness

Henry A. Giroux

> The liberation of racial identity is as much a part of the struggle against racism as the elimination of racial discrimination and inequality. That liberation will involve a revisioning of racial politics and a transformation of racial difference. It will render democracy itself much more radically pluralistic, and will make identity much more a matter of choice than of ascription. As the struggles to achieve these objectives unfold, we shall gradually recognize that the racialization of democracy is as important as the democratization of race (Winant, 1994, p. 169).

WHITENESS AND THE CONSERVATIVE BACKLASH

Within the last decade, the debate over race took an intriguing turn as whiteness became increasingly visible as a symbol of racial identity. Displaced from its widely understood status as an unnamed, universal moral referent, whiteness as a category of racial identity was appropriated by diverse conservative and right-wing groups, as well as critical scholars, as part of a broader articulation of race and difference. For a disparate group of Whites, mobilized, in part, by the moral panic generated by right-wing attacks on immigration, race-referential policies, and the welfare state, whiteness became a signifier for middle-class resistance to "taxation, to the expansion of state furnished rights of all sorts, and to integration" (Winant, 1992, p.166). Threatened by the call for minority rights, the rewriting of U. S. history from the bottom up, and the shifting racial demographics of the nations' cities, other Whites felt increasingly angry and resentful over what was viewed as an attack on their sense of individual and collective consciousness. (For an excellent analysis of this issue see Edsall & Edsall, 1992).

As whiteness came under scrutiny by various social groups—such as Black and Latina feminists, radical multiculturalists, critical race theorists, and others—as an oppressive, invisible center against which all else is measured, many Whites began to identify with the "new racism" epitomized by right-wing conservatives, such as talk show host Rush Limbaugh (e. g., Giroux, 1992a; Winant, 1994). Winning over vast audiences with the roar of the "angry White male" bitter over imagined racial injuries committed against Whites, Limbaugh's popularity suggested that race had become one of the most significant social forces of the 1980s and 1990s. In an era of unprecedented unemployment, poverty, and diminishing opportunities for most Black Americans, right-wing Whites convinced themselves of their own loss of privilege. Thus, the discourse of race became a vehicle for appeasing White anxiety and undermining the forceful legacy of racial and "social justice." For example, as the Republican Party moved to the right during the 1980s and 1990s, it capitalized on the racial fears of many Whites and launched an aggressive attack on affirmative action while successfully promoting retrograde policies designed to reduce social spending, dismantle the welfare state, and slow down the pace of racial integration (Edsall & Edsall, 1992). The progressive legacy of identity politics—with its emphasis on acknowledging the presence of new social actors who use their own social location as a resource to develop a politics that attempts to historicize and understand how identities are constructed and work as "a crucial movement to expand citizenship to people of color and other subordinated groups"—was either trivialized or dismissed as conservatives appropriated the politics of identity as a defining principle of whiteness (Yúdice, 1995). John Brenkman (1995) highlights this appropriation by claiming that "the constituency whose beliefs and fears have been most significantly molded to their racial identity in the 1980s are White (p. 14)."

A siege mentality has arisen for policing cultural boundaries and reasserting national identity. The discourse of whiteness signifies the resentment and confusion of many Whites who feel victimized and bitter, while it masks deep inequalities and exclusionary practices within the current social order. Shifting the politics of race from the discourse of White supremacy, the historical legacy of slavery and segregation, as well as the ongoing burden of racial injustice endured by African American and other minorities in the United States, politicians such as Pat Buchanan, David Duke, Jesse Helms, and Pat Robertson mobilized a new populist discourse about family, nation, traditional values, and individualism as part of a broader resistance to multicultural democracy and diverse racial culture.

In the popular media, conservatives bash Blacks for many of the social and economic problems facing the country (e. g., Giroux, 1996). Conservative columnist Mickey Kaus exemplified this sensibility when he said he wants "to live in a society where there is no alienated race and no racism, where I need not feel uncomfortable walking down the street because I'm White" (Brenkman, 1995, p. 34). As race became paramount in shaping U. S. politics and everyday life from the 1980s on, racial prejudice in its overt forms was considered a taboo. While the old racism maintained some cachet among the more vulgar, right-wing conservatives (i.e., New York City's radio talk show host Bob Grant), a new racist discourse emerged in the United States. The new racism was coded in the language of "welfare reform," "neighborhood schools," "toughness on crime," and "illegitimate births." Cleverly designed to mobilize White fears while relieving Whites of any semblance of social responsibility and commitment, the new racism served to rewrite the politics of whiteness as a "besieged" racial identity. As the racial backlash intensified in the media and other public spheres, whiteness assumed a new form of political agency that was visible in the rise of right-wing militia groups, White skinheads, and the anti-PC crusades of indignant White students and conservative academic organizations such as the National Association of Scholars and the Southern League. (See, for further discussion, Berlet, 1995; Diamond, 1995, 1996; Novick, 1995).

Rather than being invisible, as critics from the left such as Richard Dyer (1988) and bell hooks (1992) have claimed, whiteness was aggressively embraced in popular culture in order to rearticulate a sense of individual and collective identity for "besieged" Whites. Both Dyer and hooks have argued that Whites see themselves as racially transparent and reinscribe whiteness as invisible; that is, it rarely occurs to White people that they are privileged because they are White. While this argument may have been true in the 1980s, it no longer makes sense as White youth, in particular, have become increasingly sensitive to their status as Whites because of the racial politics and media exposure of race in the last few years (Dyer, 1988; hooks, 1992). Celebrated in the mass media in the 1990s, the new cartography of race has emerged as the result of an attempt to rewrite the racial legacy of the past, while recovering a mythic vision of whiteness associated with purity and innocence. Immensely popular films such as *Forrest Gump* (1994) attempted to rewrite public memory by cleansing the American past of racial tensions and endorsing "a preferred understanding of racial relations that work on the behalf of the public mourning of the 'victimized White male'" (Gresson, 1996, p. 11). Widely discussed books, such as *The Bell Curve* by Richard Herrnstein and Charles Murray (1994) and *The End of Racism* by Dinesh D'Souza (1995), revised and reaffirmed the basic principles of the eugenics debate of the 1920s and 1930s and provided a defense of racial hierarchies.

In the popular press, the discourse of racial discrimination and social inequality gave way to lurid stories about Black crime, illegal aliens taking jobs, the threat to the deficit posed by government welfare payments to single teen mothers, and the assertion that Black "gangsta" rap artists such as Snoop Doggy Dogg and Ice Cube corrupt the moral values of White suburban youth. (See, for further discussion, Dyson, 1996; Ferrell & Sanders, 1995; Fiske, 1994; Giroux, 1996; Gray, 1995; Jones & Deterline, 1994; Reeves & Campbell, 1994). While liberal academic journals such as *The New Republic* and *The Atlantic Monthly* shunned the extremist discourses of David Duke, Ralph Reed, and Jerry Falwell, they produced editorials and stories legitimating the popular perception that Black culture is a culture of crime, pathology, and moral degeneracy. The *New Republic* devoted an entire issue to an analysis of *The Bell Curve*, justifying its decision in a shameful editorial statement that declared, "The notion that there might be resilient ethnic differences in intelligence is not, we believe, an inherently racist belief" (Editorial, 1994, p. 9). Of course, the refusal to acknowledge that such a position grew historically from a eugenics movement that legitimated diverse racial hatreds as well as some of the most barbarous and atrocious massacres of the twentieth century appeared irrelevant next to the editorial's self-congratulatory assertion of intellectual flexibility. The *Atlantic Monthly* echoed similar racial fears in a barrage of sensationalist cover stories and articles about how crime, disease, gangsta rap, and unwed (Black) mothers were about to wreak havoc on "everyone—even White people in Back Bay" (Augnet, 1996, p. 14).

The tawdry representations of Black experience that these magazines produced gained increasing currency in the dominant media. Racial coding, parading as commonsense populism, associated Blacks with a series of negative equivalencies that denied racial injustice while affirming the repressed, unspeakable, racist unconscious of dominant White culture. Images of menacing Black youth, welfare mothers, and convicts, framed by the evocative rhetoric of fear-mongering journalists, helped to bolster the image of a besieged White middle-class suburban family threatened by "an alien culture and peoples who are less civilized than the native ones . . . a people who stand lower in the order of culture because they are somehow lower in the order of nature, defined by race, by color, and sometimes by genetic inheritance" (Hall, 1992, p. 13).

While the popular press was signaling the emergence of a politics of identity in which White men defined themselves as the victims of "reverse" racial prejudice, academics were digging in and producing a substantial amount of scholarship, exploring what it might mean to analyze whiteness as a social, cultural, and historical construction. Such work was characterized by various attempts to locate whiteness as a racial category and to analyze it as a site of privilege, power, and ideology. In addition, this work sought to examine critically how whiteness as a racial identity is experienced, reproduced, and addressed by those diverse White men and women who identify with its commonsense assumptions and values.

In some quarters, the call to study whiteness provoked scorn and indignation. For instance, *Time* magazine ridiculed a professor who named a standard American literature survey course she taught "White Male Writers" (Henry, 1991). *Newsweek* took a more mainstream position, constructing an image of White men in the United States as undergoing an identity crisis over their changing public image. According to David Gates (1993), writing in *Newsweek*, White males were no longer secure in an identity that had been ravaged by "feminists, multiculturalists, P.C. policepersons, affirmative-action employers, rap artists, Native Americans, Japanese tycoons, Islamic fundamentalists and Third World dictators" (p. 48). *Newsweek* further lamented the clobbering that White men were taking in the media, buttressing its argument with comments from a "rancorous" female employee as well as a prominent psychiatrist, who assured readers that, "For White men in their 30s and 40s, this is not a joke at all. Their whole future is at stake, in their minds. They're scared" (Gates, 1993, p. 51). While the demise of the power of White men seemed a bit exaggerated to the editors of *Newsweek*, they made it quite clear that the current White panic was not entirely unfounded, since Whites may find themselves in the next century living in a society consisting largely of "diverse racial and ethnic minorities" (p. 49).

WHITENESS STUDIES

Building upon the work of W.E.B. Dubois, Ralph Ellison, and James Baldwin, scholars from a wide range of disciplines, including history, cultural studies, literary studies, sociology, and speech communication, have put the "construction of 'Whiteness' on the table to be investigated, analyzed, punctured, and probed" (Fischer Fishkin, 1995, p. 430). Rejecting the assumption that an analysis of race means focusing primarily on people of color, scholars such as David Roediger (1991; 1994), Ruth Frankenberg (1993), Theodore Allen (1994), bell hooks (1992), Noel Ignatiev (1995), Toni Morrison (1992), Howard Winant (1994), Alexander Saxton (1991), and Fred Pfeil (1995) address the historical and social construction of "whiteness" across a wide spectrum of spheres, identities, and institutions, and redefine the necessity to make whiteness central to the broader arena of racial politics. (See also, Ignatiev & Garvey, 1996; Omi & Winant, 1994; Ware, 1992). While it is impossible to analyze this large body of work in any great detail, I will comment briefly on some of the theoretical directions it has taken and assess the implications of such work for those of us concerned with issues of representation, racial politics, and pedagogy.

Historians such as David Roediger, Noel Ignatiev, and Theodore Allen among others, build upon the work of previous historians of race by focusing less on the African American influences on mainstream White American culture—Southern culture, colonial American agriculture, American music, theater, literature, etc.—than on the issue of how White racial identity has been taken up, appropriated, and shaped historically in terms of how Whites narrate and represent themselves, as well as the ways in which dominant White identity influences the construction and treatment of racial "others" (e.g., Fischer Fishkin, 1995). Challenging both what it means to be White and the experience of whiteness as an often unstable, shifting process of inclusion and exclusion, these historians have rearticulated and broadened the concept of racial identity while simultaneously challenging whiteness as a site of racial, economic, and political privilege. More specifically, such work brings a revisionist history to the highly charged debates about racial and national identity central to contemporary American politics. By focusing on how whiteness, as the dominant racial identity, shaped the history of American labor at different intervals and configured historical and political relations among ethnic groups (such as the Irish), Roediger and others have thrown into sharp relief "the impact that the dominant racial identity in the United States has had not only on the treatment of racial 'others' but also on the ways that Whites think of themselves, of power, of pleasure, and of gender" (Roediger, 1994, p. 75).

Central to theoretical work on whiteness is the attempt to confront "the issue of White racial identity [and to raise] the questions of when, why and with what results so-called 'White people' have come to identify themselves as White" (p. 75). No longer the stable, self-evident, or pure essence central to modernity's self-definition, whiteness is unmasked, in the work of such historians as David Roediger and Noel Ignatiev, as an attempt to arbitrarily categorize, position, and contain the "other" within racially ordered hierarchies. Dislodged from a self-legitimating discourse grounded in a set of fixed transcendental racial categories, whiteness is analyzed as a lived, but rarely recognized, component of White racial identity and domination.

These scholars have done more than add a historical component to the discourse about whiteness; they have expanded and deepened the relevance of politicizing the debates about the interrelationship between whiteness and race. Roediger (1994), for example, provides three reasons for urging cultural critics who are involved in the social construction of race to focus their political energies on "exposing, demystifying and demeaning the particular ideology of whiteness":

The first is that, while neither whiteness nor Blackness is a scientific (or natural) racial category, the former is infinitely more false, and precisely because of that falsity, more dangerous, than the latter. The second is that in attacking the notion that whiteness and Blackness are "the same," we specifically undermine what has become, via the notion of "reverse racism," a major prop underpinning the popular refusal among Whites to face both racism and themselves. The last is that whiteness is now a particularly brittle and fragile form of social identity and it can be fought (p. 12).

The notion that whiteness can be demystified and reformulated is a theoretical motif that links historical analyses of the construction of whiteness to the work of prominent theorists in a variety of other fields. For instance, Toni Morrison (1992), in her landmark book *Playing in the Dark*, challenges critics to examine how whiteness as a literary category functions to shape and legitimate a monolithic "American identity." Morrison frames her interrogation of the imaginative construction of whiteness in the following way:

the readers of virtually all of American fiction have been positioned as White. I am interested to know what that assumption has meant to the literary imagination. When does racial "unconsciousness" or awareness of race enrich interpretive language, and when does it impoverish it? . . . What parts do the invention and development of whiteness play in the construction of what is loosely described as "American" ? (p. xii, 9)

In the field of cultural studies, Ruth Frankenberg, Richard Dyer, and bell hooks further probe the role of whiteness as a site of privilege and exclusion, recognizing that whiteness is produced differently within a variety of public spaces, as well as across the diverse categories of class, gender, sexuality, and ethnicity. Frankenberg (1993), for example, explores how whiteness as a site of racial privilege works to shape the lives and identities of a diverse group of White women. On the other hand, through analysis of the racial pedagogies at work in popular culture, Dyer (1988) challenges the representational power of whiteness "to be everything and nothing as the source of its representational power" (p. 45). He provides a theoretical service by analyzing whiteness as a guarantor of beauty and truth within the representational politics of three Hollywood films.

One of the most trenchant criticisms of whiteness comes from bell hooks, who argues that too many White scholars focus on certifiable "others" in their analysis of race, but they are doing very little "to investigate and justify all aspects of White culture from a standpoint of 'difference'" (hooks, 1990, p. 55). According to hooks, "It would be just so interesting for all those White folks who are giving Blacks their take on Blackness to let them know what's going on with whiteness" (p. 54). hooks further extends her critique by arguing that while Whites are willing to analyze how Blacks are perceived by Whites, rarely are White critics attentive to how Blacks view Whites. According to hooks, Whites refuse to see Blacks as political agents. Nor do Whites, caught up in their own racial fantasies of murder and rape, recognize that, in the Black imagination, whiteness is often associated with terror. But for hooks more is at stake than getting Whites to recognize that representations of whiteness as pure, good, benevolent, and innocent are challenged by Black imaginations' representations of whiteness as capricious, cruel, and unchecked. hooks also calls into question whiteness as an ideology by exposing its privileged readings of history, art, and broader institutional power and its politically myopic forms of cultural criticism. hooks (1992) builds upon this criticism by calling for Whites to become self-critical about how whiteness terrorizes, to "shift locations [in order] to see the world differently."

In a decisive theoretical and somewhat paradoxical twist, hooks (1992) urges Whites not to go too far in focusing on whiteness, particularly if it serves to downplay the effects of racism on Blacks. First, she argues that attempts to see racism as victimizing to Whites "in the hopes that this will act as an intervention is a misguided strategy" (p. 13). Second, disavowing the discourse of White victimization as one that fails to distinguish between racial prejudice, as it is experienced by Blacks and Whites alike, and institutional racism, which victimizes people of color, hooks agrees with the Black theologian James Cone, who argues that the only way in which Whites can become antiracist is "to destroy themselves and be born again as beautiful Black persons" (p. 14).

hooks's criticism is echoed in the field of speech communication by Thomas Nakayama and Robert Krizek, who also argue that the primary task of Whites is to demystify and unveil whiteness as a form of domination. In this case, Nakayama and Krizek (1995) go to great lengths to "deterritorialize the territory of 'White,' to expose, examine, and disrupt . . . so that like other positions it may be placed under critical analysis . . . . We seek an understanding of the ways that this rhetorical construction makes itself visible and invisible, eluding analysis yet exerting influence over everyday life" (p. 291).

Heavily indebted to the assumption that whiteness is synonymous with domination and oppression, the new scholarship on whiteness focuses largely on the critical project of unveiling the rhetorical, political, cultural, and social mechanisms through which whiteness is both invented and used to mask its power and privilege. The political thrust of such work seeks to abolish whiteness as a racial category and marker of identity. That is, central to such an effort is the attempt to strip whiteness of its historical and political power to produce, regulate, and constrain racialized others within the discursive and material relations of racial domination and subjugation. Roediger (1994) echoes this sentiment in his comment that "it is not merely that 'Whiteness' is oppressive and false; it is that 'Whiteness' is nothing but oppressive and false" (p. 13). This position is echoed by Noel Ignatiev (1995), who provocatively writes in *Race Traitor* that "the key to solving the social problems of our age is to abolish the White race . . . . So long as the White race exists, all movements against racism are doomed to fail [and] treason to 'Whiteness' is loyalty to humanity" (p. 10). Similar arguments conflating 'Whiteness' with White racism can be found in the work of Derrick Bell (1992) and Andrew Hacker (1992).

In what follows, I will analyze some of the political and pedagogical problems that flow from a critique based on the assumptions that whiteness is synonymous with domination and that the only alternative that progressive White youth have to constructing a racial identity is to, in fact, renounce their own whiteness. I develop this critique by examining three considerations. First, I focus on some of the issues at stake in understanding the racial backlash that is taking place among many White students in the United States. Second, I address how representations of whiteness in two films exemplify the limits and possibilities of analyzing its social construction. Third, I explore how these films might be used pedagogically to rearticulate a notion of whiteness that builds upon, but also moves beyond, the view of whiteness as simply a fixed position of domination. To do so, I attempt to fashion a tentative and strategic pedagogical approach to whiteness that offers students a possibility of rearticulating "whiteness," rather than either simply accepting its dominant normative assumptions or rejecting it as a racist form of identity. While White students may well feel traumatized in putting their racial identities on trial, trauma in this case can become a useful pedagogical tool in helping them locate themselves within and against the discourse and practice of racism. As a potent pedagogical tool, trauma refers to the subjectively felt effects of classroom practices that baffle, reorient, and challenge students' commonsense assumptions about race, how it shapes their lives and affects their interactions with racially diverse groups of people. Trauma represents that pedagogical moment when identities become unsettled, provoking both anxiety and the opportunity to rethink the political nature and moral content of one's own racial identity, and the roles it plays in shaping one's relationship to those who are constituted as racially "other." In short, White youth need a more critical and productive way of construing a sense of identity, agency, and race across a wide range of contexts and public spheres. However, linking whiteness to the project of radical democratic change should not be a rationale for evading racial injustice, and the deep inequalities between Blacks and Whites.

YOUTH AND THE REARTICULATION OF WHITENESS

Race increasingly matters as a defining principle of identity and culture as much for White students in the 1990s as for youth of color in the 1970s and 1980s. As a marker of difference, race significantly frames how White youth experience themselves and their relationships to a variety of public spaces marked by the presence of people of color. Diverse racial identities have become more visible and more hybrid as a result of the changing demographics of urban space and the prominence of race in hip-hop culture, fanzine magazines, MTV, television sitcoms, Hollywood films, and the emergence of Black public intellectuals in the media. As culture becomes more racially diverse, White youth increasingly become more conscious of both the ways in which subordinate others struggle to represent themselves and the necessity to define themselves in racial terms that take into account their whiteness as a marker of identity, a point of cultural attachment and historical location. In contrast to the position popular among White educators who claim that "we [Whites] do not experience ourselves as defined by our skin color" (Scheurich, 1993, p. 6), White youth have become increasingly aware of themselves as White. Two major forces affecting the racial divide have served to make whiteness more visible and fragile as a site of privilege and power, while at the same time limiting opportunities for youth to be both White and oppositional. (See, Jester, 1992; Yúdice, 1995, on the possibilities for articulating whiteness in oppositional terms). In other words, whiteness has become more visible as a privileged signifier of racial identity and, consequently, has come under attack in many quarters. However, as whiteness increasingly becomes an object of historical and critical analysis, there have been few attempts to provide a theoretical language in which White youth can refuse to reference their whiteness only through the common experience of racism and oppression. Hence, it becomes difficult for White youth to view themselves as both White and antiracist at the same time.

The first force is the emergence of identity politics in the United States from the 1960s to the present. While contradictory and diverse in its manifestations, identity politics has largely resulted in the formation, consolidation, and visibility of new group racial identities. These include groups as diverse as White youth who identify with Black youth culture and label themselves "wiggers"; feminists whose identities have been rearticulated through the racial registers of being Black, Latina, Brown, or Mestizo; and political groups such as Black Nationalists, Mexican Americans, Puerto Rican Nacionalistas, and Native Americans who assert their racial and hybrid identities as a part of a new politics of difference, representation, and social justice. These identities have emerged within a highly charged public debate on race, gender, and sexual orientation, and have made it more difficult for White youth to either ignore whiteness as a racial category or to "safely imagine that they are invisible to Black people" (hooks, 1992, p. 168). White students may see themselves as non-racist, but they no longer view themselves as colorless. As Charles Gallagher (1995) points out, whiteness has become "a salient category of self-definition emerging in response to the political and cultural challenges of other racialized groups" (p. 166).

Unfortunately, for many White youth, whose imaginations have been left fallow, unfed by a larger society's vision or quest for social justice, identity politics engendered a defensive posture. White students assumed that the only role they could play in the struggle against racism was either to renounce their whiteness and adopt the modalities of the subordinated group or to suffer the charge that any claim to White identity was tantamount to racism. Within this paradigm, racism has been configured through a politics of representation that has analyzed how Whites have constructed, stereotyped, and delegitimated racial others, but it has said practically nothing about how racial politics might address the construction of whiteness as an oppositional racial category. Moreover, while the debate within identity politics has made important theoretical gains in rewriting what it means to be Black, it has not questioned the complexity of whiteness with the same dialectical attentiveness. Although whiteness has become an object of critical scrutiny, its primary connotation appears to "signify the center which pushes out, excludes, appropriates and distorts the margins" (Jester, 1992, p. 115). Similarly, liberal ideology has provided only a one-item agenda for how Blacks and Whites might work together in the struggle for social and racial justice. It would replace their recognition of the importance of racial identities with calls for tolerance and a color-blind society.

Identity politics, in part, served as one means to undermine the possibilities for White youth to engage critically the liberal appeal to a color-blind society; it has also had the unintended consequence of reinforcing the divide between Blacks and Whites. Furthermore, the absence of an oppositional politics for antiracist pedagogies and struggles between the discourse of separatism and a power-evasive liberalism provided an opportunity for conservatives and right-wing activists to step into the fray and appropriate whiteness as part of a broader backlash against Blacks and people of color. In this case, conservatives and the far right actively engaged in the process of recovering whiteness and redefining themselves as the victims of racial antagonism, while simultaneously waging a brutal and racially coded attack against urban youth, immigrants, and the poor. Seemingly unresponsive to the needs of White youth, the White working class, and the White underclass, the discourse of whiteness was easily appropriated as part of a broader reactionary cultural politics that in its most extreme manifestations fueled the rise of White militia groups, the growing skinhead movement among White youth, and a growing anti-political-correctness movement in both higher education and the mass media.

The second force at work in reconstructing whiteness as a racial category among youth is the profound changes that have taken place regarding the visibility of Blacks in the media. While it would be foolish to equate the increased visibility of Blacks in the media with an increase in power, especially around issues of ownership, diverse representations of Black culture throughout the media have made issues of White identity inextricably more fragile and fluid. This is evident in the ways in which popular culture is increasingly being reconfigured through the music, dance, and language of hip-hop. Similarly, the emergence of Black Entertainment Television (BET), MTV, and cable television testifies to the ubiquitous presence of people of color in television dramas, sports, and music while the popular press touts the emergence of the "new" Black public intellectuals in academia. All of these changes in the media signal that Whites can no longer claim the privilege of not "seeing" Blacks and other people of color; White youth now have to confront cultural difference as a force that affects every aspect of their lives. Coupled with the rise of an incendiary racial politics, the racialization of the media culture, and growing economic fears about their future, a significant number of White American youth are increasingly experiencing a crisis of self-esteem. Similar to cultural critic Diana Jester's (1992) comment about British youth, they "do not feel that they have an 'ethnicity,' or if they do, that it's not one they feel too good about" (p. 107).

Jester (1992) further suggests that White youth have few resources for questioning and rearticulating whiteness as an identity that productively narrates their everyday experiences. This seems to be borne out in the ways in which many White college students have reacted to the racial politics of the last decade. One indication of the way in which whiteness is being negotiated among students is evident in the rising racist assaults on students of color on campuses across the United States in the last few years. As a resurgent racism becomes more respectable in the broader culture, racist acts and assaults have once again become a staple of college life.[1] At the same time, large numbers of White students appear to support the ongoing assaults on affirmative action programs that have been waged by the courts and state legislatures. Moreover, White students increasingly express a general sense of angst over racial politics and an emphatic indifference to politics in general.

Gallagher's ethnographic study of White college students suggests that many of them view the emergence of multiculturalists, feminists, and other progressive groups as an attack on whiteness and a form of reverse discrimination. For example, Gallagher (1995) writes:

It is commonly assumed among many White students that any class that addresses issues of race or racism must necessarily be anti-White. More specifically, students believe that the instructors of these classes will hold individual White students accountable for slavery, lynching, discrimination, and other heinous acts (p. 170).

Many of the White students that Gallagher interviewed did not see themselves as privileged by virtue of skin color; some went so far as to claim that, given the rise of racial preferences, Whites no longer had a fair chance when competing with minorities in the labor market. Gallagher asserts that White students are resentful over being blamed for racism and that "ignoring the ways in which Whites 'get raced' has the making of something politically dangerous . . . [and that] [W]hiteness must be addressed because the politics of race, from campus clubs to issues of crime to representation in the statehouse, permeate almost every social exchange" (pp. 182, 185). Unfortunately, Gallagher offers little in the way of suggesting how whiteness might be rearticulated in oppositional terms. In fact, he concludes by suggesting that as whiteness becomes more visible, it will be further appropriated and mediated through a racist ideology, and any notion of White solidarity will result in a reactionary politics. Hence, whiteness as a marker of identity is confined within a notion of domination and racism that leaves White youth no critical lens, vocabulary, or social imaginary through which they can see themselves as actors in creating an oppositional space to fight for equality and social justice.

Central to any pedagogical approach to race and the politics of whiteness is the recognition that race, as a set of attitudes, values, lived experiences, and affective identifications, has become a defining feature of American life. However arbitrary and mythic, dangerous and variable, the fact is that racial categories exist and shape the lives of people differently within existing inequalities of power and wealth.[2] As a central form of difference, race will neither disappear, be wished out of existence, or become somehow irrelevant in the United States and the larger global context. Howard Winant (1994) insightfully argues:

Race is a condition of individual and collective identity, a permanent, though tremendously flexible, element of social structure. Race is a means of knowing and organizing the social world; it is subject to continual contestation and reinterpretation, but it is no more likely to disappear than any other forms of human inequality and difference . . . . To rethink race is not only to recognize its permanence, but also to understand the essential test that it poses for any diverse society seeking to achieve a modicum of freedom (p. xiii).

Pedagogically, this implies providing the conditions for students to address not only how their whiteness functions in society as marker of privilege and power, but also how it can be used as a condition for expanding the ideological and material realities of democratic public life. Moreover, it is imperative that all students understand how race functions systemically as it shapes various forms of representations, social relations, and institutional structures. Rather than proposing the eradication of the concept of race itself, educators and other cultural workers need to fashion pedagogical practices that take a detour through race in order to address how whiteness might be renegotiated as a productive force within a politics of difference linked to a radical democratic project.

Analyzing whiteness as a central element of racial politics becomes useful in exploring how whiteness as a cultural practice promotes race-based hierarchies, how White racial identity structures the struggle over cultural and political resources, and how rights and responsibilities are defined, confirmed, or contested across diverse racial claims.[3] whiteness in this context becomes less a matter of creating a new form of identity politics than an attempt to rearticulate whiteness as part of a broader project of cultural, social, and political citizenship.

All students need to feel that they have a personal stake in their racial identity (however fluid, unstable, and transitory), an identity that will allow them to assert a view of political agency in which they can join with diverse groups around a notion of democratic public life that affirms racial differences through a "rearticulation of cultural, social, and political citizenship" (Yúdice, 1995, pp. 276–77). Linking identity, race, and difference to a broader vision of radical democracy suggests a number of important pedagogical considerations. First, students need to investigate the historical relationship between race and ethnicity. Historian David Roediger is right in warning against the conflation of race and ethnicity by critical theorists, especially in light of a history of ethnicity in which White immigrants saw themselves as White and ethnic. According to Roediger (1994), the claim to ethnicity among White immigrants, especially those from Europe, did not prevent them from defining their racial identities through the discourse of White separatism and supremacy. In this case, White ethnicity was not ignored by such immigrants; it was affirmed and linked in some cases to the dominant relations of racism.

The issue of racial identity can be linked to what Stuart Hall (1996) has called the "new ethnicity." (See also, Hall, 1990; 1991a; 1991b). For Hall, racial identities can be understood through the notion of ethnicity, but not the old notion of ethnicity that depends in part on the suppression of cultural difference and a separatist notion of White identity. Within the discourse of the "old identity," identity was seen as fixed and self-contained, as opposed to open, complex, and unfinished. Consequently, the "old ethnicity" was often defined as an essence that had to be protected against other forms of cultural differences in which it found itself embroiled. Hall's attempt to rewrite ethnicity as a progressive and critical concept does not fall into the theoretical trap described by

Roediger. By removing ethnicity from the traditional moorings of nationalism, racism, colonialism, and the state, Hall (1996) posits the new ethnicity as a referent for acknowledging "the place of history, language, and culture in the construction of subjectivity and identity, as well as the fact that all discourse is placed, positioned, situated, and all knowledge is contextual" (p. 29).

Extending Hall's insights about ethnicity, I suggest that the diverse subject positions, social experiences, and cultural identities that inform whiteness as a political and social construct can be rearticulated in order for students to recognize that "we all speak from a particular place, out of a particular history, out of particular experience, a particular culture without being constrained by [such] positions . . . . We are all, in that sense, ethnically located and our ethnic identities are crucial to our subjective sense of who we are" (Hall, 1996, p. 29). In Hall's (1990) terms, whiteness can be addressed not as a form of identity fashioned through a claim to purity or some universal essence, but as one that "lives with and through, not despite difference" (p. 235).

Hall provides a theoretical language for racializing whiteness without essentializing it. That is, he recognizes that whiteness is a crucial form of self-identity, "a politically and culturally constructed category, which cannot be grounded in a set of fixed trans-cutural or transcendental racial categories" (Hall, 1996, p. 443).[4] In this case, whiteness provides a shifting and complex set of attachments and identifications through which individuals and social groups understand who they are and how they are supposed to act within and across the diverse landscape of cultural difference. Hall also argues correctly that ethnicity must be defined and defended through a set of ethical and political referents that connect various democratic struggles while expanding the range and possibilities of democratic relations and practices. Within the theoretical parameters of a new ethnicity, whiteness can be read as a complex register of identity and a theory of agency defined through a politics of difference that is subject to the shifting currents of history, power, and culture. That is, whiteness can no longer be taken up as fixed, naturally grounded in a tradition or ancestry, but, as Ien Ang (1995) claims in another context, must be understood as a form of postmodern ethnicity, "experienced as a provisional and partial site of identity which must be constantly (re)invented and (re)negotiated" (p. 110).

The new ethnicity defines racial identities as multiple, porous, complex, and shifting, and in doing so provides a theoretical opening for educators and students to move beyond framing whiteness as either good or bad, racially innocent or intractably racist. whiteness in this context can be addressed through its complex relationship with other determining factors that usurp any claim to racial purity or singularity. At the same time, whiteness must be addressed within power relations that exploit its subversive potential, while not erasing the historical and political role it plays in shaping other racialized identities and social differences. Unlike the old ethnicity that posits difference in essentialist or separatist terms, Hall's notion of the new ethnicity defines identity as an ongoing act of cultural recovery, while acknowledging that any particular claim to racial identity offers no guarantees regarding political outcomes. At the same time, the new ethnicity provides a theory that allows White students to go beyond the paralysis inspired by guilt or the racism fueled by anxiety and the fear of difference. In this context, whiteness gains its meaning only in conjunction with other identities such as those informed by class, gender, age, nationality, and citizenship. For progressive Whites, "crossing over does not mean crossing out" (Erickson, p. 185), or renouncing whiteness as a form of racial identity. Whites have to learn to live with their whiteness by rearticulating it in terms that help them to formulate what it means to develop viable political coalitions and social movements. They also have to learn to engage in a critical pedagogy of self-formation that allows them to cross racial lines not in order to become Black, but to begin to forge multiracial coalitions based on a critical engagement rather than a denial of "whiteness." Whites have to unlearn those histories, ideologies, values, and social relations that allow them to "cast the Other primarily as the object of aesthetic, not moral evaluation; as a source of sensations, not responsibility . . . [forces] that tend to render human relations fragmentary and discontinuous" (Bauman, 1995, p. 155).

By positioning whiteness within a notion of cultural citizenship that politically, culturally, and socially affirms difference, students can take notice of how their whiteness functions as a racial identity. In addition, they can be critical of forms of whiteness that are structured in dominance and aligned with exploitative interests and oppressive social relations. By rearticulating whiteness as more than a form of domination, White students can construct narratives of whiteness that both challenge and, hopefully, provide a basis for transforming the dominant relationship between racial identity and citizenship, a relationship informed by an oppositional politics (e. g. hooks, 1990; 1992; Giroux, 1997; Winant, 1994). Such a political practice suggests new subject positions, alliances, commitments, and forms of solidarity between White students and others engaged in the struggle to expand the possibilities of democratic life through "a profound restructuring and reconceptualization of the power relations between cultural communities" (Shohat & Stam, 1994, p. 47). George Yúdice (1995) argues that as part of a broader project for articulating whiteness in oppositional terms, White youth must feel that they have a stake in racial politics that connects them to the struggles being waged by other groups. At the center of such struggles is both the battle over citizenship redefined through the discourse of rights and the problem of resource distribution. He writes:

This is where identity politics segues into other issues, such as tax deficits, budget cuts, lack of educational opportunities, lack of jobs, immigration policies, international trade agreements, environmental blight, lack of health care insurance, and so on. These are the areas in which middle—and working-class Whites historically have had an advantage over people of color. However, today that advantage has eroded in certain respects (p. 276).

As part of a wider attempt to engage these issues, Yúdice suggests that White youth can form alliances with other social and racial groups who recognize the need for solidarity in addressing issues of public life that undermine the quality of democracy for all groups. As White youth struggle to find a cultural and political space from which to speak and act as transformative citizens, it is important that educators address what it means pedagogically and politically to help students rearticulate whiteness as part of a democratic cultural politics. While it is imperative that a critical analysis of whiteness address its historical legacy and existing complicity with racist exclusion and oppression, it is equally crucial that such work distinguish between whiteness as a racial identity that is non-racist or antiracist and those aspects of whiteness that are racist (e.g., Frankenberg, 1993). When whiteness is discussed in educational settings, the emphasis is almost exclusively on revealing it as an ideology of privilege mediated largely through the dynamics of racism (e. g., Scheurich, 1993a; Sleeter, 1993). While such interventions are crucial in developing an antiracist pedagogy, they do not go far enough.

REPRESENTATIONS OF WHITENESS IN THE MEDIA

I want to begin to take up this pedagogical challenge by building upon James Snead's (1994, especially Chapter 10) pertinent observation that the emergence of mass visual productions in the United States requires new ways of seeing and making visible the racial structuring of White experience.[5] The electronic media—television, movies, music, and news—have become powerful pedagogical forces, veritable teaching machines in shaping the social imaginations of students in terms of how they view themselves, others, and the larger society.

Central to the formative influence of the media is a representational politics of race in which the portrayal of Black people abstracts them from their real histories while reinforcing all too familiar stereotypes ranging from lazy and shiftless to the menacing and dangerous. Recent films from a variety of genres, such as *Pulp Fiction* (1995), *Just Cause* (1995), and *Ace Ventura: When Nature Calls* (1996), offer no apologies for employing racist language, depicting Black men as rapists, or portraying Blacks as savage or subhuman. Antiracist readings of these films often position White students to define and critique racism as the product of dominant racist stereotypes that unfairly depict Black identities, experiences, histories, and social relations. As important as these critiques are in any antiracist discourse or pedagogy, they are severely limited theoretically because they do not address how whiteness as a racial identity and social construction is taught, learned, experienced, and identified within certain forms of knowledge, values, and privileges. Hollwood films rarely position audiences to question the pleasures, identifications, desires, and fears they experience as Whites viewing dominant representational politics of race. More specifically, such films rarely make problematic either the structuring principles that mobilize particular pleasures in audiences or how pleasure as a response to certain representations functions as part of a broader public discourse. At worst, such films position Whites as racial tourists, distant observers to the racist images and narratives that fill Hollywood screens. At best, such films reinforce the liberal assumption that racism is something that gives rise to Black oppression but has little or nothing to do with promoting power, racial privilege, and a sense of moral agency in the lives of Whites (Frankenberg, 1993, p. 49).

In what follows, I want to explore the pedagogical implications of examining representations of whiteness in two seemingly disparate films, *Dangerous Minds* (1995) and *Suture* (1993). Though I will focus primarily on *Dangerous Minds*, it is through a juxtaposition and intertextual reading of these films that I hope to provide some pedagogical insights for examining how whiteness as a cultural practice is learned through the representation of racialized identities; how it opens up the possibility of intellectual self-reflection; and how students might mediate critically the complex relations between whiteness and racism not by repudiating their whiteness, but by grappling with its racist legacy and its potential to be rearticulated in oppositional and transformative terms. I also want to stress that I am not suggesting that *Dangerous Minds* is a bad film and *Suture* is a good film, given their different approaches to "whiteness." Both have weaknesses that are notable. What I am suggesting is that these films are exemplary in representing dominant readings of whiteness and as cultural texts that can be used pedagogically for addressing the shortcomings of the recent scholarship on "whiteness," particularly as ways to move beyond the jaundiced view of whiteness as simply a trope of domination.

At first glance, these films appear to have nothing in common in terms of audience, genre, intention, or politics. *Dangerous Minds*, a Hollywood sleeper starring Michelle Pfeiffer, was produced for a mass audience and grossed millions for its producers within its first week. The film's popularity can be measured in part by the appearance of a pilot television series called *Dangerous Minds* that premiered in the fall of 1996. In contrast, *Suture* is an independent film that played primarily to highbrow audiences with a penchant for avant-garde cinema. While some may argue that *Dangerous Minds* is too popular and too unoriginal to be taken seriously as a pedagogical text, it is precisely because of its popularity and widespread appeal that it warrants an extended analysis. Like many Hollywood films, *Dangerous Minds* is offensive not only in terms of its racial politics, but also in its fundamentally debased depiction of teaching and education. The 1995 summer hit is also symptomatic of how seemingly "innocent" entertainment gains its popularity in taking part in a larger public discourse on race and whiteness largely informed by a right-wing and conservative notion of politics, theory, and pedagogy.

DANGEROUS MINDS AND THE PRODUCTION OF WHITENESS

Dangerous Minds resembles a long tradition of Hollywood movies recounting the sorry state of education for dispossessed kids who bear the brunt of poverty, crime, violence, and despair in the inner cities of the United States. Unlike earlier films such as *Blackboard Jungle* (1955), *To Sir With Love* (1967), and *Stand and Deliver* (1988), which also deal with the interface of schooling and the harsh realities of inner-city life, *Dangerous Minds* does more than simply narrate the story of an idealistic teacher who struggles to connect with her rowdy and disinterested students. *Dangerous Minds* functions as a dual chronicle. In the first instance, the film attempts to represent whiteness as the archetype of rationality, "tough" authority, and cultural standards in the midst of the changing racial demographics of urban space and the emergence of a resurgent racism in the highly charged politics of the 1990s. In the second instance, the film offers viewers a mix of compassion and consumerism as a solution to motivating teenagers who have long since given up on schooling as meaningful to their lives. In both instances, whiteness becomes a referent not only for rearticulating racially coded notions of teaching and learning, but also for redefining how citizenship can be constructed for students of color as a function of choice linked exclusively to the marketplace.

Providing an allegory for representing both the purpose of schooling and the politics of racial difference as they intersect within the contested space of the urban public schools, *Dangerous Minds* skillfully mobilizes race as an organizing principle to promote its narrative structure and ideological message. Black and Hispanic teenagers provide the major fault line for developing pedagogical classroom relations through which whiteness, located in the authority of the teacher, privileges itself against the racially coded images of disorder, chaos, and fear. The opposition between teacher and student, White and non-White, is clearly established in the first few scenes of the film. The opening sequence, shot in grainy monochrome, depicts a rundown urban housing project teeming with poverty, drug dealing, and imminent danger. Against this backdrop, disaffected Black and Hispanic children board a school bus that will take them to Parkmont High School and out of their crime- and drug-infested neighborhoods. This is one of the few shots in the film that provides a context for the children's lives, and the message is clear: the inner city has become a site of pathology, moral decay, and delinquency synonymous with the culture of working-class Black life. The soundtrack, featuring hip-hop music by artists such as Coolio, Sista, and Aaron Hall, is present only as a backdrop to the film.

Since the beginning of the movie is framed by racial iconography and a musical score that constructs minority students as both the objects of fear and subjects in need of discipline and control, the audience is prepared for someone to take charge. Enter LouAnne Johnson, a new teacher thrust, like a lamb led to the slaughter, into the "Academy School," a euphemism for a warehouse for students who are considered unteachable.

Dressed in frowzy tweeds and white lace, LouAnne enters her class full of high hopes to meet a room filled with Hispanic and Black kids who have brought the "worst" aspects of their culture into the classroom. Music blares amidst the clatter of students shouting, rapping, dancing, presenting LouAnne with an apparently out of control classroom in an inner-city school. Leaving the safety of her White, middle-class culture in order to teach in a place teeming with potential danger, LouAnne Johnson is presented to the audience as an innocent border crosser. This image of innocence and goodwill is used to provide White America with the comforting belief that disorder, ignorance, and chaos are always somewhere else, in that strangely homogenized, racial space known as the urban ghetto.[6] The students respond to LouAnne's attempt to greet them with the taunting epithet "White bread." Confused and unable to gain control of the class, LouAnne is accosted by a male student who makes a mockery of her authority by insulting her with a sexual innuendo. Frustrated, she leaves the class and tells Hal, a friend who teaches next door, that she has just met the "rejects from hell." He assures her that she can reach these students if she figures out how to get their attention.

These opening scenes work powerfully to link Black and Hispanic kids with the culture of criminality and danger. These scenes also make clear that whiteness as a racial identity, embodied in LouAnne Johnson, is both vulnerable and under siege, as well as the only hope these kids have for moving beyond the context and character of their racial identities. In other words, these scenes construct whiteness as a racial identity in contrast to the stereotypical portrayal of intellectually inferior, hostile, and childish Black and Hispanic kids. whiteness is thus coded as a norm for authority, orderliness, rationality, and control.

The structuring principles at work in *Dangerous Minds* perform a distinct ideological function in their attempt to cater to White consumers of popular culture. Pedagogy performs a double operation as it is used in this film. As part of the overt project, the film focuses on teaching in an inner-city school and constructs a dominant view of race as embodied in the lives of urban Black and Hispanic children. On the other hand, the hidden project of the film works pedagogically to recover and name the ideological and cultural values that construct whiteness as a dominant form of racial identity. Hollywood has been producing films about teaching for over forty years, but rarely do such films use the theme of teaching in order to legitimate a conservative view of whiteness as a besieged social formation and subordinate racial identities as a threat to public order. *Dangerous Minds* stands as an exception to the rule. The conservative and ideological implications of how whiteness is constructed in this film can be seen through a series of representations.

Dangerous Minds tells the audience nothing about the lives of the students themselves, their histories, or their experiences outside of the school. Decontextualized and dehistoricized, the cultural identities of these students appear marginal to the construction of race as an organizing principle of the film. Racial differences in this film are situated within the spatial metaphor of center and margins, with the children of color clearly occupying the margins. At the center of the film is the embellished "true story" of LouAnne Johnson, who not only overcomes her initial failure to motivate these students but also serves as a beacon of light by convincing them that who they are and what they know needs to be ditched if they are to become more civilized and cultured (and more White). Racial conflict in this context is resolved through a colonial educational model in which White paternalism and missionary zeal provide the inspiration for kids from deprived backgrounds to improve their character and sense of responsibility by reading poetry. The kids in this movie appear simply as a backdrop for expanding LouAnne's own self-consciousness and self-education; the film shows no interest in their development and ignores the opportunities for understanding their coming of age and examining how racism works in the schools and larger society. Whenever these kids do face a crisis—an unwanted pregnancy, the threat of violence, or dropping out of school—LouAnne invades their homes and private lives, using the opportunity to win the kids' allegiance or draw attention to her own divorce, physical abuse, or sense of despair. If any notion of identity occupies center stage, it is not that of the kids but that of a White woman trying to figure out how to live in a public space inhabited by racialized others.[7]

The notion of authority and agency in *Dangerous Minds* is framed within a pedagogy of "tough love" that serves to mask how racial hierarchies and structured inequality operate within the schools and connect them to the larger society. Authority in *Dangerous Minds* is asserted initially when LouAnne

Johnson shows up on the second day of class wearing a leather jacket and jeans. Reinventing herself as a military officer on leave, she further qualifies her new "tough" no-nonsense look by informing her students she is an ex-Marine who knows karate. Suggesting that fear and danger are the only emotions her students recognize as important, LouAnne crosses a racial divide by rooting her sense of authority in a traditionally racist notion of discipline and control; that is, classroom authority for subordinate groups is often based less on persuasion and dialogue and more than on threats, manipulation, and punitive action. Once she gets the group's attention, she moves onto more lofty ground and begins the arduous task of trying to develop a pedagogy that is both morally uplifting and pedagogically relevant. Choice becomes for LouAnne the theoretical axis that organizes her classroom approach. First, on the side of moral uplift (complete with a conservative nineties Whitewashing of history), she tells her students that there are no victims in her class. Presumably, this is meant as a plea to rouse their sense of agency and responsibility, but it rings entirely hollow since LouAnne has no understanding of the social and historical limits that shape their sense of agency on a daily basis. Of course, some students immediately recognize the bad faith implicit in her sermonizing call and urge her to test it with a dose of reality by living in their neighborhood for a week.

Moreover, LouAnne appears to confuse her own range of choices, predicated in part on her class and racial privileges, with those of her students, even though they lack the power and resources to negotiate their lives politically, geographically, or economically with the same ease or options. She has no sense that choice springs from power, and those who have limited power have fewer choices. The subtext here reinforces the currently popular right-wing assumption that character, merit, and self-help are the basis on which people take their place in society. Of course, within a hierarchical and social structure organized by race, as well as economic power, gender, and other key determinants, whiteness emerges as the normative basis for success, responsibility, and legitimate authority. By suggesting that White educators can ignore how larger social considerations impact on racial groups, their interrogation of White privilege, experience, and culture denies complicity with, if not responsibility for, racist ideology and structural inequalities.

Choice is not only trivialized in LouAnne's classroom; it provides the basis for a pedagogy that is as indifferent to the lives of poor inner-city kids as it is demeaning. Relying on the logic of the market to motivate her kids, LouAnne rewards classroom cooperation with candy bars, a trip to an amusement park, and dinner at a fancy restaurant. Baiting students with gimmicks and bribes does more than cast a moral shadow on the pedagogical value of such an approach or the teacher as a kind of ethical exemplar, it also makes clear how little LouAnne knows about the realities of her students' lives. Indifferent to the skills they need to survive, LouAnne is unconcerned about their experiences, interests, or cultural resources. This becomes clear in three pivotal instances in the movie.

In the first instance, LouAnne attempts to motivate the students by giving them the lyrics to Bob Dylan's "Mister Tambourine Man." Indifferent to the force of hip-hop culture (though marketing executives appeared to know the draw and impact of hip-hop on the film's audience in designing the soundtrack), her attempt to use popular culture appears as nothing less than an act of cultural ignorance and bad pedagogy. But more revealing is her attempt to relate Dylan's lyrics to one of the most cliched aspects of the students' culture, namely, violence and drugs. Not only does she ignore their cultural resources and interests, but she also frames her notion of popular culture in a text from the 1960s, almost twenty years before these kids were born. Rather than excavating the traditions, themes, and experiences that make up her students' lives in order to construct her curriculum, she simply avoids their voices altogether in shaping the content of what she teaches. Beneath this form of pedagogical violence there is also the presupposition that Whites can come into such schools and teach without theory, ignore the histories and narratives that students bring to schools, and perform miracles in children's lives by mere acts of kindness.

LouAnne's teaching is in actuality a pedagogy of diversion, one that refuses to provide students with skills that will help them address the urgent and disturbing questions of a society and a culture that in many ways ignores their humanity and well-being. These students are not taught to question the intellectual and material resources they need to address the profoundly anti-humane conditions they have to negotiate everyday. How to survive in a society, let alone remake it, is an important pedagogical question that cannot be separated from the larger issue of what it means to live in a country that is increasingly hostile to the existence of poor kids in the inner cities. But LouAnne ignores these issues and offers her students material incentives to learn, and in doing so constructs them as consuming subjects rather than social subjects eager and able to think critically in order to negotiate and transform the worlds in which they live.

LouAnne's sense of privilege also becomes evident in the boundless confidence she exhibits in her authority and moral superiority. She believes that somehow her students are answerable to her both in terms of their classroom performance and in terms of their personal lives; her role is to affirm or gently "correct" how they narrate their beliefs, experiences, and values. LouAnne takes for granted that she has a right to "save them" or run their lives without questioning her own authority and purity of intentions. Authority here functions as a way of making invisible LouAnne's own privileges as a White woman, while simultaneously allowing her to indulge in a type of moralizing commensurate with her colonizing role as a White teacher who extracts from her students love and loyalty in exchange for teaching them to be part of a system that oppresses them. Moreover, LouAnne's pedagogy does nothing to rupture her own liberalism, which shifts the focus from the real structures of oppression faced by her students to the moral dilemmas that racism and other issues raise for dominant groups. LouAnne ignores the social gravity of the problems her students face, and in doing so is largely impervious to issues regarding how racism and poverty are interwoven into the very structure and fabric of the school and dominant society. Instead, she focuses on the problems such students present to institutional authorities such as herself and how they can be mediated and resolved without having to call into question either her own racism or the ways in which schools systemically function to oppress inner-city youth.

Dangerous Minds mythically rewrites the decline of public schooling and the attack on poor, Black, and Hispanic students within a broader project that rearticulates whiteness as a model of authority, rationality, and civilized behavior. The politics of representation at work in this film reproduces a dominant view of identity and difference that has a long legacy in Hollywood films, specifically Westerns and African adventure movies. As Robin Kelley points out, the popularity of many Hollywood films is as much about constructing whiteness as it is about demonizing the alleged racialized other. He notes that within this racialized Hollywood legacy, "American Indians, Africans, and Asians represent a pre-civilized or anti-civilized existence, a threat to the hegemony of Western culture and proof that 'Whites' are superior, more noble, more intelligent" (Kelley, 1992, p. 1406). *Dangerous Minds* is an updated defense of White identity and racial hierarchies. The colonizing thrust of this narrative is highlighted through the image of Michelle Pfeiffer as a visiting White beauty queen whose success is, in part, rendered possible by market incentives and missionary talents.

Against LouAnne Johnson's benevolence and insight is juxtaposed the personality and pedagogy of Mr. Grandy, the Black principal of Parkmont High. Grandy is portrayed as an uptight, bloodless bureaucrat, a professional "wannabe" whose only interest appears to be in enforcing school rules (Hollywood's favorite stereotype for Black principals). Grandy rigidly oversees school policy and is constantly berating Johnson for bypassing the standard curriculum, generating non-traditional forms of teaching, and taking the students on unauthorized trips. As a Black man in a position of leadership, he is depicted as an obstacle to the success of his charges and ruthlessly insensitive to their needs. When Emilio visits Grandy's office to report another student who is trying to kill him, Grandy orders him out because he failed to knock on the office door. After leaving the building, Emilio is shot and killed a few blocks from the school.

Racial politics in this film are such that Black professionals come off as the real threat to learning and civilized behavior, and Whites, of course, are simply there to lend support. In contrast to Grandy, Johnson's whiteness provides the racialized referent for leadership, risk-taking, and compassion. This is borne out at the end of the film when the students tell her that they want her to remain their teacher because she represents their "light." In this context, *Dangerous Minds* reinforces the highly racialized, mainstream assumption that chaos reigns in inner-city public schools, and that White teachers alone are capable of bringing order, decency, and hope to the those on the margins of society.

SUTURING WHITENESS

Directed by David Siegel and Scott McGehee, *Suture* explores the location of identity within a dominant racial politics. Central to the politics of the film is the way in which it organizes the unfolding of its plot around two narratives. On the one hand, the directors use the discursive narrative, which develops through character dialogue and adopts the conventional form of the crime thriller. On the other hand, they construct a visual narrative that introduces racial identity as a defining principle of the movie by casting one of the two central characters as Black and the other as White. Set within a plot about murder and framed identity, *Suture* presents the story of two brothers, Vincent Towers and Clay Arlington. Under police investigation for killing his father, the rich and ruthless Vincent sets up a scheme in which he first plants his driver's license and credit cards in his working-class half-brother's billfold. He then convinces Clay to drive his

Rolls Royce to the airport. Clay does not realize that Vincent has placed a bomb in the car that can be triggered by remote control through the car phone. Vincent waits until Clay leaves for the airport and then calls him, setting off the bomb. After the explosion, Vincent leaves town assuming that the police will mistake Clay for himself. Unfortunately for Vincent, Clay survives the explosion, though he has to undergo massive reconstructive surgery on his face. In fact, the damage to Clay is so extreme that the police and doctors who attend to Clay believe that he is Vincent.

Clay survives the ordeal, but is an amnesiac and believes that he is Vincent. In fact, everyone who comes in contact with Clay believes that he is Vincent. As Clay undergoes psychoanalysis and repeated bouts of surgery, he falls in love with Renee Descartes, a beautiful and renowned plastic surgeon. In the meantime, the real Vincent breaks into his old house to kill Clay, but Clay shoots him first and disposes of his body. By the time he kills Vincent, Clay has regained his memory but refuses to slip back into his old identity and give up the identity and life he has assumed.

What is so remarkable about *Suture* is that it is mediated by a visual narrative that is completely at odds with the discursive narrative and unsettles the audience's role as "passive" spectators. Clay does not look anything like Vincent. In fact, Clay is Black, but is treated throughout the film as if he is White. In a scene fraught with irony and tension, Renee Descartes takes off Clay's bandages and she tells him that he has a Greco-Roman nose, which allegedly proves that he "isn't inclined to deviant behavior, like killing people."

Memory and identity in this film are fluid and hybridized rather than fixed and sutured. Black identity is presented as a social construction that cannot be framed in essentialist terms. Clay assumes all the markings of White experience and culture, and it is only the audience that is able to mediate his newly assumed cultural capital by virtue of his Blackness.[8] There is more at work in this film than a critique of Black essentialism; there is also the ironic representation of whiteness as both invisible to itself and, at the same time, the norm by which everything else is measured. That is, whiteness in *Suture* becomes the racial marker of identity, power, and privilege. Playing the visual narrative against the discursive narrative, *Suture* evokes a peculiar form of racial witnessing in which it exposes whiteness as an ideology, a set of experiences, and a location of privilege. But it does so not by trading in binaristic oppositions in which bad Whites oppress good Blacks, but by calling into question the racial tension between what is seen and what is heard by the audience. The discursive narrative in the film privileges language while denying the defining principle of race, but the visual narrative forces the audience to recognize the phenomenological rather than political implications of race, identity, and difference. As film critic Roy Grundmann (1994) notes, "We initially want to jump out of our seats to scream at the characters who (mis?)take Clay for Vincent, especially upon such comparative 'evidence' as videos, photos, and a police lineup with a witness who knew Vincent" (p. 24). Racial difference, in this case, is defined entirely through a representational politics of visual imagery that assails both the liberal appeal to color-blindness and a power-evading aesthetic of difference that reduces racial identities to lifestyles, marketing niches, or consumer products.

Rupturing the Hollywood cinematic tradition of presenting whiteness as an "invisible" though determining discourse, *Suture* forces the audience to recognize whiteness as a racial signifier, as an "index of social standing or rank" (Goldberg, 1993b, p. 69). But in the end, *Suture* provides no means for framing whiteness outside of the discursive and visual politics of domination. The film's attempt to develop a representational politics certainly forces the viewer to demystify and debunk whiteness as invisible, abstracted from the modalities of power and identity, but it does nothing to develop a power strategic politics—a politics that attempts to transform both ideologies and material relations of power—that refuses to accept whiteness as a racial category that has only one purpose, which is closely tied to if not defined by shifting narratives of domination and oppression. This might explain why *Suture* eventually engages in a reductionistic moralizing by suggesting that Clay should be condemned for wanting to be White, but doing so without really engaging whiteness in a more dialectical or critical fashion.

CINEMA AND THE PEDAGOGY OF WHITENESS

Dangerous Minds and *Suture* offer contrasting narratives of race that can be used pedagogically to critically deconstruct both racial othering and whiteness as part of a broader discourse on racial justice. The juxtaposition of these two films opens up a pedagogical space for reading contradictory representations of whiteness as an ideology and site of power and privilege within the discourse of what Stuart Hall has labeled the "old ethnicity." Similarly, rupturing singular definitions of whiteness provides educators with the opportunity to construct more complex models for theorizing whiteness through a multiplicity of social relations, theoretical positions, and affective identifications. In this context, whiteness can be taken up pedagogically and politically in order to enable both White and other students of color to address issues of racial identity within a new and expanded conception of ethnicity. This suggests highlighting the historical, political, and contextual nature of racial identities, not as distinct racial formations, but through their complex relationship to each other within specific relations of power. Once again, Stuart Hall elaborates on the democratic possibilities that a reconceptualized notion of ethnicity might enable students and others to analyze cultural identities as they are fashioned out of the complex web of history, power, and politics. He is worth quoting at length:

I have been arguing for new conceptions of ethnicities which recognize that people are placed in a history, in a culture, in a space, that they come from somewhere, that enunciation is always located. I have been asking whether ethnicity could be a term which would enable us to recognize that placing of enunciation in a very different way from the embattled, aggressive ethnicities that have rampaged through our world. (1995, p. 67)

Rather than being dismissed simply as a racist text by critical educators, *Dangerous Minds* should be read symptomatically for the ways in which it articulates and reproduces whiteness as a form of racial domination within the public space of the inner-city classroom. Offering an unapologetic reading of whiteness as a trope of order, rationality, insight, and beauty, *Dangerous Minds* is an important educational text for students to use in addressing how whiteness and difference are portrayed in the film, and how race consciously or unconsciously shapes their everyday experiences, attitudes, and worldviews. Pedagogically the objective is not to force students into viewing *Dangerous Minds* as either a good or bad film, but to engage the broader social conditions through which the popularity of the film has to be understood. One pedagogical task is to get students to think about how *Dangerous Minds* bears witness to the ethical and racial dilemmas that animate the larger racial and social landscape.

Students may offer a number of responses to a film such as *Dangerous Minds*. But given the popularity of the film, and the large number of favorable reviews it received in newspapers across the country, it is reasonable to assume that the range of readings available to White students will fall within a mix of mainstream liberal to conservative interpretations that, while not differing from each other substantially, might uncover interesting contradictions to be explored in classroom analyses (e.g., Chastain, 1995; Glass, 1995; Saillant, 1995). Rather than stressing that students are diverse readers of culture, it is important pedagogically to recognize and understand how the ownership and control of the apparatuses of cultural production limit the readings made widely available to students and shape the popular context from which dominant notions of racism are understood. When racist difference does enter into classroom discussion, it more than likely will focus on the disruptive behavior that Black and Hispanic students exhibit in schools. That behavior that will often be seen as characteristic of an entire social group, or as a form of cultural pathology that suggests minorities are largely to blame for the educational problems they experience. Similarly, when whiteness is destabilzed or critically addressed by students, it more than likely will be taken up within a power-evasive discourse in which White racism is often reduced to an act of individual prejudice that is neatly removed from the messy contexts of history, politics, and systemic oppression.[9] This suggests that it is unlikely that White students will recognize LouAnne's teaching approach and insistence on the value of middle-class cultural capital as a racist attempt to teach Black and Hispanic students that their own narratives, histories, and experiences are uncivilized and crude. However popular such dominant readings might be, they offer educators a prime pedagogical opportunity to interrogate and rupture their codes and ideologies. For instance, the ideological link between the privileging of White cultural capital and the ongoing, degrading representation of the other in Hollywood films may not be evident to students on a first reading of the film, but can become an object of analysis as various students in the class are provided with alternative readings. At best, *Dangerous Minds* offers White students an opportunity to engage a popular text that embodies much of what they generally learn or (mis)learn about race without initially putting their own racial identities on trial.

A viewing and analysis of *Suture* reveals a different set of claims about whiteness that raise alternative possibilities for interrogating the relationship between whiteness, race, and racism. *Suture* presents a critical reading of whiteness as a dominant social and cultural construction and attempts, through an unsettling visual narrative, to reveal how whiteness wages symbolic violence through its refusal to name its defining mechanisms of power and privilege. In doing so, *Suture* forces students, especially White students, to consider problematizing the assumption that issues regarding race and racial politics are largely about non-Whites as a social group. The dominant defense of whiteness as a universal norm is visibly thrown off balance in this film and makes whiteness a racial category open to critique. In rupturing whiteness as a racially and politically neutral code, *Suture* provides a pedagogical opportunity for educators to talk about how White experience is constructed differently within a variety of public spaces and mediated through the diverse, but related, lenses of class, gender, and sexual orientation.

Played off against each other, the two films engage in a representational politics that illuminates whiteness as a shifting, political category whose meaning can be addressed within rather than outside of the interrelationships of class, race, ethnicity, and gender. In other words, the structuring principles that inform these films as they work intertextually provide a theoretical basis for challenging whiteness as an ideological and historical construction. It is precisely the tension generated between these films that invites entrance into a pedagogy that commences with what Gayatri Spivak (1990) refers to as "moments of bafflement," that is, a pedagogy that focuses on demystifying the act and process of representing by revealing how meanings are produced within relations of power that narrate identities through history, social forms, and modes of ethical address that appear objective, universally valid, and consensual. Such a pedagogy attempts to open up questions "regarding the link between epistemology and morality: between how we get to know what we know and the moral life we aspire to lead" (Hartman, 1994, p. 28). While such pedagogical tensions do not guarantee the possibility of decentering whiteness in order to render "visible the historical and institutional structures from within which [White teachers and students] speak" (Spivak, 1990, p. 67), they do provide the pedagogical conditions for students and teachers alike to question and unlearn those aspects of whiteness that position them with the space and privileged relations of racism.

While it is impossible to predict how students will actually react to a pedagogy of bafflement that takes whiteness and race as an object of serious debate and analysis, it is important to recognize that White students will generally offer enormous resistance to analyzing critically the "normative-residual space [of] White cultural practice"—that is, those historical narratives of whiteness that misrepresent the past in order to privilege a White racist view of the present and future (Frankenberg, 1993, p. 234). Resistance in this case should be examined for the knowledge it yields, and the possibilities for interrogating its silences and refusals. Pedagogically, this suggests allowing students to air their positions on whiteness and race regardless of how messy or politically incorrect such positions might be. But there is more at stake here than providing a pedagogical space for students to narrate themselves and to speak without fear within the contexts of their own specific histories and experiences.

Rather than arguing that students simply be allowed to voice their racial politics, I am suggesting they be offered a space for dialogue and critique in which such positions can be engaged, challenged, and rearticulated through an ongoing analysis of the material realities and social relations of racism. In other words, teachers might begin such a dialogue with what students already know; they might question students' awareness of the racial and cultural differences between neighborhoods, spaces for recreation, schools, eating establishments, and other public spaces within their own communities. Issues can be raised about who can cross over into such spaces, how certain racial groups are excluded, under what circumstances, and why? Similarly, questions of cultural identity can be explored through a pedagogy of representation that analyzes how dominant and subordinate racial groups are portrayed and stereotyped in the media, press, and other aspects of the culture, and how such groups are influenced and positioned by such stereotypes. In this instance, it is important for students to understand how power and privilege mediate how different racial groups are represented.[10] Students can explore the relations between the ways in which racial identities are constructed and the broader social landscape that registers very different consequences regarding how racism actually [and differently] affects, for example, Whites and non-Whites within highly iniquitous relations of power. At the same time, teachers can point to strategies of intervention, exploring how students can exercise their sense of politics, power, and collective agency to engage and attempt to change dominant and oppressive relations of power as they affect both their everyday lives and the lives of others who struggle under the oppressive weight of racism.

The issue of making White students responsive to the politics of racial privilege is fraught with the fear and anger that accompany having to rethink one's identity. Engaging in forms of teaching that prompt White students to examine their social practices and belief systems in racial terms may work to reinforce the safe assumption that race is a stable category, a biological given, rather than a historical and cultural construction. For instance, AnnLouise Keating (1995) points out that when teaching her students to interrogate whiteness critically, many of them come away believing that all Whites were colonialists, in spite of her attempts pedagogically to distinguish between whiteness as the dominant racial and political ideology and the diverse, contingent racial positions White people take up.

In spite of the tensions and contradictions that any pedagogy of whiteness might face, it is imperative that teachers address the histories that have shaped the normative space, practices, and diverse relationships that White students have inherited through a legacy of racial privilege. Analyzing the historical legacy of whiteness as an oppressive racial force requires that students engage in a critical form of memory work, while fostering less a sullen silence or paralyzing guilt and more a sense of outrage at historical oppression and a desire for racial justice in the present. Keating illuminates the problems she faced when attempting to get White students to think critically about racism and its systemic nature and to interrogate or reverse their taken-for-granted assumptions about whiteness and racial privilege. She writes:

These reversals trigger a variety of unwelcome reactions in self-identified "White" students, reactions ranging from guilt to anger to withdrawal and despair. Instructors must be prepared to deal with these responses. The point is not to encourage feelings of personal responsibility for the slavery, decimation of indigenous peoples, land theft, and so on that occurred in the past. It is, rather, to enable students of all colors more fully to comprehend how these oppressive systems that began in the historical past continue misshaping contemporary conditions. Guilt-tripping plays no role in this process (1995, p. 915).

However, Keating is not entirely clear on how educators can avoid guilt-tripping students or to what degree they are not to be held responsible for their present attitudes within this type of pedagogy. Making whiteness rather than White racism the focus of study is an important pedagogical strategy. Analyzing whiteness opens a theoretical space for teachers and students to articulate how their own racial identities have been shaped within a broader racist culture and what responsibilities they might assume for living in a present in which Whites are accorded privileges and opportunities (though in complex and different ways) largely at the expense of other racial groups. Yet, as insightful as this strategy may prove to be, more theoretical work needs to be done to enable students to critically engage and appropriate the tools necessary for them to politicize whiteness as a racial category without closing down their own sense of identity and political agency.

While both *Dangerous Minds* and *Suture* provide an educational opportunity for students to see how dominant assumptions about whiteness can be framed and challenged, neither film addresses what it means to rearticulate whiteness in oppositional terms. Neither the portrayal of whiteness as a form of racial privilege nor as a practice of domination necessarily establishes the basis for White students to rearticulate their own whiteness in ways that go beyond their over-identification with or desire to be "Black" at the expense of their own racial identities.

I am concerned about what it means educationally for those of us who engage in an antiracist pedagogy and politics to suggest to students that whiteness can only be understood in terms of the common experience of White domination and racism. What subjectivities or points of identification become available to White students who can only imagine White experience as monolithic, self-contained, and deeply racist? What are the pedagogical and political stakes in rearticulating whiteness in anti-essentialist terms as part of a broader new discourse of ethnicity, so that White youth can understand and struggle against the long legacy of White racism while using the particularities of "their own culture as a resource for resistance, reflection, and empowerment?" (Hall, 1991a, p. 57).[11]

At the same time, there are too few attempts to develop a pedagogy of whiteness that enables White students to move beyond positions of guilt or resentment. There is a curious absence in the work on whiteness regarding how students might examine critically the construction of their own identities in order to rethink whiteness as a discourse of both critique and possibility. Educators need to connect whiteness with a new language of ethnicity, one that provides a space for White students to imagine how whiteness as an ideology and social location can be progressively appropriated as part of a broader politics of social reform. Theorizing the relationship between ethnicity and identity enables students to both locate themselves in society and construct temporary points of belonging and orientation. Central to such a task is the political and pedagogical challenge of refashioning an antiracist politics that informs a broader, radical, democratic project (e. g. Haymes, 1995; Keating, 1995).

NOTES

1. Howard J. Ehrlich (1994) estimates, from studies done by the Baltimore-based National Institute Against Prejudice and Violence, that over one million racial incidents take place each year on college campuses. See also Eflin, 1993.

2. I want to thank my colleague at Pennsylvania State University, Bernard Bell, for this insight (personal communication).

3. I think Houston Baker (1992) is instructive on this issue in arguing that race, for all of its destructive tendencies and implications, has also been used by Blacks and other people of color to gain a sense of personal and historical agency. This is not a matter of a positive image of race canceling out its negative underside. On the contrary, Baker makes a compelling case for the dialectical nature of race and its possibilities for engaging and overcoming its worse dimensions while extending and deepening the interests of a transformative and democratic polis.

4. My definition of essentialism is taken from Barry Hindess. He claims that essentialism "refers to a specific mode of analysis in which social phenomena are analyzed not in terms of their specific conditions of existence and their effects with regard to their social relations and practices but rather as the more or less adequate expression of an essence" (cited in San Juan Jr., 1991, p. 221).

5. For an analysis of the importance of race in the broader area of popular culture, two representative sources include Dyson (1993) and Giroux (1996).

6. On the localization of crime as a racial text, see Goldberg (1993a).

7. LouAnne is not interested in the stories, histories, and experiences of her students so as to become more attentive to the skills and knowledge they need to resist and transform the oppression that shapes their lives. On the contrary, she simply affirms her dominant expectations about these kids and how they should be educated while inserting herself as their savior. This becomes clear in two pivotal scenes in the film. In the first scene, LouAnne breaks up a fight between Emilio and some other students, then demands from Emilio a full explanation:

LouAnne : "Was it worth it? You like to hit people? Why? You feel angry?"

Emilio : "You're trying to figure me out. You going to try to psychologize me. I'll help you. I come from a broken home, and we're poor, okay. I see the same fucking movies you do."

LouAnne : "I'd like to help you, Emilio."

Emilio : "Thank you very much. And how you going to do that? You going to give me some good advice—just say no—you going to get me off the streets? Well, forget it. How the fuck are you going to save me from my life?"

Emilio is trying to educate LouAnne, but she is inattentive. She assumes a moralizing posture that is indifferent to the complex forces shaping Emilio's life. Nor can this Great White Hope consider that her students' histories and worldviews might be usefully incorporated into her pedagogy in order to teach kids like Emilio the survival skills and knowledge they need to cope with the conditions and contexts of their surroundings. In another exchnage, LouAnne takes Raul, a promising student, to a fancy restaurant because his group won a poetry contest. LouAnne mistakenly presupposes that it will be as easy for Raul to cross class borders as it is for her. But, Raul is uncomfortable in such a context; he tells LouAnne that, in order to dress properly and avoid humiliating himself and her, he has purchased a stolen expensive leather jacket. In this scene, there is the underlying suggestion that, to succeed in life, working-class kids such as Raul need the cultural capital of White middle-class people like LouAnne.

8. For a definition and analysis of cultural capital and its relationship to education, see my analysis of the work of Pierre Bourdieu and Jean Claude Passeron in Giroux (1983 pp. 87–96). The most detailed articulation of cultural capital can be found in Pierre Bourdieu and Jean Claude Passeron (1977); see also, Pierre Bourdieu (1984).

9. For example, in Frankenberg's (1993) study of White women, radical positions on race were in the minority; and in Gallagher's (1995) study of White college students, liberal and conservative, as opposed to radical positions largely predominated.

10. Of course, it is crucial for students not only to understand how different groups are stereotyped, but also, depending upon their resources and power, how they respond differently to such attacks, and what they can do about it when it happens. For instance, Ella Shohat and Robert Stam (1996) argue that, "The facile catch-all invocation of 'stereotypes' eludes a crucial distinction: stereotypes of some communities merely make the target group uncomfortable, but the community has the social power to combat and resist them; stereotypes of other communities participate in a continuum of prejudicial social policy and actual violence against disempowered people, placing the very body of the accused in jeopardy. Stereotypes of Polish Americans and Italian Americans, however regrettable, have not been shaped within the racial and imperial foundation of the US, and are not used to justify daily violence or structural oppression against these communities" (p. 183).

11. In this context, Hall (1991a) is not talking about Whites but Blacks. It seems to me that his point is just as relevant for rearticulating whiteness as it is for debunking the essentialized Black subject, though this should not suggest that such an appropriation take place outside of the discourse of power, history, inequality, and conflict. See also, Pfeil, 1995.

Bibliography

Aaronsohn, E. (1990). "Learning to Teach for Empowerment." *Radical Teacher,40*(2), 44–46.

Aaronsohn, E., Carter, C., and Howell, M. (1995). "Preparing Monocultural Teachers for a Multicultural World." *Equity and Excellence in Education, 28*(1), 5–9.

Aaronsohn, E., Foley, T., Holmes, J., and Wallowitz, J. (1994). "Teacher-Pleasing, Traditional Grading and Learning?" Unpublished paper.

Alba, R. D. (1990). *Ethnic identity: The transformation of White America.* New Haven, CT: Yale University Press.

Allen, T. (1994). *The invention of the White race.* London: Verso Press.Allen, W. B. (1993). "Response to 'White Discourse on White Racism.'" *Educational Researcher, 22* (8), 11–13.

Allport, G. W. (1954). *The nature of prejudice.* New York: Addison-Wesley Publishing, Inc.

Ang, I. (1995). "On Not Speaking Chinese: Postmodern Ethnicity and the Politics of Diaspora." *Social Formations, 24*(2), 110–123.

Angus, I. (1990). "Crossing the Border." *Massachusetts Review 23*(2), 32–47.

Anzaldua, G. (1987). *Borderlands/la frontera: The new Mestiza.* San Francisco: Spinsters/Aunt Lute.

Apple, M. W. (1997). "Consuming the Other: Whiteness, Education, and Cheap French Fries." In M. Fine, L. Weis, L. C. Powell, and L. M. Wong (Eds.), *Off white: Readings on race, power, and society.* New York: Routledge, pp. 121–128.

Aronowitz, S. and DiFazio, W. (1994). *The jobless future: Sci-tech and the dogma of work.* Minneapolis: University of Minnesota Press.

Augnet, C. (1996). "For Polite Reactionaries." *Transition, 6*(1), 14–34.

Baker, H. (1992). "Caliban's Triple Play." In H. L. Gates, Jr. (Ed.), *Loose canons: Notes on the culture wars.* New York: Oxford University Press, pp. 381–395.

Baldwin, J. (1963, 1988) "A Talk to Teachers." In R. Simonson and S. Walkins (Eds.), *The graywolf annual five: Multicultural literacy*. St. Paul: Graywolf Press, pp. 12–23.

Balibar, E. (1996). "Is European Citizenship Possible?" *Public Culture, 19*(1), 355–376.

Banks, J. A. (1991). *Teaching strategies for ethnic studies*. Boston: Allyn and Bacon.

Banks, J. A. (1992). "The Stages of Ethnicity." In P.A. Richard-Amato and M. A. Snow (Eds.), *The multicultural classroom: Readings for the content-area teachers*. White Plains, NY: Longman, pp. 93–101.

Banks, J. A. (1994a). *An introduction to multicultural education*. Boston: Allyn and Bacon.

Banks, J. A. (1994b). *Multiethnic education: Theory and practice* (Third Edition). Needham Heights, MA: Allyn and Bacon.

Bartolomé, L. (1994). "Beyond the methods fetish: Toward a humanizing pedagogy." *Harvard Educational Review, 64*(2), 173–194.

Batts, V.A. (1989). *Modern racism: New melody for the same old tunes*. Cambridge, MA: Visions, Inc.

Bauman, Z. (1992). *Mortality, immortality and other life strategies*. Stanford, CA: Stanford University Press.

Bauman, Z. (1995). *Life in fragments*. Oxford, England: Basil Blackwell.

Bauman, Z. (1996). "On Communitarians and Human Freedom, or, How to Square the Circle." *Theory, Culture and Society, 13*(2), 79–90.

Belenky, M. F., Clinchy, B., McGoldberger, N. R., and Tarule, J. M. (1986). *Women's ways of knowing: The development of self, voice, and mind*. NY: Basic Books, Inc.

Bell, D. (1992). *Faces at the bottom of the well: The permanence of racism*. New York: Basic Books.

Bensimon, E. M. & Soto, M. (1997). "Can we build civic life without a multiracial university?" *Change, 29*(2), 42–44.

Bennett, M. J. (1986). "A Developmental Approach to Training for Intercultural Sensitivity." *International Journal of Intercultural Relations, 10*(3), 179–196.

Berlet, C. (Ed.). (1995). *Eyes right!: Challenging the right-wing backlash*. Boston: South End Press.

Berman, M. (1982). *All that is solid melts into air*. New York: Simon and Schuster.

Bernstein, S. (1996). "Storm Rises Over Ex-Klansman in Debate." *Los Angeles Times*, September 11, A3, A14.

Bhabha, H. (1986). "Remembering Fanon." In F. Fanon, *Black skin, White masks*. London: Pluto Press, pp. 1–2.

Bhachu, P. (1996). "The Multiple Landscapes of Transnational Asian Women in the Diaspora." In V. Amit-Talai and C. Knowles (Eds.), *Re-situating identities: The politics of race, ethnicity, and culture*. Peterborough, Canada, and Essex, London: Broadview Press, pp. 283–303.

Bigelow, W. (1990). "Inside the Classroom: Social Vision and Critical Pedagogy." *Teachers College Record, 91*(3), 437–48.

Blades, R. (1987). *Chicago Sunday Times*, January 26, B7.

Boggs, C. (1995). "The God Reborn: Pondering the Revival of Russian Communism." *Los Angeles View, 10*(20), 8–11.

Bollin, G. G. and Finkel, J. (1995). "White Racial Identity as a Barrier to Understanding Diversity: A Study of Preservice Teachers." *Equity and Excellence in Education, 28*(1), 25–30.

Bonnett, A. (1996). "Anti-Racism and the Critique of White Identities." *New Community, 22*(1), 97–110.

Bourdieu, P. and Passeron, J. C. (1977). *Reproduction in education, society, and culture*. Beverly Hill, CA: Sage Publications.

Bourdieu, P. (1984). *Distinction: A social critique of the judgement of taste*. R. Nice (Trans.). Cambridge, MA: Harvard University Press.

Boston Globe. (1990). January 26, p. A7.

Bowser, B. P. and Hunt, R. G. (Eds.). (1981). *Impacts of racism on White Americans*. Beverly Hills: Sage.

Bradlee Jr., B. (1996). "The Buchanan Role: GOP Protagonist." *Boston Sunday Globe*, March 3, pp. 1/12.

Brenkman, J. (1995). "Race Publics: Civic Illiberalism, or Race After Reagan." Transition, 5 (2), 14–17.

Britzman, D. P. (1997). "Difference in a Minor Key: Some Modulations of History, Memory, and Community." In M. Fine, L. Weis, L. C. Powell, and L. M. Wong (Eds.), *Off white: Readings on race, power, and society*. New York: Routledge, pp. 29–39.

Brodie, M. (1995). "The Four Americas: Government and Social Policy Through the Eyes of America's Multi-Racial and Multi-Ethnic Society." *The Washington Post*. Cambridge: Kaiser Family Foundation and Harvard University.

Brown, D. (1971). *Bury my heart at Wounded Knee: An Indian history of the American west*. New York: Holt and Rinehart.

Bruner, J. (1990). *Acts of meaning*. Cambridge: Harvard University Press.

Bulkin, E. (1984). "Hard Ground: Jewish Identity, Racism and Anti-Semitism." E. Bulkin, M. B. Pratt and B. Smith (Eds.), *Yours in Struggle*. Brooklyn, NY: Long Haul Press, 76–92.

Camus, A. (1956). *The rebel: An essay on man in revolt*. New York: Vintage Books.

Carey, J. (Ed.) (1996). *Multicultural counseling in schools: A practical handbook*. Boston: Allyn and Bacon.

Cashmore, E. (1996). *Dictionary of race and ethnic relations* (Fourth Edition). London and New York: Routledge.

Chan, C. S. (1989). "Issues of Identity Development Among Asian-American Lesbians and Gay Men." *Journal of Counseling and Development, 68*(5), 16–20.

Chastain, S. (1995). "Dangerous Minds No Threat to this Tough Teacher." *The Times Union*, August 13, p. G1.

Chávez Chávez, R. (working paper). "A Curriculum Discourse for Achieving Equity: Implications for Teachers when Engaged with Latina and Latino Students." Unpublished paper.

Chávez Chávez, R. (1995). *Multicultural education in the everyday: A renaissance for the recommitted*. Washington, D.C.: AACTE.

Chávez Chávez, R. (1998). "Engaging the multicultural education terrain: A holographic montage for engagers." In R. Chávez Chávez and J. O'Donnell (Eds.), *Speaking the unpleasant: The politics of (non)engagement in the multicultural education terrain.* New York: State University of New York Press, pp. 102–124.

Chávez Chávez, R. & O'Donnell, J. (Eds.). (1998). *Speaking the unpleasant: The politics of (non)engagement in the multicultural education terrain.* NY: State University of New York Press.

Chomsky, Noam. (1996). *Class warfare: Interviews with David Barsamian.* Monroe, ME: Common Courage Press.

Clark, C. (1993). *Multicultural education as a tool for disarming violence: A study through in-depth participatory action research.* Unpublished dissertation.

Cone, James H. (1986). *A Black theology of liberation.* New York: Orbis Books.

Connelly, F. M. and Clandnin, D. J. (1990). "Stories of Experience and Narrative Inquiry." *Educational Researcher, 19*(5), 2–14.

Connolly, M. L. and D. A. Noumair. (1997). "The White Girl in Me, the Colored Girl in You, and the Lesbian in Us: Crossing Boundaries." In M. Fine, L. Weis, L. C. Powell, and L. M. Wong (Eds.), *Off white: Readings on race, power, and society.* New York: Routledge, pp. 322–332.

Conquergood, D. (1994). "Homeboys and Hoods: Gang Communication and Cultural Space." In L. Frey (Ed.), *Group communication in context.* Hillsdale, New Jersey: Lawrence Erlbaum Associates, pp. 23–55.

Conroy, P. (1972). *The water is wide.* Boston, MA: Houghton Mifflin Company.

Cross, W. E. Jr. (1973). "The Negro-to-Black Conversion Experience." In J. A. Ladner (Ed.), *The death of White sociology.* New York: Vintage Books, p. 267–286.

Cross, W. E. Jr. (1978). "The Thomas and Cross Models of Psychological Nigrescence: A Review." *The Journal of Black Psychology, 5*(1), 13–31.

Cruz, J. (1996). "From Farce to Tragedy: Reflections on the Reification of Race at Century's End." In A. Gordon and C. Newfield (Eds.), *Mapping multiculturalism.* Minneapolis and London: University of Minnesota Press, pp. 19–39.

Culley, M. and Portuges, C. (Eds.). (1995). *Gendered subjects: The dynamics of feminist teaching.* Boston: Routledge and Kegan Paul.

Darder, A. (1992). *Culture and power in the classroom.* South Hadley, MA: Bergin and Garvey.

Davis, A. Y. (1981). *Women, race and class.* New York: Random House.

Davis, A. Y. (1996). Unpublished speech.

Dean J. P. and Suchman, E. A. (1964). *Strangers next door: Ethnic relations in American communities.* Englewood Cliffs: Prentice-Hall.

Delgado, R. (Ed.). (1995). *Critical race theory: The cutting edge.* Philadelphia: Temple University Press.

Delgado, R. and Stefancic, J. (Eds.). (1997). *Critical White studies: Looking behind the mirror.* Philadelphia: Temple University Press.

Dennis, R. (1981). "Socialization and racism: The White experience." In Bowser, B. P. & Hunt, R. G. (Eds.), *Impacts of racism on White Americans*. Beverly Hills: Sage, pp. 112–127.

DeRosa, P. (1996). "Learning about Racism: Lessons from Oneonta and Beyond." Unpublished speech.

Diamond, S. (1995). *Roads to domination: Right-wing movements and political power in the United States*. New York: Guilford Press.

Diamond, S. (1996). *Facing the wrath*. Monroe, ME: Common Courage Press.

Douglas, F. (1972). "The Meaning of the Fourth of July to the Negro." In P. S. Foner (Ed.), *The voice of Black America, Volume 1*. New York: Capricorn Books, pp. 23–34.

D'Souza, D. (1995). *The end of racism: Principles for a multiracial society*. New York: Free Press.

Dussell, E. (1993). "Eurocentrism and Modernity." *boundary 2 20*(3), 65–77.

Dyer, R. (1988). "White," *Screen, 29*(4), 44–64.

Dyson, M. E. (1993). *Reflecting Black*. Minneapolis: University of Minnesota Press.

Dyson, M. E. (1996). *Between God and gangsta' rap*. New York: Oxford University Press.

Editorial. (1994). "The Issue." *New Republic*. October 31, p. 9.

Edsall, T. B & Edsall, M. D. (1992). *Chain reactions: The impact of race, rights, and taxes on American politics*. New York: W. W. Norton.

Eflin, M. (1993). "Race on Campus." *U. S. News and World Report*, April 19, pp. 52–56.

Ehrlich, H. J. (1994). "Reporting Ethnoviolence: Newspaper Treatment of Race and Ethnic Conflict." *Z Magazine, 6*(2), 53–60.

Erikson, E. H. (1968). *Identity, youth, and crisis*. New York: W. W. Norton.

Fanon, F. (1963). *The wretched of the earth*. New York: Grove Press.

Fanon, F. (1967). *Black skin, White masks*. New York: Grove Press.

Fay, B. (1977). "How People Change Themselves: The Relationship between Critical Theory and Its Audience." In Ball, T. (Ed.), *Political theory and praxis: New perspectives*. Minneapolis: University of Minnesota Press, pp. 200–233.

Feagin, J. R. and H. Vera. (1995). *White racism: The basics*. London: Routledge.

Ferrell, J.and Sanders, C. R.(Eds.). (1995). *Cultural criminology*. Boston: Northeastern University Press.

Fields, S. (1996). "The Most Pressing Problem is Young Super-Predators." Distributed by *Los Angeles Times* Syndicate, in *Albuquerque Journal*, October 17, p. A14.

Fischer, M. M. (1986). "Ethnicity and the Post-Modern Arts." In J. Clifford and G. E. Marcus (Eds.), *Writing culture: The poetics and politics of ethnography*. Berkeley: University of California Press. pp. 54–67.

Fischer Fishkin, S. (1995). "Interrogating 'Whiteness,' Complicating 'Blackness': Remapping American Culture," *American Quarterly, 47*(3), 428–466.

Fiske, J. (1994). *Media matters*. Minneapolis: University of Minnesota Press.

Flagg, B. (1993). "'Was Blind, But Now I See': White Race Consciousness and the Requirement of Disciminatory Intent." *Michigan Law Review, 91*(3), 953–1017.

Flores, J. (1993). *Divided Borders: Essays on Puerto Rican Identity.* Houston: Arte Publico Press.

Fordham, S. (1988). "Racelessness as a Factor in Black Students' School Success: Pragmatic Strategy or Pyrrhic Victory?" *Harvard Educational Review, 58* (1), 111–127.

Frankenberg, R. (1993). *White women, race matters: The social construction of whiteness.* Minneapolis: University of Minnesota Press.

Franklin, J. H. (1956). *The militant south.* Cambridge, MA: Harvard University Press.

Franklin, V. P. (1966). *Black self-determination, a cultural history of the faith of the fathers.* Westport, CT: Lawrence Hill & Company.

Fraser, N. (1993). "Clintonism, Welfare, and the Antisocial Wage: The Emergence of a Neoliberal Political Imaginary." *Rethinking Marxism, 6*(1), 9–23.

Freire, P. (1970). *Pedagogy of the Oppressed.* New York: Seabury Press.

Friedman, S. S. (1995). "Beyond White and Other: Relationality and Narratives of Race in Feminist Discourse." *Signs, 21*(1), 25–37.

Fromm, E. (1973). *The anatomy of human destructiveness.* New York: Fawcett Crest.

Fusco, C. (1995). *English is broken here: Notes on cultural fusion in the Americas.* New York: New Press.

Gallagher, C. A. (1994). "White Construction in the University." *Socialist Review, 94* (1/2), 165–187.

Gardiner, M. (1996). "Alterity and Ethics: A Dialogical Perspective." *Theory, Culture and Society, 13*(2), pp. 121–144.

Gardner, H. (1983). *Frames of mind: The theory of multiple intelligences.* New York: Basic Books.

Gates, D. (1993). "White Male Paranoia." *Newsweek*, March 29, p. 48.

Gay, G. (1985). "Implications of Selected Models of Ethnic Identity Development for Educators." *Journal of Negro Education, 54*(1), 43–55.

Gay, G. (1990). "Achieving Educational Equality Through Curriculum Desegregation." *Phi Delta Kappan, 72*(1), 56–62.

Geertz, C. (1973). *The Interpretation of Cultures.* New York: Basic Books.

George, L. (1993). "Gray Boys, Funky Aztecs and Honorary Homegirls." *Los Angeles Times Magazine*, Januray 17, pp. 14–19.

Glass, J. (1995). "'Dangerous Minds' Inspires Teachers." *Virginian-Pilot*, September 2, p. B1.

Giroux, H. A. (1983). *Theory and resistance in education.* Amherst, MA: Bergin & Garvey.

Giroux, H. A. (1992a). *Border Crossings: Cultural workers and the politics of education.* New York: Routledge.

Giroux, H. A. (1992b). "Post-Colonial Ruptures and Democratic Possibilities: Multiculturalism as Anti-Racist Pedagogy." *Cultural Critique.* 24(2), 5–39.

Giroux, H. A. (1993). *Living dangerously: Multiculturalism and the politics of difference.* New York: Peter Lang Publishing, Inc.

Giroux, H. A. (1996). *Fugitive cultures: Race, violence, and youth.* New York: Routledge.

Giroux, H. A. (1997a). *Channel surfing: Race talk and the destruction of today's youth.* New York: St. Martin's Press.

Giroux, H. A. (1997b). "Rewriting the discourse of racial identity: Toward a pedagogy and politics of whiteness." *Harvard Educational Review, 67*(2), 285–320.

Goldberg, D. T. (1990). "The Social Formation of Racist Discourse." In D. T. Goldberg (Ed.), *Anatomy of racism.* Minneapolis: University of Minnesota Press, pp. 295–318.

Goldberg, D. T. (1993a). "Polluting the Body Politic: Racist Discourse and the Urban Location." In M. Cross and M. Keith (Eds.), *Racism, the city and the state.* New York: Routledge, pp. 45–60.

Goldberg, D. T. (1993b). *Racist culture: Philosophy and the politics of meaning.* Cambridge: Blackwell.

Goodman, D. (1998). "Lowering the Shields: Reducing Defensiveness in Multicultural Education." In Chávez Chávez & O'Donnell (Eds.). *Speaking the unpleasant: The politics of (non)engagement in the multicultural education terrain.* New York: State University of New York Press, pp. 221–235.

Gould, S. J. (1996). *The mismeasure of man* (Second Edition). New York: W.W. Norton.

Gramsci, A. (1971). *Selections from the prison notebooks.* New York: International Publishing Company.

Gray, H. (1995). *Watching race.* Minneapolis: University of Minnesota Press.

Gresson III, A. D. (1996). "Postmodern America and the Multicultural Crisis: Reading Forrest Gump as the 'Call Back to Whiteness.'" *Taboo, 1*(1), 11–33.

Griffin, G. B. (1995). *Season of the witch: Borderlines, marginal notes.* Pasadena, CA: Trilogy Books.

Grundmann, J. (1994). "Identity Politics at Face Value: An Interview with Scott McGehee and David Siegel." *Cineaste, 20*(3), 24.

Guiner, L. (1994). *The tyranny of the majority: Fundamental fairness in representative democracy.* NY: The Free Press.

Gutiérrez, R. (1996). "The Erotic Zone Sexual Transgression on the U.S.-Mexican Border." In A. Gordon and C. Newfield (Eds.), *Mapping multiculturalism.* Minneapolis, MN: University of Minnesota Press, pp. 12–24.

Hacker, A. (1992). *Two nations, Black and White, separate, hostile, unequal.* New York: Charles Scribner's Sons.

Hale, J. (1978). "Cultural influences on learning styles of Afro-American children." In L. Morris (Ed.), *Extracting learning styles from social/cultural minorities.* Albuquerque: Southwest Teacher Corps Network, pp. 7–27.

Haley, A. (1986). *The autobiography of Malcolm X as told to Alex Haley* (Thirtieth Printing). New York: Ballatine Press.

Hall, S. (1981). "Notes on deconstructing 'the Popular.'" In R. Samauel (Ed.), *People's history and socialist theory.* London: Routledge and Kegan Paul, pp. 103–117.

Hall, S. (1990). "Cultural Identity and Diaspora." In J. Rutherford (Ed.), *Identity, community, culture, difference*. London: Lawrence and Wishart, pp. 222–237.

Hall, S. (1991a). "Ethnicity: Identity and Difference." *Radical America, 13*(4), 9–20.

Hall, S. (1991b). "Old and New Identities, Old and New Ethnicities." In A. D. King (Ed.), *Culture, globalization and the world system*. Binghamton: State University of New York Press, pp. 41–68.

Hall, S. (1992). "Race, Culture, and Communications: Looking Backward and Forward at Cultural Studies." *Rethinking Marxism, 5*(1), 13.

Hall, S. (1995). "Fantasy, Identity, Politics." In E. Carter, J. Donald, and J. Squires (Eds.), *Cultural remix*. London: Lawrence and Wishart, pp. 67–91.

Hall, S. (1996). "New Ethnicities." In D. Morley and K-H. Chen (Eds.), *Stuart Hall: Critical dialogues in cultural studies*. New York: Routledge, pp. 441–449.

Haney López, I. (1996). *White by law: The legal construction of race*. New York: New York University Press.

Hardiman, R. (1979). *White identity development*. Amherst, MA: New Perspectives, Inc.

Hardiman, R. (1982). "White Identity Development: A Process Model for Describing the Racial Consciousness of White Americans." *Dissertation Abstracts International*, 432, 104A University Microfilms No. 82–10330.

Hardiman, R. and B. W. Jackson. (1992). "Racial Identity Development: Understanding Racial Dynamics in College Classrooms and on Campus." In M. Adams (Ed.), *Promoting diversity in college classrooms: Innovative responses for the curriculum, faculty, and institutions*. San Francisco: Jossey-Bass, pp. 47–65.

Hardisty, J. (1996). "My On-again, Off-again Romance with Liberalism." *The Brown Papers 2*(7), p. 27–35.

Harris, C. I. (1993). "Whiteness as Property." *Harvard Law Review, 106*(8), 1709–1791.

Hartman, G. (1994). "Public Memory and Its Discontents." *Raritan, 8*(4), 28.

Haymes, S. N. (1995a). "Educational Reform: What Have Been the Effects of the Atempts to Improve Education Over the Last Decades? (Response essay)." In Kincheloe, J. L. & Steinberg, S. R. (Eds.), *Thirteen questions: Reframing education's conversation* (Second Edition). New York: Peter Lang Publishing, Co., pp. 239–250.

Haymes, S.N. (1995b). *Race, culture, and the city*. New York: State University of New York Press.

Helms, J. E. (1984). "Toward a Theoretical Explanation of the Effects of Race on Counseling: A Black and White Model." *The Counseling Psychologist, 12*(4), pp. 153–165.

Helms, J. E. (1990a). "Toward a Model of White Racial Identity Development." In J. E. Helms (Ed.), *Black and White racial identity: Theory, research and practice*. Westport, CT: Greenwood Press, pp. 49–66.

Helms, J. E. (Ed.). (1990b). *Black and white racial identity: Theory, research and practice*. Westport, CT: Greenwood.

Helms, J. E. (1995). "An Update of Helms's White and People of Color Racial Identity Models." In J. G. Ponterotto, J. M. Casas, L. A. Suzuki, and C. M. Alexander (Eds.), *Handbook of multicultural counseling*. Thousand Oaks, CA: Sage Publications, pp. 23–37.

Henry III, W. A. (1991). "Upside in the Groves of Academe." *Time*, April 1, pp. 66–69.

Herrnstein, R. J. and Murray, C. (1994). *The bell curve: Intelligence and class structure in American life*. New York: Free Press.

Hidalgo, F., Chávez Chávez, R., & Ramage, J. (1996). "Multicultural Education: Landscape for Reform in the 21st Century." In J. Sikula & E. Guyton (Eds.), *Handbook of teacher education*. New York: Macmillan, pp. 761–778.

Holston, J. and Appadurai, A. (1996). "Cities and Citizenship." *Public Culture, 19*(2), 187–204.

Holt, J. (1983). *How children learn*. NY: Dell.

hooks, b. (1989). *Talking back*. Boston, MA: South End Press.

hooks, b. (1990). *Yearning*. Boston: South End Press.

hooks, b. (1992). *Black looks: Race and representation*. Boston: South End Press.

hooks, b. (1993). *Teaching to transgress: Education as the practice of freedom*. New York: Routledge.

hooks, b. (1995). *Killing rage: Ending racism*. New York: Henry Holt & Company.

Howard, G. (1993). "Whites in Multicultural Education: Rethinking our Role." *Phi Delta Kappan, 75*(1), 36–41.

Hurston, Z. N. (1937). *Their eyes were watching God*. New York: Lippincott.

Hutchinson, E. O. (1994). *The assassination of the Black male image*. Los Angeles: Middle Passage Press.

Ignatiev, N. (1995). *How the Irish became White*. New York: Routledge

Ignatiev, N. and Garvey, J. (Eds.) (1996). *Race traitor*. New York: Routledge.

Ignatiev, N. (1996). "Editorial." In N. Ignatiev and J. Garvey (Eds.), *Race traitor*. New York: Routledge, p. 3–5.

Jackson, B. W. (1976a). *The function of a Black identity development theory in achieving relevance in education for Black students*. Unpublished dissertation.

Jackson, B. W. (1976b). *Black identity development*. Amherst, MA: New Perspectives, Inc.

Jackson, B. W. and R. Hardiman. (1988). "Oppression: Conceptual and Developmental Analysis." In M. Adams & L. Marchesani (Eds.), *Racial and cultural diversity, curricular content, and classroom dynamics: A manual for college teachers*. Amherst: University of Masachusetts, pp. 12–23.

Jackson, D. (1995). "Blacks vs. Whites: Through the Looking Glass." *Boston Globe*, November 1, p. B6.

Jester, D. (1992). "Roast Beef and Reggae Music: The Passing of Whiteness." *New Formations, 118*(2), 106–121.

Johnson, M. (1995). "Wanting To Be Indian: When Spiritual Searching Turns into Cultural Theft." *The Brown Papers, 1*(7), 13–22.

Jones, A. & Deterline, K. (1994). "Fear of a Rap Planet: Rappers Face Media Double Standard." *Extra, 7*(2), 20–21.

Kaye-Kantrowitz, M. (1996). "Jews in the U.S.: The Rising Costs of Whiteness." In B. Thompson and S. Tyagi (Eds.), *Names we call home: Autobiography on racial identity.* New York: Routledge, pp. 221–243.

Kaplan, C. (1990). "Deterritorializations: The Rewriting of Home and Exile in Western Feminist Discourse." In A. R. JanMohamed and D. Lloyd (Eds.), *The nature and context of minority discourse.* New York: Oxford University Press, pp. 357–368.

Karp, J. B. (1981). "The Emotional Impact and a Model for Changing Racist Attitudes." In B. P. Bowser and R. G. Hunt (Eds.), *Impacts of racism on White Americans.* Beverly Hills, CA: Sage Publications, pp. 87–96.

Katz, J. (1978). White awareness: Handbook for antiracism training. Norman: University of Oklahoma Press.

Keating, A. L. (1995). "Interrogating 'Whiteness,' (De)Constructing 'Race.'" *College English, 57*(8), 907–924.

Kelley, R. D. G. (1992). "Notes on Deconstructing 'the Folk.'" *American Historical Review 97*(5), 1406–1422.

Kinchloe, J., Pinar, W. F., & Slattery, P. (1994). "A Last Dying Chord? Toward Cultural and Educational Renewal in the South." *Curriculum Inquiry, 24*(2), 407–436.

Kinchloe, J. and Steinberg, S. (in press). *Changing multiculturalism: New times, new curriculum.* London: Open University Press.

Kohn, A. (1993). *Punished by Rewards: The trouble with gold stars, incentive plans, A's, praise, and other bribes.* Boston: Houghton Mifflin.

Kovel, J. (1984). *White racism: A psychohistory.* New York: Columbia University Press.

Kozol, J. (1991). *Savage inequalities: Children in America's schools.* New York: Crown Publishers, Inc.

Kreisberg, S. (1992). *Transforming power: Domination, empowerment and education.* New York: State University of New York Press.

Laclau, E. (1992). "Universalism, Particularism, and the Question of Identity." *October, 61*(3), 83–90.

Lash, S. (1996). "Postmodern Ethics: The Missing Ground." *Theory, Culture and Society, 13*(2), 91–104.

Lazarus, E. (1991). *Black Hills White justice: The Sioux Nation versus the United States 1775 to the present.* New York: Harper Collins Publishers.

Lipsitz, G. (1991). *Time passages: Collective memory and American popular culture.* Minneapolis: University of Minnesota Press.

Lipsitz, G. (1995). "The Possessive Investment in Whiteness: Racialized Social Democracy and the 'White' Problem in American Studies." *American Quarterly, 47*(3), 369–387.

Lipsitz, G. (1996). "'It's All Wrong, but its All Right': Creative Misunderstandings in Intercultural Communication." In A. Gordon and C. Newfield (Eds.), *Mapping multiculturalism.* Minneapolis and London: University of Minnesota Press, pp. 403–412.

Loewen, J. W. (1995). *Lies my teacher told me: Everything your American history textbook got wrong.* New York: The New Press.

Loiacano, D. K. (1989). "Gay Identity Issues Among Black Americans: Racism, Homophobia and the Need for Validation." *Journal of Counseling and Development, 68*(5), 21–25.

Lorde, A. (1984). *Sister outsider.* New York: Crossing Press.

Lott, E. (1993). "White Like ME: Racial Cross-Dressing and the Construction of American Whiteness." In A. Kaplan and D. E. Pease (Eds.), *Cultures of United States imperialism.* Durham, NC: Duke University Press, pp. 474–498.

Macedo, D. (1994). *Literacies of power.* Boulder, CO: Westview Press.

Macedo, D. and Bartolome, L. (forthcoming). "Dancing with Bigotry: The Poisoning of Racial and Ethnic Identities." In E. Torres Trueba and Y. Zou (Eds.), *Ethnic identity and power.* New York: State University of New York Press, pp. 212–234.

Manning, M.L. (1995). "Understanding Culturally Diverse Parents and Families." *Equity and Excellence in Education, 28* (1), 52–57.

Maslow, A. (1970). *Motivation and personality.* New York: Harper & Row.

Mathison, C. and Young, R. (1995). Constructivism and Multicultural Education. *Multicultural Education, 2*(1), 7–10.

McCall, A. L. (1995). "We Were Cheated! Students' Responses to a Multicultural, Social Reconstructionist Teacher Education Course." *Equity and Excellence in Education, 28*(1), 15–24.

McCarthy, C. & Critchlow, W. (Eds.). (1993). *Race identity and representation in education.* New York: Routledge.

McIntosh, P. (1983). *Interactive phases of curricular development.* Wellesley: Center for Research on Women.

McIntosh, P. (1989). "White Privilege: Unpacking the Invisible Knapsack." *Peace and Freedom, 1*(1), 10–12.

McIntosh, P. (1992). "White Privilege and Male Privilege: A Personal Account of Coming to See Correspondences Through Work in Women's Studies." In P. H. Collins and M.Andersen (Eds.), *Race, class and gender: An anthology.* Belmont, CA: Wadsworth Publishing, pp. 102–118.

McLaren, P. (1995). *Critical pedagogy and predatory culture.* London and New York: Routledge.

Mitchell, W.J.T. (Ed.). (1981). *On narrative.* Chicago: University of Chicago Press.

Morales, M. (1996). *Bilingual education: A dialogue with the Bakhtin circle.* New York: State University of New York Press.

Morrison, T. (1992). *Playing in the dark: Whiteness in the literary imagination.* Cambridge, MA: Harvard University Press.

Murphy, P. (1996). "Peregrini." *Thesis Eleven, 46*(1), 1–32.

Nakayama, T. K. & Krizek, R. L. (1995). "Whiteness: A Strategic Rhetoric." *Quarterly Journal of Speech, 81*(3), 291–309.

Nation of Islam (1991). *The secret relationship between Blacks and Jews, Volume One.* Chicago, IL: Latimer Associates.

Nestle, J. (1987). *A restricted country.* Ithaca, NY: Firebrand.

Nieto, S. (1996). *Affirming diversity: The sociopolitical context of multicultural education.* White Plains, NY: Longman.

Nieto, S. (1998). "From Claiming Hegemony to Sharing Space: Creating Community in Multicultural Courses." In Chávez Chávez, R. and O'Donnell, J. (Eds.), *Speaking the unpleasant: The politics of resistance in the multicultural education terrain.* New York: State University of New York Press, pp. 33–57.

Novik, M. (1995). *White lies, White power: The fight against White supremacy and reactionary violence.* Monroe, ME: Common Courage Press.

Oakes, J. (1985). *Keeping track: How schools structure inequality.* New Haven: Yale University Press.

O'Brien, C. C. (1996). "Thomas Jefferson: Radical and Racist." *The Atlantic Monthly, 233*(5), 53–74.

O'Donnell, J. (1995). "Toward an Antiracist Pedagogy: A Theoretical Instructional Paradigm." In A. Nava (Ed.), *Educating Americans in a multiethnic society.* New York, NY: McGraw-Hill, Inc., pp. 34–48.

Ogbu, J. (1986). "Black students' school success: Coping with the burden of 'acting White.'" *The Urban Review, 18*(3), 176–206.

Omi, M. & Winant, H. (1994). *Racial formations in the United States from the 1960s to 1990s.* New York: Routledge.

Paley, V. G. (1979). *White teacher.* Cambridge: Harvard University Press.

Payne, D. A. (1891, Reprint 1969). *History of the African Methodist Episcopal church.* Nashville, TN: AME Press.

Perea, J. F. (1995). "Los Olvidados: On the Making of Unvisible People." *New York University Law Review, 70*(4), 965–991.

Petry, A. (1946, 1974, 1985). *The street.* Boston: Beacon Press.

Pfeil, F. (1995). *White guys: Studies in postmodern domination and difference.* London: Verso Press.

Pinar, W. F. (1993). "Notes on Understanding Curriculum as a Racial Text." In C. McCarthy and W. Crichlow (Eds.), *Race, identity and representation in education.* New York: Routledge, pp. 117–134.

Pinar, W. F., Reynolds, W. M., Slattery, P. and Taubman, P. M. (1995). *Understanding curriculum.* NY: Peter Lang Publishing, Inc.

Polkinghorne, D. (1988). *Narrative knowing and the human sciences.* New York: State University of New York Press.

Powell, R. (1996). "Confronting White Hegemony." *Multicultural Education, 4*(2), 12–15.

Proctor, S. D. (1995). *The substance of things hoped for.* New York: G. P. Putnam's Sons.

Raboteau, A. J. (1992). "Retelling Carter Woodson's Story." *Journal of American History, 77*(2), 185.

Raines, H. (1977). *My soul is rested: The story of the Civil Rights Movement in the deep south.* New York: Penguin Books.

Rattansi, A. (1994). "'Western' Racisms, Ethnicities and Identities in a 'Postmodern' Frame." In A. Rattansi and S. Westwood (Eds.), *Racism, modernity and identity on the western front.* Cambridge and Oxford: Polity Press, pp. 403–412.

Reeves, J. L. & Campbell, R. (1994). *Cracked coverage: Television news, the anti-cocaine crusade, and Reagan legacy.* Durham: Duke University Press.

Rich, A. (1979). "'Disloyal to Civilization': Feminism, Racism, Gynephobia." In A. Rich (Ed.), *On lies, secrets and silences.* New York: Norton, pp. 13–29.

Rich, A. (1986). *Blood, bread, and poetry.* New York: Norton.

Rich, A. (1993). *What is found there: Notebooks on poetry and politics.* New York: W.W. Norton & Co.

Roediger, D. (1991). *The wages of whiteness.* London: Verso Press.

Roediger, D. (1994). *Toward the abolition of whiteness.* London: Verso Press.

Rorty, R. (1989). *Contingency, irony, and solidarity.* New York: Cambridge University Press.

Rosaldo, R. (1993). *Culture & truth.* Boston: Beacon Press.

Rose, W. (1992). "The Great Pretenders: Further Reflections on White Shamanism." In M. A. Jaimes (Ed.), *The state of Native America: Genocide, colonization, and resistance.* Boston: South End Press, pp. 117–138.

Rosenberg, P. M. (1997). "Underground Discourses: Exploring Whiteness in Teacher Education." In M. Fine, L. Weis, L. C. Powell, and L. M. Wong (Eds.), *Off white: Readings on race, power, and society.* New York: Routledge, pp. 79–89.

Rowe, W., Bennet, S. K., and Atkinson, D. R. (1994). "White Racial Identity Models: A Critique and Alternative Proposal." *The Counseling Psychologist,* 22(1), 129–146.

Said, E. (1985). *Orientalism.* London: Penguin.

Saillant, C. (1995). "School of Soft Knocks." *Los Angeles Times,* October 11, p. B1.

San Juan Jr., E. (1991). "The Culture of Ethnicity and the Fetish of Pluralism: A Counterhegemonic Critique." *Cultural Critique, 21*(2), 221–234.

Saxton, A. (1991). *The rise and fall of the White republic.* London: Verso Press.

Scheurich, J. J. (1993a). "Toward a White Discourse on White Racism." *Educational Researcher, 22*(8), 5–10.

Scheurich, J. J. (1993b). "A Difficult, Confusing, Painful Problem that Requires Many Voices, Many Perspectives." *Educational Researcher, 22* (8), 15–16.

Schniedewind, N. & Davidson, E. (1987). *Cooperative learning, cooperative lives: A sourcebook of learning activities for building a peaceful world.* Dubuque, IA: William. C. Brown.

Schwartz, B. (Ed.). (1993). *Educating for civic responsibility in a multicultural world.* Swarthmore, PA: Swarthmore College.

Segest, M. (1994). *Memoir of a race traitor.* Boston, MA: South End Press.

Segrest, M. (1984). *My mama's dead squirrel: Lesbian essays on southern culture.* Ithaca, NY: Firebrand Books.

Seldon, H., (1992). *The 'new' racism????: Convictions about racism in the United States of America.* Boston: Community Change, Inc.

Shohat, E. (1995). "The Struggle Over Representation: Casting, Coalitions, and the Politics of Identitfication." In R. de la Campa, E. A. Kaplan, and M. Sprinker (Eds.), *Late imperial culture.* London and New York: Verso, pp. 166–178.

Shohat, E. & Stam, R. (1994). *Unthinking eurocentrism.* New York: Routledge.

Shor, I. (1992). *Empowering education: Critical teaching for social change.* Chicago & London: The University of Chicago Press.

Simon, S. (1996). "Job Hunt's Wild Side in Russia." *Los Angeles Times*, November 23, pp. 1, 9.

Slattery, P. (1995). *Curriculum development in the postmodern era*. New York: Garland.

Sleeter, C. E. (1993). "Advancing a White Discourse: A Response to Scheuirch." *Educational Researcher, 22* (8), 13–15.

Sleeter, C. E. (1996). *Multicultural education as social activism*. New York: State University of New York Press.

Sleeter, C. E. & Grant, C. A. (1991). "Race, Class, Gender and Disability in Current Textbooks." In M. W. Apple and L. K. Christian-Smith (Eds.), *The politics of the textbook*. New York: Routledge & Chapman Hall, pp. 234–254.

Smith, L. (1961). *Killers of the dream* (Second Edition). New York: W.W. Norton and Company.

Snead, J. (1994). *White screens, Black images*. New York: Routledge.

Social Issues Training Project (1986). *Hints for the heterosexual woman*. Amherst, MA: New Perspectives, Inc.

Southern Poverty Law Center. (1996). *False patriots: The threat of antigovernment extremists*. Montgomery, Alabama.

Sprinker, D. (Ed.). (1994). *Late imperial culture*. London and New York: Verso.

Spivak, G. C. (1990). "Post-colonial critic." In S. Harasym (Ed.), *Interviews, strategies, dialogues*. New York: Routledge, pp. 67–137.

Stalvey, L. (1988). *The education of a WASP*. Madison: University of Wisconsin Press.

Stowe, D. W.(1996). "Uncolored People: The Rise of Whiteness Studies." *Lingua Franca, 6*(6), 68–77.

Sue, D. W. & Sue, D. (1990). *Counseling the culturally different: Theory and practice*. New York: John Wiley.

Takaki, R. (1987). *From different shores: Perspectives on race and culture in America*. Boston: Little, Brown, and Company.

Takaki, R. (1993). *A different mirror: A multicultural history of America*. Boston: Little, Brown and Company.

Tatum, B. D. (1992). "Talking about race, learning about racism: The application of racial identity development theory in the classroom." *Harvard Educational Review, 62*(1), 1–24.

Tatum, B. D. (1994). "Teaching White students about racism: The search for White allies and the restoration of hope." *Teachers College Record, 95*(4), 462–76.

Tatum, B. D. (1997). *Why are all the Black kids sitting together in the cafeteria? and other conversations about race*. New York: Basic Books.

Terkel, S. (1992). *Race: How Blacks and Whites think and feel about the American obsession*. New York: The New Press.

Terry, R. (1981). "The Negative Impact of White Values." In Bowser, B. P. & Hunt, R. G. (Ed.s), *Impacts of racism on White Americans*. Beverly Hills: Sage, pp. 35–47.

Terry, R. (1975). *For whites only*. Grand Rapids, WI: William B. Erdmans.

Thomas, A. and Sillen, S. (1972). *Racism and psychiatry*. New York: Brunner/Mazel.

Thompson, B. (1996a). "National, Transnational and Diasporic Feminist Theories." Unpublished speech.

Thompson, B. (1996b). "Time Traveling and Border Crossing: Reflections on White Identity." In B. Thompson and S. Tyagi (Eds.), *Names we call home: Autobiography on racial identity*. Minneapolis: University of Minnesota Press, pp. 111–125.

Thompson, B. and Tyagi, S. (1996). *Names we call home: Auotbiography on racial identity*. Minneapolis: University of Minnesota Press.

Thompson, B. and Tyagi, S. (1993). "The Politics of Inclusion: Reskilling the Academy." In S.Tyagi and B. Thompson (Eds.), *Beyond a dream deferred: Multicultural education and the politics of excellence*. Minneapolis: University of Minnesota Press, pp. 237–245.

Thompson, B. and White Women Challenging Racism. (1997). "Home/work: Antiracism Activism and the Meaning of Whiteness." In M. Fine, L. Weis, L. C. Powell, and L. M. Wong (Eds.), *Off white: Readings on race, power, and society*. New York: Routledge, pp. 354–366.

Thompson, L. (1996). Whitefolks: *Seeing America through Black eyes*. Self-Published.

Todorov, T. (1984). *The conquest of America: The question of the other*. New York: Harper and Row.

Time. (1995). "Banker to Mexico: 'Go get 'em.'" February 20, p. 9.

Trembath, P. (1996). "Aesthetics without Art or Culture: Toward an Alternative Sense of Materialist Agency." *Strategies, 9*(10), 122–151.

Van Sertima, I. (1975). *They came before Colum*bus. New York: Random House.

Van Sertima, I. (Ed). (1990). *African presence in early America*. New Brunwisk, NJ: Transaction Publishers.

Wallace, A. (1996). "Less Diversity Seen as UC Preferences End." *Los Angeles Times*, October 2, A1, 18.

Walsh, C. (1991). *Pedagogy and the struggle for voice: Issues of language, power, and schooling for Puerto Ricans*. New York: Bergin & Garvey.

Ware, V. (1992). *Beyond the pale: White women, racism, and history*. London: Verso Press.

Webster, Y. (1992). *The racialization of America*. New York: St. Martin's Press.

Weinstein, G., & Obear, K. (1992). "Bias Issues in the Classroom: Encounters with the Teaching Self." In M. Adams (Ed.), *Promoting diversity in college classrooms: Innovative responses for the curriculum, faculty, and institutions*. San Francisco: Jossey-Bass, pp. 203–214.

Wellman, D. (1993). *Portraits of White racism* (Second Edition). New York: Cambridge University Press.

Wellman, D. (1996). "Red and Black in America." In B. Thompson and S. Tyagi (Eds.), *Names we call home: Autobiography on racial identity*. New York: Routledge, pp. 13–29.

Welsch, W. (1996). "Aestheticization Processes: Phenomena, Distinctions and Prospects." *Theory, Culture and Society, 13*(2), 1–24.

Welsing, F. C. (1970). *The Cress theory of color, confrontation, and racism (white supremacy)*. Washington, D.C.: C-R Publishers.

West. C. (1993). *Keeping faith: Philosophy and race in America*. New York: Routledge.

White, D. G. (1985). *Ain't I a woman?: Female slaves in the plantation South*. New York: W. W. Norton & Company, Inc.

Williams, P. J. (1991). *The alchemy of race and rights: Diary of a law professor*. Cambridge: Harvard University Press.

Williams, R. (1970). *American society*. New York: Knopf.

Wilson, W. J. (1980). *The declining significance of race*. Chicago, IL: The University of Chicago Press.

Winant, H. (1992). "Amazing Race," *Socialist Review, 75*(19), 166–173.

Winant, H. (1994). *Racial conditions*. Minneapolis: University of Minnesota Press.

Wolfenstein, E. V. (1993). *Psychoanalytic-Marxism: Groundwork*. New York and London: Guilford Press.

Women of the South Asian Diaspora (1993). *Our feet walk the sky*. San Francisco, CA: Aunt Lute.

Wood, E. M. (1995). *Democracy against capitalism: Renewing historical materialism*. Cambridge and New York: Cambridge University Press.

Wray, M. and Newitz. A (Eds). (1997). *White trash: Race and class in America*. New York: Routledge.

Yarbro-Bejarano, Y. (1994). "Gloria Anzaldua's Borderlands/La Frontera: Cultural Studies, 'Difference,' and the Non-Unitary Subject." *Cultural Critique, 23*(4), 5–28.

Yon, M. (1995). "Educating Homeless Children in the United States." *Equity and Excellence in Education, 28*(1), 58–62.

Young, L. (1990). "A Nasty Piece of Work: A Psychoanalytic Study of Sexual and Racial Difference in 'Mona Lisa.'" In J. Rutherford (Ed.). *Identity: Community, culture, difference*. London: Lawrence & Wishart, pp. 188–206.

Young, V. (1979). "Toward an Increased Understanding of Whiteness in Relation to White Racism." Unpublished paper.

Young, W. (1969). *Beyond racism*. New York: McGraw-Hill.

Yúdice, G. (1995). "Neither Impugning Nor Disavowing Whiteness Does a Viable Politics Make: The Limits of Identity Politics." In C. Newfield and R. Strickland (Eds.), *After political correctness*. Boulder, CO: Westview Press, pp. 255–281.

Zamichow, N. (1996). "Captains Courageous Enough Not to Fight." *Los Angeles Times*, January 23, pp. 1, 9–10.

Zinn, H. (1980). *A people's history of the United States*. New York, NY: Harper & Row Publishers.

Zinn, H. (1970). *The politics of history*. Boston: Beacon Press.

Index

About the Editors and Contributors

Elizabeth Aaronsohn is an Associate Professor of Education at Central Connecticut State University. Aaronsohn was a civil rights worker for two years in Mississippi and a classroom teacher for thirty years. Her first book, *Going Against the Grain: Supporting the Student-Centered Teacher*, was published in 1996. Her on-going research includes a radical critique of traditional grading.

Christine Clark is an Assistant Professor of Curriculum and Instruction and Multicultural Education at New Mexico State University. Her area of specialty is in the development of critical multicultural, bilingual education as a tool for disarming violence in schools and communities. Her research also explores the trend in civil law toward becoming more race neutral and the trend in criminal law toward becoming more race conscious and the resulting escalation of institutionalized racism. She is currently a member of the Board of Directors of the National Association for Multicultural Education (NAME).

Arnold Cooper is Dean of the College of Education at Georgia Southern University. Dean Cooper served as a Vista Volunteer with the South Carolina Commission for Farm Workers, as a high school administrator in several rural southern school districts, and as an administrator and faculty member at two historically African American colleges. Dr. Cooper is the author of *Between Struggle and Hope: Four Black Educators in the South, 1894–1915* and numerous articles on the history of African American education.

Patti DeRosa is the President of Cross-Cultural Consultation, a consulting firm focusing on workplace and community diversity. She is also a consultant, educator, and activist with twenty years experience in social justice and anti-racism work. She has served on the faculty at Simmons College, Lesley College, and Boston University, teaching courses on racism and intercultural relations.

Mary M. Gannon is a lecturer in the School of Human Services at Springfield College in Manchester, New Hampshire. She is also a consultant for the Intergroup Relations Dialogue Project and an Ed.D. candidate in Social Justice Education at the University of Massachusetts in Amherst where her research focuses on intergroup race relations.

Henry A. Giroux is the Waterbury Chair Professor of Education at Penn State University. He has published widely in a range of academic and popular journals magazines, and newspapers. His most recent books include: *Disturbing Pleasures: Learning Popular Culture*; *Fugitive Cultures: Race and the Violence of Youth*; *Channel Surfing: Race Talk and the Destruction of American Youth*; *Pedagogy and the Politics of Hope*; and, *Education and Cultural Studies*.

Gary R. Howard is the President and Founder of the REACH Center for Multicultural Education in Seattle, Washington. Over the past twenty-five years he has provided extensive training in cultural awareness to schools, universities, and businesses throughout the United States, Canada, and Australia.

Peter McLaren is Professor in the Division of Urban Schooling at the Graduate School of Education and Information Studies, University of California, Los Angeles. He is author and editor of over twenty books on politics, pedagogy, and liberatory praxis, the most recent of which is titled, *Revolutionary Multiculturalism: Pedagogies of Dissent for the New Millennium*. A political activist, McLaren lectures worldwide. His works have been published in Spanish, Portuguese, Japanese, Hebrew, Polish, French, German and Catalan.

James O'Donnell is senior faculty in the department of Curriculum and Instruction and Coordinator of Secondary Student Teaching at New Mexico State University. He specializes in teacher education and socialization, qualitative research and evaluation, curriculum development, and multicultural education. He has taught middle school science, math, and languages arts in the midwest and in a bilingual school in Bogota, Colombia. He served as a Peace Corps volunteer in Sierra Leone, West Africa designing and conducting teacher education workshops for primary and secondary teachers. He is co-editor of the recently published book, *Speaking the Unpleasant: The Politics of (Non)Engagement in the Multicultural Education Terrain*.

Carolyn O'Grady is an Assistant Professor of Education at Gustavus Adolphus College. She is a frequent workshop facilitator for schools and small organizations on issues of diversity, including race, gender, and sexual orientation. Her research interests include education as social change, spirituality in education, and the intersection of multicultural education and service learning.

G. Pritchy Smith is a Professor of Curriculum and Instruction at the University of North Florida. He teaches courses in the sociology of education and multicultural education. He coordinates the University's Master's of Education program in Belize. He is a past vice-president of the National Association of Multicultural Education (NAME) and is currently a member of its Publications Committee. He has authored several articles on multicultural education and has conducted research on the impact of testing on the racial and ethnic composition of the nation's teaching force.

Beverly Daniel Tatum is a Professor of Psychology and Education at Mount Holyoke College. Her teaching and research interests include the psychology of racism, racial identity development among Black youth in predominantly White settings, and the impact of antiracist professional development on teacher attitudes and classroom practice. She is the author of numerous articles on these topics and the book, *"Why Are All the Black Kids Sitting Together in the Cafeteria?" and Other Conversations about Race.* She is the recipient of a two year grant from the Carnegie Corporation, a school-based demonstration project involving antiracist education for teachers, parents, and youth.

Becky Thompson is an Associate Professor of Sociology at Simmons College where she teaches courses in sociology and African American studies. She is the co-author of *A Hunger So Wide and So Deep: A Multiracial View of Women's Eating Problems* and co-editor of *Beyond a Dream Deferred: Multicultural Education and the Politics of Excellence* and *Names We Call Home: Autobiography on Racial Identity.* She is currently working on a book about White activism across decades.

David Wellman is a Professor of Community Studies at the University of California, Santa Cruz. He is also a Research Sociologist and Principal Investigator at the Institute for the Study of Social Change at the University of California, Berkeley. He has served as a member of the Working Group on Urban Policy Issues for the National Association of State Universities and Land Grant Colleges and was primary consultant for the Detroit Strategic Planning Committee, Task Force on Race and Racism. He is author of *Portraits of White Racism,* a second edition of which was published in 1993. His most recent work is titled, *The Union Makes Us Strong: Radical Unionism on the San Francisco Waterfront.* He has authored numerous articles on racism, working class culture, and sociological methods.

ISBN 0-89789-620-3

EAN

90000>

HARDCOVER BAR CODE